J P McKeon

4539 Walden

GM STILLE

BAO

THIS HOUSE
AGAINST THIS HOUSE

Books by Vincent Sheean

BETWEEN THE THUNDER AND THE SUN

BIRD OF THE WILDERNESS

NOT PEACE BUT A SWORD

A DAY OF BATTLE

THE PIECES OF A FAN

SANFELICE

PERSONAL HISTORY

THE TIDE

GOG AND MAGOG

AMERICAN AMONG THE RIFFI

ANATOMY OF VIRTUE

NEW PERSIA

THIS HOUSE
AGAINST THIS HOUSE

Vincent Sheean

O, if you raise this house against this house,
It will the wofullest division prove,
That ever fell upon this cursed earth.
Prevent it, resist it, let it not be so,
Lest child, child's children cry against you woe.

                    KING RICHARD II, IV, i.

RANDOM HOUSE · NEW YORK

FIRST PRINTING

To Irita:

and to the friends who have gone

CONTENTS

PART ONE

FREE BORN

A Meditation

And the chief captain answered, With a great sum obtained I this freedom. And Paul said, But I was free born.   *Acts*, xxii, 28.

I think I have . . . shown sufficiently clearly the basis of a democracy. I have especially desired to do so, for I believe it to be of all forms of government the most natural, and the most consonant with individual liberty. In it no one transfers his natural right so absolutely that he has no further voice in affairs; he only hands it over to the majority of a society, whereof he is a unit. Thus all men remain, as they were in the state of Nature, equals.

Spinoza, *Tractatus Theologico-Politicus*, ch. xvi.

qual ti negasse il vin della sua fiala
per la tua sete, in libertà non fora,
se non com' acqua ch' al mar non si cala.
                     Paradiso, Canto X.

§ 1

On the edges of the great verdant park there stands a hotel which has seen more than its share of these events. It is called the Hotel Trianon-Palace, and during the years between the two world wars it was a place of resort for calm moments under the trees, the tranquil lunch, the placid tea, the hour of refuge from life in the city. It was the only hotel I ever saw anywhere where cows grazed under your windows, as undisturbed as in any Alpine pasture. Once, in some interval of moving from one country to another, I passed a week or two there and had my breakfast in the window of an immense bedroom, looking at the cows. They might indeed have been the very cows which Marie Antoinette received into her intimacy, and their steady gaze through the green shadows toward the Trianon may have discerned—like the two spinsters from England who met the Queen there some decades ago—figures not visible to our coarser vision, clad in soft garments we have forgotten how to wear.

In the great dining room of the hotel, overlooking the terrace on one side and the park on the other, there used to be a marble plaque hitched somehow to the wall above the doors at one end. It said:

This House Against This House

Dans cette salle le 7 mai 1919

Monsieur GEORGES CLEMENCEAU
Président de la Conférence de la Paix
A REMIS AUX DÉLÉGUÉS DE L'ALLEMAGNE
Les Conditions
du Traité de Paix de Versailles
En présence de
Monsieur WOODROW WILSON, Président des Etats-Unis.
Monsieur LLOYD-GEORGE,
Premier Ministre de Grande-Bretagne.
Monsieur ORLANDO,
Président du Conseil des Ministres d'Italie.
Monsieur HYMANS,
Ministre des Affaires Etrangères de Belgique.
et des Représentants
de toutes les Puissances Alliées
et Associées.

The inscription was cut into the veined marble and made bright with gold. Gay garlands in bronze decorated the edges of its baroque frame. As the guests looked up from their unstinted luncheons in the 1930's ("The oysters are good today, my dear; shall we have a little champagne with them?") their eyes fell upon this legend and their minds dwelt, however fleetingly, upon some aspect of that scene years ago: the Tiger, stern and yellow, his eyes flashing from the shadow of those fierce old brows, stretching out a hand in which there lay the document, the paper, the great fat cumbersome paper, the Treaty of Versailles. And Brockdorff-Rantzau, the proud Prussian aristocrat, Count Ulrich von Brockdorff-Rantzau, taking it—ah, taking it!—with a tremor of humiliation and revolt, perhaps aware even then that his hand would refuse to sign it,

4

that others would sign and mean not a stroke of their signa-
tures, that none would thereafter obey. As it passed from the
hand of Clemenceau to the hand of Brockdorff-Rantzau it was
already dead; they might just as well have made a bonfire of it
then and there, beneath the cold pure eyes of the American
professor and the mischievous nose of the Welsh politician—
better fire than blood.

The cows are gone now. No doubt they were eaten up long
ago. I would not give much for the chances of any cow detected
in the neighborhood of Paris at the present time. The plaque
is gone too. When the German air force took over the hotel in
the spring of 1940, the first thing they did was to remove the
marble tablet. Some say it was taken to Germany as a trophy,
some that it was smashed to pieces by the infuriated airmen;
but it is not there. When I stood not long ago beneath the bare
place on the wall where it had been, the dining room was a mess
hall for high officers of the Supreme Headquarters, Allied Expeditionary Forces, and the hotel was used for their quarters.
The American mess sergeant was polite but uninformed.

"We don't know what became of the marble that was up
there," he said. "We have had other inquiries. French people
have asked. I guess it's in Germany now."

So that we can stand here by a bare wall and speak of forgotten monuments, so that we may look through this window
into the green shadows, men have died all over the earth, in all
manners and moods, in the thunder and lightning of the air as
in the cold mud of the beleaguered ditch, and many have sunk
to the far depths of the water; those are pearls that were their
eyes. Some have starved and many have labored. Young girls
have set to work in the fields of grain in summer, and old men
have gone back to the factory they had left for the evening's
repose a long time ago. The coal was produced, the steel was
produced, the food was produced, the weapons were made;
we put them into the hands of our sons, and we are here. But

down every wind that blows in the world is the echo of their sighing, the sigh of our lost youth and of those who loved them. The sun in its punctual rising can never again dispel all the shadows that dwell about us, for in one sense we take shame to be here at all when so much is gone. Ever-returning spring will lay upon us the same old enchantment, since life's obstinacy is equal to its sorrow, but with the springs that remain to us will be forever mixed the thought of those for whom no spring will come again. A certain dusty, tawny kind of sunset must always make me, at least, think of that wondrous field we had at Télepte, in Tunisia, the field where I learned what the youth of my own country could do in war; and the snow among pines and firs will mean the Ardennes, as a valley glimpsed from the air will be the Rhine; and the thunder is the guns and the lightning is the bombs; no field will ever be so vast as the fields of our B-29's in China; life recurring and continuous contains death remembered. So it always was and so it will be always, the present containing innumerable superimposed, interrelated and inextricable layers of the past, but this time there is a sort of finality about the experience, not for me only but for millions like me, who have lived the war as if each day might be the last. Such extremes are not suited to the human condition and are in themselves inimical to life. Man cannot go on like this. Peace we must have; now we must have peace, and we will have peace.

§ 2

Georges Clemenceau was born in 1841 at Mouilleron-en-Pareds, in the Vendée. He was therefore seventy-eight years old in 1919. He had journeyed far in those seventy-eight years, from the extreme Left to what was almost the extreme Right, and the old radical barnstormer, anti-clerical and Dreyfusard was now, as he stood in this room handing the thick book to the German, a personification of national patriotism. The

Germans had made him so. Nobody can pay much attention to Clemenceau's life and work without realizing that the change which took place in him from 1911 onwards was brought about by the sharp anguish of knowledge—knowledge of Germany's strength and France's weakness, of Germany's indubitable intentions, of the inevitability of the great ordeal. It was in 1911 that he became a member of the Senate's commissions for the army and for foreign affairs, and thus privy to all the information the French government possessed on these subjects. It was then that his alarm for France itself, for the soil and people beneath all parties, drove him into that attitude of tigerish patriotic energy which is his fixed pose in history. He would criticize anything and everything that weakened France: poor hospitals, bad use of manpower, bad organization, lack of guns or munitions; and he would uphold anything and everything that gave France strength—even men and institutions which he bitterly disliked. His powers of sarcasm, vituperation and assault were almost without equal in his time, and with these powers he could castigate and finally sweep away the governments which showed any hesitation; for we are in a war to the death, he kept on saying, and we must win. Thus he became Father Victory to millions of French soldiers in 1918 and went into the peace conference with a personal authority none could question. The Tiger—the Father of Victory.

Yet this was not naturally his character. The sharp tooth and claw were there, of course, and many a man carried their marks; but they were by nature used for the defense of the weak, the poor, the disinherited. Clemenceau fought anti-Semitism, the clerical reaction, imperialism, the Bank of France, all the forces of darkness, through the greater part of his life. His was by nature a philosophical and humanitarian mind. Any who care to look through his reflective work called *Au Soir de la Pensée*, published in 1925, will see with what tenderness he could re-

7

gard this and all other species. There is a sentence of poignant regret, somewhere halfway through the book, about the mother partridges he had shot in his youth when they were only protecting their young—*"qui s'offrait bruyamment à mon plomb criminel pour le salut de sa couvée."* Yet this mind and spirit, so harmonious with the widest thought of humanity in its native condition, turned into a highly tempered instrument for battle and victory, for the victory of the French nation state over the German nation state, and for the perpetuation of that victory through times unborn. This transformation of a social, humanitarian and democratic protagonist into a phenomenon of naked patriotism was the work of the Germans alone. Now, as he stood beetling at the Prussian aristocrat, beetling and growling and showing his fangs, the Tiger was so formed or transformed by the events in which he had played a great part that all memory of the international socialist had faded away, leaving a kind of quintessential residue of the purest nationalism. Moltke, Hindenburg, Ludendorff and the Kaiser Wilhelm II produced this result, willy-nilly, just as the Tiger himself (along with Poincaré and others whom he equally disliked) was to assist mightily in the production of Adolf Hitler.

David Lloyd George, who stood there and watched the fat paper pass to the reluctant hand of the German, saw the event with mixed feelings. He had not wholly agreed with the concessions and compromises to which necessity had led him in this treaty. He, too, was an old-time radical barnstormer and had started out his parliamentary career thirty years before in a position as far to the Left as was possible in the English political life of the time. He was twenty-two years younger than Clemenceau—a mere fifty-six at this moment—and the ardor of his social passion was by no means quenched. He had once in fiery words declared war on poverty in England, which, he said (in his budget speech of 1909) should become "as remote to the people of this country as the wolves which once infested its forests." He had been a tremendous innovator in society, economics and politics, introducing the first social insurance and unemployment benefits known in the west—adapted from Bismarck—and utilizing taxation as a weapon of reform; he had made the House of Lords harmless; he had attacked the problem of the land. His interests were so centered upon these great questions of internal structure that he had not attended much to the growing threat of war. At the beginning he had not even been in favor of the declaration of war, and was persuaded to vote for it only (August 3, 1914) by the violation of Belgian neutrality. Once in, he had fought the war with a tenacity equal to the Tiger's; as Chancellor of the Exchequer, as Minister of Munitions, as Secretary of State for War, and finally as Prime Minister, he had battled for all the great solutions—vastly increased production, universal conscription, quick aid from America, the unified allied command. That there were two million American soldiers in Europe at the end of the war, and that Foch commanded them as well as the British, French and all other allied troops, were achievements of Lloyd George's will and skill. He could make up his mind, and he could persuade; he could face facts and deal with them. But he did not wholly like this treaty, although it seemed to him the best that could be obtained under the circumstances. He disliked the idea of a French occupation of the left bank of the Rhine for fifteen years; he disliked the idea of turning the Saar territory over to France for the same length of time; he feared the rise of a spirit of revenge in Germany and thought these and other measures in the treaty —all concessions to Clemenceau—would foster and increase it. None knew better than he how near the Western allies (exclusive of America) had come to losing this war, and none had a shrewder idea of how insecure the American support—the support of the "associated power"—might be in times to come.

9

Nor did he wholeheartedly welcome the idea of making the League of Nations covenant a fundamental part of the treaty, although he had upheld Wilson against Clemenceau in the final dispute over this matter. And, unlike both Wilson and Clemenceau, he had a persistent notion that a treaty was, or should be, a form of agreement, and not a text imposed upon one side by the other. This uneasy sense of something fundamental lacking in the document was to make him argue through the coming weeks, and for the most part in vain, that some German petitions for modification should be considered. He did not like the Germans ("Hang the Kaiser!" was his partisans' byword) but he recognized that they existed. Sometimes he seems to have been alone in this view among the high contracting parties, as the quaint diplomatic phrase has it; for Clemenceau's acknowledgment of fact in this respect was by now too "obnubilated" (a word he liked) by fear and hatred to have any objective validity. Wilson's knowledge of Germany, as of all countries in Europe, was so exclusively bookish that he, too, often seemed to be talking of people who lived on another planet. Of the three, only the Welshman had ever actually been to Germany or paid any serious attention to German institutions, ideas or capacities. And it is quite possible, as the writings of the three of them suggest, that his was the most sincere, direct and powerful revulsion against all the slaughter and cruel waste of warfare. He had detested war even when he was fighting it most untiringly, and its realities—the dead boy in the trench, the ruined village, the weeping women—never really left his sensitive Celtic mind. Nothing could divorce Lloyd George's Welsh imagination from the life of the people. When I met him years later he was very old, and many long decades had separated him from the toil and sorrow of his people in the Welsh mining villages, but he could still argue their problems with a fire lit in youth and never altogether extinguished. As he stood there, about the same size as Clemenceau (short men, both), but pink where Clemenceau was yellow, and framed in white hair, wrinkling his nose, he must have felt that this document now passing from hand to hand was imperfect, like all things human, but that it afforded a hope, some hope at least, that a system for the preservation of peace could be created and maintained in Europe. By my reading this is what he hoped, whereas what Clemenceau hoped was that Germany could be kept permanently subjugated—a very different thing.

What Woodrow Wilson hoped was something still different. He hoped that the whole world, in all its infinite diversity of races, religions and social organization, could be brought into a parliament of mankind so as to discuss and compose the differences which lead to war. He believed that the covenant of the League of Nations, embodied in this treaty as Part I, would provide mankind with the necessary constitutional process by which this could be done. In the utmost stubbornness he defended his concept against every assault made upon it, and for month after month he struggled, not only against ideas advanced by Clemenceau and Lloyd George, but against all notions from whatever quarter—Japan, Italy, China—which threatened what he held to be supreme. He was capable of the most astonishing compromises (such as those with Japan) in order to obtain support for this concept and to write it into the whole treaty. His thought appears to have been that whatever happened to the principles listed in his Fourteen Points ("The good God only had ten," said Clemenceau) the League must come into being so that it could in time create the better world. The unfortunate thing, of course, was that Germany had signed the armistice on the basis of the Fourteen Points, from which the treaty now being handed to Brockdorff-Rantzau departed so widely, in so many notable respects, that Germans were able to say for twenty years that they had been cheated. As he stood there watching, the tall, austere man,

11

so cold and unfeeling on the surface, he must have experienced the hot surge of triumph in his spirit at one thing, his supreme victory: he had his League. He may also have felt the edge of a bitter sadness underneath this triumph, because to the League he had been obliged to sacrifice the Fourteen Points, the principles upon which he had made the war and the armistice. But it does not seem, upon any evidence accessible to me, that he had faced the possibility of defeat by his own people in his supreme purpose.[1] True, he had been home to America in the early spring, had tested the temper of the Republican majority in Congress, and had made some modifications of the League covenant to satisfy what he thought were their main contentions. But, having sacrificed so much to this one great principle—including his own popularity throughout the world—he could hardly foresee that this, too, he would lose, and his whole system come into being crippled from birth by lack of support from the country of its origin.

Wilson was in his sixty-third year at this moment. No man alive had possessed a more acute temperamental and philosophical distaste for the use of force in international affairs. He was the son of a Presbyterian minister and his lifelong devotion to moral principle had a high, cold, narrow Calvinistic note in it. He reprobated war, force, imperialism, the use of power for exploitation of the weak. Through most of his life he had lived in academic circles as a professor of jurisprudence and political economy or as president of Princeton University. His published work was critical analysis of the American political system for the most part, and it was by a

---

[1] To his daughter, Mrs. Sayre, he wrote after the armistice: "I am very tired, but not too tired, and not at all dismayed or disheartened by the recent elections. I think the Republicans will find the responsibility which they must now assume more onerous than joyful, and my expectation is that they will exercise it with some circumspection. I shall see to it that they are put in a position to realize their full responsibility, and the reckoning in 1920 may hold disappointing results for them."

—R. S. Baker, *Woodrow Wilson, Life and Letters,* vol. 5, p. 591.

series of accidents that he left such work for political action, first as Governor of New Jersey and then as President of the United States (1912). What he wished to do was to bring about reforms of a mildly liberal nature, and he did succeed in some respects—a tariff law; the Federal Reserve Act (1913); the Federal Trade Commission and an anti-trust act (1914); the introduction of an income tax as part of the tariff law, for compensatory revenue; legislation to prepare the Philippine Islands for independence. But from early in his administration he had been obliged to deal with problems of a very different nature, which his whole delicate physique and austere Calvinistic spirit found repugnant: problems involving violence and the clash of arms. The Mexican Revolution of 1911, winding its way through swift and complicated changes with both genuine and spurious forces among the people, and taking forms determined by the social and economic condition of Mexico, with heroic idealism sometimes allied to unabashed banditry of the most bloodthirsty kind, was not a process Wilson could have been expected to understand either by nature or training or experience. He did not understand it, and wavered between contradictory policies from 1914 to 1917, without pursuing the advantages of either frank intervention or resolute abstention, so that when the last American troops left Mexico in January, 1917, nothing had been achieved except a sense of grievance which survives in Mexico to this day. In the greater conflict that broke out in Europe in 1914 he was determined to be neutral, and if the Germans had consented to moderate their submarine warfare there seems little doubt that he would have been neutral to the end, whatever forebodings had been aroused in his mind by the character of German imperial militarism. In the early years of the war his notes to Great Britain on the blockade system and the freedom of the seas were at least as sharp as his notes to Germany on submarine warfare and war zones.

13

He made no preparation for war in spite of a rising sentiment throughout the nation that "preparedness" was necessary. After the Germans in April, 1916, had promised not to sink merchant ships without warning and without saving the lives of passengers, Wilson seems indeed to have felt that this difficulty was disposed of, and he fought the election that summer under banners reading "He Kept Us Out of War." He felt a sense of personal grievance and outrage—a sense to which his temperament made him peculiarly subject—when Count von Bernstorff, the German Ambassador, handed him a note on January 31st, 1917, announcing the immediate resumption of unrestricted submarine warfare. By the following April, after a series of sinkings in which many American lives were lost, we were at war with Germany.

Unlike Clemenceau and Lloyd George, who had both visited the actual front and had trudged through the stinking trenches more than once, Wilson had no personal experience whatever either of the war or of Europe. He had arrived for the first time in the preceding December, after the victory, to be greeted in London, Paris and Rome with such demonstrations of popular enthusiasm as have seldom come to any man. His eagerness for knowledge, for information and advice, seems established by the testimony of many of those who accompanied him, including the Republicans; but he grew cold and distant very quickly if he felt a fundamental antagonism toward (above all) the League of Nations or any of his ruling ideas in the persons to whom he appealed. This characteristic gave rise to the legend that he would take no advice and would delegate no responsibility—a legend contradicted by his conduct of the war, in which he had delegated all the highest responsibilities and had taken all the advice he could get—and thus contributed, when the decline began, to the rapid waning of his star. He seems to have been amazed, as Lloyd George was, at the multitude of national and racial

14

aspirations released in the world by his principle of "self-determination," which had been a great allied war cry and lay at the root of eight (at least) of the Fourteen Points. Submerged nationalities everywhere were springing into life and demanding to be heard, even in areas like Catalonia, which had never been in the war; all over the Balkans, the Middle East, Central Europe, the Alpine and Adriatic regions, bitter antagonisms and fierce assertions of national rights envenomed the air; disorders big and little broke out in many places. Clemenceau, who had always regarded these principles with a kind of sour distrust, was not surprised; he had foreseen it all; he was not above using the effects as an attack upon the ostensible cause, and the attrition of the Fourteen Points in the course of the treaty negotiation was to a considerable extent his work, aided, as he was, by objective reality at almost every turn, each new situation producing another in the endless evolution of historical dialectic, so that a mind unprepared for the operation of all these specific forces (as Wilson's clearly was) could cling with desperation to only one ruling principle and sacrifice the rest.

And indeed as he stood there watching the passage of this treaty to the hand of the Prussian, Wilson's mind must have grown somber for at least one aching moment. Part I was safe: he had his League. But the whole philosophy of international relations which he had developed in his speeches during 1918 had paid the price. This philosophy had been formulated not only in the Fourteen Points (Jan. 8, 1918, to the joint session of Congress) but also in the "Four Principles" (to Congress, Feb. 11, 1918), the "Four Ends" (July 4, 1918) and the "Five Particulars" (Sept. 27, 1918). The principles, ends and particulars thus proclaimed were of a general nature, lofty in moral tone and extremely wide in their application to the difficulties of the world. They did not actually form the basis of the armistice—that was the Fourteen Points—but they were referred to during the armistice negotiations and undoubtedly played a great part in the surge of idealistic hope which arose among victors and vanquished at the end of the war. The nature of all these declarations can be shown by any one of them—for example, the second of the "Four Principles": [1]

"That peoples and provinces are not to be bartered about from sovereignty to sovereignty as if they were chattels or pawns in a game, even the great game, now for ever discredited, of the balance of power."

To every one of these statements, unexceptionable in themselves, some insuperable objection could be made whenever a specific case arose, as had happened over and over again during the preceding months of discussion. The moment you said quite plainly, "How does that apply to Hungary?" or "How does that apply to Austria?" you found yourself immersed in not only history and geography, but human passions of the most violent character, passions which lead men to murder, arson and anarchy unless they can be controlled. Wilson was wholly unprepared for the extent and complication of the passionate nationalisms his various groups of principles had fanned into flame. He neither knew nor liked them; there was a delicacy, a fastidiousness, a temperature of the mind, which in him impeded even the understanding of such emotions, and was reinforced by his lack of previous experience of them. As he had never understood the Mexican Revolution, so he does not seem to have understood the whole exhausting tangle of racial and national repulsions in Central and Southern Europe, to which his own political philosophy had helped give such fierce new vitality.

But what he did understand was the Fourteen Points—a great state paper, one of the great state papers of all history. He understood it because it had been the result of long work

[1] The Four Principles, Four Ends, and Five Particulars, as well as the Fourteen Points, are to be found in full in the Appendix.

by trusted advisers and of his own mature reflection, not upon principle alone—which came altogether too easily to his pen —but upon principle applied to the settlement of specific problems in this specific war. Such harnessing of theory to practice was rare in Wilson's career, and in the case of the Fourteen Points it offered the whole world the prospect of a peace to which no man of good will, whatever his nationality, could conceivably object.

Few of these points now survived. The first ("Open covenants openly arrived at") had been impossible to adhere to even in the negotiation of this treaty. The body of thirty allied and associated powers had been reduced to a council of ten, and then to five and finally to three (Wilson, Clemenceau, Lloyd George) in whose secret meetings all the most important decisions had to be made. The second, on freedom of the seas "alike in peace and in war," was made subject to reservations by Great Britain from the very beginning, and was in effect a dead letter from the time it was enunciated. The third, on the removal of economic barriers between nations "so far as possible," played no part in the development of either thought or practice, even in the United States. The fourth, on the reduction of national armaments to the lowest point consistent with national safety, received lip service in treaty and covenant, and as he stood there on May 7, 1919, Wilson may indeed have thought that this point at least had been saved; but its subsequent results were little or nothing. The fifth, on an adjustment of all colonial claims in strict observance of the principle that the interests of the populations concerned must have equal weight with the equitable claims of the government whose title is to be determined—this may, indeed, be said to have resulted in the mandate system of the League of Nations, but in what way the mandates were superior to old-fashioned colonial imperialism is another question. The sixth, demanding the evacuation of all Russian

17

territory and a welcome to the new Russia "under institutions of her own choosing," with a pledge of all assistance and a strong expression of sympathy, was systematically ignored by all the powers including, after a while, Wilson's own government; they carried on a bewildering policy of small-scale intervention for another year or two, doing just enough to plant the seeds of permanent distrust in Russia and not enough to achieve whatever it was they thought they wanted. The seventh, on the restoration of Belgium, had been fully taken over by the peace treaty—so fully that some small parts of Germany were even added to the Belgian state. The eighth, on the restoration of Alsace-Lorraine, was carried out in the treaty. The ninth, on the readjustment of Italy's frontiers, was carried out not in accordance with this point, but substantially in accordance with the secret Treaty of London (1916) which had bribed Italy to enter the war on the allied side; Italy thus received some Austrian territory to which she had no right under Wilsonian principles—as well as the Greek isles of the Dodecanese. The tenth point, on the "autonomous development" of the Austro-Hungarian peoples, was transformed into a whole separate treaty creating new states and allotting populations to this or that side of new frontiers. The eleventh, on the Balkans, was substantially put into effect, with numerous debatable allotments of territories and peoples. The twelfth, on the freedom of Turkey as well as of peoples formerly subject to Turkey, was the subject of a subsequent peace treaty and was partially effective, although the opening of the Dardanelles "as a free passage to the ships and commerce of all nations" was not a clause in that treaty. The thirteenth point, on the erection of an independent Polish state including territories inhabited by "indisputably Polish populations," with free and secure access to the sea, was interpreted so generously that Poland received a huge chunk of Russian territory and the question has plagued us all to this day. The fourteenth point, on the creation of a general association of nations to guarantee great and small states alike, was that by which Wilson set most store, and he had proved during the discussions of the preceding months that he could come to terms on all the other thirteen if he could keep his fourteenth point secure and get it written into the treaty. It was there, Part I of the treaty, The Covenant of the League of Nations, in twenty-six articles.

So Count Ulrich von Brockdorff-Rantzau spoke, received his copy of the document, bowed and retired, and the representatives of the allied and associated powers were free to contemplate the cows on the green outside. Among them were many who did not feel happy about this treaty. Colonel House, who had been active in many conversations during these years and had made many journeys, was to write in his diary the day after the signing of the document: "I should have preferred a different peace. I doubt if it could have been made, for the ingredients of such a peace as I would have had were lacking in Paris." There was Marshal Foch, who was angry over his Rhine bridgeheads, and of course there was Vittorio Emanuele Orlando, soon to be voted out of office at home, who was angry because among the non-Italian territories assigned to Italy there were not included Fiume and the Yugoslav coast of the Adriatic. Among the delegations were many who would write of these things afterwards, most of them very critically indeed, since the temper of all men quickly turned against this settlement. J. M. Keynes, representative of the British Treasury at the Peace Conference, was to resign exactly one month later and devote himself to the writing of a book which came out before the end of the year (December, 1919), and shook the world's faith in the peace more effectively than any other one influence of the time. This was *The Eco-*

19

nomic Consequences of the Peace, an essay written with such skill and perception that in spite of the fact that it made reparations and economic law the center of the whole matter, it could be read with the liveliest interest by any member of the public. Along with facts and figures designed to show that a "Carthaginian Peace" was practically impossible and would overwhelm the existing order of society, Keynes gave vivid glimpses of Clemenceau, skeptical of all general principles and bent only upon the destruction of German economic and industrial and military power; of Lloyd George, "with six or seven senses not available to ordinary men," darting his sensibility about through every obstacle; of Wilson, the hero and prophet of the age, exhibiting a dull and slow-minded stubbornness in the council chamber, unfamiliar with the conditions of Europe, well behind everything that was going on, always being out-maneuvered by quicker wits and subtler spirits—"this blind and deaf Don Quixote," said Keynes, "was entering a cavern where the swift and glittering blade was in the hands of the adversary."

Then, too, the protagonists themselves were to be heard again before they went into the darkness—Wilson in speeches delivered up and down the land as he struggled to obtain support for the treaty and covenant; Clemenceau in an extraordinary valedictory, *Splendeurs et Misères d'une Victoire* (1929), a volume brimming with venom against neither Germans nor allies, but against Poincaré the President and Foch the Supreme Commander; Lloyd George in the most verbose memoirs of the age, running to no less than eight big volumes, and showing (like Clemenceau) more resentment against some of his own commanders than against anybody else. Around these, and based in large part upon them, was an epigonic literature which in part justified or officially upheld (as in R. S. Baker's *Life and Letters of Woodrow Wilson*) and ranged

20

through various shades of criticism to the post-Hitler, Nihilistic Germanophobia of Ludwig Schwarzschild. No treaty produced so varied a literature as the treaty of Versailles. Hardly any of this literature was good, but it exhibited the sharp, sudden changes of opinion in twenty years—from the time when the treaty was condemned as being too harsh toward the Germans to the time when it was condemned as being too mild toward them. Obviously these judgments were more dependent upon external events than upon rational reflection, or the same treaty could not have seemed too severe in 1920 and too generous in 1945. What had changed was not the treaty but the objective situation of Germany in Europe, and in this case the treaty—obviously—must in some way be a part of the original cause, but not all of it.

For in the inexorable operation of the historical process the treaty was soon left far behind. Brockdorff-Rantzau retired from this dining room in the Trianon-Palace Hotel with the treaty in his hand, but no sooner had he read it than he saw he could not sign it as it stood. His efforts to obtain modifications in the terms—coinciding with some qualms of conscience on the part of Lloyd George and Arthur Balfour—produced weeks of tergiversation. In particular Lloyd George felt that Upper Silesia should not be "torn out of Germany and handed over to Poland" without a plebiscite, that a fixed amount for Germany's reparations should be agreed upon, and that it would be unjust to insist upon German disarmament unless Germany's neighbors also disarmed.[1] Wilson, who had repeatedly proclaimed that the peace settlement should be made by agreement with the vanquished, had changed so much in these few months of discussion that he no longer wished to hear the Germans but insisted on the draft treaty as it stood. Clemenceau had made an agreement with him by which the

[1] Lloyd George: *Memoirs of the Peace Conference,* Vol. II.

French press was to cease its personal attacks upon the American President, and France was to give up the idea of making the Rhine her frontier; for these somewhat unequal concessions (if they were concessions) Wilson was prepared to back Clemenceau on all the rest of the treaty terms which interested France. He was also so flatly and unreasonably pro-Polish that he contested even the simplest facts of ethnography and history. Thus in wrangling and ill-temper, with liberal opinion in both England and America already in revolt, with Smuts and Balfour and Botha and Tardieu and Loucheur and Painlevé each tugging at some one point or other (Painlevé from outside the French delegation, the others from within)—and with Poincaré and Foch keeping up a steady crossfire at Clemenceau for not being extreme enough—somehow or other they called it finished. Brockdorff-Rantzau, unwilling to sign, withdrew from the German government and the treaty was signed (June 28, 1919) by a man named Hermann Muller for the German Republic.

Wilson sailed for home, his political philosophy abandoned and his prestige throughout the world (brief but overwhelming) already wrecked. Hardly a principle he had proclaimed through the war and at the outset of the peace negotiations had been carried through into practice. He pinned his faith now to the League of Nations, which would, he thought, right all the wrongs he had been unable to deal with; and in the battle for the League against recalcitrant senators, congressmen and public opinion, he wore himself out to final collapse. The treaty and the League were rejected by the American Congress, for the combination of inimical forces was too great, taking in reactionary nationalists and liberal idealists alike. The majority was small, but it was enough, and America watched the development of the next twenty years as if it had no responsibility for any of it—as if these things took place on another planet or in another age.

§ 3

If the Fourteen Points were almost wholly set aside by the treaty, and if they in practical fact produced no results, why have I referred to them as one of the great state papers of history? Can a mere statement of wishes or ideals qualify as a state paper at all? What is the historical status of such honorable velleities?

So much time has passed, so much blood has been shed, that as we look back across the ruins of the years it is difficult to see clearly now. What I see is that the Fourteen Points could have been the basis of a just and honorable peace in which Germany might have taken her place as a member of the free association of nations. This was the last chance for a very long time for such a thing to happen. Powerful elements in the German national character have always made it difficult for the humane genius to prevail among German peoples, especially since Bismarck and the empire of 1871, but the Fourteen Points offered a true opportunity for that genius to gain and keep the upper hand. If the territorial and economic settlements had followed the lines of the Fourteen Points, every encouragement would have been given to what is or has been best in the German race—those qualities of industry, ingenuity, peaceful accomplishment, which we see so admirably exemplified among the millions of Americans of German origin. By discarding the Fourteen Points (or most of them) for an old-fashioned treaty of limitless indemnities, occupations and annexations, the peacemakers created that state of sullen and resentful disintegration in Germany which imperatively called for and historically determined the rise of Adolf Hitler and the subsequent horror of the greater war.

For the Fourteen Points were not—like the Atlantic Charter—a mere enunciation of abstract principles with no clear application to specific cases. They were the most specific solutions Wilson ever proposed, and they caught the historic moment when they were objectively possible. Too much has happened since; they will never be possible again. For history is not a static thing, proceeding according to blueprints, diagrams and Euclidean theorems. It moves dialectically, each situation producing a new one by a series of contradictions and resolutions. It is not necessary to follow Hegel or Marx to see that this is concretely true. Napoleon said of battles: "No precise rules can be laid down. Everything depends upon the character of the general, his abilities, his weakness, the quality of his troops, the range of their weapons, the weather and a thousand other circumstances which never repeat themselves." And what is true of battle, physical, military battle, is true of the clash of historic forces on their way; everything depends upon a thousand circumstances which never repeat themselves. The opportunity of 1919 will never—I say never —come again.

What, then, was this Treaty of Versailles which Brockdorff-Rantzau carried away with him from the dining room of the Trianon-Palace Hotel on May 7, 1919?

Part I was the covenant of the League of Nations, in twenty-six articles. It provided for a league of self-governing states (originally the signatories to this treaty) with an assembly and a council, a permanent secretariat, and a permanent seat at Geneva. It provided for consideration of the reduction of armaments at least every ten years, some form of supervision of the private enterprise of munitions and implements of war, and a military, naval and air commission to advise on these matters. The members of the League undertook to "respect and preserve as against external aggression" (Article 10) the "territorial integrity and existing political independence of all Members of the League." Other articles provided for inquiry and arbitration of disputes, the establishment of a Permanent Court of International Justice, procedure for the discussion of disputes, protection for labor and for native in-habitants of controlled territories, and set up the mandate system for territories not ready for self-government.

Part II settled the boundaries of Germany, which were mainly natural and ethnographical in the West, but political and sentimental in the East, giving Poland some German terri-tory and a corridor to the sea through East Prussia. Part III, the "political clauses for Europe," restored Belgium (with the German districts of Eupen and Malmedy thrown in) and an independent Luxemburg outside the German customs union; it neutralized the east bank of the Rhine for fifty kilometers and all the west bank, in which no German fortification or armed force could exist; the coal mines of the Saar Basin were ceded to France in "full and absolute possession"—the govern-ment of the Saar to be in the hands of a League commission for fifteen years, when a plebiscite would be held; it restored Alsace-Lorraine to France, with numerous clauses intended to cut that province economically from Germany; it created the Czechoslovak, Polish and Austrian states with new frontiers, providing for a plebiscite in Upper Silesia. It also reserved Memel for subsequent decision by the allies, created Danzig as a free city under the protection of the League, and abrogated the Treaty of Brest-Litovsk between Germany and Russia.

Part IV, on German rights and interests outside Germany, made the Germans give up all their overseas possessions in favor of the allies. (These were subsequently allotted under the mandate system—the African colonies to Italy, France and England, the Pacific isles to Japan.) Germany also surrendered all special rights and concessions in China, Siam, Liberia, Morocco, Egypt, Turkey and Bulgaria, and turned over her rights, privileges and properties in the province of Shantung to Japan.

Part V, the military, naval and air clauses, cut the German land army to a maximum of one hundred thousand men to be recruited by voluntary enlistment, reduced the navy to thirty-six ships of all classes, specifically excluding submarines, and named fifteen thousand as the maximum personnel of the whole German navy, including administrative and other land offices. The rest of the German ships were to be turned over to the allied powers. The construction of submarines was forbidden in Germany; the manufacture of arms and munitions was restricted to certain approved factories and was subject to allied control. Germany was to have no military or naval aircraft of any kind; all in existence were to be turned over to the allies. An interallied control commission was set up to see that these military, naval and air clauses were enforced.

Part VI was on war prisoners and the graves of the dead; Part VII "solemnly arraigned" William II of Hohenzollern and demanded that the German government turn over material for use in his trial as a war criminal.

Part VIII, on reparations, declared Germany and her allies to be responsible for all damage done to the allied and associated powers in this war, which was imposed upon them by German aggression. (This "war guilt" clause was one of those to which Germans objected most violently in the next two decades.) A reparations commission (interallied) was set up to deal with Germany's payments and to hear just pleas in this regard. Twenty billion marks gold (five billion dollars) were to be paid in 1919, 1920 and the first four months of 1921. The rest was more or less a blank check, the amounts to be settled later.

The reparations clauses, with their annexes, were immensely long and complicated. They reposed upon the declaration of Germany's war guilt and upon the principle that the allied and associated powers were entitled to get back everything their citizens had lost in the war (exclusive of military expenditure). Thus was enumerated everything from ships to sows, from dyestuffs to coal, from stallions and fillies and milch cows to sulphate of ammonia and ocean cables and the Triptych of the Mystic Lamb by the brothers Van Eyck.

Part IX contained the financial and Part X the economic clauses. Germany assumed the cost of the armies of occupation and of the cash payments of reparations, and the succession states (or those to whom German territory was annexed) were to pay a portion of the old German state debt. There were special clauses for Alsace-Lorraine, for Turkey (Germany's share of the Ottoman debt) and other particular situations. The economic clauses, detailed in the extreme, regulated customs, shipping, insurance, contracts, debts and property, with a general tendency to make allied decisions and allied courts the final authority in any question at issue.

Part XI was on aerial navigation, and gave the allies the same rights in Germany as German aircraft had enjoyed. Part XII, on ports, waterways and railways, gave the allies rights of free transit in Germany and payments equal to those of German nationals, with a declaration of international status for the Elbe, Oder, Niemen and Danube. A special section gave France special rights to water power, German shipping and ports, and water for irrigation purposes from the Rhine and Moselle.

Part XIII set up the International Labor Office under the League, for the regulation of the conditions of work and the protection of the interests of the worker. Its provisions were extremely humanitarian and idealistic so far as the words went. Part XIV was on guarantees of the execution of the treaty (allied military occupation of certain areas for certain periods up to fifteen years). Part XV, the last, contained miscellaneous provisions, such as a blanket recognition by Germany of any treaties to be made subsequently between the allies and those powers which had fought on Germany's side in the war (Austria, Hungary, Bulgaria, Turkey).

This, then, was the Treaty of Versailles. It was, to begin

27

with, not a treaty at all—that is, it was not a document providing terms of settlement by agreement between two parties. It was a settlement negotiated between the victors, without consultation of the vanquished. It was, in fact, a *Diktat*, as Hitler and practically all other Germans were to call it for the next twenty years, a settlement dictated by the conqueror. In this fundamental respect it violated Wilson's principles in general, and in particular it was in direct contradiction to the second and third of the "Four Principles," and the third of the "Four Ends."

Aside from this general, fundamental invalidity, it departed so far and so often from the Fourteen Points (upon which Germany had made the armistice) that it was child's play for any German nationalist agitator, not Hitler alone but much milder and more reasonable politicians, to represent it as a gigantic swindle inflicted upon the German people. Polemicists writing twenty and twenty-five years later without an adequate comprehension of the fluidity of history were to say (like Ludwig Schwarzschild) that the treaty was too weak, too gentle, too much influenced by liberal idealism and humanitarianism and without enough familiarity with the irredeemable ferocity of the German barbarian. Such criticism was not heard at the time of the treaty or for years afterwards. It was only after the treaty—this treaty—had played its great historic role in creating a new situation from which Adolf Hitler was the inevitable product, and events of twenty years had flowed with dialectical certainty to the most extreme assertion of German tribal ambition, that the emotions of 1940, particularly among those who had most severely suffered from Nazi cruelty, re-interpreted the events of 1918-1920 and discovered that the Treaty of Versailles was a "good" treaty.

It was not a "good" treaty. It was not a treaty at all. It was a dictated settlement which was, by and large, about as bad as it could be, because it violated every proclaimed principle and ideal without obtaining the advantages of real control over the Germans. It could not rally the support of any important public opinion in any country; it was never applied as a whole, and after the defection of America it rapidly began to fall apart as a system.

A "good" treaty could have been made in 1918-1919 on the basis of the Fourteen Points. It is just possible. The worst thing about the Treaty of Versailles is that it made this sort of peace, a peace of justice based upon principles accepted by all men of good will, quite outside the possibilities thereafter. Once such terrible forces have been set in motion, the further results, after innumerable new situations have arisen, cannot be used as a justification of old errors. Buchenwald and Dachau are not arguments in favor of the Treaty of Versailles, because they did not exist in 1919. The errors of Versailles must take their place upon the stage of history in their right place, their chronological position, contributing their concrete results at a stage in the development when no man could foresee, or did foresee, the eventual ruins of the Ukraine, the horrors of Dachau or the death struggle in East and West.

§ 4

I came to the Trianon-Palace Hotel at Versailles last spring from some days spent in Cologne. All winter I had been with Patton's army going toward the Rhine, and many conversations with German prisoners, many scenes of death in the snow and actions grimly performed were alive in my most recent memory. The ruins of Cologne had made an impression much more painful than might have been expected because of the words, the random, ordinary words of ordinary people, which I had caught on the wing as I visited there.

In the old days when we went to Cologne on the Paris-Berlin or the Berlin-Paris Express we got out at the most

29

animated railway station in Germany. If it was spring or summer the women were selling flowers up and down the platform; at any season they were selling newspapers, magazines, books and candy. The stop was always a fairly lengthy one, and many a passenger who never set foot outside the immediate neighborhood of the railway station has had at least a bird's-eye view of the cathedral square beside the Rhine. The arrangement of the cathedral and railroad station put the show window of Cologne, so to speak, at the disposal of the casual traveler bound for Berlin or Warsaw or Moscow on quite other business, and it may be said that Cologne was probably the most glimpsed, if not the most visited, of Germany's cities.

The cathedral was the center of the town physically as well as in most other respects. That is, Cologne was built in a half-moon around that cathedral, which, for the greater part of the city's long history, was itself only an idea imperfectly suggested. It was not actually constructed, carried out in full, until the nineteenth century, and then in the frigid architectural correctness of a Hohenzollern professor copying the great Gothic styles of France. But lifeless and model-like as it was, the structure which the Kaiser William II opened in 1880 was somehow the fruition or modern statement of a dream which had been implicit in the life of Cologne for centuries. We find even Heinrich Heine writing, in the *Dichterliebe,* about the "great, holy cathedral," at a time when it did not yet exist, when in fact it had only a fourteenth-century choir and the later foundations of a transept and façade. But this extremely rudimentary cathedral, this sketch in stone, awaiting its completion through the centuries, had so taken possession of the minds of those who dwelt in the city that at all periods Cologne has been conscious of its central monument, has built around and toward that one hublike center, just as if the great Gothic dream had come to pass in the only century when it was really possible, the thirteenth. Thus the great city brooded for centuries upon a falsehood, like an earnest hen set upon a china egg.

And in fact most of Cologne's other eggs were china too. Never was a city more badgered by archeologists, antiquarians, architects, restorers and chambers of commerce. What the nineteenth century did to Gothic Cologne was a triumph of zeal, erudition and civic pride, but it left hardly a Gothic or romanesque or even baroque church unrestored. The sinister dates 1870, 1880, 1885, are strewn across the relics of its past, and the development of the sprawling commercial and industrial city coincided with a pedantic effort to prop up and set forth everything that still possessed a stone or a line or a suggestion of less prosaic moments in its history. The prosperous and thick-necked burghers of the bouncing Hohenzollern days, touched to nostalgia by music or beer or the good wine of the Rhine Valley, were trying to buy back a past that had gone forever.

We used to humor this civic antiquarianism by an occasional visit to the synthetic monuments which were its pride, but in truth what I always liked best in Cologne was the peculiar flavor of its contemporary life. When I say contemporary I speak of the years before Hitler, the last good years, perhaps, which the Rhineland capital will know for a very long time. What distinguished Rhenish from other North German life was its simpler and more unaffected appreciation of pleasure, of all the pleasures of life, music and wine and food and friends. It was neither solemn nor feverish. Sometimes when Berlin called for madder music and stronger wine—I speak of the 1920's—one had the impression of being in an insane asylum. And except for a very few restaurants in Berlin, Munich and Hamburg, good eating and drinking, as distinguished from gluttony, were never widely understood in North Germany. The fashions and manners of the women in Berlin, when they were not simply a form of upholstery, had a touch of the same madness. The North German spirit seemed on the whole too serious, too intent, to be capable of moderation, and as it turned to metaphysical thinking, false science and fanatical politics, so its attitude toward pleasure, when it had time for pleasure, was tinged with madness and decay. Who, who ever knew them, could forget the cabarets of Berlin in the 1920's?

As against this unequal and immoderate pursuit of pleasure could be opposed, in those days, the simpler gaieties of Cologne, a provincial capital which did not consider itself to be Prussian and had always lived its own life. Cologne at its best, such as on an evening when something really good was being performed at the opera house, was capable of suggesting both Paris and Vienna—suggesting them only, and with a good strong Rhenish accent, but at any rate seldom suggesting Berlin. Everything was fairly early, as I remember, and the night clubs of the town were not rampant at any time, but there was a straightforward and genuine enjoyment of music, dancing, food and drink, a recognition of the place of pleasure in ordinary life, and with this, perhaps as a result of it, a simpler and more natural good taste than was common elsewhere in Northern Germany. This had its effect upon everything from women's clothes to the decoration of a restaurant, and although it would be absurd to suggest that Cologne ever rivaled Vienna, for example, in any such respects, yet it is certainly true that the charm of life did exist here in its own distinctive way. And with the great, beautiful river to dignify everything it touched, spring and summer could give Cologne another special quality to set it off from the general stodgy unattractiveness of German cities.

This time I did not enter Cologne by either of the old ways, right or left of the Rhine, for the railway was gone and the station no longer existed. Among these ruins, the most extensive I had ever seen up to that moment, many streets were

32

partly filled with rubble, many were completely lost in the general devastation. It was difficult to pass through any whole street from beginning to end, except on the very wide Ring Boulevard built in the nineteenth century along the line of the semi-circular wall which once enclosed the medieval city. The first impression, as you drove in from west or north, was one of unimaginable desolation. For mile after mile the houses stood or fell in every stage of ruin. None was untouched; many were only rubbish; even those which still stood were mostly hollowed out by explosives and fire. Whatever we expected —and everybody knew Cologne had been bombed from the air for three years—the reality was bound to stun us at first; wreckage on such a scale is something for which no previous experience had prepared us. I thought I had seen bomb destruction in Spain, China, France, Belgium, England, all of it brought about by the tenants of these houses or their allies. But after seeing Cologne I was aware that the weapon they themselves brought into existence was the most terrible punishment visited upon them. And from these hundreds of acres of rubble and ruin arose one aching question: Did they understand this? Did they know how this awe-inspiring catastrophe came upon them? Did they learn anything from it?

I was afraid not.

The Venloer Strasse is one of the spokes of the wheel which is Cologne. Coming through that long drive in a jeep we saw few civilians, a shabby and cringing few, picking their way amidst the ruins. It seemed hard to believe that any human beings would willingly stay in this doomed city, and yet the military government officials told me the final count would be something like a hundred thousand. This was what was left of eight hundred thousand, and under the circumstances it seemed a lot. Discounting any Nazi agents who might have been left for espionage or other party work, it was only reasonable to suppose that seventy-five or eighty per cent of those who stayed were anti-Nazis or at least non-Nazis, since by remaining in the city they were deliberately disobeying an order of the Nazi government and party. And precisely for this reason what they said to me appalled me, for if these people, ordinary men and women who had never much liked the Nazi fantasy or believed in it, these people who were its victims, had not learned their lesson, what hope was there for convincing the rest?

"Poor Germany," they say, "did not have enough airplanes. We have known for a long time that the war was lost. There was too much force against us."

Poor Germany, indeed!

The Venloer Strasse leads directly into the Ring Boulevard, which bears different names at different stages of its semi-circular stretch around the inner city. At the Military Government headquarters just where the Kaiser Wilhelm Ring meets the Hohenzollern Ring, we consulted maps and officials, received admonitions and cautions. We were not to go here or there; such and such a place was under machine-gun fire from across the river; the mortars had been falling just here and just there. (For this and a few more days, Cologne was still in the front line.) The last remnants of the Watch on the Rhine were just over the sparkling water in the suburb called Deutz. Now, even now as we stood in front of maps and spoke reasonably of such mad things, the despairing crackle of machine guns could be heard—this at a moment when at a hundred other points, north and south of Cologne, the American and British armies were rolling far beyond the Rhine into Germany. Although those German companies across the water in Deutz might not know it yet, the Rhine had ceased to be a great natural barrier. They were to be engulfed soon in a tide greater than the Rhine. What barrier, indeed, is valid now?

All circumstances weighed, it seemed to me that my jeep tour of Cologne would yield some concept of the city's fate if I pursued the Ring boulevards around to the Severin Tor, one of the still extant gates of the old city, and then went up the Severin Strasse, the High Street in fact, to the Cathedral. This, with a side jaunt to the Nazi University, was the plan, and in spite of the ruins I had already seen, it still seemed possible.

The Ring boulevards were one long spacious street, tree-lined and opulent, in the days before Hitler. The traffic lanes were separated by a well-planted garden space in the old days, like the Champs Elysées in Paris or Park Avenue in New York. Now the middle space was arid and the trees along the side, when they stood at all, seemed withered and black. Along both sides of the Ring were the shops, offices and apartment buildings of prosperous people, those who owned and managed the factories to the north, the banks in the center, the shipping and insurance interests of the city. Now the boulevard was lined with ruin, rubbish and ruin. The pompous names it bore seemed to emphasize the devastation on every hand. This was the Kaiser Wilhelm II Ring, and in the middle of the garden space down its center there still stood a statue of his wife, Empress Augusta, headless and mutilated by bomb blast.

From the Kaiser Wilhelm II to the Hohenzollern Ring, and from the Hohenzollern to the Hapsburg Ring, we passed almost without knowing it. The wreck of buildings on each side was so complete that seldom were the street signs left at the corners, and we marked our progress chiefly by means of the map. In the debris on one side was a painted sign, one of those the Nazis put up all over Germany and Europe. It said, in staring black upon a wall which jutted from the surrounding rubbish, *"Was hast du fuer Deutschland getan?"* What have you done for Germany? What, indeed?

Before us loomed a familiar gray hulk, the Opera House. By now we were in the Hohenstaufen Ring—the Hapsburgs had only a very small section of this elegant boulevard named after them. On the right was the bulging arcaded front, the pompous roof, of a theater which used to be one of the best in Germany. The Cologne Opera was on a smaller scale than those in Berlin, Munich and Dresden, but it could hold its own with the best of them in good productions of, for example, Mozart. It was in this opera house that I first heard a Mozart opera. It was *The Marriage of Figaro* and the performance was given in the winter of 1922-1923, at the time of the French occupation of the Ruhr. I was in Cologne, like dozens of other press correspondents of greater age and experience, to report the doings of the Rhineland Separatist movement which the French then patronized. Those were times of crisis, supposedly, in the Rhineland, and the great war of 1914-1918 was still a vivid memory. People I knew in Cologne used to tell me of the food shortages they had undergone, and of the terrors of bombing from the air, although by 1922 any trace of damage (if there ever was any) had been removed.

The performance at the opera that night was characteristic of the best in German stage techniques, careful and precise, with resourceful staging and admirable musicianship. I even remember the singer who sang the part of Susanne, a soprano called Emmy Senff-Thiess, whom I never saw again. It was a kind of revelation to me, who had hitherto seen only the carelessly slung-together kind of opera performances we have in America, to discover what could be done with great music and a little intelligence. The audience, too, so silent and enraptured, was something new in my experience. I went away —like most of the Germans—singing, and repaired to the Dom Hotel to discuss it all with a friend over a bottle of Rhine wine.

Now the big gray opera house was gutted, its roof open to every wind that blew, its insides burned out and filled with rubble. The arcades and the bulging front still stood, and on one side the stage door was still firmly shut. On it was a sign put up by the American army: "Danger. Typhus Fever. Off Limits." The colonnade had a rubbish heap beneath each arch.

Beyond the opera house, on the right, was the big church of the Sacred Heart of Jesus, its walls and spire alone standing. Even this was a triumph of endurance for this particular spot, since practically everything else in the neighborhood was reduced almost to dust. In the Barbarossa Platz, to which we came next, not a wall was intact, not a street sign to be seen. This was merely rubbish on four sides, and the fountain that used to play in the middle of the open space seemed to have vanished with no trace.

Here was where I headed off down the Luxemburg Strasse to the outer part of the city on a visit to the new university. Most of the streets leading to it were, I had been told, filled with fallen masonry, but through the Luxemburg Strasse one could get to the general neighborhood and then pick a way around through the debris. This street, another spoke in the wheel, led out past the South Station of the Cologne-Bonn Railway into a new quarter which was once all apartment buildings. Shells of these remain, and a few civilians were to be seen moving in and out of the cellars or first floors, but the general picture of desolation was the same as in the rest of the city. Off to the right, in an area less often bombed than the city's center, were the huge modern buildings of the Cologne University.

These gray, barrack-like structures had most of their walls and some of their roofs intact, although all were considerably damaged in some night bombings of October, 1944. I left the jeep in the broad space before the main university building and went in, pausing on the broad steps to look at the stylized Nazi eagle and swastika over the entrance.

Here, I thought, is the crux of the matter. For at the very entrance of the main building of the university, in a sort of

37

golden niche no visitor could possibly miss, was inscribed the Nazi credo: *"Alles Wissen soll der Nation dienen."* All knowledge shall serve the nation.

Here, when they built the structure in 1934, the Nazis stated the essential belief in which they perverted all German science and philosophy. Knowledge must no longer exist for itself, as a means of reaching truth, for the enlightenment and solace of mankind, or, as the medieval scholastics had it, for the greater glory of God. No: it exists for the nation, for the German nation, which is identified with the sanguinary and tribal fanaticism of the National Socialist Party.

Under such a banner no university could be possible, and we are scarcely surprised to learn that Cologne University never lived up to its spacious and expensive pretensions. Older schools, such as Heidelberg and Bonn, could keep some vestiges of learning even in the midst of Nazi tyranny. Cologne was doomed from the beginning because it did not become a great modern university until the blight had already descended. The dates over the doorway are as illusory as most other archeological or historical data in Cologne. They say 1388-1934, but actually the old school founded in 1388 had nothing whatever to do with the new Nazi university, less even than the Gothic foundations had to do with the Hohenzollern cathedral.

I wandered around through deserted lecture halls in which the furniture was intact and the windows gone. In the main auditorium, which seats 1500 people, the stage was ornamented with an American flag and a sign saying "Presented by U.S.O. Shows." As I wandered back down the high echoing hall I ran into a small, worried elderly man who presented himself as the housemaster, or, in fact, janitor.

Yes, he said, the university had been untouched by all the bombings until last October. It was too far out of the center of the city and too far from any railroad or factory or bridge.

When the Cologne Opera was destroyed in June, 1943, the opera company moved out to the university and gave its performances in the big auditorium, twice or sometimes three times a week. It had been necessary to enlarge the stage and to take out some front rows of the orchestra seats to make room for the musicians. When the Opera was not playing, the big auditorium was used for theater and cinema performances. But the university itself "suffered" in October, and these performances came to an end. They were resumed on March 13, 1945, by the Americans, and Miss Lily Pons—the intrepid and indefatigable—had sung there only a few nights before to a crowded audience of soldiers.

The use of the word "suffered" (*gelitten*) as meaning bombed, struck upon my ear.

"When you say suffered," I remarked, "have you any idea of what the cities of other countries have suffered from the Germans? Do you know anything about the bombings of Rotterdam or Warsaw or London or Bristol?"

"Yes," the old man said, "but these things we knew only from the newspapers."

"But do you Cologne people realize that what you have suffered is an exact and logical consequence of what you made others suffer earlier?"

"I don't know about that," he said. "We heard only one side, propaganda in newspapers. But we knew that we had lost the war."

"Do you remember that Hitler promised in a radio speech in the autumn of 1940 that he would erase every city in England? Using the word '*ausradieren*'—erase?"

"Yes," said the old man, cackling suddenly, "but we also know that he didn't have the rubber to do the erasing. It was the Englanders who had the rubber!"

"When did you know that you had lost the war?" I asked.

"After the Blitzkrieg was over," he said. "We always knew

39

our ground soldiers were good. We understood that we could win a Blitzkrieg. But we are too poor to afford a big air force. We could not win against such an air force."

I was almost speechless with exasperation. What was the use of telling him that we had had no air force to speak of until we were forced to build one? What was the use of recalling, to this all-too-convenient German memory, the fact that the German air force ruled the skies only five years ago?

It reminded me of the German cleaning woman at the press camp who said, "Ah, poor Germany! We had no chance against such power!" Or of the other German who told me that Germany had been forced to make war because the Americans, British and Russians were in league against her. The cart before the horse, the cart always before the horse, German reasoning and German memory in precisely the same state today as they were in 1922, arguing that the result caused the cause. Germany had created our air force, had created our alliance with Russia and England, and then, before the accomplished fact, argued backwards. This was the way it always had been and it seemed that this might be the way it always would be.

The old man was cackling on.

"As soon as so many allies came in against us," he said, "we knew it was no use. Many dogs mean death to the hare."

He was quoting an old proverb, *Viele Hunde sind des Hasen Tod,* one of those tags of peasant wisdom with which most Germans can face practically any catastrophe and escape a feeling of responsibility for it.

There was no use talking to this man. There was no use talking about the essential problems to any German I had yet met, war prisoner or civilian. It seemed to me that the primary necessity in this affair was to show the German people the chain of cause and effect, show them by every means in our power and before we lived much longer. For the really staggering thing in the whole affair is that they acknowledged

40

not only no guilt, but no responsibility, and in the very moment when they throw off the responsibility onto Hitler and
the Nazis they also absolve them by saying, "They should have
known they could not win against such power."

Power? Power? Who was it had the power five years ago?
Who was it that made power the only standard of action or
value?

We turned from the university and made our way back into
the center of the city.

The Ring brought us to the Severin Tor, one of the surviving gates of the medieval wall. This—like the Roman archways
at Trier, like so many odd remnants of a much earlier day—
seems to have had no damage at all, and stands much as it always did amidst the surrounding ruin. Through the old gate
we headed up the Severin Strasse for the High Street and the
cathedral.

This was once the main shopping street of Cologne, but before we had gone far I realized that it was useless to try to
identify anything here. One rubbish heap followed another;
the road was blocked by rubbish and we were obliged to turn
into another street and then another, left or right, darting
and twisting and winding in the jeep tracks which traversed
the ruins rather in the way a sheep goes over a hill. Occasionally street signs remained on the corners of the hollowed-out
buildings, but oftener they, too, had disappeared. Enough
high walls remained between here and the river to screen
the jeep tracks from observation, but there came at last a point
at which the American patrols stopped us.

"You can't take a jeep any further," they said. "It will be
fired on. They can drop a mortar very easily on anything
they see."

And so we went along on foot toward St. Agatha and the
Minoriten Church, ignoring the unpleasant smells and pausing cautiously at each intersection to be sure we were not

41

observed. To right and left were the wrecks of all Cologne's reconstructed Gothic. But the G.I.'s intervened again: on this route we could not reach the cathedral.

"You can't go out there," they said. "You'll only draw fire. Go back and approach the cathedral from the other side, from the front, and you can see all you want."

So we regained the jeep and wound our way again through a trail marked by our predecessors, a trail to which the map no longer seemed to have any application. In this wilderness it was so easy to get lost that we came out, finally, not far from our original point of departure—in fact, in the Ring again, in a square near the Opera House. Here the Americans had put up a square sign quoting one of Hitler's celebrated boasts and its English translation. It said: *"Gebt mir fünf Jahre und ihr werdet Deutschland nicht wieder erkennen."* Give me five years and you will not recognize Germany again.

Down from the Ring on the Christoph and Gereon Streets —one street which changes names from time to time—we came at last to the cathedral square. The Church of St. Gereon, parts of which are Romanesque and others still older, now is walls alone; it was here that the legendary Gereon and his companions of the Theban Legion were supposed to have suffered death under the Emperor Diocletian in 286 for refusing to abjure Christianity. Here, too, Helena, the mother of Constantine, once built a basilica on the site of the present nave. The big banks and the German state post office which line the street nearest the cathedral looked almost undamaged, except for their blank windows; they were all sealed up and guarded now by American sentries.

As we came to the edge of the cathedral square and stood with relative caution before that famous model we were in plain view of the Germans on the other side of the river. There was the bridge, there the sparkling Rhine, blue-white in the light of a suave Palm Sunday noon. The sky gleamed through

42

the holes in the cathedral roof. Part of the façade was damaged. Aside from this, the black lines of the pseudo-Gothic church arose as before, geometrically neat and lifeless. It bore the same relation to the cathedrals of Amiens and Chartres as a mechanical heart does to the living organ. But this was Palm Sunday, a day on which those steps would once have been thronged with the devout Rhinelanders carrying branches, and now they were at last as dead and empty as the architecture above them. The crackle of machine-gun fire sounded out over the square and we got back to the American army signs. They said: "Sightseers, stay away. You will only draw fire. We risk our lives 24 hours every day. Do you?"

Over on the other side of the wrecked railway station, up a small and narrow street, was the Church of St. Ursula, one of the ancient monuments of the city. (Of course it was restored in 1891.) Here the tomb of the British Princess Ursula, who with her eleven thousand virgins was sacrificed to save the Roman colony from the Huns, has been venerated for centuries. Today there were walls and nothing else. From one breach could be seen a gleam of gold, a remnant of mosaic. On the intact door of the shell there was a sign put up by American army authority: "Historic monument. Do not touch."

It reminded me of a ruder but equally futile sign I had seen amidst the debris of the Severin Strasse. It was on a doorway which was partially intact although the house behind it was hardly more than dust. It said: *"Achtung! Bissender Hund!"* Beware. Biting dog.

We had seen enough. What if the Ford factory, up in the northern suburbs, was by some extraordinary accident undamaged? The Farina headquarters, over on the other side of the cathedral, the home of the Cologne water which traveled the world over, was a wreck; one factory more or less could make little difference. I did not even think it mattered much

43

that the synthetic Gothic cathedral had been substantially saved from destruction. What mattered was that air bombardment had systematically wiped out a city with all its main organs of life, traffic, industry, culture and commerce, had done so upon a German plan and German example, and with the purpose of teaching the Germans once for all that they must give up the dream of conquering other peoples. Had this end been achieved?

I had no doubt of the extraordinary military effectiveness of the bombardments. The marshaling yards at the South Station, wreckage not of stone but of steel, would alone be proof of this. The wilderness of ruins proved that it could be done. But had this conveyed anything whatever to the German mind?

Here I doubted and wondered. There is something quite beyond reason or common sense in the German feeling of superiority and inferiority. These very people who today would speak to you of "poor Germany" were the same ones who went to the film theaters and applauded wildly in 1940 when films were shown of the destruction of Warsaw and Rotterdam by German bombing. They did not connect. They were never taught to connect. When they had the power it was right for them to assault and devastate every part of the non-German world which they could possibly reach. Now that their power was exhausted and ours was at its height, they wept among their ruins and lamented, not for the madness which led them out to conquer the world, but for the relative weakness which prevented their accomplishing that end. They did not see that this result was inevitable from the moment that they submitted to, or acquiesced in, when they did not actively support, the Nazi plan for a subjugation of all other peoples. Here in the ruins of Cologne it was impossible not to think of all the other ruins that covered the face of Germany, and of the strange passion of strength and weakness that brought them about. We had to think of those words at the end of *Mein Kampf:*

"Ein Staat, der im Zeitalter der Rassenvergiftung sich der Pflege seiner besten rassischen Elemente widmet, muss eines Tages zum Herrn der Erde werden."

Masters of the Earth?

The words echoed strangely in the narrow street beside St. Ursula's Church. Two old women were walking down the street arm in arm, like the blind leading the blind. Their faces were dulled and whitened by suffering. The stubborn and stupid people, forever at the mercy of any prince or fakir who could arouse their sense of superiority, lapsed into despair and self-pity when their efforts came to nothing. If we could fill that gap, if we could somehow make them understand that this result came from that cause, the thing might perhaps not happen again very soon. This was all we could do for the ghosts of our own youth who died in the skies over Cologne to teach a lesson so grim, so bitter, so ill-comprehended. Along the roads to and from this city we had passed blue-and-white signs, neatly lettered and with arrows pointing off: "American cemetery. Four miles." This, too, it had cost; and in the time which was now at hand we had to find, with thought and reason, some way to make the living understand.

§ 5

To come back in space to this room in the Trianon-Palace Hotel at Versailles took a long journey—through Africa, Italy, France and part of Germany. To come back historically to this point, to live again through the opportunity of 1919, was no longer possible; that chance was forever gone. Remembering Cologne, remembering the hundreds of Germans to whom I had talked in the campaigns of the winter and spring—remembering, too, the faces of our dead soldiers, and the look of the platoon strung out on the hillside—it seemed to me that some fundamentally new way of approaching the problem of the peace must be found, some way profoundly different from the spirit which animated the conversations of Versailles. For what happened, in simple fact, in this room? A "treaty" of an antiquated pattern, departing very widely from the conditions of the armistice, was handed to the delegates of a demoralized but still powerful nation, who were told in polite but firm tones that they could make "observations," but essentially no changes in this document.

"This cannot be the time or place for superfluous words," Clemenceau said to them.[1] "The hour has come for the heavy settlement of accounts. You have asked us for peace. We are prepared to accord it to you."

In his brief speech, which Lloyd George[2] characterized as "a few short but perfectly courteous sentences," Clemenceau was on his feet. It had been expected that when he sat down Count von Brockdorff-Rantzau would also rise to reply. Instead of doing so, he "leisurely or nervously unfolded a manuscript document and, after a painful interval of strained silence, proceeded from his seat to read it page by page in a loud, harsh and defiant voice. His conduct was regarded as an insult to the Assembly and especially to its aged President."

At this point, Lloyd George tells us, President Wilson's mind "closed with a snap," and he turned to the British Prime Minister to say: "Isn't it just like them?"

Years later Lloyd George heard "the real explanation." It was that Brockdorff-Rantzau was so everwhelmed by nervousness that he could not rise from his chair. He made an effort to do so, but the trembling of his knees was such that he had to sink back again. Lloyd George records his interpretation that, as a Foreign Office official who had never faced any au-

---

1 Clemenceau: *Discours de Paix,* p. 89.
2 In *Memoirs of the Peace Conference.*

dience before, the Prussian aristocrat was simply overcome by "stage fright."

The German speech rejected the exclusive war guilt of Germany and rejected also the contention that in the conduct of the war Germany alone had been at fault. It suggested a neutral commission to investigate war guilt and war atrocities, and went on to an eloquent appeal to the "principles of the President of the United States of America as a basis for peace." Brockdorff-Rantzau accepted the obligation to restore Belgium and the devastated regions of Northern France, but warned that a peace "which cannot be defended in the name of justice before the whole world would continually call forth fresh resistance." He must have been thinking of himself when he added: "No one could sign it with a clear conscience, for it would be impossible of fulfillment. No one could undertake the guarantee of fulfillment which its signature would imply."

In the following weeks, with their crises and resignations, General Smuts of South Africa seems to have had the most obstinate and accurate finger for the weakest points of the treaty. He was ready to take almost any fixed sum for reparations, even one which might be demonstrably too low, in order to get the German agreement to a definite sum. He objected to occupations and annexations, particularly the military occupation of an area which it was proposed to exploit industrially. He found these two notions "incompatible ideas," and probably he was right. He seems almost to have foreseen the "passive resistance," the invention of a few years later which did, in the end, defeat the military occupation of the Ruhr and the Rhineland. Throughout he appears to have been animated by the concept, which Wilson had so impressively stated and so quickly forgotten, that a treaty was an *agreement* between two parties.

All this, and the occasional qualms of Balfour and Lloyd George, along with repeated appeals by many delegates to the principles of Wilson, counted for very little. Very little came of the observations and memoranda of the German delegates. The Tiger, red in tooth and claw, had already made his bargains with both Wilson and (tacitly) with Lloyd George. He had already been so generous to Britain with the German ships and colonies that England was no longer in a position to complain of the size of France's reparations bill; he had already promised Wilson the main reward, support of the Covenant of the League, and Wilson was tired, impatient, perhaps a little bored, and wanted to go home. So, with very little modification except for a few districts in the East, and only one important amendment (the Silesian plebiscite) the treaty was signed on June 28, 1919.

Often in this room years later I was to look at that marble tablet with its gold lettering and wonder what might have happened if the Treaty of Versailles had been a real treaty and if it had conformed to the proclaimed principles of the allied war. If, for example, it had not been handed to the German delegates in a hotel dining room, but negotiated with them, point by point, in the Palace of Versailles itself (where the allied delegations met on state occasions) or in the French Foreign Office, or in some other suitable place, would it have been greatly different? If it had adhered to the Fourteen Points and all the Wilsonian principles it would obviously have been a very different document, but would it have been any more binding? As a *Diktat* it could not be psychologically binding; as a swindle—which in one important respect it was—it afforded every opportunity for the agitators and fakirs of succeeding years to arouse the passions of the German people. *Diktat* and swindle it was called by others before Hitler (many in the American and British nations used a similar language), but he was to bring these accusations to a very high pitch of hysterical suggestion, extracting out of the Germans of the 1930's, overwrought as they were by the unparalleled disintegration of their country, an almost maniacal force of will to power.

All this is gone now. Now it is no longer possible to negotiate with the Germans; there is no German who can negotiate in the name of Germany. Everything has changed. The effort to make a comprehensive peace settlement of the kind made at Versailles would not only be stupid now, but it would be impossible. So much blood has flowed over the earth, so many weary years of suffering have broken the bodies and spirits of untold millions, that the objective realities no longer bear any relation to the situation which faced the victors in 1919. Wholly new elements have come into the world, such as the Union of Socialist Soviet Republics. What one can or cannot do with the Germans depends most of all upon what we singly and together think of our common destiny, its possibilities, limitations and dangers, as well as of Germany and the Germans. They are only one element of our problem. They were once its center, but that time is past. Our attitude toward them now must be based upon considerations which do not immediately arise from the nature of the Germans, but rather from the relation of the Germans to the other forces of the coming age.

And still, the nature of the Germans is the physical basis of these relations, on one side at least. What have we thought, in life, of this German people? How have our views changed with the situations which are superimposed one upon the other in the passage of time? We have read much in recent years about a "soft peace" and a "hard peace" with Germany—inapplicable words, hollow and meaningless words—and always the proponents of the one or the other base their case upon what they think of the German people. This case, for or against, is made up very largely of the polemicists' own experience with that people or conclusions drawn from such experience. Standing here in the dining room of the Trianon-Palace Hotel, in the empty room where the potentates once handed out their terms of settlement, I, an ordinary American of forty-five, without a drop of German blood, but with no inherited dislike or distrust of Germans, must try to think back over what I have had to feel toward that people up to this moment. Oh, not all of it—not all the way; such explorations of the jungle of the past must be partial and afford sometimes no more than tantalizing glimpses of what once was passion or prejudice or fear; but with Cologne fresh in my mind from yesterday, and three years of war lying heavy upon me, how did I come to this point, to this hour?

§ 6

In the town where I was born, in the middle of Illinois, there were not many Germans. What few there were belonged to the most respected elements in the life of the town—comfortable retired farmers, a doctor and a druggist. There may have been eight or ten in all who were known to me as Germans originally from Germany, and I looked on them with considerable awe. Germany had in those days the charms of music and poetry, the prestige of great learning and superb imperial power.

The leading druggist in our town was from Bavaria and I went to school with his sons, who were completely Americanized and spoke German badly. With them I used to frequent the drugstore after school, and my earliest acquaintance with anything really German was the reading of the North German Lloyd bulletin which came there every week. I suppose the druggist must have been on some German propaganda list, or list of propaganda centers, because he received these leaflets regularly and they were free for the asking.

The North German Lloyd bulletin—I think that was its official name—was a publication intended primarily to encourage Americans to visit Germany on North German Lloyd ships. But to achieve this purpose it naturally had to present all that was most picturesque or beautiful in Germany, and to do it in the most favorable way. Thus I made acquaintance, at the age of seven or eight, with Rhineland castles on high hills, with medieval gateways and Bavarian lakes, Tyrolean waterfalls and old Heidelberg. All this was presented in a greenish or brownish process of some kind. It might have been rotogravure or whatever, before 1914, was the ancestor of rotogravure. The green photographs were particularly lovely, and I used to look at them for hours at a time. Later on, when I came to know more about Germany, the North German Lloyd fascination grew a little less compelling, but up until the time when it ceased to arrive—sometime in 1916, I suppose —that bulletin was still something I had to look at regularly. The stately ships which figured in its pages, the *Kronprinzessin Cecilie* and the *Kaiserin Augusta,* and later on the *Vaterland* and *Bismarck,* were more real in my mind than any others then, and had far more enchantment than any vessels I ever saw in after years.

Along with the picturesque and the historic, the North German Lloyd bulletin also provided a regular dose of photographs and information about the German imperial family. There would be pictures of the Kaiser reviewing troops, getting on or off a ship, opening a canal, and of all the members of his family doing the same worthy things. I suppose that in a rather innocent and non-political way this publication was sheer propaganda, but in those days the word was not in common use and the suspicion with which we regard the thing had not arisen. I know that I, at least, accepted all the North German Lloyd had to give me with sheer joy as a window on a remote and beautiful world.

When I got to high school I studied the German language, the only modern one taught in our town. Our first teacher was the pastor of the Lutheran church, an irascible little man who spoke little English in a comic accent. With him we got through some kind of grammar and read a bit of poetry, mostly Heine and Schiller. I remember particularly *Wilhelm Tell*, upon which we spent many weeks. Later on the Lutheran pastor was succeeded by an American lady of German origin, who had been to Germany the preceding summer—the summer when the great war broke out—and told us many stories of her adventures getting home. This lady was distinctly a "propagandist," because she loved Germany and wanted Germany to win the war. She taught us German songs in class, including "Die Wacht am Rhein" and "Deutschland ueber Alles." It seems odd now to think of classes of young Americans in the Middle West, hardly any of them of Teutonic origin, lustily bawling out these hymns of German nationalism.

But by this time I had derived, from history courses and much reading, a fairly good idea of the dangers inherent in German militarism. It used to give me great pleasure to bait this German teacher by asking an apparently innocent question which led her into contradictions or overstatements and made her ridiculous. A certain amount of feeling had already been engendered even in our town by the pretensions of German imperialism, and although up to 1916 we were not violently pro-ally, I think most of us were at least hoping that Germany would not win the war.

The submarine campaign ended all that, and no more German was taught in the school. By the time the war was over and I could have returned to German studies in college, I was already more interested in French and Italian. I did, however —we nearly all did—take courses in German philosophy, in which the ideas of eighteenth- and early nineteenth-century German thinkers were expounded to us and we had to do a certain amount of reading. Almost any course in philosophy naturally abounded in references to the German philosophers, and a proportion of the German culture seeped in by that means, in translation. I think at that time we all made a sharp separation in our minds between German militarism and imperialism, against which our elder brothers had been fighting, and the German culture and music which we loved. And it was quite obvious to us all that the one had killed the other —in other words, that the rise of German imperialism under Bismarck signified the end of the original and fecund period of German culture. No great figure in philosophy, poetry or music arose under the German empire; all was the mailed fist and the disciplined mind. We understood so much years ago, but had no idea to what lengths this mailed fist could eventually go.

It was after the peace treaty that I and a great many of my contemporaries became passionately pro-German. The feeling rose to its height in 1922 when the French occupied the Ruhr and Rhineland territories. The Rhineland had been occupied by Belgian, French, British and American troops. Relations between the Anglo-American occupying troops and the population had been good; there had been many marriages and much friendship. Then the Americans and British went out and the French took their places.

By this time I was a budding foreign correspondent. I had been engaged on the day of Mussolini's march on Rome by the Paris correspondent of the Chicago *Tribune;* his chief reason for employing me was that I could speak Italian. I did not, however, go to Italy after all, and my first assignment as a foreign correspondent was to go to the Ruhr and Rhineland when the Separatist movement broke out.

The French had occupied the Ruhr territory some months before (autumn, 1922) as security for the payment of reparations. The Germans had then gone into "passive resistance," which meant that they refused to work in the coal mines or steel mills or on the railroads. It was an extremely successful campaign which in reality defeated the purposes of the French occupation and conquered the sympathies of the greater part of the world.

Along with this, the French were supporting a "Rhineland separatist" movement, led by native Rhinelanders who made armed attacks upon the German civil and police authorities. Pitched battles on a small scale took place in Duisburg, Duesseldorf, Krefeld, Aachen and other places. The first shooting I ever saw close up was at Aachen—Aachen, which now lies in ruins. On successive days I saw fighting in most of the Rhineland towns, as far down as Coblentz, where the American occupying army had once had its headquarters and had left pleasant memories. Like practically every other American or British correspondent, I was enraged at the unfairness of the French methods and felt extremely sorry for the modest, kind and friendly Germans. While we were going through this agitation in the Rhineland we heard of a *putsch,* an attempted coup d'état or revolt of some sort, which took place in a beer hall in Munich and was led by a maniac called Adolf Hitler. The German Republican authorities put down the disturbance, jailed the maniac, and we thought that would be the last we should ever hear of him. While he was in jail he wrote a book called *Mein Kampf,* to which we all had to pay a good deal of attention afterwards.

The pro-German nature of my own feelings and of those of practically all my contemporaries was unquestionably sincere and based upon a sense of justice. It was also based upon something which seems to me incontestable, that Americans by and large tend to like Germans under normal conditions. We thought the French harsh, unjust, mercenary and greedy, and we thought the Germans a simple and likable people who had suffered great historic misfortunes. These were not only my opinions; these were extremely prevalent opinions in 1922-1923. They were indeed so prevalent that they eventually took control even in France and forced a reversal of Poincaré's

German policy. Hitler was probably bound to occur, in some form, but another policy in the early 1920's might have made it difficult for him to achieve a following.

From the Rhineland days we went into a new era of Franco-German relations. This was the 1924-1926 era of Herriot and MacDonald, the beginning of an attempt to get Germany back into the concert of nations. Most people have forgotten all about it now, but in 1924 Herriot and MacDonald tried to evolve a protocol for world peace which would strengthen the League of Nations and eventually get a world organization rather like the one created at San Francisco. They failed, of course, and there followed a period of direct negotiation between the French and Germans, dominated by Briand and Stresemann. I never thought Stresemann much more than a tool of the German governing classes, but Briand seemed to me, as he did to all of us, a perfectly sincere lover of peace. He was a weary old man, and lazy besides, and always willing to resign his office if anybody said boo to him, but he did try for peaceful arrangements with Germany. In that period my generation of Americans became pro-French again, because the French sincerity was clear and the German sincerity was not. All sorts of disquieting signs began in Germany, among them the creation of a highly skilled skeleton army and the drilling of various military "societies." German social disintegration had gone so far that none of us (I am talking chiefly of foreign correspondents) expected a revival of German power in the immediate future, but the possibilities were beginning to be apparent. What was more apparent was that the Weimar Republic itself was playing a sort of progressive game with the Western powers; whenever Stresemann made a gain, he waited a while and then tried for another. This threw a strange light over every negotiation and made the permanence of any arrangement with the Germans seem doubtful.

Then, of course, came Hitler's call to power by President

von Hindenburg on January 30th, 1933, followed by a rapid destruction of the institutions of republican Germany. The Nazi state which emerged, modeled in some respects upon Mussolini's Fascism, quickly displayed its military character by the creation of war industries, attacks upon the Versailles system, and the evolution of an air force which five years later was without an equal in the world. The speed with which Germany re-militarized was indeed prodigious and the Western nations were paralyzed by fear and unbelief. They did not want to believe what was happening under their eyes, and as usual they were governed by people so busy trying to get re-elected that they had no time to read anything. It is apparently the historic fact (although it appears impossible) that Neville Chamberlain, for instance, never read *Mein Kampf* until after the Munich agreement.

During the ten years 1925-1935 I was fairly often in Germany for one reason or another connected with my profession. I did not actually work there at any time, but coming and going from Russia, Persia, Scandinavia, I passed enough time in Berlin to see something of what was going on. The extravagant profiteering and social disintegration of the Weimar Republic, with its weird mixture of champagne, starvation, drugs and violence, were quite well known to me. We used to follow the mad murder stories of the day with a sort of uncomprehending wonder—the butcher of Hamburg, who made sausages out of little boys; the fantastic sexual crimes all over the country; the rise of violence among the workers and their division into opposing bands. It was impossible to have anything but a sort of impatient, unsympathetic pity for the Germans as a whole during that period. They seemed bent on destroying each other and themselves. On the one hand they produced monsters of capitalistic speculation, such as Hugo Stinnes, and on the other hand they produced slum gangs of the utmost cruelty and degradation. Nowhere else in the world have I ever seen cocaine openly sold in a night club as if it were cigarettes. Nowhere else, except in the Weimar Republic, was it possible to see such a range and profusion of professional prostitution. Berlin in 1930 made Paris seem positively puritanical in comparison. And with all this, the political parties were unable to agree on any kind of program; governments succeeded each other without making the slightest difference to anybody but the professional politicians; the birth rate went slithering down (it has been declining since the creation of the German Empire) and the intelligent or sincere workers had obviously lost faith in the future.

At this period most of us agreed upon one thing which was definitely good in Germany, and it was about the only thing. That was the theater, including music. The plays of Ernst Toller, the Communist or Socialist poet who afterwards killed himself in New York; the productions at the Berlin, Munich and Dresden opera houses; the Berlin Philharmonic Orchestra under Furtwaengler—these were things unequaled elsewhere. German stage production reached a perfection quite unknown in the West, and rivaled only by the theaters of Moscow. Perhaps it might be said that what was left of the German spirit was taking refuge in canvas and grease-paint, in a sort of flight from the horror of contemporary life. Certainly such intelligent and civilized Germans as I knew were not happy people and had little hope in them. I had a few friends in Berlin—weary and cynical from early youth; I suppose they were thrown into the German army afterwards, willy-nilly, but I am sure they had not the heart to make any resistance to Nazism or anything else.

At the same time important scientific work was being done in Germany, a surprising amount of it by Jews. Professor Einstein was a nationally respected figure, and the municipality of Berlin gave him a house out on the Wannsee for his fiftieth birthday. Max Planck and others were doing important original work in physics; Richard Strauss was still writing rather good music of a post-Straussian order. I had little contact with university circles, but every journalist has to be aware of these things, and my impression was that outside of physical science and astronomy there was nothing original being done. Psychology and psychoanalysis, of course, flourished on the grandest scale, but if I may confess to a prejudice, it seems to me that any unusual development in these sciences is a symptom of disease rather than of intellectual activity. Certainly the Germany of the Weimar Republic must have been a psychoanalyst's dream.

During this period an extremely astute piece of financial juggling had been going on. Germany wiped out her entire internal debt by inflation, then stabilized the currency and proceeded to take care of the external debt—and industry at home—by borrowing from the French, British and Americans. Vast loans were floated, very successfully, under the Dawes and Young plans. German industry was put into mechanically good running order by these operations and was held back mainly by the need for more and more markets. Although what Hitler took over in 1933 was a socially diseased people, at the same time he got a powerful and in parts brand-new industrial machine and what was almost a clean slate financially. These were formidable advantages which he knew how to use. And the German bankers and industrialists were eager to be used in exchange for his pledge to put an end to social disintegration.

How "pro-German" were any of us in 1925-1935? I think the question hardly arose at that time. We liked some Germans whom we happened to know, and disliked others. For the nation as a whole we could not have much sympathy, but neither could we have much fear. All the machinery was there, actually, for Hitler to use in his swift and terrible development of military might; it had been put there by the German general

staff, the bankers and the industrialists. But it was masked by
the chaotic and apparently hopeless condition of German society, pulled every which way by opposing forces and apparently unable to regenerate or unite itself. I think I, all this
time, looked at Germany as a spectacle, without any clear
realization that I and all my brothers and children would be
involved in its development.

Then—about a year after Hitler's seizure of power—I came
to my senses and saw what all this was leading to. In successive
years my sense of the tragic inevitability of these events grew
sharper and sharper; at times it was unbearably painful, because it was so difficult to make anybody in the Western
nations realize this danger in time. There were a lot of foreign
correspondents who felt the same thing in the same way and
who tried, as I did, to speak up. I suppose we were thought to
be calamity-howlers of one sort or another; and of course it
is true that to the generality of mankind nothing is real until
it has happened. You can see an avalanche coming down a
hillside, and you can hear its roar, but a deaf man who has his
back turned neither sees it nor hears it, and will not believe
you if you tell him.

How did we feel about Germany in 1935-1939, that is,
during the period when Hitler was quite openly preparing to
conquer the whole of Europe and eventually the world?

I saw the process going on with sheer horror, and nobody has
kept a more undeviating course of opposition to it than I
and a half dozen like-minded colleagues. But I did have an
illusion, parted with very late and most regretfully. This was
that there existed powerful anti-Nazi forces within the German people, who would be our allies in the inevitable struggle,
and to whom we could entrust the inevitable ruins when the
whole thing was over.

This illusion was based on long acquaintance with some
German workers and intellectuals of the democratic and Left

parties. Indeed most Germans I ever knew were in this category, with the exception of a few aristocratic diplomats and officials. Germans are not all brutes, and everybody with any considerable or lengthy acquaintance with Germany must have known charming, witty and civilized people. In addition to that—which is a sort of drawing-room judgment—I had also known, in Austria, Czechoslovakia, Spain and China, brave and honest Germans who fought for freedom. Nobody could ever forget how they fought in Spain. These were exiles, of course—Social Democrats, Communists, Republicans of one kind or another, and there were Jews among them as well. But they were certainly brave and honest men and they saved Madrid in 1936—the German Brigade, and no other, was the best-trained part of Miaja's forces. The commander of the international brigades—of which there was a whole division in 1938—was a German, a stern and unflinching opponent of Nazism on every field. He went on to do us great service in this war and there are hundreds like him scattered over the earth.

But that is just the point, and that is why my illusion of the anti-Nazi German forces is no more. There are hundreds of these brave and honest Germans, but they do not count at all in a nation of seventy million people who followed Hitler through six years of Hunnish and degrading war. The Jews, as either a force or a constructive element in German society, were wiped out; most of the brave and honest Social Democrats went into exile or were destroyed in Germany, since there was little hope for most of them to "go underground." And the rest, all the cultivated and fair-minded Germans whom one used to meet in Berlin and Munich, simply acquiesced in the most inhuman scheme of racial dictatorship ever evolved on earth. In so doing they lost their social existence and value, along with their self-respect.

An example would show best what I mean. In Cologne, not

60

long since, a friend of mine, an American lady who works for the military government, actually found an anti-Nazi intellectual, a surviving Social Democrat. This was a schoolteacher of about fifty, a woman who had been to jail in the early days of the Nazi regime and had survived since then by keeping very silent and letting her friends and relatives in the police department protect her. She was an intelligent, civilized German woman who abhorred the whole Nazi process and really understood the course and inevitable results of the war. After a long talk with my friend, she said:

"It has been wonderful to talk like this after so many years. In your work you must get around a lot and talk to a lot of Germans. If you ever find any who think the same way we do, would you give them my address so that we could meet? I don't know anybody I can talk to any more."

In other words, this intelligent woman of fifty ceased to exist as a social force because she had nobody with whom she could communicate. Such minds, if they exist in Germany in any numbers, have been so long isolated and afraid that they are as if canceled out of the society.

In the last winter and spring of the war, in the Third Army, I was of course seeing Germans every day, both prisoners of war and civilians in the territories our army entered. During the preceding two and a half years I had seen a good many other German prisoners, when I was an officer in our own army. And the result of this rather extensive experience was this: I never encountered one single German who had any sense of social responsibility in the vast historical crime of Hitlerism. Not one.

And for this reason, of course, I could not believe that any genuinely democratic force existed in Germany. I could not maintain that the people I talked to in that last winter and spring were typical or characteristic; they were not a poll. They were just anybody I happened to meet. But what I must

61

maintain is that if in months of talking to Germans, even Catholic Rhineland Germans, who never were Nazis—and even the most ordinary old workmen and peasant women—if in all this time I did not find one single one who showed any sense of social responsibility, then there could be no hope for a democratic force in that country.

You would be able to discover intellectuals, of course, who understood the history of the past ten years. But their appalling weakness canceled them out as a social force. They were like the schoolteacher who had nobody to talk to.

It would be foolish to pretend that intellectual life in Germany ceased with the advent of Hitler. I went through ruined houses in Cologne and Trier and other cities where there were swastikas all over the place and where, nevertheless, the most forbidden democratic and Socialist literature was on the bookshelves or lying amidst the rubbish. Even Nazis read books, and their own literature was so wretchedly dull that they had to read ours. But whatever sort of life this gave to their minds, it was furtive and solitary; it had no social value and could have no result. By definition a society consists of individuals cohering and associated in action, and the activity of a single mind sealed off from the rest can have social existence only if it is expressed in words written or spoken, or in acts explicit upon the stage of history. In no other way could the thought of a hermit dwell even statically in the collective mind; in no other way has the thought of the past subsisted; and since this way was impossible in Hitler's Germany, the minds which silently rebelled were isolated and annulled, hermit minds with no outlet or inlet, no communication and no progeny. The dead Goethe, the forbidden Heine, the half-tolerated Tolstoy and Shakespeare, along with those parts of Kant and Hegel which had to be accepted in order to obtain the rest, carried more germs of truth to German thought than any effort of the intellectuals in Hitler's day. That is why, when a

62

German intellectual dares to assert that he never followed National Socialist doctrine, one is forced to answer him in Hitler's words: if this is so, *Was hast du heute fuer Deutschland getan?*

To Versailles we come after a long journey. In my own case this journey through peace and war started afar off, on the plains of Illinois, with no feeling toward Germany except one of childish admiration for a beautiful country and a gifted people. Opinion and sentiment veered this way and that through the years, determined by events, new situations born out of the womb of time—pro-German during the dark days which saw Hitler's beginnings, in the early 1920's, pro-French during the years when an effort was being made by France to obtain a peaceful solution, apathetic and discouraged during the confusion which preceded Hitler's seizure of power; then, with Hitler, sharply anxious and alarmed for the whole future of our world so desperately threatened. In all this I was perhaps typical, and certainly not much out of the *Zeitgeist* of my contemporaries except, perhaps, in the painful acuity with which I experienced some of its phases.

Here, then, there can be no question of "good Germans" or of "bad Germans," no thought of the ferocious unredeemable barbarian any more than of the enlightened and all-loving poet or of the supreme creator of music. The dilemma of Arminius and Hitler on one side, Goethe and Beethoven on the other, does not exist for a mind which has grown used to regarding history as a dialectical process. One's own personal experience shows above all that opinion and sentiment vary with the situations which form them and toward which they are directed. So far as I am concerned I have no passion and no prejudice left with respect to the Germans—no fear, no love, no hate. They are a people which, for certain definite reasons of geography, climate, tradition and historical determinism have shown great aptitude for tribal unity and aggressiveness, along with great mass suggestibility in the hands of their dervishes. These qualities have caused them to play a part of the first importance in the history of the world between 1871 and 1945. Among persons now living, there are very few whose daily lives—even in remote parts of the planet—have not been affected in some way by the successive surges of German ambition, German delusion and German despair. The psychopathology of such a people has led them to ruin on a scale never seen before in modern times, and has—thus we see it in the glass which separates us from twilight in the park of the Trianon—summoned up new shapes and shadows upon the film of our future. No situation, of all those in which they played so primary a part, will repeat itself in the time to come. These vanquished Germans have taken their place in the chain of cause and effect, and their recurrence in that endless concatenation will be in new forms or not at all, since much that they have now produced in their wake has made their resumption of a primary causational pretension forever impossible.

§ 7

We can see how true this is—how far along the chain of cause and effect we have come since 1919—if we try, here and now in the dining room of the Trianon-Palace Hotel, to reproduce in contemporary terms the scene which was played there so many years ago. However absurd it may be, we must put in the place of Clemenceau, Wilson, Lloyd George, Orlando and Hymans, and of "all the Representatives of the Allied and Associated Powers," our contemporary equivalents. Thus we obtain General Charles de Gaulle, Mr. Harry S. Truman, Mr. Clement Attlee, somebody like Signor Parri or Signor Nenni for Italy, and M. Van Zeeland or M. Spaak for Belgium.

What instantly appears, if we do this, is the glaring absence of the principal European power, Soviet Russia. Even if we were to assume that Russia signed not as an ally, but as an "associated power," as America did in 1919, it would still be inconceivable that the Russian representative should not be in the list of principal signatories. This observation alone —the first we should be obliged to make if we tried to re-enact the scene of 1919—points out the most enormous change in the alignment of forces brought about during the process now ended.

But there are other observations that would crowd in upon us as we surveyed that impossible scene. General Charles de Gaulle as President of the Conference . . . ?

General de Gaulle, whose personal qualities need not enter into the hypothesis, is the self-appointed ruler of a state which no longer possesses the vital or material force to play a leading part in the affairs of the world. Nobody knows whether he is a president, a prime minister, or a generalissimo; his constitutional position is uncertain; the position of his state is precarious and is made more so by a persistent xenophobia combined with restless assertions of dubious power. The claims of France, difficult enough to digest in 1919 after a war in which the French people had made cruel sacrifices, would be almost insupportable under contemporary conditions unless they suited the political objectives or desires of the powers which fought the war. Clemenceau never tired of reminding the Americans and British that France had been in the forefront of battle; General de Gaulle uses the same language without any regard to the fundamental nature of the change which has taken place.

The American President, without experience in foreign affairs, has only the prestige given by his high office and the power of his country; to most of the world he was recently unknown and has only slowly begun to fill out the outlines so boldly sketched by his predecessor.

One British Prime Minister, whose appeal to the imagination of the world was powerful in 1940 and 1941—and who in those days was ready for the most original and daring improvisations to conciliate the democratic forces in all countries —became in the era of victory almost the villain of the play, antagonizing popular opinion first in this nation and then in that, speaking a dictatorial and imperialistic language which shocked even his own supporters, and causing the allied partisans in many European countries to wonder why they risked so much in such a cause. Thus he was to be succeeded before the war's end by Mr. Clement Attlee: after fire comes ashes.

Italy? In these terms, in spite of much effort on the allied side in the last year and a half of the war, Italy no longer exists. If there is an Italy at the peace conference it will be on the other side, accepting humbly, or rejecting in despair, whatever the powers decide to bestow.

Belgium, in any meeting of the allied and associated powers, would, in future, be little more than an additional vote for Great Britain. And "all the Representatives of the Allied and Associated Powers" would group themselves either about Great Britain or about that great absent element, that force which could not appear on the scene at all if we modeled it upon May 7th, 1919.

Last, and most startling, in the place of Brockdorff-Rantzau and the German delegation there would be nothing. Germany no longer exists. There could be found some sorry remnants of National Socialism to accept a treaty, or some vestiges of Social Democracy to carry it out, if the victors chose to explore the ruins for such instruments. In objective fact, what exists is an area which once was Germany and is now four separate zones of military occupation. No central German government is likely to exist under this military occupation, nor is any central German government with both authority and popular support conceivable under the conditions to be foreseen in the next few years.

By transposing the scene of May 7th, 1919, into contemporary terms, we have, I think, demonstrated the absurdity of any such performance today. If we see de Gaulle, Truman, Attlee and a Belgian or a Brazilian handing out the terms of a peace settlement to some Germany which is not even there, in the absence of a Russia which substantially won the war, we have seen sheer fantasy, and we have perceived that a Treaty of Versailles is at the present time impossible.

For which the forces of history be thanked.

§ 8

The new situation produced by the conflict of 1939-1945 is one in which Soviet Russia is the principal European power, inheriting great elements of the powers of Germany, Austria, Italy and France as well as a considerable part of the extra-European, tutelary or admonitory prestige of Great Britain with respect to Europe. Great Britain, although impoverished and weakened by the struggle, retains a great maritime and imperial establishment along with concomitant unsolved problems which make its permanence in the present form doubtful. Industrially, economically and in some military and naval respects—such as air power—the United States of America emerges as the mightiest single nation of the age, with a future which would seem to be limited only by its capacity to adapt itself to changes as they take place.

But the single nation is no longer the unit of historical conflict and progress. Concepts of social economy also have profoundly influenced the behavior of men in these years, even when imperfectly apprehended. In the crudest and simplest form of statement such concepts, aided by geography and material forces all along the line (the elements of historical movement), would tend to drive the nations into two rival or opposing systems which would divide the world be-

tween them: the system upon which the Soviet Union has
been built, and that which has brought the United States to
its present position. It is my conviction that no such division
of the world is necessary or desirable, that the two systems are
susceptible of modification, that synthesis is the inevitable law
of development, and that those who try to set forth or encourage a *deliberate* antagonism between capitalism as it
stands in America and socialism as it stands in the Soviet Union
are enemies of humanity, not to be distinguished fundamentally from the disciples of Adolf Hitler. To discern the nature
of these two systems and to make the opposition historically
fruitful—in peace and production, not in war—is the task of
the coming years. How shallow and misleading most of the
cruder statements of this opposition are may be seen in the
words used to describe the two systems—the "Russian system"
and "the American way of life." The "Russian" system was
evolved by Germans, the "American way of life" by Englishmen. Successive modifications, taking place naturally in the
historical process, have made American capitalism very different from its English parent, as the Soviet system is very
different from the stateless and classless socialism of Marx.
Some parts of the Soviet system (such as the Soviet itself) were
deep in the mind and tradition of the Russian people centuries before Marx. Some parts of American capitalism—its
divorce from territorial ambition; its emphasis on technological advance; its desire for small profits on large production
rather than large profits on small production—are socially and
economically so different in degree from English capitalist
practice as to be objectively different in kind. In the unceasing
movement and change to which these forces are subjected in
their natural development, the introduction of artificial, ma-
lignant and deliberate incitations to conflict can only be the
work of anti-historical, Hitleristic minds which have perceived
some tiny part of the truth and endeavor to bring about catas-

trophic solutions through an inability to grasp the extent of the whole.

From the point of view at which we have placed ourselves for these reflections—the dining room of the Trianon-Palace Hotel at Versailles—it is not possible to survey the entire range of a prospect so novel. What we can see clearly is that the effective elimination of many states during this war of 1939-1945 has radically altered our way of making a peace settlement. Germany is no longer a Western problem; Germany is no longer even the central problem of the peace; Germany's relation to the rest of Europe and of the world is what is to be determined, and this only as part of our own compact with the Soviet Union. Never again will a handful of statesmen gather in this room to hand over a set of terms to sullen or resentful Germans. Before we can even think of a peace treaty we must create the Germany with which we are to make it— and we can only create that Germany in agreement with the Soviet Union, which occupies half of the German soil, and which won in blood and sacrifice much more than half of the German victory.

What this meant in concrete fact, I thought, watching the shadows gather in the park of the Trianon, is that we should undertake to study and understand what Russia wants with regard to Germany, and to adjust our conceptions, accommodate and integrate them with the Russian conceptions. We ought never to attempt to create one sort of Germany in the zones we occupy and let another sort of Germany be created in the zones the Russians occupy. The conflicts would be unending, and might indeed involve us in worse difficulties than we have yet had. We ought to make a tremendous effort to agree with the Russians upon a system of education for the German people from childhood, as well as upon some form of nonpolitical administration which could be carried on by the Germans themselves. Political government of Germans by Germans is

69

out of the question for years to come. This means that in the special case which the Germans made out of themselves our concepts of democratic process and free election do not apply. The Germans should be treated as what they are, a people politically unborn. It seems likely that before long the Russians will want to set up some sort of simulacrum of a Socialist government in their area, even if only to open flower shows and agricultural exhibitions. If they insisted upon it, we should make no objection, because the thing is irrelevant anyhow. What concerns us is the education of the German child and the formation of the German mind with respect to its place in the world.

Even now, remembering the Germans of the war's last winter and spring, I did not think we had anything to teach the Germans about the facts of human history and development. They knew all the facts, and their industrious research had greatly contributed to our common store of knowledge. What they ought to be taught is the meaning of the facts. It would be merely silly if a captain in the military government organization should attempt to reorganize the University of Heidelberg. What is needed is an attack upon the primary education, from which everything else comes. All the best we have to give should be devoted to this problem, in agreement with Russia. When we disagree it should be argued out, however long it might take, until a synthesis—or at any rate a compromise—could be reached. A house divided against itself cannot stand.

It did not seem to me that in making these reflections I was going beyond the limits set by common sense, experience and recorded history. There was no hatred in it. Every German of value—whatever kind of value—has known the animal suggestibility of his people with regard to social or political organization. Goethe knew it and said it; Heine said it rather hysterically; Bismarck said it with grim and bitter realism;

70

even Hitler said it over and over again. Prince von Buelow, Bismarck's successor, who was a tired and arrogant old aristocrat without strength but with great perception, said it most plainly of all. He remarked in his memoirs that God had given so many gifts to the German people that He was obliged in common justice to withhold one thing, which was a political sense.

For this reason—a reason only too well established by recorded fact—I should expect the Russians to be cautious in the revival of German political life, and to treat such governments or administrations as may be set up (even if they should be Socialist or Communist) with the most extreme suspicion and vigilant surveillance. Great purposes would be served if we could do the same. Punishment of Germany and the Germans for war crimes may be severe and prolonged, but must come to an end sometime, and it is at that further point that the utmost skill, tact and imaginative understanding are required of the occupying powers to bring their points of view into harmony. For a permanent partition of Germany, involving the creation of an area which might be called the Teutonic Marches, with the Eastern part tending toward absorption into the Soviet Union and the Western part tending toward subjection to occidental capitalism, would be the worst outcome of all. The natural inclinations and necessities of Great Britain and America must cause their interest in Western Germany to decline extremely soon and leave that essential area of heavy industry, the heart of continental Europe, to be preyed upon by French imperialism—the weakest of contemporary imperialisms and therefore the most unreasonable, captious and uneconomic, the most certain to produce external conflict and internal revolt. The disorders, not to say wars, inevitable upon such an outcome should be obvious to every mind, but we know from the past that the obvious is

71

often veiled from our governing potentates until it overwhelms them.

In this room I used to lunch on Sundays during a war which hardly touched the inner recesses of governing minds in the Western democratic states. Even the French Socialists in the earlier part of the Spanish Civil War appeared to have no conception of its determining power upon their own fate. Léon Blum, a Socialist Prime Minister, actually invented (upon a British suggestion as it would seem) the system of non-intervention which strangled the Spanish Republic for lack of supplies and enabled Hitler, Mussolini and their lackey Franco to win the first great victory of their war. While this victory was taking place—a laboratory test or dress rehearsal for the German victories in Poland and France—the parliamentary rulers of England and France met with the representatives of Hitler and Mussolini periodically to accept assurances that such was not the case. Russia was being thrown back upon isolationism in every meeting of this sinister and foolish non-intervention committee, and the Western powers were losing their Eastern front—to be lost definitively at Munich. All this time, particularly in 1938, I was rubbed raw with apprehension, especially on every return from embattled Spain. It was a perpetual surprise to discover how little French people knew or cared about the wild beasts on their doorstep. In this room the skillful waiters came and went, the flowers bloomed discreetly on the white tables, and on a Sunday in springtime you would see scented people and hear soft laughter which took no account of the terror and tragedy in store.

Now the room was a mess hall for higher officers of SHAEF —the Supreme Headquarters, Allied Expeditionary Forces. So completely Anglo-American was this organization that you would hardly ever see a Frenchman in any of its numerous quarters or headquarters, except perhaps in the role of inter-

preter or liaison officer or censor. France, which commanded
on land in the war of 1914-1918, was almost absent from the
war of 1939-1945, except for a month of unavailing and panicky struggle in the spring of 1940. Helpful as the Résistance
Française had been, it was no more than helpful, and then
only after an actual invasion of France had taken place on a
huge scale with heavy losses in American and British and
Canadian lives. The military role of France (the "first military
power of Europe") in the allied victory had been minor indeed. Without a recognition of this fact one could not begin
to understand the objective situation. It was obscured by every
sort of sentimentality and refusal to face facts, but the truth
was that France would have been liberated if not a single
Frenchman had lifted a finger to bring about that result. One
could see this without minimizing the bravery of those who
had risked their lives to help themselves and us. The allies,
governed at many turns of events by the melancholy ancestral
tenderness which afflicts us all with respect to France, gave
every opportunity for the French to assume a role they could
not actually fill—as when Patton outflanked Paris and compelled the Germans to withdraw, then sent in his single French
division (Leclerc's) to obtain the appearance of victory. For
this we obtained no gratitude, except in the first two or three
days of delirium, and expected no gratitude; gratitude is not
a political sentiment; now, as I looked through the glass at the
darkling green toward the Trianon, I reflected that the Germans themselves were hardly more unpopular in France than
the Americans, and all our difficulties in the effort to make a
peace were magnified and confused by the agitation of the
heirs to Clemenceau, who dreamed of the past and made
rhetoric about the future, unaware—alas!—of the present.

Never mind. Let us leave this room. Let us go to a place
where we can meet Russians and talk of what to do.

But here again, even as we take our leave to go elsewhere and speak in other terms (as it might be at San Francisco, at Berlin, at Moscow) the long shadows of the unbroken immemorial Western past lie over us and make heavy our reluctant feet. Everything from Parmenides and Pythagoras to the public library on the Kansas plain has cast our minds through all the ages upon the way of freedom, a concept which in spite of its insufficiency toward determined situations in complex industrial societies has still forever and always and again today set alight the fires of our will and desire. This is the meaning and direction of that continuous tradition which the human spirit has kept alive in our Western world through the centuries, dwindling or wasting away under slave cultures and eras of catastrophe but never wholly vanishing from the minds of men whose most trivial folk tales and minor customs bear the mark of Greece and Rome. It would be only too easy to discern the breaks and blanks, to excoriate the imperfections, the gross contradictions, and thus to sustain a thesis according to which the love of freedom in Western man has been accompanied by an ever-resurgent propensity to enslave others, but in truth no such expression of greed and arrogance has at any time gone without sharp, penetrating protest from the contemporary conscience and has in every instance arisen from social and economic conditions which, changing with the flux of time, have in turn caused it to pass away, giving place to institutions informed by the undying spirit of liberty and law even when their application is impeded by the specters of greed and thus become contradictions in their turn. So it was with human slavery in the American states, which, when it was canceled after a frightful struggle, took ever lighter and more tolerable forms considered from the point of view of the original evil, but ever still remained contradictory to the law which abolished it and to the successive laws which have endeavored to enfranchise the slaves' descendants and receive them into the society without statement of difference. It would serve no purpose whatever to deny the existence of such contradictions in the very center of the freedom-loving systems of the West. Their glare is so powerful that for many eyes it makes invisible the larger good which these contradictions contradict. That larger good, in sum, is the freedom to sustain the struggle for freedom—and this is so much the condition of life as it has been understood by the Western mind through the ages that none among us dares to deny it even in the midst of the most insidious attack upon it. Amongst us there is no evil which cannot be named and made the object of a social effort, major or minor, toward eradication. Just as the thinking mind (the Ego, the Self) has to postulate its own existence before it can think of objects—or must at least accept its own existence as reciprocal with that of the objects—so our society is compelled by its historical nature and sustained secular psychological condition to postulate or accept the struggle for freedom as inseparable from its own existence and vitally identical with it, looking upon the ever-changing terms and fortunes of single struggles, social, economic, political and intellectual, as the whole looks upon the part, or as the single Ego looks upon the objects perceptually received as part of its life. This society has engendered rebellion and re-absorbed it countless times, usually after the death of the rebels and in a form they would scarcely have recognized, but seldom indeed has it extirpated any form of heresy which substantially appeared. The Waldenses and the Hussites—not to speak of the Jews—survived storms of persecution and still live today. Institutions socially established in the West but inimical by nature to the idea of freedom, such as the Church of Rome, have learned to make their peace with it as they make their peace with all of man's fundamental character, because otherwise

75

they could not continue to exist. Authority is curbed in our society not by the laws that aim to do so, but by this live cognition which, lying in the very essence of our social existence and indistinguishable from it, is forever alert to repel attack. Thus with us the idea of freedom hangs like the sword of Damocles over the neck of power.

How pervasive and unconscious is this freedom to struggle, to dissent and rebel, to demand ever and ever larger freedoms, to assault the citadels of authority in season and out, to disagree or agree, participate or abstain, is nowhere more apparent than in the behavior of Americans, British, French, Belgians, Dutchmen, Norwegians—in a word, of Western man —in times of crisis. The powers to which we submit at such periods are subjected to a critical and censorious attention which never sleeps, and of which they are continuously aware. The British government in 1940 was made all-powerful by a law, passed through the Commons in a single reading, which placed all persons and all property at the disposal of the state. Draconian as this law was, it received only the most partial application under the incessant vigilance of the House of Commons, which at no time surrendered its right to review action and debate principles. The American President, Mr. Roosevelt, received and exerted very comprehensive powers from 1941 (and even before) to the time of his death, creating whole new organs of rule by executive order, but he was extremely sensitive—as all who knew him can bear witness—to criticisms freely printed in the untrammeled press, and sometimes was known to have altered his course under pressures which had no constitutional origin but nevertheless were brought into being by the consciousness of the people. And, to delve into the particulars of behavior, what soldier in the American or British armies has not heard the most radical and vituperative criticism of his own government in campfire conversations? Was not Mr. Roosevelt the favorite subject for comic entertainers and imitators in the American army, as Mr. Churchill was in the British? These were unconscious expressions of what, in teleological language, could be called the soul's heritage, the innate psychopolitical muscle-flexing bondlessness of self-assertion in the individual Western man.

This man is not so free as he thinks, it is quite true; material determinism of innumerable kinds (physiological, biochemical, geographical, social, political, economic and the rest, not to speak of the experiential effects of these causes which in turn cause further effects) binds him with invisible chains of which he is only sporadically and serially aware. If he felt all his chains at once he would not greatly care to live. But he does experience the positive sensation of freedom with respect to his society, and it cannot be said to be more illusory than any other psychological experience of importance to the individual, such as love, ambition or intellection, since its reality is empirically perceived, not taught. This man *feels* free. To convince him that he is not, you are obliged to bedevil him with every branch and leaf of the tree of human knowledge, and harangue him with philosophical concepts as well, and, when you have done, the feeling may be a little wan and limp, but it will still be there.

A percept so obstinate, positive and general must be admitted as reality in the kind and to the degree that it is effective (i.e., produces or influences action), which is, at the very least, psychologically. Since the man *feels* free, he *is* free, at least in his own mind. He breathes a breezy, independent air and is not afraid to entertain ideas and reflections which run counter to those officially consecrated by institutions, majorities or laws. In the experience of these heirs to the tradition of freedom practically every part of the social structure has at some time or other been attacked, and the conflicts have ended dialectically, with a synthesis, such as resulted from the attempt to enforce religious uniformity in the Western world and the rebellion against it; that synthesis has retained much of the power of organized religion in general under a great diversity of specific forms and with a hollow core where once there dwelt the principle of absolute authority by divine delegation. At the present time in those parts of the Graeco-Roman world which are not under military occupation (like Italy and Greece) or Fascist dictatorship (like Spain) a man can, if he wishes to submit to some mild social disapproval, go out into the street and deny the existence of God; unless he interfered with the traffic he could do so with impunity. And yet there was a time, not so very long ago as the lifetime of humanity runs, when it meant prison or lingering death to express any doubt even of the transubstantiation—that is, of the doctrine that the bread and wine of the Christian sacrament are in actual fact the living flesh and actual blood of Jesus of Nazareth. Less than nine hundred years ago a saintly and learned divine, the monk Berengarius of Tours and Chartres, who, without denying the "real presence" (as it is called in Anglican theology), was unable to convince himself metaphysically of the true *nature* of the substance, suffered years of ecclesiastical persecution on that account, although he was in every other respect a devout proponent of the whole body of church doctrine. Today it would be difficult to find any member of any church who fully accepted and profoundly believed everything he is supposed by that church's theology to believe; much that was once vital is now dead wood and is tacitly so recognized by the incidence of the church's emphasis, fleeing theology as the mother of doubt and taking refuge in ethics; we have Catholic Socialists in many countries, and in Italy of late we have seen the attempt to create a Catholic Communist Party; the greatest and most sustained effort made in history to break down the identity of Western culture with the struggle for ever-increasing freedom was clearly that made by the Church of Rome and, much less philosophically or effectively, by some of its offspring, but that, too, has failed. What remains is the certainty that the inheritors of this almost endocrine obsession value it more highly than any other part of the social baggage passed on through the centuries. For this one thing it is possible to unite the most disparate groups in a passionate, if temporary, concentration of effort, and freedom under law is still, in the mind of the whole West, the highest good known to associations of men.

It has become allied with the notion of democracy since the eighteenth century, just as it was in various ancient periods, but its development in England—for long its most fertile ground—was not originally so; indeed it was only partly polit-ical, and had its strongest and deepest roots in the demand for civil rights, where a man's freedom as man (rather than as political animal) is most at stake. Such things as *habeas corpus* and trial by jury, taken for granted lo these many cen-turies by unthinking Anglo-Saxons, have created the climate of freedom in which political rights naturally grow up for all men and ultimately appear to overshadow all the rest. In the result, as Western man surveys his estate, democracy and free-dom seem inextricable, it is difficult to the point of impossi-bility to think of one without the other, and the Western mind is made numb by the novelty of a system which, like that of the Soviet Union, proposes to give unparalleled effect to the one by annihilating the other—sets out, that is, to create a social, economic, intellectual and political democracy so uni-versal and profound that it would far surpass anything we have ever known in that direction, but does so largely by means of the abolition of practically everything which we could easily recognize as freedom. The Western mind is so unready, indeed so unable, to make the logical disjunction here between de-mocracy and freedom that it falls into pathetic confusion when it attempts to understand a scheme based upon that disjunc-tion. Thus we hear on one hand critics who deny any element of either democracy or freedom to the Soviet system, bringing out all the most vulgar details (the vodka at Kremlin banquets, the wages of ballerinas, etc., etc.) in an attempt to prove that these peripheral and statistically insignificant expenditures constitute tyrannical extravagance and a disregard for the people's wants; whereas on the other hand we hear ignorant, well-meaning Western apologists for the Soviet system arguing (as no Russian would dream of doing) that freedom does actually exist under that system in a purer form than in our own. The fact is, of course, that the Russians have no historical experience of freedom, no genuine understanding of it or desire for it, and have on the whole regarded it as the easiest of all the sacrifices they have made to the better world of which they dream. The secular obsession of the Western world for the idea of freedom, the identification of society with the struggle for more and more freedom, the continuous and by now practically organic consciousness of Western man as free man, all this means nothing to the Russians and never did.

How, then, as we leave this room on the eighteenth-century park, how are we prepared for the rendezvous to which we go?

As Americans we are perhaps a little more prepared than we are as English, French or Belgians, because the Americans have had a more extensive "practical" civilization than their older brethren, a greater acquaintance with machines, techniques, engineering concepts, diffused among much larger classes of the population. An American soldier's chief astonishment with his allies has always been that they have to be taught to ride a bicycle, to drive a car, to use a Diesel engine or any other of the objects they have received under the lend-and-lease arrangements. It is rare to find an American male without some technical proficiency. This is both symptom and effect of a great industrial development and becomes in its turn a cause of further development, along with the material conditions which make it possible. In this respect (techniques, machines) the American culture and consequently the American mind are by and large better fitted to meet the Russian than any other, because the American already has what the Russian wants and expresses what the Russian wishes his society to express, technological optimism in its highest form. But the American is philosophically less prepared than his English counterpart for the task, because his natural confidence (satisfaction with his own methods) gives little room for the reception of novel concepts. Novelty from outside the Western circle, novelty from a "backward" nation such as Russia, comes veiled in doubt to the American mind, whereas Englishmen of the requisite intellectual level have long been accustomed to considering ideas, whatever their origin, only as a rule to reject them or modify them in accordance with English prejudices, but at any rate viewing them thoughtfully and all together. The American men who are likely to have the chief part in that conversation with the Russians which will occupy the next ten years or so are men who will be able to talk easily and eagerly, in a wash of mutual comprehension, on specific practical matters concerned with the exchange and regulation of tangible objects, the disposal of goods and values, the flow of trade, the division of responsibilities; but when, as happens again and again with men who (like the Russian commissars) are still close to and conscious of their origins in philosophic theory, the question discussed touches upon a larger area of abstract thinking, we should expect to see comprehension cease and bewilderment set in. The points of departure are so far apart that it becomes difficult to keep the rendezvous at all, once the problems are transferred to the realm of general thought in which American politicians are so noticeably ill at ease. For the thing to remember is that the ideas I have been trying to state—the freedom to struggle for freedom as Western man's social Ego and therefore identical with his society itself; this social Ego further mixed, inextricably, with the idea of democracy—are *unconscious* in the collective mind of the West and scarcely emerge in statement at all except in threadbare inherited aphorisms and rhetorical flourishes. Their reality expresses itself not by dialectical proliferation, as other ideas do, but by the ordinary acts of life in which Western man *behaves* like a free man, says and does what he likes or protests against any restraint upon his right to do so. This very day the Boston daily newspaper which occasionally reaches my house contains on its first page, along with the news of war in the Pacific and politics in Washington, no less than three headlines concerned with the incessant assertion of freedom on the part of our citizens. In one, some adherents of a cult calling itself "Jehovah's Witnesses" demanded an injunction to prevent a municipality from restricting its right to distribute leaflets from door to door—a right which, it would appear, had previously been upheld in a decision by the Supreme Court of the United States; in another, a man sought legal action to keep his neighbor's children from making too much noise, and failed; in another, soldiers who had smuggled an Italian boy protégé into the country were appealing successfully for aid in keeping him here—aid which involved the alteration of a law; such is the behavior of men who *feel* themselves free and therefore *are* free, philosophically speaking, within the limits materially determined.

This idea of freedom is utterly alien to the Russian mind. You can search in vain through the Russian literature for any clear expression even of the desire for freedom in the Western sense. Russian social democracy did express that desire in cloudy terms at the turn of the last century (1890-1905) but obviously as a mere concession to Europeanism and always very much behind the ruling requirements of party discipline, ideological correctness, etc., etc. The polemical literature of the time—the works of Lenin in particular—show that free-

82

dom, both civil and political, was not what William James called a "live option" at all, because it was not sufficiently important to be made the subject of even one vigorous argument: this in a literature which rises to boiling point over the tiniest questions of Marxian orthodoxy or party procedure. What is so striking in the polemical publications of a party which, by contagion from its European counterparts, had to include some aspiration toward freedom in its formal statements of aims, becomes even more striking in the imaginative literature which expresses the spirit of a people. The word freedom (*svoboda*) was for a long time blacked out of the Russian dictionaries permitted to be publicly sold under the Tsarist regime, and the forms in which the idea occurs from Gogol to Tolstoy are peculiarly unlike anything we could recognize by that name. Freedom for the serfs? Yes, but in what form, and what did it mean? It meant the *right to own land*. Scarcely anything else, even in Turgenev, the most Western of great Russian writers. Freedom in the novels of Tolstoy most often meant either the individual freedom to love or the individual freedom to escape from love. In Dostoyevsky it became so metaphysical—as in *The Idiot,* for instance—that it had practically no social meaning. And in all these writers, including Gogol himself, the implicit great aspiration often confounded with "freedom" and completely obscuring it was the creation of a new Russian society. That desire—to create anew, *ab ovo* —runs through the whole of Russian literature and gives it much of its singular majesty and power; but it has nothing to do with the innate freedom-determined social Ego of the West.

The *national* or *collective* freedom—that is, the freedom of the Russian soil and people from dominion by the foreigner —is of course precisely the same in Russian literature as it is in any other, but this simple patriotic emotion is not at all what is meant by the freedom of man in Western society. Patriotic emotion is common to all societies, even the least free, except under conditions of the most abject material misery and disintegration, and even then (as we have seen in such wretched countries as Ireland) it is likely to flourish fanatically when sufficiently canalized. The Russian national or collective "freedom" in this sense is the same as that of the Serbs, Mexicans, Chinese or any other people which does not like foreigners and would rather have slavery under native masters than liberty and happiness under a beneficent, but foreign, rule. Russian legend and folk music also has another concept of freedom: that which is expressed in the song "Stenka Razin," for example, the Volga bandit who enjoyed a princess and threw her to the waves when she interfered with his work: this is a class concept and again bears no relation to what we have taken as our highest social good and individual benefit from society in the West.

At the present moment the Russian concept of freedom, in so far as one exists, does not touch upon civil or political rights. Education and the life of the mind are free to all in Russia if they do not go beyond the doctrinal limits of state philosophy. Freedom to live and work, to receive education up to the quantitative or qualitative degree decided upon by authority, to express individual aptitudes in appropriate activity—all this no doubt exists, but is circumscribed (to our way of thinking and feeling—not to the Russian) by an inability at any turn to assert fundamental dissent, to attack established authority or question official opinion. Russians apparently believe that a state regime which relieves the individual of any need to think about it releases his powers as never before, and bestows a new freedom singularly sweet and strong for the active citizen. This may indeed be true for artists, imaginative writers, exceptional workers with no special desire for original or speculative thought, but in what way it can become true for the generality of mankind remains to be seen. Russian friends have explained

84

to me that the abolition of politics—of any possible serious dissent, that is—is practically equivalent to the abolition of the state in the true Marxian sense: and yet this runs so counter to the most blatant observed facts, the supremacy of the state, the omnipotence of the police, the exclusively state-dictated forms of trial, that no Western mind can follow such self-delusive reasoning without a great many ironic footnotes. And yet the quality of those who so reasoned was such that I am convinced they believed what they were saying; and under the conditions at present obtaining, with all things situated just as they are today, this is true for them although it is not true for me.

We go, then, to speak an unknown language in a strange place, and what makes the adventure exhilarant in prospect is that we know there are innumerable points upon which we already agree although we have not yet discovered it. In two and a half years on air fields throughout the world I found that those who understood aircraft needed no language to talk to each other. It is when the specific touches upon those larger areas behind us—all those centuries which are our point of departure—that we must take thought, recognize our differences and endeavor by an exercise of the imagination not to gloss them over, never to gloss them over, but to understand them as they are at both terms of the antithesis where true antithesis appears. The brave Scythians we go to meet have never touched our historical society at any point save at Byzantium, the tangential, uncharacteristic, hieratic Byzantium, and briefly at the close of the nineteenth century (up to 1905) in the socialist doctrines of Marx and Engels. At both points these strong, drastic men embraced with passion what the West had to give, transforming it in each case utterly, so that Mount Athos and the British Museum eventuated respectively in Russian village mysticism and Russian presidial Communism. All the rest, from Plato to Bergson or Croce in philosophy and from Themistocles to Winston Churchill in political action, has taken place on a scene invisible to them and without interest for the few, simple and powerful concepts under which they choose to regulate their collective existence. They are a living example of Trotsky's "law of combined development," whereas we are the evolutionary product of centuries of struggle in one direction: we are the heirs of the ages, if you like, and they have sprung fully armed from the brow of Zeus.

The light fails now through the trees; we must go before dark. We leave behind us those nineteenth-century illusions which brought *"Monsieur Georges Clemenceau, Président de la Conférence de la Paix,"* along with *"Monsieur Woodrow Wilson, Président des Etats-Unis, Monsieur Lloyd-George, Premier Ministre de Grande-Bretagne,"* and all the others, into this hall to present a treaty of peace to the vanquished Germans. We know now that Germany's relation with the rest of the world is a function of that world's own relations, and that we cannot possibly expect to treat the German question any longer as an isolated phenomenon. The agreement between America and Russia is the main thing: if we have this on the German question we shall have it on many others, most others, and if America and Russia agree there will be little difficulty obtaining the agreement of Great Britain and its satellites. This is not merely because of the combined power of America and Russia, immense though that is; it is also, and perhaps primarily, because there are few points in which England and America are not *a priori* in agreement. The agreement, the harmony between them, is deeper than ordinarily appears on any surface, because it is quite independent of the single opinions of men and refers back (perhaps unconsciously) to all that brings both to life; whatever happens during the coming dialogue between Russia and the West, it is hardly to be supposed that America and England can seriously dis-

86

agree on anything of radical importance. The exception, a conspicuous one, is of course imperialism, in which the British form (a frank but on the whole benign rule to those who do not revolt against it) is unlike the disguised American form and therefore seems morally wrong to great sections of the American population who are unaware that an American form exists. There are no doubt evil men in England as in other countries, we reflect, who would like to embroil America with Russia for the sake of their own profit, but if such there be, they must surely be more stupid even than evil, because a conflict so gigantic would drag England in and, this time, there can be little doubt, down, whatever the issue of the struggle. The other danger to the Anglo-American harmony—aside from the hearty natural dislike between these two peoples, which is of a family nature and does little harm—comes from an endeavor on the part of extreme Tory elements in England to commit the United States to courses of policy which the American nation as a whole will never approve. This has already taken place in Italy and Greece and unless the Americans are vigilant it might easily happen again. But at the point of time in which we stand, taking our leave of the Trianon, indeed of all Versailles, it seems doubtful if the Tories will be able to commit even their own government to such courses for much longer; their days, too, are numbered.

The treaties upon which we have mused in this room all took their names from the royal palaces and gardens which luxurious despots in the seventeenth and eighteenth centuries built for their own ease and for the pleasures of ostentation: Versailles, St. Germain, Trianon. The Treaty of St. Germain with Austria and the Treaty of the Trianon with Hungary were modeled upon the Treaty of Versailles and were completed in the following autumn; again, like the Versailles Treaty, they attempted to rule upon a vast mass of detail, awarding everything from heifers and art objects and historical documents to the states created out of the debris of the Austro-Hungarian empire. Was there any reason for choosing Versailles, St. Germain and the Trianon for the signing of these treaties and for the names they bore during the brief period during which they were applied? No, we may be sure; the reason was no different from that which induced Churchill, Truman and Stalin to meet at Potsdam in the summer of 1945, the mere material convenience of large houses and many rooms. But the French palaces which gave their names to the treaties of 1919 do set up certain echoes in the caverns of the mind: St. Germain means the youth of Louis XIV, the exile of James II Stuart and Mary of Modena, the royal hunt; Versailles is Louis XIV in his utmost splendor, dominating Europe, as it is also the folly of Montespan and the calculated bigotry of Maintenon; Trianon is Marie-Antoinette and her cows. All that is very far away in time and even more remote in manners of thought and behavior. When we think of Jeannette de Pompadour sitting in that small cabinet on the ground floor at Versailles and writing little admonitory notes to ambassadors and princes ("Remind the Holy Father of the Thirty Years' War," she wrote to Choiseul when he was French ambassador to the Vatican), we see how interplanetary space is scarcely more dizzying than the distance which separates men's systems of action over a mere two hundred years. Mme. de Pompadour and Choiseul—Stalin and Vishinsky: they have little besides the ink and paper in common. The power of France on the continent of Europe was scarcely less during the seventeenth and eighteenth centuries than is that of Russia today, but in what frivolity and extravagance was it thrown to the winds! The twilight that is thickening through the trees hides not only the great branches of oak and elm, but the sun-king and the sun of another age.

88

§ 10

Called back at the very door by a persistent hissing noise in the shadows, we turn and peer and hesitate, for the hours have passed and the SHAEF officers must be given their messhall for the evening meal. What is this last call upon our departing attention? What are these small obsequious forms which incline from the median, left hand in right, and utter the sound of inhaled saliva? Why, can it be—indeed it is—it is our friends, our dear friends, the Marquis Saionji (soon to be Prince), the Baron (soon to be Count) Makino, the Viscount Chinda, Mr. Matsui and Mr. Ijuin; how could we have forgotten them? Have they been here all the time?

Yes, indeed, all the time.

They have watched the Tiger's claw point the treaty into the hand of the Prussian; they saw the Prussian's knees tremble as he tried to rise; they overheard Wilson's aside to Lloyd George ("Isn't that just like them?") and they even saw the look of distaste upon the faces of delegates here and there among the dignitaries, Smuts, Botha, Orlando; they have missed nothing of all this. And on the whole they have had more reason to be satisfied than anybody else present at the long conversations which ended in the treaty handed to Brock-dorff-Rantzau in this room. These shades so dimly seen across the lustrous floor have been able to congratulate themselves upon the most formidable diplomatic victories obtained at the whole peace conference. Their exertions, after all, had been little: they had merely taken Germany's possessions in the Far East in 1914 without much trouble, outposts that could not be defended by a power so far away. These outposts were Tsingtao and the Kiao-Chiao area of China, so easy (so very easy) to make into a base for the conquest or control of all Shantung; there were also the Marshall, Pelew, Caroline and Mariana islands, very convenient, very nice to have, especially in the case of a naval war. Under the mandate system which dear President Wilson had so thoughtfully provided it would be quite simple for Japan to take over these islands, fortify them or not, according to their usefulness, and allow them to play their part in the sacred destiny of the divine people. But even more satisfactory to minds which could contemplate a long future were the events which had so securely established Japan on the mainland of Asia during this war, and which, although not mentioned in the peace treaties, had been the subject of amiable private agreements between the powers. Europe and America had been too preoccupied in 1915 to pay much attention to China; it had been relatively child's play to present the Twenty-One Demands to old Yuan Shih-kai and obtain Shantung, Manchuria, Eastern Mongolia, special rights in Fukien, priority for Japanese advisers and Japanese capital in the development of China. Port Arthur and Dairen were pretty prizes; so were the South Manchurian Railway and the Antung-Mukden Railway. In a few brief months, while the Western powers were looking in another direction, Japan obtained all those immense advantages for which, essentially, her wars of 1894 against China and of 1904-1905 against Russia had been fought, but which at the time they were fought did not produce the longed-for fruit because the world was too vigilant. China was now helpless; Russia was nearly so, or the Japanese diplomats cajoled themselves into thinking that this might soon be the case. Japanese troops were at Chita and Irkutsk; the "government" of Kolchak, supported by Japan and her Western allies, had been proclaimed at Omsk the year before. Japanese soldiers would soon—within a few months—occupy Northern Sakhalin, and for those who, like Saionji and Makino, saw the destiny of the divine people as supreme in all Asia, the future was indeed bright. Dear President Wilson, so interested in his League of Nations—sssss! wonderful institution, League of Nations, sssss!

—was willing to pass over all this, to avert his eyes, except in the matter of Shantung, where he agreed to recognize Japan's special status, and to do so, why? So that Japan would support the League, which indeed at that moment Japan could not have afforded to stay out of under any circumstances.

Kimmochi Saionji was seventy years old in 1919; he had been born in medieval Japan and before he died (at ninety-one) the modernized, though still sacred, empire had made its compact with National Socialist Germany. In any country a life so long would have encompassed many changes; in Japan it saw the swift passage from bow-and-arrow feudalism, handicrafts and complete seclusion to a highly industrialized and ambitious maritime empire bent upon expansion and conquest. Saionji was four years old when Commodore Perry paid the momentous visit to Japan; he was nineteen when the Tokugawa era ended and he became commander-in-chief of the imperial forces (still with bow-and-arrow). As a young man he accompanied Ito to Europe to learn the political customs of the pale strangers who had wrought such changes by breaking down the walls of the hermit kingdom, and, having learned, he made use of the parliamentary system in various capacities, twice as prime minister. When Prince Hirohito began the Showa reign (1926) Saionji was to attain the special dignity, partly by mere longevity, attached to the Genrō of Meiji, of whom he was the last. What was to make the Showa reign memorable to world history, and catastrophic to the Japanese, took place one year after Saionji's death: the attack upon the American fleet at Pearl Harbor in Hawaii. Whether the old man would have approved of a gamble so tremendous, on the risky assurance of German victory in Europe, or whether he would have been able to restrain those who had set their minds upon it, are questions not to be answered now; but what is certain is that his objection would have been for reasons of caution only, and not for reasons of principle. In principle Saionji and his party (the Seiyukai) wholly supported the expansionist adventures, the dreams of imperial grandeur and the financial and commercial elephantiasis for which they were largely responsible in the beginning. Like all of the "moderates" belonging to the old feudal aristocracy, Prince Saionji owned precisely the same set of notions about Japan's future as the most rabid patriotic maniac, differing from them only in matters of method and on questions of risk. With all this he had been able to adjust the formal ceremonious dignity of a medieval Japanese noble to the manners and charms of Western society, so that few Japanese diplomatists or ruling personages come off better in the memoirs of their Western friends.

Those Western friends were, of course, numerous. Aside from the alliance with Great Britain—which was to be abrogated within two years—Japanese diplomacy in the Meiji reign had conquered the good opinion of the whole West, aside, perhaps, from Russia, by dint of sedulous application to Western schematic or conventionalized behavior without, of course, any attempt to penetrate the original meaning of such forms. There was something which appealed to Western imaginations in the sudden emergence of this island empire into the general current of life, with its extraordinary orderly revolution and its quick adaptation to techniques three or four hundred years in advance of its own. It is to be remembered that Theodore Roosevelt's purposes in convening the peace conference of Portsmouth (1905) were not merely pacific; there is good evidence that he wanted the Russo-Japanese War to end with Japan in the advantageous position given by the recent victories, which a prolongation of the war might have threatened. He certainly digested the Korean policy without a qualm, and his admiration of the "brave little people" was widespread in his day in America. Wilson's doctrines were violated at every point by Japanese policy toward Russia and

China in 1915-1919, and yet he, too, was willing to permit
Saionji, Ishii, Makino and anybody else who hissed enough
and talked enough to persuade him that there was no danger
in it. Aside from the rather naive admiration for Japanese
achievement, Americans, like Europeans, appear to have suffered from the belief that Japan's ambitions were not serious
—were a matter of religious ritual and folk custom, quaint and
indeed beautiful in their formal expression but not to be taken
au pied de la lettre so far as the grown-up diplomacy and
realistic arrangements of the truly "great" powers were concerned. One must be indulgent, my dear friend; these Orien-
tals are like children, you know; they attach such importance
to words and gestures . . . Have you read Lafcadio Hearn?
It is easy to imagine Lord Dufferin, Mr. John Hay, M. Jules
Cambon and others of those who directed policy in the early
part of this century wearily flicking over the documents which
built up Japan's imperial status and pushing them to one
corner of the desk, so as not to interfere with the more vital
questions to be settled—the Banat of Temesvar, the status of
Bosnia and Herzegovina, the marriage of the Archduke. It
was by indulgence toward the new Oriental power that Japan
was allowed to send troops in with the Western allies at the
time of the Boxer rebellion in Peking; it was a general con-
descending kindliness which fostered Japanese greed in Manchuria, Mongolia and Fukien. A village fair in the Balkans
seemed more important, to this generation of Europeans, than
any Japanese plan on the mainland of Asia. In one sense they
were right, because the village fair in the Balkans did produce
the monstrous conflagration of 1914-1918; and in the next generation (that of Wilson, Clemenceau and Lloyd George) the
conflagration occupied all minds to the practical exclusion of
everything else, so that it was possible for Japan to make enormous strides without being obstructed or, in fact, even noticed.

Two episodes in the process, we reflect in the gathering

darkness, showed what has been proved abundantly on other scenes throughout this century: that international journalism was more alert than international statesmanship. In the first episode two correspondents resident in Peking, Mr. G. E. Morrison of the London *Times* and Mr. Frederick Moore of the Associated Press of America received from Yuan Shih-kai the text of the Twenty-One Demands presented by Japan—demands which had been made in secret and accompanied by an ultimatum (1915) which would have effectively ended the independence of China if carried out in every detail without opposition. Both in London and in New York these demands were regarded as so startling that they could not be true; the British Foreign Office and the American State Department did what they usually do in such cases—denied the whole thing. The Associated Press cabled Mr. Moore that in future they wanted "news, not rumors." It was months before the truth in the matter was permitted to leak out, supporting in full what the two correspondents had originally said. In the second episode (1919) the outraged Chinese delegation to the peace conference, having been unable to get a sympathetic hearing with Wilson, Clemenceau or Lloyd George, and aware that the agreements and understandings reached in hotel rooms were all favorable to Japan in the design to dominate China, gave the text of the Treaty of Versailles to a correspondent for the Chicago *Tribune* while the document was still secret. It was taken to America on a fast ship and was read out, word for word, into the minutes of the United States Senate by Medill McCormick before the world at large had a text at all. The emphasis given in this second case, as in the first, was upon the dangers inherent in Japanese ambition—dangers which the responsible statesmen of the period were inclined to flout as being of no real consequence to the world at large. It may also be said that the functional and competitive alertness of journalism deserved no credit for these revelations, since they did not primarily come from conscience, sense of justice, political awareness or foresight, but merely from the desire to get news; but this begs the question, because whatever the causes, in effect journalism *was* more awake than statesmanship. It is to be remembered that the British Foreign Office and the American State Department actually *did not believe* the Twenty-One Demands to exist in fact; they were too ill-informed and too slouchy-minded to be prepared for the reality of Japan's ambition. Journalism may be excessively credulous in some respects but at least it did not rule out what was to be one of the determining elements in the evolution of the world forces during the first half of the twentieth century.

It was to take thousands upon thousands of American lives to undo the work of these polite little gentlemen in the shadows. When the course of Japanese foreign policy since 1894— or, in fact, since 1874—is objectively surveyed, it can be seen to present greater homogeneity, continuity and internal logic than any other foreign policy known to us in modern times. It was never the toy of partisan politics or personal ambition; it was never affected by the rivalries inevitable in domestic affairs. From the time when the hermit empire abandoned its self-imposed isolation and, coming out into the current of life, made haste to learn the industrial and military techniques of the Western world, the face Japan turned toward that world has never altered. In early days it was necessary to accept unequal treaties of the kind that had been forced also upon China, Turkey, Persia and other Eastern states; but these did not last long with the resourceful, determined and unwavering Japanese. By 1874 Japan, having undergone considerable salutary revolution in six or seven years, was ready to begin the outward push, starting with the Ryukyu Islands down toward Formosa, which was annexed after the war of 1894; the next step was in the north, Korea, then Manchuria and Mon-

golia; China itself was now to be gobbled up under the
Twenty-One Demands. There was never the slightest difference between Japanese on any of these expanding operations
except upon questions of method, risk and detail. In principle
all Japanese were here as one, although in internal questions
they differed almost as much—above the fundamental religious
and patriotic base—as Westerners do. The puzzle in retrospect
is *why*, when the whole course of modern Japan has been as
easy to read as a multiplication table and was always just as
irrefutable, *why* did the Western politicians or (to adopt the
term which for some reason has become eulogistic in English)
"statesmen," refuse to give it its full weight in the calculation
of forces? Why this indulgence, this sympathetic admiration
for the "brave little people," when in fact Japan was systematically infringing every rule of national conduct which the Western powers, themselves uneasily conscious of a lurid past in
that respect, were now attempting to give the force of law?

The explanation I find is one which does not apply to Japan
alone, but to every question involved in the relations between
governments throughout the world during the modern era,
up to and including a large part of the war which began in
1939. It is this: the men who directed affairs, particularly
foreign affairs, in the great states of the West, were never con-
ditioned to think of the world as a whole. They considered one
problem at a time and hoped like Micawber that "something
would turn up" before they had to face the next. When they
were busy over Bosnia and Herzegovina they did not have
the agility or the training to think of Mongolia and Manchuria; they had "spheres" in their minds, when in reality we
live on only one sphere; they could not see that "Near East"
and "Far East" and "Adriatic" and "Baltic" were coming
nearer and nearer to each other with vertiginous speed. Few
of them were men of any technical knowledge, and the inventions which shrank the world in this century were never con-

temporaneously understood in their sociological or historical context: statesmanship was thus always far behind the obscure designers, engineers, electrical experimenters and technological dreamers who gave the age its primary material character. There was and is a refusal on the part of foreign offices in the West to recognize connections between questions which are geographically separated: what has Poland, they would say, to do with Argentina? This kind of childish pigeonholing of matters vital to the life and work of the human race is inherited from ages when, in fact, the parts of the earth could be effectively separated from each other and dealt with one by one. Our foreign ministers and secretaries of state too often have been like the little boy who admits that two plus two equals four in arithmetic, but cannot see how this has any application to his actual life—or like Hegel's case of the man who wanted fruit in the abstract but refused to accept cherries, pears or grapes. The fact that what applies in Bosnia and Herzegovina might also apply in Argentina or Manchuria is something quite new to the state department-foreign office level of consciousness. It took cataclysmic action and reaction by Germans, Japanese and Russians between them to alter this state of affairs, at least on the highest plane, so that it was possible for Roosevelt, Churchill and Stalin to speak of the entire world for perhaps the first time in modern history. Hitler had, of course, *thought* in such terms throughout his life; it was one essential part of his genius, and his debt in this respect to Haushofer and "geopolitics" is one concerned more with form than with content. The tendency on the part of trivial minds after the victory to rob Hitler (a crazed genius, but a genius) of any element of masterly and original creation should not blind what is intelligent among us to the truth: he did teach the West that the world was one. He knew this far more certainly than did Mussolini, for example—a cleverer man, a more "normal" man and originally a stronger one—but it

97

did not keep him from being utilized, and perhaps in the final analysis ruined, by an Oriental ambition which he no doubt considered he could deal with in due course after the eventual victory.

For Japan never, by my reading, accepted any view of the world in which one-ness was diverse and multifarious. The literature and religion of the Japanese make no allowance for the existence of the West at all. Astute Japanese have studied the West in every aspect accessible to them, but not with the recognition of permanence in Western achievement. What is ultimately true for the Japanese as the aim of history is the unity of all men under the sacred Emperor—a sort of combination, perhaps, of the Church of Rome and the Roman Empire—with Japanese everywhere as the ruling force. Thus the Japanese diplomatists took Hitler's victories and Hitler's alliance as instrumental in their ultimate purposes, since the German danger immobilized the whole of British and American force at the time, but any Germano-Japanese victory would have resulted in an unappeasable opposition between the victors. Japanese Shintoism could make no room for Germany, however much the secular mind of Japan admired the Germans, and the National Socialist theory of racial purity could not accommodate an Asiatic master-people. The association of the two was a provisional arrangement corresponding to temporary necessities in their separate but kindred ambitions, against which England, Russia and the United States were the principal resistance; in the autumn of 1941, thanks to the stupendous victories of the German army, it seemed possible that a twin effort might revise the whole structure of the world, and it has always seemed to me that a daring prosecution of the original scheme might have so resulted. In other words, if Japan had not subsided upon her vast victories in Asia, but had proceeded to attack Siberia in the spring or summer of 1942, risking the consequences, risking everything at once, there might have been a collapse of Russia—not probably, but possibly—which would have rendered a victory of the Anglo-Americans out of the question. But the polite and ferocious small men whose brains could conceive and execute schemes of such magnitude as the exploiting suzerainty of East Asia and the destruction of American naval power balked at the final touch which would have brought the conspiracy to logical completion, the attack on Russia. Perhaps too many men like Saionji—dead, of course, by that time, but Konoye or Ishii or another of the breed—felt that the island empire had already dared too much; perhaps success had had an opiate effect, and time no longer seemed to press; in any case by the end of 1942 it was too late and the whole tide of the war had changed. The summer of 1942, up to the first of September, while Stalingrad hung on like grim death and we waited from day to day for the Japanese attack on Siberia, was the really dreadful moment of decision, but the little men could not take the leap. Their whole ghastly gamble, restrained at the last and most useless moment by caution or uncertainty, put me in mind of the idle rhyme scrawled (so legend says) by Walter Raleigh and Elizabeth Tudor with cutting diamonds on a window at Windsor:

> *I fain would climb, but I fear to fall.*
> *If thine heart fail thee, climb not at all.*

By now, as we stand in the gathering darkness and take our leave, the results of the throw were all too obvious for the small men, the polite and hissing little men who had so shrewdly studied and so seriously misjudged the forces of the West. They had built their whole scheme upon German victory, and the German victory had crumbled to nothing—Germany was in ruins. At the close of the 1914-1918 war they had profited exceedingly by the slovenly patchwork of the peace. All they had to do, Saionji and Makino and the suave, London-combed Chinda, was to pay their court to "dear President Wilson and dear Mr. Lloyd George," keeping their eye out for any convenient ally who might appear in the development of the inevitable results of error. They cared nothing for any of these pale foreigners whose technical skills they aped; an alliance with England at one time, with Germany at another, served the ends of the sacred empire equally and could equally be abandoned if it seemed profitable to do so. The League of Nations was to be used if possible, especially as it offered a stage upon which Japan could play the part of a modern great power and lie in wait for opportunities. But the great design of expansion on the mainland of Asia at the expense of China and Russia was never to be obscured by any permutation or combination of temporary forces and sentiments, any more than the oceanic dream, the domination of the Pacific, was to fade or die. The favoring circumstance in all this was that generations of great men held the highest offices in the West, from Theodore Roosevelt to Franklin Roosevelt, from Lord Salisbury to Winston Churchill, from Delcassé to Clemenceau to the wretched Daladier, without ever thoroughly becoming aware of the perilous watcher at the gates, the small and cautious watcher who would spring when the opportunity offered.

Now that we go to meet the Russians, what shall we say to them of these hissing shadows, these afterthoughts of the Western peace and war? No voice would dare *demand* of Russia, after the unimaginable sacrifices made for the defeat of Germany, to repeat the operation so as to ease and hasten our victory over Japan. But the hope is undeniable, and we shall have it in mind whether it takes form in words or not, for the Japanese are the natural enemies of Russia, we tell ourselves, and the only rulers in the West who have consistently known this danger throughout the present century were the Russians, Tsarist and Bolshevik alike, from Izvolsky to Molotov, who are—thus we reflect in awareness of our own inconsistency, if

100

inconsistency it is—Western with respect to Japan as they are un-Western with respect to us. There they lie between an Orient and an Occident which they touch or refrain from touching as they please, a land mass larger than the surface of the moon, a population which (if it is Western at all) is the only Western population that shows a rising birth rate, and a social system as different from one as it is from the other. To assume the dominant position in East Asia which belongs rightfully to the greatest of Asiatic land powers, the Soviet Union had to enter the Eastern war and be present at the Eastern peace; but would the results be greatly different afterwards if this came to pass? Would not the claims of Russia be undeniable even if Russia had not participated in the war at all? Had the Russians not held the greatest of Japan's land armies immobilized on the Russian frontier since the very beginning of the war and before? As we think of these circumstances we seem to hear the voice of Stalin echoing from March, 1939, saying—what was it, now?—that he did not propose to pull chestnuts out of the fire for anybody. It depends, one supposes, on how desirable are the chestnuts and what chance there is of keeping them afterwards.

In any case we know that the Eastern war was made upon a hypothesis arising out of the Western war, and we were right —our supreme directors were supremely right—in fighting the Western war first. They were perhaps urged on to do so by Stalin (we seem to have heard echoes of the kind from Teheran) but it was in any case the only strategy, because the Japanese gamble from the very beginning depended upon the war in the West. Once the war in the West was won, there remained not the faintest material possibility for any outcome except surrender for the Japanese, no matter how obstinately they might prolong the struggle. Our soldiers in the East could not be expected to understand the necessity of this strategy, which left them for three long years fighting with insufficient means,

but there was the hard certainty that if Germany won in
Europe (which means, if Germany won over Russia) there
could be no practical or discernible way of winning the war
at all for the United States and England. The greater enemy
had to be annihilated before it was possible to turn upon the
lesser. A division of forces would have prolonged the war and
made victory doubtful, and a concentration upon the East
would have been worst of all, producing in all likelihood both
a victorious Germany and an inimical Russia, the two least desirable of all results in this century for the American and
British groups of states. Thus by a concurrence of circumstances which generations to come will study in all their complexity, the minds of Churchill and Roosevelt were turned—
perhaps under military advice, perhaps not altogether; perhaps under Stalin's urging and perhaps only partly; but most
of all, I think, through the new habit of thinking of the world
as a whole—toward the only possible grand strategy, that which
was followed, even though it appeared objectively to serve the
interests of Russia and thus had always seemed to Hitler impossible. To his last day Hitler refused to believe in the
Anglo-Russian-American alliance (Lucifer, son of the morning!) and pinned his dying hope to a clash between his enemies. That he was proved wrong is perhaps the greatest of the
debts we owe to Roosevelt and Churchill, both of whom saw,
I think, that the outcome of any hesitation might have been
the welding of German skill and German power with the
power and resources of Russia, a combination against which
years of bloody combat might well have been unavailing.

The small men have lost, too, and the face of Asia has
changed. In the appointment we are now to keep, for some
years to come, those who control the affairs of Europe will also
control the affairs of Asia. It will not be possible to make a
peace treaty, like that of Versailles, in which the whole Asiatic
continent is involved merely by implication, a surrender by

Germany there, a providential cloak by the League of Nations there, a few amiable concessions in hotel rooms to the desires of this or that negotiator. It will be necessary to take account of the relation between Europe and Asia and of the vast hyphen between them which is Soviet Russia; it will be necessary to take account of the desires of the Asiatic peoples. The one clearly life-giving role which Japan played upon the stage of twentieth-century history was that of champion for the Asiatic peoples. The part was played for a variety of reasons, some of which were undoubtedly sincere and not invented for the advantage of the sacred empire. In the early part of the century the Asiatics, stirred by the sharp rise of Japan, tended to look upon the Japanese as their spokesmen in the world; there were times when Japanese diplomacy accepted this responsibility with a certain disinterested elevation of concept, even against immediate Japanese advantage; such an instance took place here at Versailles when the Japanese delegation attempted to get the principle of racial equality written into the covenant of the League of Nations. In this, their one altruistic (or partly altruistic) effort, they made their one failure; the vote was seventeen to eleven; in all that concerned their plans for aggressive expansion on the territory of their neighbors they obtained what they wanted.

Such a part in our coming dialogue will be played no longer by Japan, which will not be heard, and only in the most formal sense by China; it will be played by Soviet Russia, which is already (and for years past) prepared to assume it. And across this area of thought and action lies India like a spongy and amorphous question mark, distorting whatever may be said or done in the older styles of Western diplomacy, demanding, in all its exasperating weakness, a solution which does not date from the 1880's. Clearly these are immensities: we are not ready for a peace treaty at all because too much must be settled if anything is to be settled. Thus we go to talk, to dis-

103

cuss, to arrange, to simplify if possible, but above all to try to see the world whole and establish its indivisible peace under the recognized diversity of our forms. Our conversation may take years; let it be so; but let us not with undue haste try to get too much on paper before we know what it is we want. Let the heifers and sheep, the historical documents, the works of art and the sulphate of ammonia and the milch cows all stay in the treaty of Versailles, where they belong; let us try to get broad and enduring agreements with our allies upon principles, and the milch cows will take care of themselves. And it might be well to remember how dangerous it is to allow an ally which, like Japan in the last war, has done little except inherit the spoils of our victory, to lie in wait and seize upon everything that may fail to interest us or be overlooked in the magnitude of our peacemaking. The German obsessions of Clemenceau we leave here; they are of no current significance, because what is done in Germany must be a part of what is done everywhere, throughout Europe and Asia, for the creation—not in rude haste, but as the conditions permit—of a peace settlement in which the great historical dialogue of America and Russia can take place in fruitful tranquillity, unthreatened by the waning passions of tribe and territory which, at a time not too far distant may perhaps be seen, and as a result of that dialogue, to vanish at last from the earth.

§ 11

The conspiracy of the Fascist-Nazi-Shinto Axis was artificial and anti-historical and, as such, was, according to the philosophical concepts implicit in everything we have said in this place, bound to fail. Against it we pitched an alliance created by the forces of nature and history which for that reason was bound to succeed. Tribal tyranny is particularly temporary, and all tyranny, as Spinoza says, is impermanent; the nature of the faith Hitler taught was responsible both for his momentary success and his final defeat. The absurdity of combined effort by a state built on the superiority-phantasm of "Aryan" racial purity and a state built by Oriental religiosity around a living god was apparent even during the war and even to Germans and Japanese; they availed themselves of each other and that was all. Between them the unhappy Italy of Fascism was like a small boy on a bicycle attempting to hang onto a speeding car. On our side historical forces—mainly, be it admitted, the enemy—drove together those great entities which many among us have for years believed in as the guardians of the world's future, the United States, England, China and Russia. The diversity here is obvious, but great fundamental principles of historicity flow together in our common aspiration toward democracy and freedom. What Western man understands by freedom, the most precious of his social possessions and in fact the essence of his social Self, is not at all what Russians understand by it (in our sense there is no freedom in Russia) but this cannot impede his recognition of the fact that the Russians have labored mightily, with inconceivable sacrifices, to create a more thoroughgoing democracy than any we have yet known in the West. The direction of their effort, in spite of the vast disparity in methods, is the same as our own. They pursue the greatest good of the greatest number. Leaving out the contradictions created by territorial imperialism (which are by nature impermanent) the whole effort of England for almost a thousand years has been in precisely the same direction. In American society there are also contradictions (the sub-citizen status of the Negroes in many states, for example) which cast shadows upon our freedom. But capitalism and socialism are less permanent than the great confluent forces upon which they are borne: the mind of Western man in its main recognizable and continuous characters was formed long before capitalism, just as Russian sovietism and communal aspiration are far older than scientific Marxism. These economic schemata may rise and fall, will inevitably be lost in change upon change upon change as new forces come up to the surface of life, but the rivers of our life still flow to the same sea.

In this the American has one final obligation which, real or imaginary, is too much a part of his historical personality to be shed in the era now at hand. He *feels* free: to the Russian who, conscious of suffering and sacrifice on a scale never known in modern times, says to him, "With a great sum obtained I this freedom," the American still answers, like Paul, "But I was free born." He has the natural inclination to wish this freedom generalized as much as his influence can bring it about, and therewith a prejudice against any form of life in which its fundamental importance is not recognized. He also feels rich, and, collectively, *is* rich with the wealth of a magnificently dowered land mass which has seen the growth of industrial power unequaled on the planet: this, too, lies upon him in part like an obligation, in part like a privilege. (It would be nonsense to deny that it gives Americans pleasure to give, and give very generously; the example of the Japanese earthquake in 1923 is irrefutable.) Morally he is in sympathy with those lines of Dante which serve as epigraph to these reflections:

> *qual ti negasse il vin della sua fiala*
> *per la tua sete, in libertà non fora,*
> *se non com' acqua ch' al mar non si cala.*

He who refuses wine from his flask for thy thirst is no more in freedom than water which flows not to the sea.

The third epigraph to these reflections, from Spinoza, suggests the American's belief that democracy is the political state nearest the state of Nature and most permissive of individual liberty; therefore, for him, the best state: and here, too, he is likely to offer wine from his flask. Thus, once he has overcome

106

the disposition toward a merely self-contained and self-suffi-
cient existence in the midst of a less fortunate world, all his
impulses run into generosity and didacticism as being most in
conformity with the moral obligation he feels or imagines to
have been laid upon him in his birth as an American. Such
generosity, such didacticism, sometimes can be very hard to
bear: resentment and suspicion greet it more often than gratitude, and the familiar notion in Europe and Asia of the long-
nosed American with bread in one hand and a tract in the
other corresponds to a kind of truth. Since it is so, let it be so:
recognizing these characteristics, perhaps we can extricate the
best there is in them from former associations with capitalist
greed, religious or sectarian ambition and political arrogance,
with some or all of which they have been mixed at times in
Asia and South America. We shall unquestionably meet other
generosities, other didacticisms, but if every opposition we
encounter should be on such ground there would be little in
the immediate prospect to fear.

So, the jeep is waiting, the soup is on the table, the lights
have gone on in the dining room behind the sheets of glimmering glass. Over the park darkness and silence have folded
in upon the great oaks, beneath whose shade in hot past sum-
mers hands fair and dead once milked the pensive cow; darkness falls upon the far fountains at the other end, in the Versailles gardens, as it falls tonight on the soft marble that crowns
the brown Acropolis, on the ruins of the Queen's Hall in London and the Ponte Vecchio in Florence, on the bomber factory at Willow Run and the grainfields of the Ukraine, the
present and the past, the living and the dead: such a night
comes gently after the weary day.

We must rise early in the morning, for we have an appointment.

107

PART TWO

GLIMPSES OF THE WAR

A Narrative

For I have always borne that laudable Partialitie to
my own Country, which Dionysius Halicarnassensis
with so much Justice recommends to an Historian.
Gulliver's Travels, Part II.

(The lengthened shadow of a man
Is history, said Emerson
Who had not seen the silhouette
Of Sweeney straddled in the sun.)
Sweeney Erect (T. S. Eliot).

CHAPTER I

BON JOUR!

Best draw my sword; and if mine enemy
But fear the sword like me, he'll scarcely look on 't.
CYMBELINE, I, ii.

WHEN WE WEIGHED anchor in Hampton Roads it was the
dark of the night before dawn on Sunday, October 23rd, 1942.
Although we did not know it, at the same moment Montgomery was beginning his assault upon Rommel's positions
at El Alamein in the Egyptian desert. In our cabin, where
twelve officers slept in layers of three—six bunks to a side—
there were two or three who called out sleepily when we felt
the lumbering, groaning movement of the ship and heard the
noise of the engines; one, I think, got up and went on deck
to see what could be seen. Most of us turned over and went
to sleep again.

Some hours later, when I came on deck, we were moving
slowly northeast along the receding coastline, heading for a
rendezvous with other parts of the convoy. So we told each
other knowingly, although I doubt if any of us really knew
what the arrangements were. All this part of the expedition
—the movement of the convoy—was a naval matter and officers
of the air and ground forces knew only its general lines. To
the west the coast of Virginia (if it was Virginia) was rapidly
growing dimmer in a greenish silver mist. To the east and
north were ships, ships, ships; never in my life had I seen so
many ships. They changed their positions from time to time,

111

forged ahead or fell back or swung to one side or the other, in accordance with orders signaled to them by fluttering pennants from the command ships of the convoy's sections. The *Ancon,* which I was to know very well in later days, appeared to be our command ship and winked its signals to us and others from morning to night.

From the moment we left Hampton Roads we expected attack from German submarines. In 1942 the German submarine was a most formidable weapon. In the spring it had invaded the St. Lawrence River and the mouth of the Mississippi; when I was in training at Miami Beach it had sunk a merchant vessel not far offshore, and the burning hulk could be seen by thousands; for some time it had seriously imperiled our communications in the Caribbean, including those with our own territory of Puerto Rico. These things we all knew but did not mention, because the ravages of the undersea enemy were too great a worry to be made public. Above all we were not to let the general population know how close beset we were by the enemy, who had actually laid mines in the harbor of New York—so bold was he, and we so unprepared.

Now we hardly ever looked out over the dancing water to the innumerable ships of our convoy without expecting to see a sudden wild burst of smoke and flame arise from one of them. Seldom did we go to bed without wondering if we would be blown out in the night. We were to throw nothing—neither cigarette ends nor orange peelings nor paper—overboard, lest the trail of such rubbish lead the enemy to us. We observed radio silence; we were forbidden to use electric razors; there were innumerable other rules and regulations to ensure that this immense concourse of ships could pass over the broad ocean without being detected. And, mysterious as it seemed to me then (and still seems), we sailed for sixteen days and sixteen nights, over a vast expanse of sea with huge roundabout movements, hundreds upon hundreds of such ships, and apparently were never detected—not only not attacked; absence of attack might have been due to many causes, including German prudence before our numbers; but actually not even detected. This was what I reluctantly came to believe upon the evidence afterwards, that which I accumulated in Africa and Europe. Our landing, the first large-scale combat landing in our history, was a complete surprise.

The ship I was on was called the *Glue*. Its real name was the *Elizabeth Stanton,* and it belonged (I think) to the McCormack Line, for combined passenger and freight service on the Pacific coast. It had been converted into a transport in the rough and speedy method of 1942, with every inch of space utilized for the accommodation of a human body. I was to see other transports later and marvel at the amount of comfort they could combine with great crowding, but the "good ship *Glue,*" as we invariably called it, was no yacht.

In my cabin we twelve were officers of rank; four of us were "of field grade," which is to say majors, and the rest captains, except for one pale boy who spent the entire voyage in his bunk being sick—he was a lieutenant of field artillery. We were allowed to have with us, along with the accoutrements considered necessary for the landing, only our musette bags: which meant that we soon developed the useful pastime of washing our own clothing. There was a bathroom just down the passage, with four or five showers and toilets and a spigot which gave forth steam and hot water; there was also a convenient bucket. At no time during the passage could you go into that bathroom without seeing at least one officer busily washing out his clothes in the bucket. You had to dodge the laundry lines going in and out of the latrine, and the underclothing and handkerchiefs were spread liberally to dry on all the bunks. We would have spread wash-lines on the decks if the navy had allowed it. For, of course, we had little to do, and the constant washing afforded an occupation. I doubt if any of us was so clean again for many months.

There were forty-six Air Corps enlisted men—aside from Signal Corps men who had their own officers—on the ship. They were all part of our headquarters squadron and were quartered together in the bowels of the ship. We had three majors (myself one), two of them from headquarters intelligence; and we had two headquarters pilots for our flight section. Amongst these five officers Dave Radam (Major Radam, the major with most seniority and least age) partitioned such work as there was. One of us was officer of the day each day beginning at noon and had to see that our men were properly quartered, fed and cared for. This was not always such an easy task, for our men were in a tiny minority on the ship and usually had to take the dirty end of the stick. They were made to wait to the very last to be fed, and had the supreme outrage of standing in line for hours while infantrymen known to them actually succeeded in going through the line twice. They also were quartered in the deepest, darkest and altogether least desirable part of the ship's underworld, where there was an odor which drove most of them out on deck for the greater part of the day. At night they were obliged to be in their quarters, which must have been (as I knew from their letters) downright offensive to most of them. When I first crawled down all those ladders and was conducted through innumerable crowded gangways to the bottommost hole where they lay, I was startled indeed. Our own quarters had seemed crowded at first—comfortable enough after a day or so—and our junior officers' quarters, with thirty in an enclosure, had seemed "really rugged" (as we used to say). But this was the black hole of Calcutta.

And yet, as the days passed in exquisite weather and everybody got used to the ship, even the black hole of Calcutta was not so bad. The boys had a sort of hammock arrangement—

114

canvas bunks swung from steel pipes in layers of four, all close together with narrow lanes between sets of eight or twelve. How they stowed away their barracks bags was a mystery, but with those barracks bags they actually had more property than the officers were allowed, and above all they had plenty of paper and ink. Although at first they did not even know where we were going, and realized that wherever it was would be a long way off, they started writing letters the very first day and kept it up indefatigably until the dawn of D-day itself. Dave Radam did not like to ask the young pilots to read their letters, so it was up to him and to me to censor them all. We divided the job between us, and the astonishing thing was how much they could write about nothing at all—the sea, the food, the passage of time, their memories of meetings in the past.

Our forty-six men were, of course, the least important on the ship. They were air corps troops, and headquarters men at that. Consequently we could not demand for them any priority over the combat infantry and artillery troops which filled the ship. They had to wait for everything. But we did succeed in getting for them some kind of alternation on the waiting with other non-combat units, so that they did not pass quite their entire day in line watching others get fed.

Dave Radam was vehement on such questions as this. He was a small, merry-eyed officer in his early thirties, who had been in the army for twelve years and much of that time in the infantry. He was Jewish, and was inclined in his rare moments of depression to think that for this reason he had not been pushed forward more in the army; but I never saw any sign of such prejudice, and indeed he did well throughout the time I knew him. His infectious grin and readiness to take the whole business lightly made him a most excellent comrade at all times, but he could shout with the best of them when it came to such matters as the feeding of the men.

"God damn it," he would bellow in a voice surprising for

115

his size, "my men have as much right to eat as anybody else on this stinking old tub. If you can't feed 'em for Christ's sake don't make 'em stand in line all day. Where's your God damned system? Can't you run relays on different bells?"

He was an excellent poker player, and the game in the officers' mess started, if I am not mistaken, on the very first night after dinner. We were pretty well served, I thought, in the officers' mess, and we must have been because the naval officers (or some of them) actually ate with us, which I never saw again on any transport except the luxurious *Ancon*. Crowding there was, and there were relays, and sometimes not enough of one thing to go round for everybody, but we fared immensely better than our men. They ate out of their mess-kits at long tables in a very smelly hall amidships which always seemed to be awash with water. After long standing (and pushing) in line, they received food which they unanimously disliked. I doubt if I ever read a soldier's letter on the ship which did not complain of the food. Much of this, perhaps, was due to the fact that this was their first experience of war conditions; such complaints grew rarer in the next two years.

The good ship *Glue* (that was its code name and at first we knew no other) was loaded with troops and attached troops of the Fifteenth Regiment of the Third Infantry Division. Thus early I made acquaintance with the blue-and-white striped patch of that magnificent division, which I was never to see again throughout the war without a stir of vicarious pride. We had chiefly the Second Battalion of the Fifteenth Regiment, commanded by Bill Billings, then a major and soon afterwards a lieutenant-colonel. Two of the company commanders were among our cabin-mates, and most of the officers with whom we played poker or walked the deck were in or attached to the battalion. At first I was taken aback by their conviction that the Third Division was the best in the army,

116

but before long I accepted this as being the truth for them, although not necessarily objectively true. I had always heard, of course, that the good soldier was one who believed his own unit to be best—"the best platoon in the best company in the best battalion in the best regiment of the best God damned division"—but I never actually ran into this belief in its pure, unself-conscious form until I sailed the good ship *Glue*. Afterwards I was to see it again in the Fifth Division, as in the Ninetieth and the Forty-fifth and others, but never with so great a sense of wonder as in those first days.

The Third Division had been doing amphibious operations in maneuvers for a year and a half. Most of this hard work had been done on the Pacific coast and the division had only recently been transferred to the Atlantic to resume the same weary exercise in Chesapeake Bay. The division had been for a long time faced toward Japan; the Fifteenth Regiment was the one from Tientsin; and it is perhaps not surprising that many of the G.I.'s, even though they sailed from Virginia, were convinced that we were on our way to the Pacific islands. The Guadalcanal landing had taken place on the preceding August 7th and the battle was still going on (it was, precisely at this time, in a critical stage).

It was therefore an astonishment to the whole ship when the sealed orders were opened, twenty-four hours out, to discover that we were bound for French Morocco. I, as an intelligence officer from the Air Staff, had been aware of the Torch plan (as we called it) for some time, and had been assigned to it for the past three weeks; the orders were not news to me. But I could see that in this particular division a certain confusion of mind had set in because of the conviction they all had that they were bound for the South Seas. Many, even among the officers, were very hazy about the exact status or area of French Morocco. The conversations at table showed bewilderment: were the Germans in Morocco? Were we at war with the French? What were we going to do in Morocco if we made a successful landing?

The War Department's booklets on French Morocco were circulated widely on the ship the next day and a little of the confusion lifted. Those War Department booklets—with which I had nothing to do—seemed to me, then and since, a creditable achievement. They were subjected to all manner of ridicule in the army afterwards because they were based upon what was generally true, and of course every soldier had some particular instance which contradicted the general truth. Our G.I.'s had not enough experience to know how a particular instance may fly against general truth without disproving it. For example, the booklets repeatedly warned the men against any trifling with veiled women in Arab countries, and the men afterwards learned that many Arab whores wore veils; their response was to say that the War Department booklet was wrong, whereas in fact it was right—super-abundantly right, as various incidents in Africa unfortunately testified. A year later a wounded soldier, on the deck of a transport going home after the Tunisian victory, came over to me and said: "Colonel, remember those talks you gave us on the way over on the *Glue?* You said we were to lay off Arab women. Well, Colonel, sir, I've got to tell you that the only Arab women I ever saw to speak to always said to me 'Fuckee, Fuckee, fitty cents.' I think you had it wrong there."

As soon as the sealed orders had been opened I went down to the black hole of Calcutta (Dave Radam's idea) to explain to our own men what French Morocco was and what we were supposed to do there. I perched on the top of one layer of bunks and talked to the boys sprawled out on all the others. I told them we were not at war with France and did not intend to be; that the French of all factions were our friends; that France had been the first to suffer in this war in the West, and had split up in great misery of internal disputes, but that we

118

had nothing to do with all that; we hoped they would join us, but if they resisted our landings we would have to fight for it and try to get them to join us afterwards. This (which was the policy as I understood it) was extremely difficult to explain. The only thing more difficult in my experience was the Italian armistice, made on the eve of the Salerno landing a year later, which confused our G.I.'s even more than the French policy. I also had to tell them that Morocco was a French Protectorate, inhabited by Arabs of mixed race, and how circumspectly they must behave with regard to Arab women, mosques, or anything connected with the Moslem religion. They asked endless questions. What was a Protectorate? How did the French get to Africa in the first place? Were the Germans in Africa too? Would the French fight us inch by inch, or only by a token resistance, or would they join the Germans against us? What kind of a town was Casablanca? What did people eat in Morocco? What was the Moslem religion?

After this seance I was pounced upon by every company commander on the ship to go through the same performance with his men. Night after night I did this, not because it was any part of my assigned duties, but because the sheer unfamiliarity of the country to which we were going was so great. Even the officers knew little or nothing about it, and many of the men had not even heard its name before. Excepting young Buckner of the Signal Corps—younger son of General Simon Bolivar Buckner of Alaska, killed in 1945 on Okinawa—I was the only officer on the ship who had ever been in Morocco, and even young Buckner remembered little from a two-day visit to Casablanca. I would go down to the mess hall after dinner at night and face a company of soldiers crowded together on benches, puzzled, serious, wondering soldiers who had many questions. And in truth it was not hard to understand their bewilderment, for instead of attacking any of the enemies who had declared war upon us, German, Japanese or

Italian, we had set forth to make a landing upon soil we considered friendly but were prepared to treat as unfriendly, depending upon what happened when we got there. I had occasion then, at the very outset, to discover what was confirmed again and again in the next two and a half years—that the American soldier was quite willing to fight his country's enemies but was continually being confused, through no fault of his own, as to who they were.

In each company there were two or three soldiers less politically innocent than the rest. (The number of these steadily increased to the end of the war.) These political literates would ask me what General de Gaulle had to do with this expedition, what we expected the Vichy government to do, and whether Pétain might be expected to order the French fleet out against us. It was my military duty to reply that we had nothing to do with the disagreements between French people, that we hoped they would all be friendly to us, and that we did know, quite decisively and accurately, those among them—very few—who were sold out to the Germans. Aside from those few, we were to assume that all French people were our friends, even though, for one reason or another, they might be ordered to resist our landing and might obey for a day or so.

This proved one of the most difficult concepts to introduce into the soldier's mind, not unnaturally.

"Major, sir, do you mean that they'll be shooting at us one day and we got to be friends with them the next?"

"Major, sir, if they kill us and we kill them how can we be friends afterwards?"

"Major, sir, if we are their friends why do they obey any German orders or Vichy orders to shoot at us?"

I did carefully say, several times over, that to the best of our knowledge and belief there were no Germans in Morocco, and that it would be difficult for German infantry or artillery to get there in time for our landing; the most we might expect,

120

I said, was German air force which might be flown down across Spain if Hitler had the warning in time. (I did not know how perfectly our secret had been kept; living in the midst of the secret myself, seeing always people who were working upon it, it had sometimes seemed to me in Washington that it must be a matter of public knowledge and that the Germans would have ample warning.) My boys, the ones I talked to, certainly were told often enough that there were no German troops in Africa. After the landing on D-day, and for several days more Americans were continually asking, "Where are the Germans?" and mistaking Frenchmen for Germans, but I do not believe that any who did so belonged to the Fifteenth Regiment of the Third Division—or attached troops.

Among the attached troops was a Field Artillery unit commanded by a young major we called Sailor Byrne. He was called Sailor because he had been at Annapolis a year before he saw the light and transferred to West Point. This admirable young officer had a serious, reflective turn of mind, was imbued with military history and tradition, and perceived the immensity of the event in which he was now participating—the first American Armada, the first surge of our national power across the seas. To many of our men and officers this convoy, which was in reality a full-fledged invasion, did not seem different from other convoys they had heard of from their fathers or elder brothers in the other war; the vast difference between actual invasion (combat landings) and the mere transport of troops across water, had not yet become apparent to them. Sailor Byrne understood what a new thing it was, what an innovation in our own national practice and what a landmark in the history of the whole world. We talked of it, not verbosely or fluently but in terms explicit enough to make ourselves understood. He had a copy of Steve Benét's poem, *John Brown's Body*, which he kept by him like a sort of Bible; he consented to lend it to me, but I could tell that he did so with reluctance. He said that it was his favorite book, which he had read many times since the first time at West Point. Steve had once gone to West Point to talk to the cadets when Sailor Byrne was there and had made a deep impression. When I said—tentatively, since such echoes from another world always seemed strange and not quite decent in the army—that I had known Steve for many years, Major Byrne gave me the book, wondering, I saw, how I could possibly have the honor of Steve's acquaintance without having read his poem.

I am glad I had not read it until then. For up to that time I had not, in forty-two years, been properly prepared for it. You had to know how these people, of all sorts and conditions, would come together in obedience to a feeling too deep for their own utterance, before you could properly understand Steve's poem. Aside from the few West Pointers, most of the officers on this ship were volunteers of one kind or another; so were many of the men. Steve's Pennsylvania farmers and the rest, the fighters of that other war so long ago, were of the same breed and recognizably so. Above all, his concept of their reason for action, running through the whole poem, was akin to that which had brought these men together. Sitting on a cot on deck, or lying on my bunk at the top of the heap in our cabin, right under the ceiling, I read the poem through and re-read it by favorite parts before I returned it to Sailor Byrne. He took it back with a glow at my appreciation.

"It's the best book I know," he said.

I wanted to write Steve about this, because something about the fortune of that poem on the toiling, crowded transport, where other officers and men read it or had read it, and it seemed to give them something special for the task ahead, would have appealed to him; but before I got around to it he had died. He must have known anyhow, without my penny's worth of tribute, what his poem meant to all Americans in a time of peril.

During these days the commanding officers of the regiment, battalion and company were studying their orders and maps with the utmost seriousness. We had detailed contour maps, road maps, photographs and some superb aerial photographic mosaics. One such mosaic had been made in our own office (the Air Support Headquarters in Washington) from photographs taken by an American camera in a high-flying Spitfire very recently, and flown to us from England. Dave Radam was the chief author of this mosaic, of which we were very proud. Afterwards when the French had become our allies and saw this mosaic, with its exact reproduction of every feature and every defense on the whole Atlantic coast of Morocco, they were astonished; they had never known their coast was being photographed. With their antiquated methods and equipment it was difficult for them even to understand how we could obtain such results. The picture was (like all mosaics) a long strip pieced together out of a large number of photographs taken at almost incredible speed from an immense height, as it might be (for instance) three or four thousand a minute from twenty-five thousand feet, and yet it displayed every coastal feature in exquisite detail. This kind of photography, along with electromagnetic detection and orientation devices, remained to the end the war's greatest mystery to me, and one which will make me to the end of my days credulous toward any new invention of physical science, however impossible it may seem at first.

As the halcyon days passed a feeling of tension grew perceptible among all on the ship. It must be remembered that we had had no experience of victory anywhere up to this moment. The war had gone badly for us and for our allies everywhere. At this moment we were hanging on by the skin of our teeth at Guadalcanal—the only offensive we had yet dared anywhere, and that a small one; the Russians, having retreated for a year, were fighting like grim death at Stalingrad. The British had had no permanent successes anywhere, nothing but an unbroken series of defeats in all parts of the world, saved only by the brilliant and beautiful defiance of the Spitfire over the cliffs of Dover. Practically speaking, Germany and Japan (and even Italy) had had everything their own way in every enterprise they had undertaken. Except for a few officers who had served in the last war, there was nobody in our convoy with experience of combat, and even these officers knew nothing at first hand of the contemporary conditions. I doubt if any American ever believed that we could lose the war; to this day most Americans have failed to realize how near we came to losing it; consequently there was no expectation of defeat, but neither was there the same absolute assurance of victory which came in the later stages. It was a moment of immense critical importance in the world's history—the moment of El Alamein, of Guadalcanal, of Stalingrad.

The proof of our unvictorious frame of mind came precisely in our reception of the news that began to come in by radio. (We could receive, even if we could not send.) Montgomery's triumph at El Alamein seemed quite flatly too good to be true. We could not understand how Rommel had been able to drive the British all the way back to the gates of Alexandria only to be beaten there. We thought that our high command was giving us a deliberately rose-colored version of events in order to encourage us for the task ahead. We combed the communiqués carefully for what might "lie behind" the bald statements, and I remember occasions when Bill Billings and I systematically rewrote the radio bulletins, in conversation, to make them mean what we thought they probably did mean. The same was true of Guadalcanal, where, just before my departure from Washington, things had been touch-and-go. The night before I left Washington for the port of embarkation, Mr. Knox, the Secretary of the Navy, had come to dinner at Bill Donovan's house, where I was staying. He and Bill (General Donovan) had been serious and worried. The Japanese were throwing in more than they could really afford, and we with our handful of B-17's, scant troops and over-worked ships, were hard-pressed indeed.

So also with Stalingrad. I knew perfectly well that Stalingrad was supposed to fall (according to Hitler's plan) on September first, at which point the Germans hoped that Japan would attack Siberia. If this had occurred—the German army cross-ing the Volga and the Japanese moving west—a collapse of Russia would have been possible, and with such a disaster we could never have won the war. This is what I thought then and still think. But even though Stalingrad had not fallen on September first, and the bitter desperation of the Russian struggle had astonished the world, I still did not feel sure that the Germans were stopped there. Nor did any of our other officers. Consequently the good news from Stalingrad—like that from El Alamein and Guadalcanal—left us doubtful and won-dering, hoping of course, but not sure. We had not the habit of good news.

In retrospect one can see very plainly that these months (August-November, 1942) were the turning point of the war. Our gallant attack at Guadalcanal with slim forces, mounted before we were really ready for it, indisputably gave the Japa-nese cause for reflection and made them cool toward the project of invading Siberia. This was its purpose; the Guadal-canal landing on August 7th was to forestall the Siberian at-tack of September first, and did help to achieve that purpose. Most of all, the failure of the Germans to cross the Volga at Stalingrad sounded the knell of their hopes in Russia and ended the possibility of Japanese attack. Along with this, Montgomery's victory at El Alamein, followed by his rapid advance through the desert and our landings in North Africa, warned the Germans that they were going to have to fight (at last) on two fronts at once. In the grand strategy of the war, these events, Guadalcanal, El Alamein and the African landings, although small in comparison to the Russian campaign, had the crucial effect of reinforcing the effect of the Stalingrad epic and compelling a revision of the German concept of victory.

And indeed from the end of that year (1942) onward, neither the Germans nor the Japanese ever achieved another victory of strategic importance.

All this we did not know, could not know, on the convoy. I knew a great deal more than most of my friends, because I had been in the War Department all summer, reading reports and cables from everywhere; I knew our African plan; I had watched the build-up, as we called it, for Montgomery's attack. The transfer of our fighter groups to Egypt had been one of the things we brooded over most anxiously. One Sunday in late July when I was on duty alone in the A-2 (Air Staff, intelligence) section in the War Department, the White House telephoned to ask whether or not we had any news of the makeshift carrier on which we were sending our P-40's to Africa. I was afraid to answer even the White House, so fanatical were we all in those days about security, and said that I would inquire and call them back. The calm secret passage to Egypt of our P-40's and B-25's—two fighter groups and one bomber group—was another of those things which seemed, at the time, almost too good to be true.

Yet, although I had had all these opportunities of knowing the pieces of the pattern, I had not put them all together. It was only on the highest level that the grand strategy was known. Now, after the event, it is easy for laymen to say that our success was inevitable and that we should have been even bolder; it was easy for the Russians, in the depths of their awful struggle, to blame us for not doing more; but at the time, with what ships we had and what air force we had and what trained troops we had, I never could see that we were not doing our utmost. We had a colossal coastline to protect and the submarines were actually coming into our rivers; in the preceding winter Japanese submarines had shelled our Western coast; we were not quite certain about German air bombardment, particularly the Focke-Wulf 123; enemy activities in Latin-America were a perpetual anxiety. Under such conditions for us to launch out as far as we did was a daring enterprise, carried out according to magistral conceptions which saw the war as a whole and the world as a whole. I have always felt sure that we owed this to Roosevelt and Churchill; I have never known to which more than to the other. Those who in the War and Navy Departments had any contact with the preparation for these various expeditions will remember that in every case our most experienced professional experts thought we were attempting too much on too little, and I well remember the chilling words I got from a high G-2 officer on the day I joined the secret staff of Torch: "It's a good plan," he said, "but I wish we weren't doing it on a shoestring." And a friend in A-2 who had worked on the plan but was not going on the expedition used to refer to two of us who were going as "the living corpses."

So, on the convoy, as the moment of decision approached, a tension of nerve and even physical sinew became noticeable. The company commanders, after getting firmly fixed in their heads what they were supposed to do, began to call platoon leaders and sergeants together to lay down the law to them. Never were maps more relentlessly memorized. There was probably an exaggerated emphasis on preparation because this was in fact our first attempt at anything so big and because all hands were battle virgins. As intelligence officers we felt ashamed not to be able to tell them what enemy forces they were about to meet, but although we knew everything about the French—right down to the political sympathies of their

127

junior commanders—we had no means of knowing how soon the Germans would get warning or what they would be able to do. I privately expected them to do something through Spain and shall always think that this is what they should have done; their choice of Tunisia was a cardinal error based on the idea that Montgomery was more dangerous than the Americans. Montgomery was indeed dangerous to them, but so, as they found out in due course, were the Americans.

We all thought that we were making a huge detour to the South Atlantic, with a feint at Dakar to deceive the enemy. To this day I do not know whether this happened or not; it was what we thought was happening. Day after day the exquisite weather lured us all on to the highest reaches of the ship—the highest, that is, to which mere army men had access. Endlessly we watched the changing of positions in the convoy, speculated about the big ships and the little, felt happy at the occasional sight of one of our battle-wagons, wondered where the submarines were. I was developing an interest, reprehensible but not to be controlled, in the letters of our soldiers. Never afterwards, I am glad to say, was I obliged to read our men's letters; that task belongs properly to company or squadron officers, and is not to be envied, because it encourages the delights of the eavesdropper. One boy of nineteen wrote to his girl at least once every day in language of such intensity that I was at a loss to find a parallel; Alfred de Musset, Adrienne Lecouvreur, the sonnets of Shakespeare, the love letters in the Thompson-Bywater murder case—all these notable outpourings of romantic adoration came to mind but were not quite right because they had not the same freshness and secret, single aim. The literary quality of those letters, their sheer command of language, struck me every day anew, and I have often wondered if their author lived to be happy in that love, to write again, or perished in some routine incident of the war. Many of the boys wrote baldly, samely, day after day, so

128

that one marveled that their mothers and sweethearts could tell one letter from another. One soldier wrote practically the same letter to a number of girls in different places. The quality of the letter to the soldier friend, to the younger brother, to the mother and to the father, was so strongly characterized that it could be distinguished at once without a glance at the heading. Some were priggish and some reckless and many were dull; but through them all, as the days wore on, there appeared the same note of farewell.

This I had glimpsed before, as a war correspondent in other wars, and was to know often again as a soldier: the valedictory feeling of all men on the eve of battle. Love, religion, property, concupiscence and sad admonitory counsels all played a part in these farewells, which reached their climax in the letters written on the night before D-day. It would be easy to ridicule such feeling on the part of men who were not in the combat infantry and who thus (according to the recent school of war reporting) incurred no risk. But as a matter of fact in a combat landing risks are about equal for everybody engaged, and of our "non-combat" headquarters squadron one boy was crushed on the landing net and two (on another ship) were blown to kingdom come by a torpedo; so I cannot take their adieu to life so lightly.

On the night before D-day I heard Pasha Bitar give his last orders and recommendations to his platoon leaders and sergeants. The Pasha was a company commander, one of those in our cabin. His lean, clever face and big dark eyes suggested the Syrian ancestry which was responsible for his nickname. He could speak a little Arabic, a few simple words in the Syrian accent, and as soon as our destination had been announced he began furbishing up everything he could remember of the language. Pasha was a good soldier, a superlatively good soldier. He was quite unaffectedly sure that K Company of the Second Battalion of the Fifteenth Infantry was the best com-

129

pany in the whole army, and I learned that in the eyes of K
Company Captain Emil Bitar—"the Captain"—was the finest
of all leaders. His orders were explicit, based on the most pains-
taking study of his own part in the plan. "And any son of a bitch
who does this or that will get this or that," he would tell them
in his cutting voice, fiercely indignant at the thought of the
contingency against which he warned them. The Pasha was
killed in Sicily, leading his men on the north road. Of those
company and platoon commanders to whom we owe the winning of the war in its most concrete aspect, Pasha was a type,
perhaps *the* type; such he has remained in my memory.

Everybody on the ship was busy cleaning guns on the day
before D-day. We were all, including officers, to land with full
field equipment and a tommy-gun. With the impregnated
clothing, gas masks, head nets, first-aid kits and innumerable
odds and ends which then constituted full field equipment,
we had a load of eighty-seven pounds strapped to our backs
for the descent over the nets to the landing boat. That is perhaps why so many of us drowned. In theory there were no non-
combatants; every soldier was to land and fight. It was the most
cumbersome outfit imaginable for such a purpose, and one of
the first lessons of our African D-day was that it had to be
reduced. It always seemed to me strange that the authorities
in the War Department had not realized this earlier; they
could have found out by trying to put the stuff on their backs
and walk downstairs in the Munitions Building, without any
experiment on landing nets. Dave Radam strapped me into
my pack two or three times on that day, roaring with laughter
at the lumbering enormity thus created. "All Air Corps
troops," according to the dispositions made in the last days
before D-day, were to land after the assault infantry or upon
signaled orders from the *Ancon*, our sectional command ship.
"Air Corps troops" included, besides our headquarters squad-

130

ron (or the part we had aboard), a whole Signal Corps battalion and an observation squadron without its aircraft.

Our own aircraft were on an improvised carrier—one of those converted merchantmen we used so much at the time—with a catapult on it, and were to be thrown off into the air as soon as we had somewhere for them to land on shore. This was the advance section of the 33rd Fighter Group, under Colonel W. O. Momyer; the next section was to arrive by the same catapult system on D-plus-five, under Phil Cochran. This 33rd Group, which I was to know much better thereafter, was the only fighter group we had with us; others were to come from England, and for the landing itself we had naval aviation alone. I had carried the sealed orders, escape kits and last-minute instructions on board the carrier the night before we sailed, and knew how dubiously our airmen regarded the scheme of throwing them off into the air with no possibility of return; throughout the journey, whenever we saw the flat-top moving into our line of vision, we thought of that moment of the catapult and were chilled. One of the reasons why that high G-2 officer (and others as well) considered that we were doing Torch on a shoestring was that our air plan was so extremely daring. It had to be daring. We had no airfields and therefore had to fly ships in as best we could and hope that the airfields would be captured in time. If the Luftwaffe had been present in force—well, there is no use talking about that, because it wasn't present at all.

I confess to sleeping very soundly on the night before D-day, so that Dave Radam had to work on me with vigor before I got up. He did so at an agreed hour (three o'clock in the morning, I believe), and when we struggled up on deck it was pitch dark. The infantry soldiers were lined up ready to go over the side, although every time anybody showed a flashlight there were curses and orders to black it out. The ship was rolling at anchor and there were no sounds across the water.

131

Of all those other ships, those hundreds of other ships, nothing at first could be seen. Then, as our eyes grew keener or the darkness slightly lightened, we could see the shadows of shapes against the dark. The Higgins boats, the small landing boats, bumped against the side of the ship; they had been lowered and were waiting. I had wanted to land with my new friends of the infantry and field artillery, particularly with Sailor Byrne, on the theory that my French would be useful to them. Sailor said I could bargain with the local farmer for the use of his mule to pull guns with; this was our plan, but we had to ask permission by wig-wag signal from my superior officer on the *Ancon*. The signal came back, not long after first light, to say that I was to wait and land with "Air Corps troops."

Before first light the first doughboys went over the side and down the nets. How silently that was accomplished could hardly be conveyed in words. In the murmuring darkness I could not distinguish a single order, a single shout or noisy movement, and yet when the sea grew lighter we could see them streaking away toward the shore, boatload after boatload of them, hunchbacked with their field equipment and clinging to their tommy-guns. The coast toward which they were directed was a mere black line in the pale shadowy light. We knew that it was, or should be, Fedala, above Casablanca.

The guns began with the first crack of dawn. What guns they were, or where, we did not know as we stood on that crowded deck. I knew in the course of the day that they were the French naval guns from Casablanca harbor and the shore battery opposite us at Fedala, smothered at times in the thunder of our own guns from the ships. As the day brightened in brilliant pale colors (pale pink, pale gold and blue) we could see the whole expanse of water between the ships and the shore dotted with the landing boats making their way to appointed places, Red Beach Number One, Red Beach Number Two, and the others. The crackle of small arms fire broke out now and then, but most of all it was in waves of thunder, the thunder of the naval guns, that the battle came to us. We had not the remotest notion of what was going on. Dave and I stood and watched the sun come up and wondered how the landing had been. By no means all of our infantry friends had landed yet; we went in to breakfast and talked excitedly to them about what we had heard or guessed. The companies disappeared over the side during the morning until the whole Second Battalion had gone. All the infantry and field artillery went by mid-afternoon, and still the guns roared and still we had no order to land. We grew weary indeed on the deck, with that crushing load on our backs, and by noon the Air Corps officers at least, in defiance of rule, had deposited packs on bunks. To get to or from the cabin we had to go through various gangways in which our remaining G.I.'s, oblivious of the battle, were crouched on the floor over the inevitable dice game. One of our boys sent fifteen hundred dollars home as a result of the crap game on the journey over; from a pay of fifty dollars a month this did not seem bad. Dave and I finally, toward the end of one of the longest days in our lives, crawled into our bunks and went to sleep. The guns were still going on, as they did intermittently for the next two days and nights.

At about sunset we saw one of our ships rushing up and down in maneuvers which we assumed to be naval battle. We were then told over the loudspeaker (which had started operating during the afternoon) that this was the *Augusta*, being attacked by two French destroyers which had sallied out from the port of Casablanca. All I could see of the battle was the rushing course of the *Augusta*, much smoke and much noise; we heard that the French destroyers were sunk. Our naval aircraft were coming and going throughout the day, executing their missions on the Casablanca and Marrakech airfields, the ships in Casablanca harbor, the targets appointed; of their attack we could see nothing. Afterwards in Casablanca I was

133

told by many civilians of how they had watched the whole battle from the roofs of their houses, but I who must have been, I suppose, in the midst of it or at least in it, saw nothing that I understood.

In the early evening we received our orders to land and stood for a long time on deck in full field equipment, but something had gone wrong; we were ordered to stand down again. It was a very dark night pierced by the flame of guns and sudden conflagration from mysterious explosions. One tremendous one, we were told or imagined, was the blowing up of a French munitions dump near Fedala, opposite us. We heard that the French navy was fighting desperately, the army with much less vigor, and that the battery north of Fedala had been silenced; we wondered vaguely what had happened to the President's proclamation, to the political arrangements, to the *coup de main* at Rabat, to the landings at Port Lyautey and Safi, but these things we were not to learn for several days. In the darkness and confusion on deck it was all we could do to keep our Air Corps units together so that we could land when ordered. Finally the word came: we were to go over the side.

This was a perilous enterprise in itself, quite aside from any battle excitement or danger from hostile fire. In the pitch darkness with eighty-seven pounds on our backs we had to leg it over the rail and down the swaying landing net to a boat which could barely be discerned below. Several boys were crushed on the nets (on this and other ships), as the swell was great and the boats sometimes rose high and collided violently with the ship's side. Some men got stuck halfway down and could neither go further nor get back to the ship. The swell off that coast is always strong, and was stronger than usual that night. Dave Radam, as ranking Air Corps officer, was giving the orders for our landing, but his voice did not carry quite as far as that of a long-legged, slow-smiling captain called Zemurray,

134

whose bellow was quite simply the loudest sound I have ever heard from a human throat. This Zemurray (who was, in army language, a wonderful guy) was outsize in every way, with enormous hands and feet and a barrel chest. He commanded the observation squadron we had with us, which—since our observation aircraft and techniques were obsolete anyhow—was soon merged into an A-20 group, and it was in an A-20 that he was killed some weeks later on patrol out toward Spanish Morocco. On that night his voice came to our rescue and marshaled our troops, our odds and ends of Air Corps troops, over the side and down the net and into the boat, warning and cajoling when necessary (especially for those who got stuck) and sometimes physically aiding the awkward or unlucky. The Third Division troops had made dozens of practice landings like this; our boys had never seen a net before. Moreover, most of ours were specialists of one kind or another (office, signals, radar, electricians and so on) and had never fired a tommy-gun except for the once required of all members of Torch before embarkation. Somehow they got over the side and were herded to the bow of the boat and threw off their Mae Wests—the elegant American Navy version of that useful garment, which we had worn all the way over—into a pile where they lay glimmering in the occasional flashlight, like so many fish.

And it was a fishing boat we were on—a French fishing boat from Toulon, which had been commandeered by some of our naval officers during the day. Its French sailors were still on it, with an American naval ensign trying to direct operations from the bridge in a language he hoped they would understand. Somehow or other they shoved off, with violent outbursts of language among the French sailors, and we made for the shore.

In the dark, cool night there had been many errors, and we, too, lost our way. There was much shouting back and forth among the French sailors, and unless I am mistaken the naval

135

ensign had his revolver out at one moment, but the course was recovered at last and we came bumping and sliding in to the pier at the port of Fedala. I was talking to one of the French sailors on the way in. When I asked if he was glad to see us he said he did not know; were we really Americans or were we British disguised as Americans? I said we were really Americans. He muttered and chewed for a while, and when I demanded what he was saying, he replied, "Americans are all right." (*Les Américains, ça nous est égal.*) After a pause he added, *"Nous ne voulons pas d'Anglais."* (We don't want any English.) Obviously he was, like the overwhelming majority of Frenchmen, a victim of the unceasing propaganda which represented Britain's attacks at Dakar, Madagascar, Syria and elsewhere as imperialist aggression against France. For days afterwards I encountered both French and Arabs who asked the same question: were we really Americans or were we British in disguise?

The pier was inky black; we knew when we were there because we crashed broadside against it, swung out and were drawn in again. Dave Radam found his way to me through the crowded bodies in the dark.

"What ought we to do?" he asked. "I don't know where this pier is. We're supposed to report at Red Beach Number Two, but where is it from here?"

"I don't know," said I. "How can we tell where this pier is? Better get off and have a council of war."

With the aid of our flashlights—sparingly used, as we had no idea where the French guns were and they were still firing —we got ashore and walked down the pier to what seemed to be some kind of freight yard. Great bales lay about here in mountainous piles; they were, we decided, bales of cork. The firing seemed to come from the left, the north, and that way also, in all probability, was the town. The observation squadron under Zemurray went marching off into the darkness to

136

look for shelter, and found it in a warehouse about a hundred yards up the road. Dave and I examined our maps with a flashlight, and looked longingly at something outlined in green and entitled, "Municipal Park." It was in the middle of the town of Fedala. However, to get there in the darkness while so much firing was going on seemed a task beyond our powers. We decided to sleep where we were until first light and then try to get to Red Beach Number Two.

We bedded our men down in the cork piles, wherever they could find a place. It was fantastically cold for the time of year, and there was much moaning and groaning (as in a herd of camels) before we got to sleep. I slept hardly at all. The whole episode, America's return across the Atlantic, had so stirred my imagination that neither weariness nor cold could drive it out of my mind. The guns were still occasionally going off, all through the night, and there were strange lights on the shadowy sea.

Soon after dawn Dave and I were up, routing the men out. We ate some K-rations and then crawled into our field packs again. Dave, with a crinkle of malice around his eyes, said:

"Now, this is your country. I don't know how the fighting has gone, and I don't understand the damned policy. We're supposed to be friends unless they shoot at us, is that it? Well, what do we do now? To get to Red Beach Number Two we've got to go right through the God damned town. Are we friends or enemies? Is it an assault or what?"

Our forty-six headquarters squadron men would have been rather at a loss as to how you began an assault.

"In my opinion," said I, "we should just walk through the town by the quickest way, only not in formation and not with tommy-guns ready. Just say 'Bon jour' to everybody we meet, and keep on going until we get to Red Beach Number Two."

Dave had a good laugh and then fell in with it. As he said, we had no idea of the situation or of whether we were friends

137

or enemies to the people of the town. He called our forty-six men to attention and explained.

"It's route march," he said, "and remember that everybody we meet is a friend unless proved otherwise. Say '*Bon jour*' to everybody."

They practiced it with many a laugh, half merriment and half nerves. And then, in the pink-and-gold light of the early morning, we started our promenade across the scene of battle. At the gates of the port a startled Arab saluted us and we saluted gravely while our men chorused "*Bon jour.*" Another Arab or two eyed us gravely in the next street, and in a minute or two our troop—more like a gaggle of geese than a troop— was in the town of Fedala, where we made a left turn through the main street. Here there were a few Frenchmen and French-women about, hurrying down the street—perhaps getting home after twenty-four hours of shelter somewhere or other; for we had seen evidences of our naval bombardment as we came along. To each of these our men dutifully said "*Bon jour,*" and each of them, after a moment's astonishment, replied in the same words. One Frenchman who was taking down the boards from the glass on a café near the center of the town shouted some welcoming words to us and waved his hand. Otherwise our passage through Fedala might have been that of any group of worthy citizens up a trifle early.

In the middle of the town we came to the Municipal Park, which looked like an excellent bivouac for troops and was (then, but not for much longer) quite empty. Dave and I debated on the possibility of staking out a claim, but decided that our orders to report to Red Beach Number Two must come first. So we went on to the north on the main street, lined with white walls with bougainvillaea tumbling over their tops. At one point we passed the gateway of the Miramar Hotel and called a halt. We knew that this was the principal hotel of the resort and had served as quarters for the German Armistice Commission for Morocco. An American sentry of the Third Division—the Second Regiment, not the Fifteenth—stood on guard at the gate. Dave and I went in, only to find that the kitchen of the hotel had been hit by one of our naval shells and some of our own men wounded. We came on out again in a hurry, as the Third Division troops inside were in no mood for visitors.

On the broad highway to the beach, lined with palms, we were making our way quite cheerfully (in spite of the packs on our backs) when we encountered some troops of the Third Division advancing toward us. They were newly landed members of the Second Regiment who were advancing from tree to tree in open skirmish formation, as they had been taught during the preceding year-and-a-half of training for action in the South Pacific. They were not at all sure who or what we were, and summoned us to halt and give the password. (It was "Georgie!" and the answer was "Patton!") When they found out who we were they allowed us to pass, in some disgust, as our straggling advent—obviously from the very town upon which they were advancing with such caution—was contrary to all rules of jungle warfare.

At this point, just as we were passing the newcomers from the Third Division, right in front of a barracks of Senegalese soldiers who were calmly preparing their breakfast, two aircraft came over and the air was filled with the clamor of guns. All of us jumped for ditches and trees, the jungle-trained Third Division, our Air Corps stragglers, and the Senegalese enemy in the cage opposite. Then Dave and I looked at the airplanes. The cry had gone up "Messerschmitt 110!" because these aircraft had two engines. But as they were incredibly slow—practically stationary, in fact—they could scarcely have been German at all, and in fact their slowness was such that our anti-aircraft fire, calculated for quite different speeds, did not touch them. When they disappeared we believed them to be what in fact they were, antiquated machines of the French Air Force. They had dropped no bombs and were no doubt out for observation.

Radam and I had a good laugh on this one and the Third Division boys continued their advance, leaping from tree to tree down the road to town.

"I'll bet you anything," I said to him, continuing my interpretation of our policy in Africa, "that the enemy over there will carry our God damned fardels for us if we ask him."

Dave was game and we went over to the enclosure—a sort of cage—where the Senegalese soldiers were preparing their breakfast. A French lieutenant, very nonchalant and trying to look as if he had never heard an airplane, was emerging from a nearby ditch.

"Would your men be willing to carry some baggage for us if we asked them?" I inquired of this officer. "We could give them something for it."

"Certainly, *mon—mon commandant*," the lieutenant said, saluting smartly and guessing wildly at our rank. "How many men would you require?"

"We'll come back and get them afterwards," I said. "We have to go and report first."

It did not seem quite right to arrive at Red Beach Number Two in the midst of the battle with the enemy carrying our field packs, otherwise Dave and I would have taken on the Senegalese right away, as our load was heavy. But we struggled on just a little longer, and there, behold, was a sandy beach with American soldiers moving about and some faces that we recognized. There was Johnny Pabst, there was Colonel Young, there were others. We plowed through the sand toward a beach house and reported to Colonel Young.

At this point some American navy planes came over and our anti-aircraft guns started to fire at them furiously. Dave

140

raced down to a gun emplacement dug in the sand and yelled at the gunner.

"Stop, you fool! Stop, God damn it! Those are our own planes!"

He kept on firing as if he had heard nothing. Fortunately his aim was no good.

We stood about in the sand for about an hour. It appeared that General Patton, the commander of the Western Task Force, had been detained on the naval flagship through most of D-day by the naval battle; it seemed that the battery at Fedala was silenced, but the naval battle was still going on off Casablanca; the Third Division was closing in on the city from this side, and the Second Armored Division was coming up from Safi. No news of Port Lyautey; no news of our political arrangements or of the *coup de main* at Rabat.

There was a Frenchman in a sort of soft-drink stand on the beach who kept offering us all wine, oranges, tangerines and food. His wife and two children were with him.

"Why were you so long getting here?" he asked us again and again. "Take wine. Take oranges. We are glad to see you. Ah, the dirty Germans! We were glad to see them go."

I heard then or later in the day how Colonel Ratay—our fierce-looking assistant G-2, whom I had first known years before when he was military attaché in Peking—had captured the German Armistice Commission in the Miramar Hotel the day before, having as his chief cohort no other than young Dick Ryan from New York, a lad who was commissioned second lieutenant and got the Silver Star for that day's work. All the French seemed to know that the hated Armistice Commission had been captured and sent out to the ships for transport to America. They would have preferred to see them shot.

Finally Colonel Young gave us leave to take our men back to town and get them a bivouac and find quarters for ourselves. He would be in the Miramar Hotel, he said, but as we had

141

already learned that it was reserved for General Patton and his staff, we had little hope of finding a place there.

"We can put the men in the park," Dave said, "and if we can get those Senegalese to haul all our stuff for us we can stay there too."

"There's bound to be another hotel," said I wisely. "Let us just go and register. After all, we are friends and not enemies."

So we returned to the town, still carrying our eighty-seven pound packs, and took a corner of the park for the men. Not far away was a building which bore the sign "Hôtel de France." It looked like innumerable French provincial hotels in the South, with a graveled garden, oleanders and bougainvillaea. We had Colonel Dickinson, the headquarters doctor, with us by now, and the three of us walked into the dining room of the Hôtel de France like cash customers.

The proprietor was a small, plump Alsatian named Schneider, who received us with such enthusiasm that it was very easy to forget the sound of the guns from the sea.

"Certainly, why, certainly, gentlemen, you shall have the best we can find. The house is full, but we'll find something. Ah, how glad we are that you have come! We have heard rumors of an expedition, some kind of expedition, but we thought it was English. Let me show you the rooms, *messieurs* —and then perhaps you would join me in something?"

Radam and I took one room, Dickinson another; and when we came downstairs M. Schneider had produced some very good champagne—"the last of the good champagne, the last bottle"—to do us honor. He kept on producing the last bottle at intervals during the period when I knew him, and months later when I went back to Fedala on a flying visit he had just had a new son and produced another last bottle to mark the occasion.

142

The first few days at Fedala were what I was to recognize only in retrospect as characteristic of the army moving in. To me, an incorrigible civilian, everything seemed confusion; and yet an extraordinary number of things were accomplished in the midst of all this hullabaloo. For example, the unloading of the ships began on D-day and continued throughout the three days of hostilities. On D-plus-1 quarters and headquarters for Patton's staff were established at the Miramar Hotel, and the staff sections began operating. Communications on the first two days were bad, but once we had some means of knowing what was going on at Lyautey and elsewhere, we saw that the landing had gone off much as we had expected—some resistance at first, sporadic and diminishing, followed by a tendency to make friends. After all, the French authorities had no means of knowing the strength or intention of our expedition, and after the experiences of Dieppe and Dakar they were not inclined to risk everything on support of a mere commando raid. When they saw our tanks and trucks coming off the ships they rapidly came to the conclusion that we meant business, and by the third day they were ready for an armistice.

Fighting had been restricted to the Fedala battery, snipers along the Casablanca road, and some unidentified fire on the outskirts of Casablanca, so far as the ground action was concerned. The French bombers at Marrakech had never gone into action, giving as their reason (to their superior officers) that the mud was too deep for a take-off. In our area no French regular troops were engaged at all; they were all like our Senegalese friends, who stayed in their quarters and made breakfast. Orders had gone to the general at Marrakech (Henri Martin) to move his division against us and he had (we heard) refused to move. The only sharp fighting and the only surprise were provided by the French navy at the Casablanca base. Admiral Michelier kept up a battle against us for three days, disregarding even the orders of his superior, the Resident-

General Noguès, to cease firing. As a result he lost the flotilla he commanded.

Dave and I got our Senegalese, a string of six of them, to follow us down to the port on D-plus-2. There we sought out our belongings, and those of Colonel Dickinson, in the midst of a scene which appeared to be bedlam itself. The ships were being unloaded as rapidly as possible and a throng of red-fezzed Arabs had been hired to fetch and carry. When we found our bedding rolls and barracks bags and other accoutrements we loaded them up on the willing Senegalese and marched back to the Hôtel de France. A more unmilitary combat landing has probably never taken place, but the Senegalese seemed overjoyed at ten francs apiece.

At the Hôtel Miramar, where our air general and his immediate staff were installed with Patton's, I had some slight duties every day, chiefly those concerned with the speaking of French. Among the prisoners taken on the first day was the chief of the French naval aviation, a narrow-faced, elderly officer with white hair who kept on saying, over and over again, "What a misunderstanding!" I tried to get him to tell me what he meant. He said that if the French authorities had known we were coming in force they would never have resisted at all; that we should have taken some means of letting them know. He said they were obliged to resist lest our expedition be a failure and dire punishment fall on them thereafter. His whole concern appeared to be not with the rights and wrongs of the matter, but with what would be the best course for the authorities in power so as to retain their power. This I afterwards found to be the principal characteristic of French colonial officials, both civilian and military.

An armistice was signed between General Patton and General Noguès at the Hôtel Miramar on November 11th. I saw them come and go but had nothing to do with the matter; Charlie Codman, then a major and afterwards lieutenant-

144

colonel and Patton's chief aide in Sicily, France and Germany, was the French-speaking officer involved. Our air general— John K. Cannon, of whom much hereafter—was not present at this settlement and we made a sort of aviation armistice of our own two days later.

In the opening days I had had little to do, and when I learned that the French air commander, General Lahoulle, wanted a meeting with our air commander, I volunteered in writing to go as interpreter. General Cannon, whom I had never seen except once when I reported for duty on Torch in the War Department, replied with a curt scrawl: "Be here at 8 tomor. row morning."

We had a command car which "Jonesy" found for us by sheer genius at scrounging. Jonesy I was to know better in many places during the war; he was a slim, light-hearted Texan named C. D. Jones, then a major, who was a colonel and commander of a bomb group when he was shot down in Northern Italy two years later. He had served under General Cannon at Mitchell Field and was one of that General's many worshipers.

"Git your ass in that car quick before somebody grabs it," was his way of announcing the arrangements. "Uncle Joe'll be down right away. Now look mighty important or some son of a bitch'll come along and take the car away from us."

There were very few jeeps or command cars available, and none of our own had landed yet; Jonesy had found one belonging to some infantry outfit and, by the exuberance of his magnetism plus a liberal use of General Cannon's name, had lured it away from the bewildered soldier in charge. The General came down and climbed in beside the driver, with Jonesy and me in the back.

It was a curious drive, our first over that road which I was to know so well. Part of the Second Armored Division had moved up part of the way, but Rabat itself was not yet occupied

145

and only one or two American jeeps had yet been seen there. All along the way, from the fields, from the crossroads, from the occasional farmhouse or inn, Arabs and Frenchmen waved at us; girls leaned out of windows and threw kisses; in one or two places flags were waved. When we came into Rabat everybody who chanced to be in the streets stopped to wave hands and yell something or other—*"Vive l'Amérique,"* perhaps. This was nothing, indeed, compared to the scenes of welcome we were to see thereafter, but it was the first, and I found myself unreasonably touched. I knew even then that the joy would not last, but it gave us all, I think, a strange new glow.

The trim prettiness of Rabat, all white villas and gardens, was not for us that day; the policeman on duty near the Résidence directed us to the Air-Maroc headquarters about ten minutes outside the town on another road. Here, at a pink gate before a walled enclosure, French (not Arab) sentries presented arms and our command car rolled in over a graveled drive to the headquarters building. Here, on the steps, we were greeted by General Lahoulle.

He was an extremely polite, rather stiltedly formal old air officer who seemed always to be wearing his left glove and holding the right even when he was not. I think he was sincerely glad to see the Americans in Morocco even though he did not, at that time, entertain great hope of our winning the war against Germany. His record in the war of 1914-1918 was one of the finest, and his dislike of the Germans was keen. However, like a great many commanding officers under the regular establishment, he had grown fond of his own position, which was extremely comfortable and afforded him much social consideration in the placid colonial capital. His charm of manner and willingness to yield on any matter we considered essential made all our dealings with him pleasant—pleasanter, indeed, than some of his watch-dog aides would have wished.

146

We went into Lahoulle's office and there and then drew up a set of conditions for aviation in Morocco. The preliminaries were courteous but brief; General Cannon obviously had no desire to waste time. In his dry, slow voice he enumerated the points upon which he requested agreement, and I translated. Each point produced an argument, some of them consternation. For example: we started by stating that control of the air in Morocco from now on until further notice must belong to the American military, specifically to the XII Air Support Command which General Cannon commanded. This meant that no flights of French aircraft, military or civilian, could take place without specific permission of General Cannon, so that our warning net, anti-aircraft and so on could be advised in time.

General Lahoulle protested. The government of a huge territory like Morocco, without railroads and with only a skeleton road system, depended to a large extent upon the use of small liaison aircraft every day. The task of maintaining order and governing the country fell upon the French, by our own declarations, and this would be impossible without the use of aircraft. General Cannon said he would authorize such liaison flights for government purposes whenever the request was made in time—say a day in advance—so that our systems could be warned; but that for the moment all French aircraft in Morocco must be grounded. Military flights, even for training, were to be temporarily forbidden. General Lahoulle argued the point for some time, but gave in. If he had not done so the "incidents" (i.e., examples of our anti-aircraft or our fighter airplanes attacking French planes in the air) would have been innumerable, owing to the edginess of new troops in a new country after such a peppery reception as we had had.

The other questions (use of airfields, utilization of French aviation mechanics and workshops, sharing of certain fields, etc., etc.) were taken up one by one and disposed of, all in a

tone of the most complete courtesy but resolution on the part
of General Cannon. I was busy translating back and forth and
noting the points of agreement as they were reached, but I had
ample time to observe the characters of the French and American commanders: Lahoulle a phenomenon not of this era
at all, a suave and rather ornate exterior upon a basis of simplicity amounting to innocence, his exquisite manners veiling
an inner uncertainty not only of political situations but even
of the material with which he had to deal, the science of air
power; and Cannon, dry, hard and sure, aware of his military
necessities in every detail and determined to ignore everything
else. It was obvious that the French General had no real conception of the radar systems by which we traced aircraft in
the air, although he had vaguely heard of them; the French
in Africa depended upon such antique arrangements as Arab
watchers on hilltops, with a communications net (if it could
be called a net) by land telephone wires.

The interview came to an end with an exchange of compli-
ments in which I was rather surprised to find my own General
as skillful as the Frenchman. I did not know then that General
Cannon had had diplomatic experience as head of air missions
in Argentina and Europe, and that he had a natural gift for
tactful expression, finding as if by instinct the right word and
the right turn of phrase which flattered without giving any
pledge or commitment. This was my first experience of the
quality of this commander, which, as time went on, impressed
me more and more: the caution which knew how to be daring
upon occasion, the dry manner which concealed the warm
heart, the complete concentration upon the job in hand. I
knew nothing of Cannon then, and found his dryness and
hardness very chilling, so that I was afraid (then and for long
afterwards) to speak to him unless I was first spoken to; it
would have startled me to be told with what esteem and devotion I was one day to regard him.

Thus we made our air armistice in Morocco. I spent hours writing up my notes, which became a paper of four single-spaced typewritten pages covering every point of the agreement. That was the basis of our relations with the French air authorities until General Cannon went to the front to take over the Bomber Command and took me with him at the beginning of January. The questions which arose were endless —quite aside from the detail of French government liaison flights, which became a daily routine of some inconvenience until, later on, our General authorized the French to resume their traffic on certain routes without previous warning. Airfields and workshops, the training of French aviators, the treatment to be accorded the volunteers who trickled in upon us from all sides, the co-ordination of air warning systems—all these and a dozen other questions kept us busy. There were very few officers or men who knew any French at all in our command—besides myself there was only Dewitt Sage, then a major, in our headquarters—and consequently this work chiefly devolved upon me. I was busy throughout the day and sometimes through a good part of the night, and at no time in the army did I ever feel so genuinely useful. Perhaps this experience of being extremely busy and useful—of being, if I may say so, almost the center of the work done at our headquarters, since everything depended upon our arrangements with the French—spoiled me permanently for army life, in which by the nature of things there are long periods of inactivity and many men for every job. In headquarters staffs, particularly, there are so many officers who have nothing whatever to do in periods of waiting that boredom becomes the chief bane of life. I never had time to be bored during those first two months in Morocco.

One night at about this time, while we were still at Fedala but after the armistice had been signed—and I believe it was the night of November 13th, after my return from Rabat with the General—Dave and I were standing with some other officers on the roof terrace of the Miramar Hotel to watch the sunset over the crowded ocean. Our ships were dotted about over the whole expanse, some outside moving up and down, some nearer in and motionless. Suddenly we saw an explosion, and then another; they were not near enough for us to be sure what they were, but the same thought came into every head: submarines? It did not seem possible that German submarines could creep so far in through all our convoy and its escort, and yet that smoke and flame meant something ominous. We could find out nothing just then, and Radam and I walked back to the Hôtel de France for supper—we were living and eating like civilians, he and I and Dickinson, and paying like civilians—with bewilderment upon us. We had supper with M. Schneider, the proprietor, who discovered that this was Colonel Dickinson's birthday and consequently felt the need to offer another bottle (the last) of the good champagne. By this time we knew that some ships had been torpedoed, but we were also told to stay away from the port where the work of rescue was being impeded by crowds. We were endeavoring to be gay about Dickinson's birthday, over a substratum of disquiet, when there came a thunderous knock at the glass door of the restaurant on the garden side. Supper had been at about nine o'clock (the dark fell late), and it was now perhaps eleven at night. Schneider went to the door, could understand nothing, and called me. When I got to the crack he had left open I saw some reason for his bewilderment. A young naval officer with face begrimed by dirt and oil, his cap askew and khaki uniform unrecognizable, stood there and stared. "I've got a lot of people here," he said in an exhausted voice. "They are survivors of the torpedoings. I don't know how many. Can you take forty or fifty here?"

"Bring them in," I said hastily, and explained to M. Schneider.

There were no lights in Fedala then: the electricity had been shot out by our naval bombardment. We had been sitting in the big dining room over one table with a candle. Its spaces were murky and it looked enormous. M. Schneider sprang to arms, found some more candles behind the counter and set them out at vantage points throughout the room while the survivors filed in silently. They were almost all very wet and made little pools of water where they stood. None were wounded: the wounded had been taken to the Casino in the Municipal Park and to the Hotel Miramar. But in spite of the army and navy blankets which they clutched about them over their wet clothing, these able-bodied survivors were shivering and chattering and many seemed shaken by nervous exhaustion. They had been blown into the water of the port and had none of them been very long in the water, but from the water to this point they had been some time in the cold night wind. M. Schneider rightly said that what they needed first was something hot to drink; he rang bells and shouted mightily until his Arabs, five or six of them, had emerged from the hovels where they lived behind the hotel. He set them to work boiling water for hot coffee—imitation coffee, mostly roasted barley, since that was all he had—and hot chocolate. Two great pots of the liquids were prepared and brought into the dimly lit room. Radam, Dickinson and I were skirmishing about to find quarters for so many men, which was difficult in a small hotel. We were more than ready to surrender our own beds but we hardly dared ask Frenchmen to do the same; the one attempt we made was not well received, and a French officer —surgeon-general of the French army in Morocco—had indeed died in his room there that evening, from an accident with American military traffic. No doubt if somebody had called all the French officers together and made them a fiery speech full of words like *gloire* and *puissance,* they would have got out of bed, but none of us felt equal to such an effort. So our poor

151

seamen stood and shivered and guzzled their imitation coffee while we assembled blankets and straw and tried to get them warm quarters in unoccupied and bedless rooms. At some point just about then, while they were drinking the welcome warm liquid, one of them started to sing that mawkish anthem, "God Bless America," which I had always vigorously disliked before. They all joined in with rough voices half in tune and half not. It made a great rumbling noise in the dark room with the splotches of yellow light here and there from M. Schneider's tallow candles. The scene and the sound were unbearably moving. I suppose they were all so glad to be alive after such an experience that the song came out of their depths as a signal of gratitude. Whatever it was, it immobilized us all for a few minutes, while the whole war, past and future, how far we had come and how much farther we had to go, pressed suddenly upon our minds.

Dave and I put as many seamen as we could into our room. There was one double bed and one single one in the room and I think we got three sailors into the double, one in the single. Dickinson, of course, gave up his room too. We all slept on the floor that night. In the morning one of the sailors in our room said he would be going back to New York immediately, having lost his ship, and was there anything he could do for me? I said he might telephone my wife, and gave him the number; to my surprise, weeks later, I found that he had done so.

At the Miramar the badly wounded were on stretchers in the hall. The burns were terrible—those were the worst cases by far. There were many more in the little Municipal Casino. I believe five ships went in that submarine raid, a daring and successful operation for the German. Immediately thereafter our ships dispersed and various other precautions were taken so that such a thing never happened again on this coast, although individual German prowlers did get straggling mer-

chant ships along there from time to time for another year
or so.

Our headquarters squadron had by this time all assembled
in a factory and warehouse outside the town on the Casablanca
road. The senior staff officers, with the General, were at the
Miramar and Dave and I, as mavericks, stayed on at the Hôtel
de France. The junior officers and even some of the seniors
were with the squadron out at the warehouse. (We had, scattered through the whole convoy, a fighter wing and a bomber
wing, that is, their commanding officers and staffs, although
their aircraft were, except for the 33rd Fighter Group, all to
come from England.) One day very soon after these events the
order was given for us all to move into Casablanca, bag and
baggage, where quarters and headquarters were to be set up.
We had enough jeeps, command cars and trucks by this time
to make the move, although it had required some fairly sharp
work on the part of our supply people to see that our vehicles
were not abstracted by other outfits. (Our headquarters doctor even found that some of our ambulances had been so removed, and the Air Corps insignia painted over.)

A word of explanation may be necessary for the layman.
We were the XII Air Support Command (an expression afterwards abandoned in favor of "Tactical Air Command," or
Tac). We were a part of the Twelfth Air Force, which consisted of four commands—Fighter, Bomber and Service, besides
Air Support. In the evolution of the air forces the Twelfth
later operated as part of the North African Air Forces (which
included the British units as well) and still later of the Mediterranean Allied Air Forces; and during the same evolution
its Bomber Command became the Fifteenth Air Force, devoted exclusively to heavy bombardment and escort. At the
moment of our landing in Africa all of the Twelfth Air Force,
that is, all its other commands and its headquarters, centered
at Algiers; we, the XII Air Support Command, were the only

153

air unit in Morocco. Generals Spaatz and Doolittle commanded at Algiers; General Cannon commanded in Morocco until he went forward to take the XII Bomber Command.

On a cold, sunny day we loaded up on a jeep and made the brief run to Casablanca, where the astuteness of our staff officers had found for us the best quarters in the town. The Hôtel Transatlantique, which I remembered well—I had stayed there years before—was ours. Through the many changes which occurred during the next years it always remained an Air Corps hotel and is to this day requisitioned by our Air Transport Command. Our headquarters had been assigned to an office building in the Rue de l'Aviation Française, with our bomb wing across the street and our fighter wing out on the airfield. The Western Task Force was more opulent in its headquarters, the Royal Dutch Shell building, the finest commercial office in Casablanca, and less fortunate in its main hotel, the Majestic. Our squadron had to bivouac in the Parc Lyautey, which had an edifice or two for mess, showers and stores. This was neither so cold nor so wet as the areas assigned other troops—the anti-aircraft units on the north road, for example, or the Third Division in the Forêt de la Mamora above Rabat—but it was conspicuously less comfortable than the officers' hotels. I was to know again and again, in the next two years, this hurry and scurry and scramble for quarters and headquarters at the taking of every town on our way, this disparity between the ranks, this subsidence or decline of spirit after the objective had been achieved and another period of preparation set in. In Morocco I was busy, but even there I wondered at the anti-climax of success, with its train of wonder at so much effort come to so little. Perhaps if we had more fully or more exactly known our general policy, the big and firm lines upon which we were conducting the war, each such high point of advance would not have been followed by such invariable disillusionment; but left in the dark as we were—

as all were, for the highest ranks among us had no more idea than we did, and rather less in some cases—it was not to be expected that the pulse of D-day could be sustained.

The Arab city of Casablanca was out of bounds, Old and New Medina alike. In the French town, with its one main street (the Rue de la Gare) and a net of subsidiary streets alongside, we soon exhausted every familiarity and chance of exploitation. I am told that every ounce of French perfume was bought up within the first week, and I know that the French brandy (as distinguished from some curious Moroccan brew) disappeared in a month. Within a matter of days the barbers had adopted American habits, with hot towels and the like, along with American prices; the little Arab boys had begun to run riot in the streets with their "shoe-shine, shoe-shine," G.I. clothes and equipment appeared in the most extraordinary places among the most unlikely people, and chewing gum was abroad like a pestilence; the venereal rate among our troops began to rise. The one broad main street of the whitewashed town was filled before curfew with American soldiers and sailors staring, laughing, making jokes under the arcades, and every hotel of any comfort at all, along with every office that could possibly be taken, had been requisitioned for us. These were the signs which grew into a system, the aftermath of our coming. The wintry swell of the gray ocean off the flat coast alone reminded us of the significance of the Western Task Force, the first American invasion of the Old World.

CHAPTER II

PRIDE AND PREJUDICE

Let all things be done decently and in order.
I CORINTHIANS, 14, 40.

*Nous n'étions qu'une poignée d'hommes, mais
nous emportions avec nous l'âme immortelle
de la France.*   CHARLES DE GAULLE

In THE COURSE of the war various episodes and incidents
in our progress came under censure at home, but nothing so
much as our policy in North Africa toward the French. This
was assailed by all the pundits of the press, who, from a safe
distance, thought it monstrous of us not to dislodge the established French authorities, flout the opinion of the vast majority of Frenchmen, and by main force install the dictatorship
of a group of exiles who clustered around the person or name
of General Charles de Gaulle.

When the clouds and smoke have all cleared away this will
surely appear to have been one of the oddest fancies of ill-
informed quixotic liberalism in our time. We were at war with
the most formidable of all military powers. General de Gaulle
was in 1942 almost unknown to the generality of ordinary
Frenchmen; his star in France only began to rise after our
occupation of North Africa and the German occupation of all
France which immediately followed. De Gaulle had no position whatever in the constitutional or legal sense: he was
merely an officer who felt and said that in him—outside of

156

France—reposed the true soul of France. The overwhelming majority of Frenchmen (most French people now, even Gaullistes, would say the practical totality) supported Marshal Pétain from the time of the armistice until the Pétain-Hitler meeting at Montoire (October, 1940), and only began to flinch when the Vichy government took on the color of a puppet regime for Germany. Even when French hearts and minds grew anxious or cold toward Pétain they still did not turn to de Gaulle: he was too little known, too uncertain a quantity, and as a voice on the British radio he struck too monotonously upon the note of national pride without a single practical suggestion for the people who actually lived day in and day out under the dominion of an all-powerful conqueror. Later, a very large part of the French public was taught to regard de Gaulle as a traitor who had fired upon the troops of the French Republic in Dakar, in Madagascar and in Syria; he became known to this public in 1942 for the first time, in the role of a rebel during a time of his country's worst ordeal.

What our liberal opinion at home (and in England, too) demanded was that we go into Africa with the Cross of Lorraine at our masthead, overthrow all the established order, and force de Gaulle upon the French. From a military point of view this was flatly impossible. We had no time to waste fighting the French, nor were we experienced enough to carry through a campaign for the occupation of such immense territories as those of Morocco, Algeria and Tunisia. We had determined upon our course in advance: all Frenchmen were our friends if they wished to be, and our enemies were the Germans. It was our purpose to get at the Germans as soon as possible by means of North Africa. Even as it was—with only a slight resistance on the part of the French—we were so disorganized and so slow in getting our supply lines established that we could not undertake the Tunisian campaign in earnest until the following spring. Any soldier who was in Tunisia and ate spam twice a day, or lived (as we did for weeks) on British rations, or tried to get warm clothing when there was none, would be able to bear this out. We simply had no time to waste on French civil war when our enemy was pouring forces into Tunisia, Spain was an ever-present threat, and we desperately needed six months' time to build up our air forces and artillery, our supplies and munitions, for the critical battle.

This was what General Eisenhower patiently attempted to explain to the all-knowing press at the time, and I have never seen a shred of logic or common sense in any argument against it.

But aside from the military necessities, it would have been a political blunder to force de Gaulle on the French. They did not want him. Many units of their regular forces would have fought us with passion if we had attempted to bring him in. The fact that these same units, these very officers and many of their men, were wearing the Cross of Lorraine in their buttonholes a year later has no bearing on the facts. The Cross of Lorraine is at present worn by persons who, to my certain knowledge, regarded de Gaulle as a traitor in 1942 and said so violently and often. The same persons will discard that emblem if a change in the situation makes it obsolete. Most French people are like most people everywhere, accepting their national regime without undue thought, concerned most of all with the problems of food, shelter and a modicum of individual happiness. Their defeat in 1940 had been tremendous. They regarded it not merely as the defeat of France but as the end of the war, and seem to have grown more and more irritated with the British for keeping up what seemed to them a senseless and hopeless struggle. In addition to all this, the generality of Frenchmen regarded de Gaulle as a tool of the British—unaware that his obligations to them had made him more bitterly anti-British than they were themselves—and would have resented any attempt to import a de Gaulle dictatorship as an infringement of their sovereignty more blatant than that of the Germans at Vichy. Under such circumstances, for us who profess belief in democracy to impose de Gaulle would have been madness.

What we did was to temporize, to put all the pressure we could on the regime in Africa to abolish Vichy legislation, and thus to pave the way for de Gaulle's self-imposition as soon as the Tunisian victory was over. De Gaulle had all the cards in his hand; all he had to do was to wait a little. Between two absolutely illegal regimes, that of Pétain inside France and that of de Gaulle outside, time and the allied victories would inevitably turn the French toward that regime which seemed to them on the victorious end, particularly as the detestation of the Germans was universal and hereditary among them. In their profound xenophobia the French have given us a superabundance of evidence that they love us not, that nothing we may ever do for them will extract a word of gratitude, that our most generous impulses are, in their minds, mere reflexes of our crafty and far-seeing selfishness, and that all our careless and unthinking behavior (as of our G.I.'s, for instance) is part of a deliberate policy and plan; but in spite of all this, ample experience has proved that they hate the Germans more than they do us. (I speak of the generality; the individual exceptions are many.) With or without a Gaulliste symbolism and banner, they would have turned to us as most of the so-called "Vichy" people did, because we represented the chance to escape from the German yoke.

All this is civilian reasoning, and I came to it by reflection after the event. When we first landed in Africa it never occurred to me that anybody could consider our course wrong. It seemed to me so obviously right—more than right: the only conceivable course under the circumstances—that I never debated the matter. The Gaullistes I knew understood it then (that is, those who were on the spot), and their whole problem was to contain themselves in patience for a few months until we were ready for them. It was only afterwards, in sheer amazement, that I saw the American newspapers and periodicals in some part (snippets sent over, or copies encountered by accident) and discovered that by some occult reasoning the press considered us to have been doing a great wrong. When I first saw some of these press articles I was mystified, as it did not seem to me that any reasonable adult could take such a point of view, and some of those who signed the articles (Freda Kirchwey, Edgar Ansell Mowrer and others) were known to me for years as sensible persons. I could only conclude what is, clearly, the truth, that these critics had no real knowledge of the situation. If they had read even the one-hundredth part of the detailed reports upon which we prepared our African expedition—reports from every part of a huge country and from all sorts and conditions of men—they would have been shaken in their simple Gaulliste fury. They none of them realized that Gaullisme was premature in 1942 for all but exiles, and that the overwhelming majority of stay-at-home Frenchmen regarded de Gaulle as an officer who had fired on his own flag when they had heard of him at all. Nor did they have the faintest notion of our military situation. Like most civilian Americans they seem to have thought we had only to wave a wand and our armies and navies would be invincible. Most of all they had the extraordinary and quite indefensible belief that anybody who had supported Marshal Pétain—which is to say, all Frenchmen except three or four thousand—was necessarily a traitor to something which they called "France." This sort of writing, which projected an idea like "France" with no relation to the will or mind of the forty million living Frenchmen, seemed to me, in the very midst of these difficulties, no less than infuriating, particularly among protagonists of the democratic principle. Under precisely the same

160

kind of reasoning we could make Father Divine's disciples the dictators of the United States, or the Doukhobors supreme in Canada.

It will be said that by stating the case in this way I ignore the moral purity and power of de Gaulle's cause and the moral issue at large. I do not contest de Gaulle's austere and noble courage, the intensity of his patriotism or the single-mindedness of his devotion throughout the darkest days. But I do not regard them as relevant to the objective situation we faced. It is true that as our victory became more manifest there was nothing to impede the rise of de Gaulle's star—this was obvious from 1940—but up until we had proved our ability to win the war such was not the case. In truth he merely had to wait. This he was unable to do, and his partisans in America and England set up the most unholy clamor throughout the winter of 1942-1943 to make it impossible for him to wait even if he had so desired. As a purely incidental result there was a campaign of vilification against the principal instruments of our African policy, notably Robert Murphy. As I read the venomous tirades printed in the so-called "liberal" weeklies about Murphy, I could hardly believe that they could be thinking of the same person: Bob, who was our only friend in diplomatic circles in Paris during the darkest days of the Spanish war; Bob who risked his neck more deliberately and coolly on D-day than any soldier, in order to save American lives; Bob who had labored like a slave, in danger and difficulty, for two whole years in order to ease our passage across Africa to get at the Germans. So much of what he did is still secret so that he bears, perhaps will always bear, some kind of odious association for those who elected to make him the villain of the piece. But the gross injustice in the affair was that these same critics who attacked Bob in terms very close to criminal libel did not utter a pertinent word against the President, the Secretary of State or the Combined Chiefs of Staff, of whose

161

policy Bob was the instrument. A soldier is always easier to attack than a general.

Along with Bob Murphy, the other villain for our blind-folded Quixotes of the press was indeed a general, but French: General Giraud. Giraud, an officer of the simplest bravery and honor, had little political intelligence and no ambition whatever, but he was respected by the French army as few of their generals were; he was also known (which General de Gaulle was not yet in 1942 among most Frenchmen). His remarkable escape from a German prison made him available for us at the right time, and he was chosen by our high command to effect the transition from a Vichy to a pro-Allied regime. He came in with us whole-heartedly, and any officer who had to deal with both would testify that we got far more unquestioning co-operation in military matters from General Giraud than we ever did afterwards. His eager, single-minded interest in victory over the Germans was apparent in the most ordinary conversation with him. He had no interest in politics and scarcely put up a struggle against de Gaulle's claim (after the Tunisian victory) to supreme authority. Yet our press chose to represent Giraud as a schemer of doubtful character, a "Vichy" general (he had nothing to do with Vichy) and even, in one memorable blunder by a press columnist, as a pro-German agent who had whipped Noguès and Morocco into line in 1940 for the Hitler armistice. (This error was quite simple: it was *Gouraud* not Giraud who had gone to Morocco in 1940; but nothing was too extreme for the press at home to believe and state in this affair.) The crowning absurdity came when the American press invented the term "Giraudiste" as an epithet to describe those people who were not Gaullistes but were pro-Allied anyhow. There were never any "Giraudistes." The term was quite meaningless, but to this day one hears it in such backwaters of 1940 *émigré* Gaullisme as the Waldorf-Astoria in New York or the Ritz in London.

162

It often seemed—and seems to this day—that the fanaticism aroused by de Gaulle among the so-called "liberals" of England and the United States was out of all proportion to the reality of the situation. It took extreme and unjust forms which could not be defended under any circumstances, even if de Gaulle had been a Messiah straight from heaven. The brave Arabs who fought in Italy under French officers were called "Gaulliste" troops in the American press, for example, although most of them had never heard of de Gaulle and most of their officers detested that leader. The identical Arabs had been called "Vichy" troops when they were under the command of Giraud. The whole thing was a sort of tempest in a teapot, which affected chiefly those polemicists who daily argue a point in print at white-hot temperatures regardless of facts. The process was clear and inevitable and I know of nobody in Africa who did not see it from the start. We could not possibly bring de Gaulle in to begin with, but his advent was as certain as the sun's rising, in due course. From the moment we got to Casablanca there was no doubt of the outcome—no doubt in any mind, from one end to the other of the range of opinion. All we wished to do was to get on with our war against Germany with the least possible friction, delay and irrelevant confusion; it was a simple practical matter, and once we had won the victory it was of no consequence to us how much political uproar there was in Algiers.

I suggest two possible explanations for the press campaign which so sorely misled our public during the winter of 1942-1943: first, the "liberals" were in mid-war without any convenient excuse for that righteous indignation by which they live, and the supposed wrongs done de Gaulle gave them such an excuse; second, they were grossly misinformed both about de Gaulle himself and his movement and about the temper of the great majority of Frenchmen. They thought de Gaulle a "liberal," for example—an almost inconceivable mistake, but one which seems to have been made in good faith. They also seem to have believed, for no apparent reason, that a majority of the French regarded de Gaulle as their leader. This was certainly not true either in 1942 or at any other time up to the liberation of France by the Anglo-American expedition. The Résistance Française accepted de Gaulle's leadership *after* the liberation, as much for lack of anything better as through any enthusiasm toward that general. De Gaulle himself has stated his own truth about himself and his movement: "We were only a handful of men, but we carried away with us the immortal soul of France." In this conception, which is philosophically indistinguishable from that of any other mystically self-appointed leader such as Mussolini or Hitler, the element which deceived the naive and concealed the essence of the matter was the militant patriotism. On our side, those who considered themselves capable of divining the exact geographical position of "the immortal soul of France" took it away from some forty million Frenchmen and located it neatly in the pocket of Charles de Gaulle, because it suited us better there. That "the immortal soul of France" might conceivably lie in France itself, either among people too old and tired to fight or among their rising revolutionary generation, was not taken into account.

And the anti-Gaullistes—all French, of course; there were none to be found in England or America—were just as exasperating, although more pitiable because their misinformation was more glaring. Many of them actually believed Charles de Gaulle, that Jesuit imperialist, to be a Jew, a Freemason and a Communist. Such was the Vichy legend assiduously propagated and accepted among those who knew no better. It was very currently believed among the French that de Gaulle's role in Syria and Madagascar had been that of cat's-paw for the British, and that the British would never surrender those territories in the unlikely event of an allied victory. It was taken as axiomatic that de Gaulle's support came from an unholy alliance of great finance capital ("La Banque") and Bolshevism. He was supposed to have been responsible for the British attack upon the French fleet at Mers-el-Kebir on July 3, 1940, for the attack at Dakar later the same year, for the Syrian and Madagascar affairs and for the British bombings in France, all of which put a formidable number of French dead upon his record. Among regular French army and navy officers the thought that he had fired upon the flag of the French Republic was particularly abhorrent and needed no Vichy or German propaganda to make it more so. The very limited nature of de Gaulle's responsibility in any of these events was imperfectly understood even among his adherents and not at all by the general French public. If an affair so tenebrous could ever be brought wholly into the light of day, it would be of the utmost advantage to history to have the facts of the relations between General de Gaulle and the British government published in a Blue Book with all original documents and dispatches. It would then be seen at what point he learned of these various British operations and what part he took in them and in what way. There remains in France, submerged by de Gaulle's present appearance of success, a powerful and widespread resentment against him for this whole sequence of incidents; the publication of the documents might clear some of this away. But in 1942 even the most incontrovertible proof would have meant nothing to the convinced anti-Gaulliste French: they were hurt, sore, passionate in their suffering, convinced that next to the abhorred Germans, their worst enemies were the British and the "traitor" de Gaulle.

I came up against this every day. It was my duty to deal with the French aviation authorities in innumerable questions from morning to night. During the whole of this rather experimental period (November and December, 1942) the effort to

165

apply our policy of firm friendliness to all Frenchmen who were with us in the war was handicapped by inexperience. We had no book of rules to go upon. In my own strictly limited sphere I had to improvise precedents, or get my General to improvise them, time after time. Practically all Frenchmen, in and out of the army, wished for our success in the war; not very many believed in it at the beginning, but the flood of our equipment into the country began to convince them before the end of the year. In the course of my experience I knew only one French officer who seemed dangerously devoted to Marshal Pétain—that is, so devoted that the passage of weeks did not cause him to change his tune. He was of so little importance in the military hierarchy that he has slipped on, unperceived, into the Gaulliste ranks now, and no doubt sports the Cross of Lorraine on his coat, but his conversation was fascinating to me as an example of the extreme Laval-Vichy point of view. He considered the American and British troops in Africa to be in precisely the same position as the Germans in France. He established procedure in dealing with us upon the analogy with the German Armistice Commission, discussed those gentlemen without rancor, informed me that many of his friends thought we had come to Africa to "drag France into the war," and said that the V-signs which were beginning to appear on blank walls were "presumably for a British victory." His neutrality, considering that his wife and family were in German-occupied France even before November 8th, was curiously perfect. It was a little too much for the French authorities after a while and they appointed another officer in his stead —a strongly pro-Allied officer whose wife was an American.

I have since discovered that some of the French officers with whom I had to deal in those early weeks considered themselves secretly Gaulliste all the time. In one case there can be no doubt of it; he was a part of the plan and I had the proof afterwards; but it must be said that most of these concealed their opinions very well. It had been illegal to profess adherence to General de Gaulle up to our arrival in Africa. This circumstance aroused terrific ire among the American enthusiasts, but I never saw how the Vichy policy could have been applied otherwise; the French government had to be one thing or the other, either in favor of Pétain's conciliation of the Germans or in favor of de Gaulle's hostility toward them. Upon our arrival the Gaulliste prisoners were released and the laws against "dissidence" were no longer applied; the Jews picked up heart and demonstrated in the streets; the Alsace-Lorraine Association, dealing with the many refugees from the unhappy provinces, which had been kept undercover by Vichy for fear of angering the Germans, was now allowed to function with public support; the long, sorry job of clearing out the concentration camps (filled with Germans, Austrians, Jews, Social Democrats of all nations, Spanish Republicans and others who for any reason displeased either the Nazis or Vichy) began under American pressure, specifically that of Bob Murphy. None of this went fast enough for those fire-eaters at home who wanted us to kick out all the local authorities and do the job ourselves or bring in de Gaulle; and nevertheless it was all done in about seven months, done decently and in order, and without public disturbance.

So far as the concentration camps were concerned I could see no reason why the work did not proceed more quickly. It was difficult to find places for all the thousands of those interned, but in view of the fact that practically all were anti-Fascists of the most indisputable kind, our interest and duty alike demanded speed. We did eventually find places on our airfields for a large number of the Spanish Republicans; many were taken into Mexico; the Germans and Austrians found a certain amount of employment with us; the local French economy did not have to absorb many. But this argument—that there was no place to put them when they were released—did serve to delay an act of justice which the logic of our war demanded and which we did, in fact, request of the French authorities as soon as our occupation by agreement had become a fact. The mere labor of checking over the records of those interned and separating the anti-Fascist sufferers from ordinary criminals took many weeks, according to my friends involved in this matter, but in the meanwhile neither the food nor the treatment of the interned improved much for a good while. All these camps were, of course, under the French internal administration and all we could do was keep on asking the French to act. Neither before nor during the war—nor at any other time known to me—has the French treatment of prisoners been distinguished by its humaneness, but proceeding, as we always did, with strict regard for French independence and pride, we could not very well say so.

Our work had nothing to do, on the surface at any rate, with politics. General Cannon was concerned with getting his flying units in from England, putting them through some necessary training and re-equipment and moving them toward the front as soon as possible. This involved the use of airfields, repair shops and mechanics belonging to the French. The only airfield in Morocco which stood up under the merciless winter rains was that at Casablanca. We had to put down steel mats at lesser fields and watch them sink into the mud. Our A-20 group came in at the Médiouna field near Casablanca and, with the exception of the Tafaraoui field near Oran, I never saw a muddier hole. We had no rights at Marrakech under our original agreement, and only asked for them later when our need for fields became greater. On our side we were continually demanding of the French more room, more help of one sort or another (sites for live bombing; slow aircraft for tow-targets; sites for air gunnery practice, and so on). On their side they were very soon requesting chances to engage in the war as active combatants. I do not think their elder and superior officers had much warlike ambition, but they were continually being pressed by the younger men to obtain equipment from the Americans and get into the fray. I believe some of the older officers were startled at this in the beginning; they had long since lost the spirit of combat; but some whiff of their own youth came back with the passing weeks, and there came a time when we hardly ever saw General Lahoulle that he was not asking for opportunities for his young men to fight.

As a matter of fact we had these requests too, and in the most unorthodox ways. Young men came to our headquarters to say that they were half-trained or partly trained on French aircraft and wanted to join us to be trained on American planes. They had no faith in their specific local authorities—or they had been suspected of Gaullisme and thought there would be a prejudice against them on that account—or they had lost faith in French leadership altogether and wanted to entrust themselves to us. Once I made bold to write a memorandum to General Cannon in this sense: there are young men coming to us every day who feel, rightly or wrongly, that they can never join the fight through the regular French authorities; can we take care of them in any way? The General wrote across this memorandum, in firm blue crayon, DO NOT MIX IN POLITICS. He underlined the *not* so as to make his point quite plain. He was thoroughly aware of the delicacy of our course between the eggshells of pride and the prickles of prejudice. The only solution for a soldier was to keep firmly in mind the one single objective and try to ignore, with all politeness and consideration, whatever irrelevant complications our friends chose to put in our path. But whenever it did not involve a pledge or a reference of any sort to politics, General Cannon seized opportunities to oblige the French as they presented themselves, particularly in whatever concerned the preparation of French pilots for combat. In this I was an eager as

169

sistant. I believe we were the first—on the Cazès air base—to check out French pilots on our P-40's, with Jacques de Montravel and others; at the same time or a little later our Phil Cochran was checking out Marin La Meslée and some of the other celebrated French fighter pilots at Rabat, where the sorely tried 2/7 Group of French fighter planes, which had the most brilliant record of all in the campaign of May, 1940, was now stationed. On our own base at Cazès we had the 2/5 Group, containing two escadrilles, the Lafayette and the Stork (*Cigogne*). The Lafayette Escadrille, formed in the 1914-1918 war as a unit of American pilots in the French service, had remained through the years as a French air force unit proud of its origin and tradition. Its insignia was the head of a Sioux Indian painted on the aircraft. With its sister escadrille, the other half of the same group, it had been assigned the defense of Casablanca and one of its pilots had been shot down protecting the Cazès air base against the attack of our naval aviation. General Cannon early distinguished the members of this unit; they were the first to try out our P-40's (they had flown P-36's before); and the idea of equipping them as the first French unit to go into combat along with ours germinated very early in our stay at Casablanca. It was brusquely taken up by higher authority in Algiers a month later and one escadrille (thirteen aircraft) suddenly was given planes taken from our own 33rd Fighter Group and sent into combat without other equipment—a circumstance which merits the telling in its place. But during those early days in Morocco, when we had no authority to give the French anything, even information, it was a diplomatic task of considerable intricacy to maintain that friendship in which we believed without yielding anything on our own side.

For example, the French became anxious to learn everything they could about our aircraft, particularly P-40 and B-25, the two which they learned from the press were going to be the first given to French pilots and crews. (We were always reading such things in the press, perhaps from Washington and perhaps from London, when we knew nothing whatever on the subject.) Most of our headquarters officers and a good many of our pilots and crews had a deep distrust of the French. In some cases (as with some of the Signal Corps people) this distrust amounted to a mania; if a Frenchman was heard telephoning in his own language from his own airfield there would always be somebody, ignorant of that language, who was sure that this was a code message to German spies. For weeks we were uncertain how much we could tell the French and to what degree they were effectively our allies. From the very beginning I had been sure that they were with us; I had lived for so much of my life in France that I simply did not believe (and do not believe now) that more than the merest handful of Frenchmen sincerely supported the Germans. What was cloudy and vague about Vichy was far more inclusive than what was downright base and treacherous. Given the opportunity, most young Frenchmen were avid to get at the Germans. But in view of our peppery reception on November 8th this was not so apparent to most of our officers, who were inclined to regard the French as probable enemies or extremely doubtful friends. On one occasion a French liaison officer who had come to our headquarters to see me on business got lost and wandered into our A-3 room, from which he was ordered out again with angry words. He fortunately was a devoted friend—a young ensign who was secretly a Gaulliste all the while—and attached no great importance to the incident. Some of our staff officers actually objected, at first, to the presence of any French officer in our headquarters at any time. General Cannon uniformly supported me in any such matter, and the exquisite courtesy of his manner toward the French did a lot to smooth over the early difficulties. More serious, because it went to the root of the matter, was the question of what technical information we could give the French. In the very early days I gave them silhouettes and published data on our aircraft—the sort of thing which could be bought in any aviation magazine—and told them what combat groups we had in this immediate area. Not to do so would have been ridiculous, since they were using the same airfields we did and could have obtained the information merely by looking. I also diagramed for them our air-force organization and our chain of command. But beyond this I did not dare go without specific authorization, which, in those early days, was not forthcoming. They wanted our "tech orders," of course, and weeks passed in a sort of miasma of uncertainty upon this relatively minor matter. Technical orders ("tech orders") are the data on the structure and operation of aircraft, carried in the aircraft on all flights. In French the term used is *"notices d'utilisation,"* a phrase so different that at first I had no idea of what the French pilots were talking about. "Buckshot" Taylor, a pilot who was then in our A-3 section, was able to guess what they meant through pilot's instinct, although he knew not a word of French; he was invaluable to me in those two months, going over technical points with patience and kindliness, explaining everything that our regulations allowed us to explain, and often smoothing over difficulties by the sheer directness and simplicity of a pilot's temperament. I remarked then and ever afterwards that men intent upon a technical problem scarcely need language for communication; they have a fund of common knowledge which transcends language, and above all they have the psychological oneness which is independent of nationality. When I afterwards saw Phil Cochran checking out French pilots on P-39's without a word, and American and Russian pilots (still later) carrying on lively conversations over the same aircraft without a word in common, I realized that there were some things more important than language.

One of my jobs in the very beginning was to go over every inch of the Cazès air base and decide, by agreement with the French, which buildings, areas and equipment we were to use. They had some small antique liaison aircraft (mostly Goëlands) and two fighter escadrilles on the field; they also used it for trimotored Dewoitine transport planes of two sizes, one about as big as our C-47 and the other smaller, for shorter flights. I think they only had three of the big Dewoitines, which did the desert flight from Algiers to Dakar, but they kept their biggest and best hangar for them. We had grounded all their aircraft in the beginning and many of our officers saw no reason why we should not take over the whole airfield, especially as our plans called for the arrival of a large number of combat aircraft here. In deference to French pride, General Cannon decided that the eastern side of the field (the Air-Maroc or French military aviation side) should be retained by them while we took the western, or civil aviation, side. By good luck the commander of our base at the very beginning was Colonel Fordyce, a huge, good-natured Texan who afterwards commanded a B-26 group and was killed in Tunisia. He fell in with the idea that we should make our arrangements as amiably as possible, and with many a roaring joke and slap on the back we divided up the "facilities" (detestable word then coming into universal use) between us. Our Fighter Wing, which expected more activity than it enjoyed on this base, had to have a headquarters on the field as well, and it was not long before the Transport Command began to flood in upon us. The minute, innumerable and ticklish problems involved in such "co-habitation," as the French called it, may be imagined; it would be tedious to relate them all. Frequently they were of that tiny, unimportant but infinitely exasperating nature which ruins the relations between men because it emphasizes a larger misunderstanding.

One such involved the French use of radio. Our Signal

173

Corps people had been so thoroughly indoctrinated with the rules of security that they did not want any Frenchmen, soldiers or civilians, to send or receive radio signals. They took over the French radio installations and set up their own equipment. Consequently when we did authorize French flights of any length it proved infinitely difficult to persuade the Signal Corps men on the field to make them possible. Specific orders from General Cannon and from the head of the Signal Corps in the Western Task Force were at first required for every such operation. I was constantly having to drop everything, hop into a jeep and rush for the airfield to keep the Americans and French from coming to blows over some such thing. The flight of the Governor-General of French West Africa, Boisson, to a council of war with Darlan and Giraud in Algiers was a case in point. This Boisson (now in jail) may have been a scoundrel or not; that was none of our business. What mattered was that our high command wanted him in Algiers for a meeting which was to decide the union of all French Africa in our support for the winning of the war. In view of the importance (at that time) of Dakar to the Air Corps, our interest in getting the man to Algiers was obvious. He could not cross the desert in his Dewoitine without radio signals, and our Signal Corps people would not permit the radio signals. They never did understand the case, and only obeyed finally on the most explicit orders from on high. I discovered that the root cause of the matter was that they could not understand a word of French and assumed all French conversation or signals to be of a treacherous nature.

Of course much of the difficulty came from unfamiliarity. Our men and officers hardly knew where they were. Most of them had never heard the French language before and had never met a Frenchman. The geography and politics of Africa were a mystery to them, and they did not fully understand the exiguous nature and condition of our own forces. We were, after all, merely perched on a few spots around the edges of an immense territory, and aside from Casablanca and Lyautey we were not really "occupying" Morocco at all. In French West Africa at that time we had nothing whatever. We wanted a base at Dakar, and got it afterwards, but we could not take these things by force because we did not have the force; we had to get them by agreement. The hours I spent in weary argument with captains and majors over our relations with the French during those first weeks should be put to my credit when the roll is called up yonder, for it was far from easy. Our junior officers at first thought they were in conquered country and that they could "requisition" (i.e., simply take) anything they happened to want. Their answer to any objection was always the same: "Let them go somewhere else." The fact was that in Casablanca, crowded with war refugees from France and all Europe, there was usually nowhere "else" to go except the ocean or the desert *bled*. We paid for everything we got in French Africa, paid abundantly, profusely, over and over again, but the trouble was that the money did not mean much. Nobody had confidence in the franc and there was nothing to be bought with it anyhow. The Arab day laborer had bundles of francs he had earned in the past year or so, but he would much rather have had a piece of cotton cloth to make himself a shirt. Under such circumstances the most lavish generosity with money could not recompense the dispossessed householder or businessman. And at the same time we had to have room to work in, if we were to win the war. This dilemma filled the days.

"We just get settled down in a place and get started to work," I heard a Signal Corps officer say one day, "when some shit of a staff major comes along and throws us out because the God damned French have got to have the house. What kind of a war is this?"

I was practically always the staff major referred to, and with

175

the best will in the world was never able to satisfy all hands in an argument. I appealed to General Cannon as seldom as possible, but there came times when nothing else would do except a direct order from him, and when it was necessary I went to him. His dry humor, his philosophic calm and his fundamental knowledge of the whole situation above or beneath its component parts made every such appeal a relief and an encouragement. My respect for the quality of this commander grew with every week that passed, and by mid-December my chief personal anxiety was that when he went to the front— which we all assumed would happen before long—he would not take me with him. I was quite ready to do any job that might be considered useful, and had entered the army for that purpose, but without the understanding and support of a commanding general no task of the kind I was engaged in could be carried out in this army. It was too fluid and unpredictable; it was treated in none of the little manuals we had from the War Department to govern our military activity; it was an essentially psychological or even political enterprise. Moreover our policy was understood, if at all, only on the higher levels, and the incomprehension all the way down, on both the French and the American sides, was all but insurmountable. As William James says, "the end is defined beforehand in most cases only as a general direction, along which all sorts of novelties and surprises lie in wait." It was these novelties and surprises which constituted the material of my work.

The first German air raid provided a good many such novelties and surprises. It came on Christmas night and was probably a reconnaissance or trial mission, since no bombs fell. On the night of December 30th it was repeated in earnest, and bombs plastered some parts of the town, notably the New Medina where thousands of Arabs lived. The port of Casablanca had been working day and night to unload the supplies we needed for the coming campaign, and after the first weeks

176

of blackout it was ablaze with light because we needed the supplies in a hurry. We were all mystified at the German reluctance to bomb us. Casablanca was the principal port for our undertaking; Algiers was distinctly secondary, and yet Algiers was bombed at this period fairly regularly and Casablanca was untouched. We knew that it could be reached from Bordeaux by the long-range Focke-Wulfs stationed there, even if fields in near-by Spain were not used. Our Fighter Wing, which was in charge of defense, had made a formal and very sketchy agreement with the French naval authorities who controlled the French warning system; I think we paid one visit to the French admiral and discussed a few points without pooling our information or resources. We had no great respect for the French system anyhow, since it consisted of Arab watchers on hillsides connected by land telephones. Our own very modern radar equipment was set up north of the city and we relied upon it.

What we had not been told, or had insufficiently understood, was that the French admiral had beside his bed in naval headquarters a switch which cut off all the electricity for the whole city and district of Casablanca. On Christmas night, at the first alarm, which had at that time not even reached us in our headquarters, he pulled the switch and plunged the whole area into darkness, after sounding a siren. The scramble for candles, the attempt to work the unfamiliar machine of our defense in total darkness, the general confusion and dismay, made the night memorable and pointed up the necessity for some more comprehensive understanding with the French about what to do in an air raid. Our nervous sentries shot pretty recklessly that night, and I was very lucky indeed to get from my quarters to my post at the Western Task Force without wounds. As usual, we were besieged the next day by reports of mysterious light signals flashing to the Germans, etc.,

177

etc.—a thing which happens after every air raid throughout the world.

In the midst of this alarm, while I was sitting at the G-2 telephone in the darkness, a call came through from Algiers. My function in air raids was to get to G-2 of the Western Task Force and stay there as liaison with the Air Support Command. The G-2 duty officer had left the room and asked me to mind the telephone. There were nowhere near enough candles in the big building and this room was in total darkness. I picked up the telephone and Algiers said: "This is AFHQ, Colonel X speaking. Who is that?" I identified myself. The voice then said: "You are to get in touch with Psychological Warfare immediately and tell them that Admiral Darlan has been assassinated. Tell them that they can say this *and nothing more*. This goes for all radio and newspapers." Click.

I sat there for a moment, musing. The city was dark and silent. It was a very curious moment. Then I picked up the telephone and asked for the Hotel Plaza, where "Psychological Warfare"—specifically, my old friend Jay Allen—lived. When I got him I said: "Admiral Darlan has been assassinated. You can say that *and nothing more*. This goes for all newspapers and radio." Jay thought I was joking and began to elaborate on the supposed fantasy, making up further episodes and developments. I was fearful of such japery on a G-2 telephone; civilians never understand anything in war, I reflected, even the most intelligent of them. I cut him short, repeated the instructions ("Admiral Darlan has been assassinated. You can say that *and nothing more*."), and hung up. Jay had been one of the most violent of those who thought we should shoot all Frenchmen in power and install a new lot, but I had never expected him to air his views on a G-2 telephone. In the result he waited a while, still thinking I was making a Christmas joke, and after a quarter of an hour he called G-2 and got the same instructions from a ground officer; then he believed them.

All troops throughout Africa had been consigned to barracks that afternoon; the high command was afraid of some clash or violent movement as a result of the Darlan assassination. Admiral Darlan, a clever, vain and ambitious man with a flexible sense of honor, had chanced to be in Africa at the moment of our landings. As he was Vice-Commander of all French forces—sea, land and air, and thus ranked next to Pétain in the Vichy regime—it was important to get him to join us as early as possible—either this or waste months in a pointless war against France. He was cajoled and threatened into taking position for us, and all the provincial governors were summoned by him to Algiers to be whipped into line. But Darlan was not quite good enough; for example, although he ordered the fleet at Toulon to join us, it disobeyed and finally had to scuttle itself to avoid being taken by the Germans. Darlan's popularity in France had never been perceptible, and there were many stories of his contrast to the adored Pétain in that respect. Now that we had compounded with him for the sake of saving some thousands of American lives (a detail our "liberals" scorned), he had become the devil incarnate for all Gaullistes, and in the end a Gaulliste youth shot him as he entered the Winter Palace in Algiers on Christmas morning. He was no great loss; we were now much better off without him; but so much passion had been aroused by these events that the consequences of his assassination were not to be foreseen. As it turned out during the next day or so there was no need for anxiety. In a long and checkered experience I have never seen anybody whose disappearance from the human drama caused so little regret as Darlan's.

The next air-raid alarm took place at about three o'clock in the morning of December 30th, and this time it was the real thing. I dressed and scurried along to the Western Task Force around the corner. This time there were plenty of candles and a full attendance of special and general-staff officers—engineers, chemical warfare, medical corps and all the rest, as well as the staff sections and Air Corps liaison, which was I. General Gaffey, commander of the military area of Casablanca—afterwards of the Fourth Armored Division and, in the final victory in Germany, a corps commander—was there, wandering between the telephone and the opened window. The anti-aircraft guns were booming away and the sky was dazzling with crisscross lines of fire. The brilliance of the spectacle almost took away one's consciousness of the thunderous bombs which fell from time to time, sometimes quite nearby. General Gaffey suddenly turned from the window and snapped: "Air Corps!" I got to him through the obscurity and saluted. "How many night fighters have we got in this area?" he asked. "None, sir," I said. He growled, cleared his throat and snapped again: "Why not?" I was stumped at this one. "I don't know, sir," I said. He walked up and down for a moment and then said: "Are you sure we have no night fighters?" I said: "Unless they came in today, I am quite sure." He was not satisfied. "Verify that," he said.

I went to the telephone and called the Air Support Command, feeling very foolish indeed. "General Gaffey wishes me to verify that we have no night fighters in the Casablanca area," I said. "Will you verify it?" Colonel Young came to the telephone and said: "It is verified." I went back to the General and reported. He stood for a while at the window looking at the incredible pyrotechnics outside.

"Why can't the day fighters go up at night?" he asked.

I tell this story not as against General Gaffey; I am sure with actual practice he learned a great deal more about air force afterwards. But at the time, in our very beginning, not many of our ground generals understood these things in any detail. I was obliged to make a stumbling and awkward explanation of the difference between day and night fighters—special radio job—we have not the equipment—it's mostly British—Algiers

has them all—and so on. Five minutes later the telephone rang
for Gaffey: it was from Patton, Commander of the Western
Task Force, and I could tell by Gaffey's answers that Patton
was asking precisely the same series of questions. Gaffey passed
on to him exactly what I had just said. I stood in a dark corner
and wondered how such things could be; if I had not been
there myself I might not have believed it. Before the next year
was out our ground generals were as familiar with the Air
Force weapons as necessity required, but to the very end there
were always strange lacunæ in their knowledge, strange notions and misconceptions which changing situations brought
into relief and which fully justified the maintenance of operational control in the hands of air officers.

Life in Casablanca was pleasant enough for a staff officer
from the moment we arrived. The French residents of the
town were friendly and hospitable; our consulate—huge at
that time—had a considerable life of its own; we were quartered in the most comfortable hotel, with friends in all the
others, ground officers at the Majestic, naval officers at the
Plaza. I had to be a great deal on air fields or in the camps of
our men, but if I had lived the regular life of the staff officer
between the hotel and headquarters it would have been not
greatly different from an office job in New York. I grew impatient with our dormitory system after a while and got permission to find a room of my own. (The principal discomfort
of army life to me was always its lack of privacy.) Just at this
time Teddy Culbertson, who had come over with us on D-day
as the only civilian, for a Civil Affairs job which did not materialize, was the social center of Franco-American life in Casablanca. Nobody knew precisely what his function was, but
he had been in the American consulate before this expedition
and was afterwards the Lend-Lease officer for Morocco. I conjecture that if we had been obliged to fight the French instead
of getting them to join us, he would have been a sort of

181

A.M.G. officer for whatever area we could hold. At any rate, on Wednesdays or perhaps Thursdays he had a "day" to which French and Americans of the official world were bidden in large numbers. Patton sometimes went; Noguès went; even General Cannon once went there for a few minutes, in spite of his dislike of "parties." In this friendly atmosphere I met M. and Mme. Jean de Mareuil, possessors of a flat in the Rue Savorgnan de Brazza, who offered me a room, and I took it.

My habitation *chez les Mareuil* was at the same time a place of material refuge and a haven of civil custom in the midst of our regulated life. Jean and his wife were reflective, cultivated and amiable people with whom I agreed on practically no known point of politics, philosophy or society, but our endless arguments had the merit of abstracting my mind from those details in which it spent its hours of duty. The Mareuils were Catholic Royalists, aloof from the struggles of the Third Republic and convinced that a different order of French society would have made them unnecessary. They were both patriotic nationalists, but Jean in particular regarded the ruin of France as a process which had been begun by the great revolution of 1789. To a mind which, like mine, thought of that upheaval as the origin of the modern world, his point of view repaid investigation, and I came to the conclusion that it was indeed one of the purest patriotic fervor: the great revolution may have fertilized the world but it weakened and divided France and was therefore evil, he said. His dislike of the *émigrés* in the present French crisis was acute, but was accompanied by a freely expressed respect for combat units such as that of Leclerc in the desert. Marshal Pétain the Mareuils regarded as "a prisoner of the Germans," and I found that this view was almost universal among the French I encountered in 1942 and even in 1943. The *émigré* vision of the old Marshal as an abject traitor did not receive acceptance among French people either in France or in Africa until a later date. I enjoyed the debate with the Mareuils as I enjoyed their generous hospitality (as this was not an official billet I was regarded as a guest and could in no way repay them); and at intervals thereafter, on the way to and from Italy, India, France, I was to see them again with the same pleasure. Their indefatigable little Berber servant, Ali, who came from the hills near Marrakech and was a model of Moslem devotion, their overflowing bookshelves, their balcony over the white city, their little lunches and the aroma of Paris which clung to their conversation, all taken together made up for me a precious retreat from the army.

Sometimes I felt heartily ashamed of the comfort to which we had so quickly accommodated ourselves in Casablanca. On fields like that at Médiouna I saw our combat units, replete with spam, contesting with the cold and the mud; our own squadron was cold and wet that winter in the Parc Lyautey in the heart of the city. One night toward the end of this period an old young friend, Wells Lewis, came to dinner with me at our mess. He was a first lieutenant in an anti-aircraft battalion; I had known him since his childhood; he was the son of Sinclair Lewis and after Harvard, Mexico and an experience with the press, accompanied by various intellectual adventures, he had enlisted in the infantry as a private. That was in the autumn of 1940 after the bombing of London. He was now a very fine young officer, military beyond our habit in the Air Corps, who saluted me and called me "Sir" until I laughed him out of it. Wells had been very adult, "sophisticated" as they say, and rather spoiled, in the glimpses I had had of him as a young man in New York before he went into the army. He knew almost too much about music, literature and history, and with his good looks and his economic advantages life did not present sufficient resistance to him. His great decision, over a year before we were attacked at Pearl Harbor, had distilled something new out of the recesses of his char-

183

acter: he had hardened, simplified, grown younger and more serious, inside and out, so that not a trace of the *flaneur* or dilettante remained. Just as he had physically altered into a superb specimen of military carriage, so his mind had sharpened and concentrated and thrown off non-essentials. I had seen him last in a box at the Town Hall in New York—Marcia Davenport's box—at a recital by Zimbalist, two or more years before; now his talk revealed no consciousness of the existence of such far-off things. He was in a headquarters battery out on the north road toward Fedala, living in the mud and the rain, and his only fear was that he might be left there for the duration of the war, doing practically nothing: for a headquarters battery, without guns, is scarcely a hive of activity in the absence of air raids. Wells spoke such excellent French, and so few of our officers did, that I thought he might be more usefully employed elsewhere, and actually did take some steps looking toward such a solution afterwards but they came to nothing. In the end his ability was discerned, he became a general's aide in France and was killed there in 1944.

That night when he dined at our mess was one of those Casablanca evenings of penetrating cold and driving rain. The temperatures were not notably low in Casablanca, but the wind and the rain had a way of injecting the cold into one's bones. Wells had hitch-hiked into the town for this meal, which was rather an occasion in his life in the ditch by the road. Dewitt Sage and I got our headquarters jeep to take him part of the way back, but the driver was afraid to go beyond the barrier because his vehicle was on duty. Wells said cheerfully that he had walked it before and could walk it again. It was midnight and there was little chance that he could find a truck or jeep going in his direction. The last I saw of him he was trudging off northward in the rain. He was a fine young officer.

Once at the height of the muddy season I had to go to Marrakech in a hurry at the call of the French Deuxième Bureau. I took an A-20 from the field at Médiouna, flew to Marrakech and got what I had come for (a hair-raising business of espionage). After this the French G-2 officer took me in to see General Martin, the commander there, whose division was later to be completely equipped by the Americans and was the first French (i.e., Arab) division in combat. Martin said, with some delicacy and hesitation, that there were no American officers in Marrakech, that General Giraud was arriving that afternoon and that he would be very happy if some American officer would be present at the reception. Would I be able to do so? I replied that I had no uniform with me (I was in field jacket and boots; nothing else was suited to the mud of the airfields). The General did not like to insist, but he kept coming back to the subject; I gathered that the presence of an American —any American—would greatly solace his anxious heart. I said that I would fly back to Casablanca, get my uniform, and return for the reception. This seemed at first a strange waste of the nation's gasoline, but as I saw the occasion through I realized that the General was quite right: it was almost essential that some American officer be present at these ceremonies because Giraud's whole mission was to win the important center of Marrakech over to his program of full participation in the war. The mere presence of an American uniform served to remind many of these satraps big and little, who were almost isolated from the world in their Barbary palaces, that there was a war to be won.

I think my pilot, a youth named Marsha, got more pleasure out of that expedition than he had had from anything for a long time. His bombardment group had been hurled from Iceland to England to Médiouna before it quite knew where it was; it had lived in the mud for about three weeks without much hope of issue; hot water and decent food were things of memory. He got his uniform and I got mine; by five that evening we were back again on the field at Marrakech, where I found, to my astonishment, an array of some twenty-five or thirty of our aircraft, B-26's. These were the first B-26's to arrive in the theater of operations and although we had expected them, we certainly did not expect them at this moment or on this airfield. I learned from my friends at the French air base that they had appeared in a cloud over the field at the precise moment when General Giraud, escorted by two French fighter aircraft, was coming in to land. It was at first assumed that the American bombers had been sent as a demonstration, as a delicate compliment to Giraud; only when the planes landed was it discovered that their pilots had never heard of Giraud and only wanted a place to sleep, wash and eat. The French at the Marrakech air base were always able to do miracles for us, and they had found the necessary beds and food and other accommodation. Marsha and I obtained a French air force car and made our way to the palace of the Pasha of Marrakech for the Giraud reception.

The streets approaching the Pasha's palace were lined with people, mostly Oriental Jews in their black caps and caftans, who had turned out to cheer Giraud. It was already dark and the narrow, dirty lanes of the old Arab city were lit up weirdly by our headlights as children, chickens and dogs scurried out of the way. I had been to Marrakech several times but my pilot had not, and everything about the spectacle filled him with wonder. "Gee!" he said. At the Pasha's palace we were led by slaves down a long, blue-tiled corridor and across a court-yard in which a fountain was playing. The rain had stopped and the new moon was up. "Gee!" said the pilot. We entered a rectangular room piled thick with rugs, with a sort of padded bench around the walls. On chairs in the middle of the assembly—small in number but exalted in rank—sat General Giraud and the Pasha of Marrakech, El Glaoui.

This important feudatory, whose mother was said to have

been a Senegalese slave, was very dark-skinned but had the aquiline Arab features for a substructure. He was tall and remarkably agile, as I found out afterwards; he could shoot from a galloping horse and accomplish all the other feats of Arab prowess as well in his age (he was seventy, at least, they said) as many did in their youth. His wealth was uncounted; like most of the Arab princes he kept whole dynasties of Jewish bankers to take care of it, and never knew what he possessed so long as he had everything that he wanted when he wanted it. The Jewish bankers (I knew one of them) grew rich on this system, but their money and even their lives were not secure. As an economic system it left much to be desired, since the poor Arab peasants who supplied all this wealth were systematically exploited without any regard for humanity or rational production. The Pasha was lord not only of Marrakech but of all the Berber tribes of the mountains, and the French had treated him with a circumspection measured by the trouble he would be able to cause them if he so desired. Thus since 1912 he had known few restraints so long as he accommodated the Protectorate in its principal requirements, financial and military, and kept the peace. But he had a mischievous, irrepressible longing for the wild warfare of his people, perhaps a nostalgia for ancestral freedom, and months later there was an occasion when he discovered that I had been with Abd el-Krim in the Rif war in 1925 and questioned me narrowly about it. The Rif people were his kinsmen, he said with unction, and he had followed their struggle as closely as he could.

On the evening when he received Giraud the tall, pink-faced old Frenchman and the dark mountain prince were affability itself. Their conversation merited preservation as an example of polite inanity. Giraud said at least five times that it made him feel young to see the Pasha again, since he had first met El Glaoui in the days of his youth; and El Glaoui kept on repeating that he was honored, more than honored, to have the visit of Giraud. There were sweetmeats of a dozen different kinds, almond milk and sherbets and nuts, cigarettes and thick coffee. The actual mission of Giraud (to raise new troops in the mountains) was of course never mentioned, nor did any allusion to the complicated skulduggery of the recruiting system take place. Si Ibrahim, the suave and cultivated son of the Pasha, whose French education had given him not only language but the ability to fill it out with thought when necessary, was conspicuously silent.

The Pasha's reception was followed by the official French dinner. Spahis stood rigidly at attention with drawn swords as we entered and the long table was lined with French officers of all ranks. I sat among aides-de-camp and derived much benefit from their conversation. Giraud's aide, across the table, had made the escape from France to Africa with his master in a submarine and obviously adored the old man in a rather belligerent way. The aide to Noguès, who sat next to me, was a scrawny boy with a monocle who seemed to take a skeptical view of the hero and contrived to let this be known without downright rudeness during the course of talk. The fourragères and decorations, the gold braid and the flowers, made all this seem remote from any circumstance of war. Indeed Marrakech was at this period, more than Casablanca and even more than Rabat, withdrawn from the current of those events which embroiled the world. The dreamy Arab city in its filth and splendor was too far removed from ordinary routes of trade and travel to maintain much interest in Europe; newspapers were very old by the time they got here; French officials or refugees who had the luck to get to Marrakech were glad to forget the stresses and strains they had left behind. All this was to change within a few months under the inundation of our aircraft, which for at least a year made Marrakech one of

188

the capitals of the war, but at the end of 1942 the metamorphosis had not begun.

On my return to the Mamounia Hotel I saw its beginning. The Mamounia, built and operated by the Compagnie Générale Transatlantique, must surely be one of the most wonderful hotels in existence, placed so that its bedrooms and their balconies look out upon the blue-and-white peaks of the Atlas Mountains. There was food in Marrakech in 1942 and the Mamounia had men who could cook it. It also had hot water and huge, luxurious bathtubs. Our B-26 pilots and crews who had arrived unexpectedly that afternoon had taken one look at the Mamounia and elected to stay there, all of them. Since there was not room for all of them they got their bedding rolls and moved in three and four and even five in a room, so as not to be obliged to go anywhere else. (There were two or three modern hotels in the city, but one look at the narrow, dirty streets of the Arab town was enough for these newcomers: they would have the Mamounia, which stood apart in its own garden, or nothing.) They had dined well and had been able to drink a little from the rapidly vanishing stock of the Mamounia bar. One of the boys could play the piano and did so. Some of the French air force officers brought their wives, sisters or daughters in to meet the Americans; the Americans wanted to dance; a dance ensued. This was the first time most of the Frenchwomen had danced since the defeat in the spring of 1940; under Pétain's regime dancing was abolished in sign of national mourning or national penitence, I was never sure which. As I sat there in the huge hall of the Mamounia and watched the dancing and listened to the laughter I was taken back to other days and places before so many catastrophes fell upon us—to the France we loved in days that are no more.

There was one uncompromisingly Gaulliste milieu in Casablanca which I found sympathetic during the end of my station there and frequented when I could. That was the Alsace-Lorraine Association and its chiefs. I had originally been sent to a Christmas festivity of this organization as the representative of General Patton. I obeyed this order like any other, expecting nothing in particular. Actually the festival was almost unbearably moving. Refugees and the children of refugees were being given a Christmas party, as nearly as possible in the manner of their homeland, but in sign of the bondage of their families in Alsace the trees were undecorated and the children's presents were ranged around them. I dined with one or two of the organizers of this association afterwards and heard their stories. These were simple, honest people who had no resemblance whatever to the gilded Gaullistes one had grown accustomed to in the luxury hotels of London and New York. They looked to General de Gaulle, but even more to the Americans, I believe, to cancel Hitler's annexation of the tragic provinces and restore them to France. The refugees were all persons who had refused to accept German citizenship and had then been forced to move into other French provinces and from there to Africa. All had relatives who for reasons of age or illness or sheer discouragement had consented to remain at home and become German citizens. These Alsatians and Lorrainers had no faith or trust in any French authority whatever except those they did not know, the Gaulliste *émigrés*. They were apolitical, gregarious and emotional to a high degree, and one of the most touching things about them was that some of those who loathed the Germans most were unable to speak French without a strong German accent. Their fondness for their own peasant costume, for their own cooking and ways of living, was more important than any political thinking to them. One man said to me with tears in his eyes: "This wine was grown on my grandmother's hillside, not three hundred yards from where I was born. I have kept it

190

for ten years. I want to drink it now to America and to Alsace-Lorraine."

A rather bewildering storm center in Casablanca was my friend Jay Allen, the head of the Psychological Warfare section. He was usually in some sort of battle with the military, particularly the G-2 section of the Western Task Force, as well as with the local French authorities. Jay did not approve of our policy in Africa at all, and said so loud and long. He had no patience with any of what he called the "Vichy people," which meant all members of the French administration so far as I could tell, and this applied not only to political personages but also to those thousands of state servants who were there before there was any Vichy government, and who remained there after de Gaulle came in. If a Frenchman happened to say a short word to Jay for any reason he always attributed a political motive to it. But his quarters and headquarters, at the Plaza Hotel and next door, were one of the liveliest centers of uproar in the whole region, and Jay's battles (for example, his struggle to obtain control of the Rabat radio station) were the most diverting episodes of the period. He had an expanding collection of men and women of all nationalities working for him, among them for a while young Archie Roosevelt, the only American officer I ever knew who troubled to find out what the Arabs were thinking of all this. (Archie said, when he was transferred to Jay: "Here we go! From San Juan Hill to Psychological Warfare in two generations!") Jay was probably much too positive and independent a personality for his task, which in essence consisted of applying a policy of which he thoroughly disapproved to the most sensitive membranes of opinion. He resigned toward the end of the winter, having caused more heat and excitement during his term of office than all the rest of the psychological warriors put together. It is a curious tribute to his vitality that officers of much higher rank came and went without leaving a

191

trace on the memory of anybody in Casablanca, but it is hardly possible to go there at all, even now, without being asked for news of Jay.

The year ended with General Cannon absent, and ominous rumors began to reach us that he would not return. Our combat units were already being moved to the front in Tunisia; the 33rd Fighter Group had been gone for some weeks, the A-20's were moving, the B-26's had spent but a few days in our command. We were on the verge of becoming a headquarters without aircraft or fighting units, and stagnation was about to set in. In two months we had accomplished a good deal in the way of getting units in, fitting them out and sending them forward, and my part in all this had not been negligible since so much depended on a daily relationship with the French; I was never to be so busy or so useful again in the army. Even so we all felt the pull toward the front where our see-saw campaign of insufficient forces against a skillful enemy was getting under way. Thus it was with joy that I received the order, on January 4, 1943, to join General Cannon in the Bomber Command.

CHAPTER III

TÉLEPTE

After the kingfisher's wing
Has answered light to light, and is silent, the light is still
At the still point of the turning world.

T. S. Eliot: *Burnt Norton*

THE FULFILLMENT of our air forces in the time since then has already dimmed the memory of what we had and could do in the winter of 1942-1943, when the enemy equaled or surpassed us in power as he overshadowed us in experience. Not only in the desperate South Pacific, but also in North Africa—which, among the theaters of operations, had first claim on supplies at that time—we were hard pressed to sustain the offensive and even to keep our advanced airfields against constant attack from the air and on the ground. Rations and personal equipment left almost everything to be desired; those were the days when the prepared meat which owns to the celebrated name of spam became a byword in the army; that was the time when the British had to come to our aid with many items, and instead of our own supremely desired coffee we had their black tea to drink morning and evening. In the front areas we had no cigarettes at times, few at other times; we were very short of every means of transport; such things as shoes and warm clothing were at a premium for the only time in this theater. I remember one cold afternoon in January (1943) on the field at Youks-les-Bains near the Algerian-Tunisian frontier, when an incursion of Messerschmitts drove me into the same ditch with a boy, a B-25 pilot, whose trousers were not only grimy but ragged. He asked me, as we made conversation in a lull of waiting, where he could get some new G.I. trousers. I suggested the quartermaster's stores at Constantine. "They haven't got any," he said. In the African and European theaters such a state of affairs seldom, if ever, came to pass again. In the later stages the supply of personal equipment kept up nearer to the front than is usual in other armies, and a regiment withdrawn from the line for a few days had not far to go to get what it wanted—while our squadrons in the air forces, of course, reached the point eventually of having just about everything on their own fields.

Such was not the case in our first winter overseas. When General Cannon took the Bomber Command its heavy striking force consisted of two B-17 groups (the 97th and 101st, both transferred to us from the Eighth Air Force in England), with two fighter groups for escort (the First and 14th). The B-26 groups, two of them, were just coming into combat, and we had two B-25 groups for shipping sweeps and other medium work. This was the nucleus of the mighty armada which became the Strategical Air Force under General Doolittle and the Fifteenth Air Force afterwards. It need hardly be said that maintenance difficulties were greater than they were ever to be thereafter, and as a result no unit had as high an operational proportion on any one day as our air force doctrine prescribed. Not only supply, but weather prediction, navigational aids and all the rest of the complex machinery of a modern air force existed more on paper than in reality. In this rather nuclear stage, rapidly developing as it was and adjusting to the needs of the campaign, it seems to me that we did remarkably well during the months of January and February, 1943. Day after day the airfields and docks at Tunis, Bizerte and Gabès were bombed, the toll on enemy shipping (chiefly Italian—the Germans sacrificed a great part of the Italian mer-

chant marine at this stage) grew heavy, and we even reached
out across the sea and began the bombardment of enemy fields
in Sicily and Sardinia. The first combat mission I was ever on
was our first overseas mission in this air force—the bombing
of the German-Italian air and sea-plane bases at Cagliari in
Sardinia (January 23, 1943). The Luftwaffe had accepted the
challenge immediately upon our landing in North Africa and
had shifted fighter and bomber units down to Sicily and Tunisia to meet us; it was air war on of course a smaller scale,
but more equal terms, than we were to encounter afterwards.

The terms were not always equal in the first months, either.
A serious effort on the part of the Luftwaffe had done great
damage to the ports of Bône and Philippeville on the Mediterranean, and Algiers had received some intermittent atten
tion as well. Most of this was done at night, but in those days
the Luftwaffe was not afraid of day bombing either, and some
of our fields were repeatedly visited. A lively respect for Ju-88
and Me-109 (particularly, of course, for the latter) had grown
up in the brief weeks of our African experience, and had engendered a tendency toward rumor and over-estimating the
enemy. When I got into the B-17 at Casablanca to fly up to
Constantine, a pilot on the field told me that I would find that
city a wreck. "Jerry bombed the bejeezus out of it yesterday,"
he said. Where he got this I never knew, for Constantine was
never bombed at any time; such latrine rumors, in an air age,
can spread over a whole continent in two or three days.

The XII Bomber Command had its headquarters in the
classical museum on the hill at Constantine, the last prefec-
ture of Algeria on the Tunisian frontier. The city was picturesque to a degree, on its high hill surrounded on three sides
by a deep ravine—what we would call a canyon—and no less
than four natural bridges or archways of stone to connect it
with the surrounding plateau. The ancient kings of Numidia
had no doubt found this admirable for purposes of defense;

we found it admirable to behold at first, but the unending slopes and steps of the town soon exhausted our esthetic pleasure, and the usual American comment was, "Why in hell did they build the town here?" The staff was quartered in a hotel which at times had hot water but which otherwise was as cold as any airfield, and the town's population (normally about a hundred thousand, but much swollen by war refugees) was not only cold but increasingly hungry. The breakdown of transport produced such anomalies as the rotting of great quantities of oranges in this area while others did without any fruit; the fertile plain of Philippeville, teeming with food, could not even get its produce into the city in any quantity. We had the usual delicate intimations from practically all the official French that practically all the others had been too friendly with the German Armistice Commission; the word "traitor," so seldom used in other countries, was bandied about. My duties, aside from dealing with the French and British authorities, consisted in developing what target information I could from French sources to supplement what we already had; and in the course of them I encountered an engineer of the Ponts et Chaussées who—for reasons into which I did not inquire—had a partially heated apartment and an extra room. For the rest of my stay in Constantine I dwelt under the hospitable roof of M. and Mme. Bargoni, hard by the museum which was our headquarters, and again I discovered that it was impossible to repay them in any way for the kindness they showed me. This amiable young couple had a farm near the Philippeville dam and sometimes had treasures of lamb and water cress, butter and wine, brought up from there; on such occasions they would ask their aging colonel —now already surfeited with spam—to lunch or dinner, and thus I hope laid up merit in their specific heaven, since they would take no recompense on earth.

The "chain of command," as we call it, had a few knots in

it just then; we were in the midst of one of our reorganizations, and it was not yet sure just what was to come out of it. Most of the higher staffs were in Algiers, with our Bomber Command in Constantine and the Fighter Command at Tebessa as the most forward elements. Strictly speaking, we had nothing to do with the Fighter Command, and I might have seen nothing of it had it not been for the arrival of the Lafayette Escadrille. General Cannon had a certain responsibility for this escadrille, which he had equipped and sent forward from Casablanca, and when it was assigned to the field at Télepte I went down there to see what I could do to ease its transition into American service.

Stories about the field at Télepte had been drifting across the other fields of Africa for almost a month now. They were mostly wild stories of guerrilla warfare, never very specific, in which Colonel Raff and his paratroopers, Phil Cochran and his P-40's, Colonel Momyer and his 33rd Fighter Group, were all involved without a precise separation of their roles or indeed much idea of what they were doing. We knew that Télepte was "rugged," and that this was "the real war," but beyond that, and the obvious crystallization of a legend which would go on for a long time, not many of us knew how things were going down Gafsa way. We were aware that the ground forces in the area were exiguous in the extreme (Raff's parachute cowboys were about the sum total in January) and that the Germans were feeling out the ground, dropping marauders with parachutes, sending out little penetrations here and there; but of the actual Wild West quality of the thing we could form no adequate notion in the atmosphere of a headquarters. Indeed I think it takes a special effort of the imagination to see the quality of any action, even the most orthodox, in the prim typewritten lines of a regulation military report; but from Télepte, of course, even these aids were lacking.

I got down to Tebessa on the daily courier which carried

the mail, arriving, as it happened, just in time for the evening air raid by Ju-88's. General Craig ("Pinky" to the Air Corps) had his quarters and headquarters in a farmhouse outside the ancient walled town. This was the Fighter Command, where cases boldly labeled "Fragmentation Bombs" served as desks and chairs, and bedding-rolls were stacked up in the corridors. There were field telephones and at least one or two type-writers, but otherwise nothing looked weighty or permanent, and for the first time I had the sensation of being somewhere in the approaches to a "front," a place where the enemy was near and threatening. Craig told me he expected the Lafayette Escadrille to fly in from Algiers at almost any time, and introduced me to Momyer and Cochran, who had arrived a short time before to make a report.

Momyer I had met in the holy of holies in Washington, the intelligence room of the special headquarters of Torch. He had been young, intent and worried, having just learned the plan under which he was to be catapulted off an improvised carrier as commander of our only fighter group. (It did sound like the most foolhardy of plans, coldly stated.) Now he seemed much older, a little tired, still worried, and had withdrawn behind thick curtains of reserve, protected by a pipe which seldom got far away from his mouth and thus seemed to obviate the necessity for much speech. At twenty-seven, handsome, brave and experienced (he had been also in the Egyptian desert) he was already one of the most notable of our fighter pilots; he was to win many ribbons of the allied nations before his combat duty was over; his success as a group commander carried on through the Sicilian and Italian campaigns. At this moment, and during the whole period at Télepte, he was contending with a phenomenon which was nobody's fault except, perhaps, that of nature itself. His deputy commander —to borrow a term from higher echelons—was Phil Cochran, whose extraordinary personality and talent attracted so much attention that it sometimes worked an injustice upon the commander.

This was the first time I had seen Cochran: a short, cocky figure in fleece-lined flying jacket, unshaven and rather belligerent, with a shock of prematurely graying hair and uneven teeth. He was about thirty-three then, I think, but looked older or younger, depending upon circumstances. Afterwards in Washington I was astonished to see him young and small; at Télepte I saw him ageless and sizeless, a kind of electrical disturbance in human form but without any of the defined human attributes. He dominated his world down there—say from Tebessa onwards—like a trainer in a stable, and it was strange to see him afterwards under other conditions returning to the norm. In his own area, the wild lands where he was king, he was without self-consciousness or afterthought. His talk poured out in a sparkling flood, voluminous and bright at once, or dried up to prolonged silence, just as he pleased; he slept and ate as he pleased (once I saw him go without food for a day, through unwillingness to be bored by it) and his clothes, appearance, manners, language and discipline were whatever conditions, whim or hazard determined, without reference to army regulations or customs. His concentration upon the problems of his field, his aircraft, his area of patrol, his "kids," was quite exceptional. It was a physical wrench for him to take his mind away from them long enough to think of anything else, and you could see the movement into a new world when this occurred, as was seldom. There was so much strut and dash and instinctive romantic style about Cochran that the first impulse of almost any observer was to distrust its authenticity. Such a character must have been composed, you felt, and although its effect was great its intent was dubious. Only under the pressure of events, in the contingencies of life and death, quick decisions, resolved and enacted sacrifice, did this *panache* take its right place as the simple external manifestation of an electromagnetic reality, the temperament of a born combat leader. When you saw Cochran surrounded by the adoration of the fighter pilots and the obedience of everybody in the area—including many men, British, French and Americans, who in no sense came under his command—you recognized the existence of a special self-imposing mechanism of leadership independent of any effort or intention, a kind of natural force manifesting itself through a cocky little pilot from Erie, Pa. The truth of the matter was that Cochran had no official status in the 33rd Fighter Group; there was no such thing as a "deputy commander," and he was not operations officer (S-3); nor was he a squadron commander. His story had been as peculiar as his present status. He had formed a celebrated fighter squadron at Groton—the squadron which afterwards grew into the 57th Fighter Group and went to Egypt under the command of Art Salisbury and piled up a tremendous record. Cochran, Salisbury and "Little John" Alison had been three musketeers of the P-40 in those days, determined to fight and win the war together. Salisbury had ended up in Egypt, Alison in China and Russia, Cochran here.[1] An illness on Cochran's part had removed him from circulation just as the group commands were being settled for overseas duty, and he was called to Washington by "Uncle Joe" (General Cannon) only a very short time before we set sail for Africa. Uncle Joe asked him if he could take an ungrateful and difficult job, the command of a makeshift squadron of half-trained pilots whom he would have to lick into shape after they were landed in Africa, to be used as replacements. Phil said yes, and thus acquired the so-called "joker" squadron of the 33rd Fighter Group, which he trained with feverish zeal at Rabat for a few weeks after our landing. He took parts of it up forward to Télepte when the field there

---

[1] Cochran and Alison worked together in Burma in 1944, in "Cochran's Air Commandos" under Wingate.

200

was occupied on December 9th or 10th, but the main reliance in those earliest days was upon the 58th squadron, the only one which had its full strength there. Meanwhile the group commander (Momyer) had been busy elsewhere, trying to get his group together, and by the time he took command at Télepte Phil had already, in some mysterious way, infected the very ground of the place with the delusion that it belonged to him. His uncertain status was an advantage in one way because it enabled him to do everything, or a little of everything, and there was no problem of operations, intelligence, administration or supply into which he did not stick his snub Irish nose and quick, commanding wit. His command was what is called "a natural"—there was no reason for it, no basis for it, but it existed as if by physical law and it never would have occurred to anybody to question it. In the patrols of the wild country, the scanty fighter protection which it was possible to give ground patrols or bodies of troops, the exploration of roads and the harassing of German ground communications, Phil had in a very few weeks built up a technique not only for himself but had imparted it to all the pilots on the field, so that the game of cops and robbers could be played with equal fury by all hands.

But in referring to it as a game I do not mean to suggest that it was ever taken lightly. The competitive spirit between squadrons and between the individual pilots was high, and there was a good deal of the natural bravado of extreme youth; but there was no mawkish nonsense about death. Death was a hard, cruel, disgusting reality, and they saw it very often, inflicted it sometimes, lived under the permanent likelihood of having it inflicted upon them. The German fighter strength in Tunisia, at least in this wild lower part where there was no real front, was a variable quantity, and when you went out in the morning you never knew if you were going to be jumped by none or one or twelve. Death and wounds were real, and

I never heard any heroical balderdash about them. This was war (and life) reduced to extremely simple terms. The boys lived two-by-two in holes in the ground, with their pup-tents over them—holes which they of course dug for themselves when they were not flying—and ate twice a day, usually spam and British tea. There was no town, there were no diversions of any sort, no buildings on the field, no movies, none of the innumerable mitigating arrangements which were afterwards contrived for them in Italy and France. It was bitter cold at night and none too warm in the daytime on the great Tunisian plain. Supplies of every kind were low because ammunition and gasoline took up the available transport. Phil Cochran had lately introduced the novelty of what was called "skip bombing," and his use of the P-40 was substantially that which in later stages became universal with that aircraft—in other words, he made it a fighter-bomber. He was a lone ranger himself, and had "stooged around" over this part of Tunisia so much that he was able to give profuse instruction on the terrain, and actually to correct the maps which—in Africa— were never very scientific at best, and could not, even if they had been good, keep up with the changing sands and waters of an unstable physiography.

Some of this Phil disclosed in flashes as he and I and Momyer sped down the way from Tebessa. The wintry plain was empty and wide under the many colors of the late afternoon sky; the road climbed to the Pass of Dernaia, which, with the Kasserine Pass a little farther north, pierced the mountain range and channeled all traffic to Tunisia. When we got through the Dernaia Pass both Cochran and Momyer gave frequent glances up into the sky and drove at full speed; this road had been a favorite resort for wandering Messerschmitts in search of something to subject to their machine guns. I had had time, the night before, to look at the Byzantine wall of Tebessa, with the Roman arch of Caracalla set into it, and even to walk

202

around the basilica and forum; when I mentioned these monuments I discovered that neither Momyer nor Cochran had ever had time to look at them. "We come up to Tebessa as seldom as possible," Cochran explained, "and say our piece and get to hell out again." They had the single-mindedness which comes of the awareness of life and death poised, delicately poised at every moment of the day and night, ready to drop decisively for friend or foe, and along with this the slight, unconscious resentment of interests or desires at variance with it.

The country looked like the American West in, say, certain areas of Montana or Wyoming, except for a greater apparent aridity and a tendency to dribble off into Arizona or New Mexico at the edges. Some of the boys from Western Texas, as I was to learn later, considered it to be like their own country with all favorable aspects removed. It was neither outright desert nor arable country, but a border plain between the two, with an aridity probably due originally to man's extravagance (deforestation and the like) and redeemable by man's ingenuity and labor whenever these might become available. Straight down the Tebessa-Télepte road we went (I think it is Route Nationale No. 12) and after something under an hour's drive found ourselves at the crossroads where this highway met the Kasserine-Gafsa road. A detachment of French engineers from one of the Tunisian commands had some long, low barracks on one side of the crossroads (southwest); on the other side, embraced between the two highways, was the huge plain of the Télepte airfield. Cochran was a great stickler for dispersal, as all air commanders are in times of difficulty, and the squadrons were spread out over an enormous area, their foxholes and bigger dugouts carefully disguised, their aircraft scattered and concealed. Part of a whole group of P-39's had been flown in and tucked away on the slopes of a southern hill beyond the field in such a way that they could not be seen from the air, and it was Cochran's hope to spring them as a surprise

203

on the enemy some day when he was least expecting it. There were some A-20's at the extreme northern end of the field (two squadrons, I think), and these also accepted the unconventional but extremely effective command of Cochran, who had no shadow of legal right to exercise it over them. The main strength and importance of the field lay in its P-40's, of which one full squadron, the 58th, was on the near (western) side of the field, and another, the 59th, had just flown in and had dug its holes on the southeastern extremity. (The 60th squadron at this time was not on the field, having been moved back to Youks.) This extreme dispersal gave an enormous perimeter, which would have been difficult to defend against ground attack, but it had been adopted because the chief danger came from the air. When I remembered the crowded fields in the Philippines and Hawaii just before Pearl Harbor this arrangement seemed to me very good.

It was dusk when we arrived, a tawny, lingering dusk with elements of the sunset still splashed through it, and the work of the field was over for the day. Cochran told me I might as well put my bedding-roll on the floor of his dugout. "The Château Cochran," he said, "is about the best hotel on the field." It had just been completed and was about as good a structure as you would ever see of its kind. On the outside nothing was visible but a sandy hillock with tufts of desert scrub, a camouflage upon which the inmates worked at intervals during the next few days; but inside it had two rooms, a wooden floor (great luxury), a stove, two telephones and electric lights. The main room was used for operations and intelligence during the day. It had a long table at one side and some big maps on the wall. At night its wooden floor accommodated the bedding-rolls of a number of inmates—Bob Wiley, the intelligence officer, A. J. Liebling of the *New Yorker*, who was to write a series of articles on the field, Hal Norgaard of the Associated Press, Bill Lamb, the assistant intelligence officer, myself and a floating population which varied from day to day. In the inner room there were actually cots for Cochran and some others. Momyer had a dugout of his own a little farther down toward the field, but I doubt if his or any other was quite so complete as this. The château owed its existence to the work of everybody who lived in it, but the moving spirit was Léon Capelan, the French liaison officer, a thin, bright, indefatigable creature whose talents at scrounging, building, cooking, arranging and combining would have been hard to equal anywhere. Léon, a lieutenant in the French artillery, was technically stationed at Kasserine, I believe, but he spent a great deal of his time in the Château Cochran or in motion between it and the French army headquarters up the Tebessa road; his job was to maintain the liaison between General Juin, who commanded in this area, and the Télepte field which had the only aircraft in Southern Tunisia.

Léon was on hand for our arrival and was determined to make an occasion because the Lafayette Escadrille had just arrived on the field. He had put them up for the night in the French engineers' barracks at the crossroads, but it was his idea that their advent should be signalized by a really outstanding dinner in Cochran's dugout. He had amassed the materials for this dinner from all over the countryside—a chicken, some wine, some this and that, all things difficult to find—and combined them with army rations in a succulent mess cooked on the stove in the corner. The French aviators arrived in time for the great meal—not the whole escadrille, but its commander, Kostia Rozanoff, with his deputy Stellin and Jacques de Montravel—and proceeded to give their escadrille toast in the red Tunisian wine.

The dugout was, of course, packed by this time, and it was none too commodious at the best of times. We sat where we could and consumed Léon's remarkable meal, while Rozanoff and his officers made the acquaintance of Momyer, Cochran and the rest. Kostia Rozanoff was of Russian origin but seemed as thoroughly French as *moules marinières,* with a vocabulary as rich and racy in its own idiom as Cochran's was in ours. General Cannon had found him in command of the "Sioux," the Lafayette Escadrille, with its sister escadrille called La Cigogne, The Stork (the two together forming the French Fighter Group 2/5). Stellin, his deputy, had been air attaché in Berlin and spoke excellent English and German, had a talent for mimicry and (like most of the pilots) a low opinion of the high-ranking French officers of the moment; this, as they were nearly all to be changed with the entry of de Gaulle into power, presumably did him no harm. Jacques de Montravel was one of the best of the young pilots and was known to most of the high officers in the Western Task Force as the husband of a very attractive wife—the center of any dinner party for our generals in the early days. (The Comtesse de Montravel was so "like an American girl," they all thought.) This was the trio in charge of our first experiment in the use of a French force in an American unit. The escadrille had been given thirteen P-40's—lifted from the 59th squadron of this very group, the 33rd—and sent to the front without any other equipment, with not enough ground crews to ensure their own maintenance or ordinary army housekeeping, and without means of ground transport. Under the circumstances, in spite of the air of cordial welcome in the smoke-filled dugout, it was already apparent on that first night that there would be difficulties. For one thing, the French were nearly all past the age which we considered suitable for fighter pilots, and their ideas were of a very classical nature—*la chasse pure,* with certain distinct acrobatic maneuvers to be executed in combat with the enemy—which did not at all fit in with the techniques we had found necessary with the P-40. Anybody who tried to do *la chasse pure* in a P-40 against an Me-109 was bound to end badly, as Cochran tried to explain to them. One had the impression, listening to the talk that first night, that they would find it awkward to accommodate themselves to our ways: the notion of carrying a bomb on a fighter plane, for example, seemed almost to shock them, and they did not appear—in spite of all the politeness—to be sufficiently attentive to Cochran's ideas, which, after all, had been formed in the daily combat experience of this aircraft in this present situation. *La chasse pure*, the dazzling coloratura of the air, was what they had all been trained for, and there was an ominous undertow of certainty that until they had tried it against the much greater virtuosity of the Messerschmitt they would not learn how to fight a P-40 properly.

In the morning I found that this awkwardness at adjustment was going to apply to a number of other things as well. They had slept (rather uncomfortably, I believe) with makeshift arrangements at the French barracks. The Americans all slept in holes on the field, because Cochran had early discovered that the French barracks up on the road made an easy target for the German airmen. I had occupied one corner of the larger room in the Château Cochran and slept well, thanks to an air mattress which was my chief treasure for the first year and a half of my service. It was the only air mattress my wife had been able to find in Washington before the expedition sailed, and it was an oddity indeed to look at, one side bright green and the other bright orange; it was, in fact, something intended for sport on the ocean wave, a sort of surf-riding mattress; but so long as I had it I was the envy of all, for with this object in the bedding-roll it was possible to sleep comfortably anywhere, in any ditch or corner.

When I went to see the escadrille in the morning I had certain instructions from Cochran to carry out. They were going to have to dig in somewhere, and the sooner the better; they were going to have to make their housekeeping arrangements somehow, as best they could; in another day or so they would

207

be expected to take their part in the daily missions, the defense of the field and all the rest. Rozanoff and the others greeted this with good-natured surprise. I think it had really never occurred to them, "star" pilots of *la chasse pure,* used to the conditions of metropolitan France and of comfortable Morocco, that they would ever be asked to use a pick and shovel. I explained to them that our pilots had dug their own holes in the ground, and that in these conditions we did not attach much importance to rank. The point was abundantly proved when I took the French officers to breakfast at a field kitchen on the plain (the 58th squadron's mess) where they stood in line with their mess-kits with our G.I.'s and found that they survived the experience very well.

That afternoon I was prospecting down the field with Rozanoff, Stellin, Villasèque ("Boa," they called him—a long, dark, growling youth who commanded the Lafayette Escadrille itself and was one of their best) and the others. We visited some of the dugouts to see how they were contrived for comfort and efficiency. Rozanoff would have to have one with a telephone in it for his command post, and I was trying to get them used to the idea of shifting for themselves. There was a bulldozer on the field—just one—and I had tried in vain during the morning to run down the engineering officer who had charge of it so as to lend it to the French. We had come out of one dugout and were looking for another when a flight of eight Ju-88's appeared from the northwest or southwest (vaguely from the sun) and bombed the field. They had an escort of Me-109's and swept down upon us before we had any notion that they were there. The first news of their advent was provided by the exploding bombs and the rattle of machine-gun fire. We scattered, of course, and the plain looked singularly flat and naked as we scrambled for cover. I got behind a big truck and saw what I did see from that rather ill-advised shelter, which was in itself often a target for the Me-109's.

The protection of the field was entrusted to four planes, according to a system Cochran had adopted: two from the 58th squadron were in the air, patrolling, when the attack came, and two from the 59th were alerted on the ground, ready to take off. The 59th squadron was the one which had only reached the front a few days before, and, having surrendered thirteen of its aircraft to the Lafayette group, it only had five aircraft operational on this afternoon. Two boys who had never been in combat before (Lieutenants Scholl and Raddin of the 59th) shot down a Ju-88 each, flying straight into the enemy formation. A third Ju-88 was shot down by a pilot of the 58th (Lieutenant Bounds). The bombs fell on the runway and alongside; one A-20 down at the northern end of the field, half dismantled for the mechanics to work on it, was burned up; nobody was injured on the ground. The thunder and lightning lasted only a few minutes, of course, and columns of smoke just beyond the field in the Kasserine direction showed where the Ju-88's had gone down.

General Juin wanted some air cover the next morning for a movement of his troops. The Germans had inexplicably evacuated a valley and some hills at Djebel Bouda Boud and he was going to occupy them with his Moroccan riflemen. He asked for three hours' cover but the shortage of planes was such that he could only be given an hour and a half—the first forty-five minutes by Cochran and some pilots of the 58th, the next forty-five minutes by Villasèque and five other French pilots. The task of finding transport for the Frenchmen and getting them to their planes, after a hasty and inadequate breakfast, was much more onerous than it sounds; they were very inept at the scrounging business we found necessary under these conditions, and besides there were no more than two or three of them who could speak or understand English. Villasèque, for example, did not know a word. They got off and back without mishap, executed their mission of cover for the ground troops and saw nothing at all except some shells bursting on the hillside beneath them. While they were gone the other airmen—marshaled by their chaplain, the Padre, one of the most active and cheerful little men you would meet anywhere —started the unaccustomed task of digging in the earth at the extreme south end of the field, where Cochran's dispersal plan placed them. After roaming from one end to the other of the immense plain I found the engineering officer, who promised the loan of a bull-dozer for the next day but not now. There was nothing on the field in more constant demand than that bull-dozer. For the moment my French friends were obliged to begin their digging career with no better aids than two picks and three or four shovels; one of the picks broke almost at once, and the pilots and mechanics—willing enough now that they understood the situation—stood about and awaited their turn at the available tools.

The problem was virtually insoluble and was, in fact, not satisfactorily dealt with until some months later when the whole 2/5 Group, three escadrilles including the Lafayette, was brought back to Morocco and completely outfitted with the T.B.A. (table of basic allowances) of an American unit. As Rozanoff stood on the field at Télepte in January he had fifty men for a theoretical thirteen planes; one of his planes had been left at Maison Blanche (the Algiers field) with engine trouble, and two others had turned back on their way to Tunisia under the same pretext. (It was only afterwards that we learned how these two pilots, longing for home, had quite simply flown to France in their P-40's and had been received as heroes by the Vichy authorities.) Ten planes had flown in to Télepte, therefore, and Rozanoff spent hours every day trying to find out on the field telephone what had happened to his other three. But even for the ten P-40's he had, his fifty men were inadequate. He had no communications people, none for supply, only four armament men (Americans used two to a plane) and nobody to do any of the innumerable varieties of work to keep up half a squadron. The only way his planes could be maintained properly was by asking the 59th squadron—to whom they belonged, from whom they had been taken—to care for them. This was, of course, adding insult to injury. The guns on the P-40's Rozanoff had had not been cleaned since the Americans had last cleaned them at Casablanca a week before. And with all this, there were no jeeps or trucks or any form of transport available for the French. The base headquarters colonel, who was establishing himself also in the red barracks of the French engineers, allowed them to use a Chevrolet car, a civilian car unsuited to the rough going on that trackless field. This was, intermittently, their means of locomotion, and at other times they walked. When the patrols and alerts and missions began, with the runway and mess and quarters all at great distances from each other, this was an inhuman *corvée* for anybody, and the wonder was that they got anything done even approximately on time.

That evening, as we were digesting this situation as philosophically as we could, Cochran gave us a dazzling exhibition of that sixth sense or electronic gland which contributed so mightily to his legend. "The Germans will come over just after dark tonight," he said. He had his reasons for thinking so, I have no doubt—perhaps they had tried everything else; perhaps they were working through the hours; in any case I am certain that Cochran's "hunches," as he called them, often were based upon a half-conscious but quite reasonable perception of how the enemy was working. He took a patrol up at a later hour than was usual for the P-40's—the regular sunset patrol, only later than customary—and kept them up until it had grown quite dark. At this point, just when the dusk had thickened into night, the Germans arrived.

It was a hair-raising engagement of which we could, naturally, see nothing at all from the ground. Cochran's patrol apparently intercepted the Ju-88's somewhere east of the field; some got through and some did not; bombs fell helter-skelter, not properly aimed and most of them not on the field at all. After the furious little battle was over there arose a new problem: how to get the P-40's down again. There were a couple of flare-pots put out on the runway and some tracer bullets from anti-aircraft were used to outline the field, but in the complete darkness of the early night it was not easy for the young pilots, most of whom were without much experience; every landing was a breathless affair. One pilot stayed up for a long time and finally confessed himself lost in the dark. I was at the control by then (ground-to-air radio was in a hole near the runway) and heard the struggle to get the pilot down. Finally Cochran, who had brought his plane in first, took off again to guide the new pilot home. Chrisman, commander of the 58th squadron, was on the radio and his voice was calm, reassuring, full of confidence. "Lieutenant, Lieutenant Thomas," he said, "you'll see a P-40 right in front of you in a minute. That'll be Major Cochran. He knows this field pretty well. You just follow him in and you'll be all right." Cochran made a long detour to the south, down Gafsa way, it seemed, before he could get the lost boy firmly attached to his tail so as to lead him in for the landing.

When they all gathered around the control in the darkness, with an occasional flashlight going on and then instantly dimmed by some angry command, the air was full of electricity. All talked at once, but dominating the babel was Cochran's excited voice, his language defying transcription, his temperament going off in all directions like a catherine-wheel. He had abundantly justified his hunch: two Ju-88's, so far as we could make out, had been shot down. Phil was sure he had shot down one himself, but he would not claim it because he had no means of proving it without a search of the whole plain in the morning. This colloquy in the darkness among a handful of pilots had all the excitement of a mob scene at a moment of crisis—the aftermath of successful fighting of an unprecedented order, which left even the participants amazed to be alive. When Joe Liebling and I walked back to the dugout we agreed that this was a pretty startling airfield.

On the next day (the 14th) there was only one German attack, at 7:30 in the morning. It consisted of about seven Me-109's who strafed the field, but were engaged by the dawn patrol coming and going. No planes were lost by either side, but the necessity for maintaining patrols at all hours from first to last light was wearing on both pilots and ships; with the P-39's still concealed and inactive, the field was running short of operational machines. Momyer and Cochran therefore decided to use the French for defense of the field on the following morning.

On that night I slept in the operations dugout, abandoning my bed-roll and enviable mattress, and have seldom been colder in my life. The object was partly to be sure of the escadrille's schedule in the early morning and partly so as to be able to get the French telephone messages which warned of approaching Germans. The French outposts up the valley, at Kasserine and beyond, warned us when they could—when the telephone worked—but since nobody knew French there was a good deal of misunderstanding. Before dawn Rozanoff came cursing and growling into the tent, his breath steaming in front of him, and took the ground-to-air radio for the dawn patrol. At 7:30 he turned it over to me, as he was to take up the next patrol and had to get into flying clothes. At a few minutes before 8 o'clock the French telephone (from Sidi Bou Zid, I think) announced the approach of a formation of Messerschmitts, and I jumped from the operations dugout to the control "tower," a hole in the ground in front of it, to warn the six French planes then in the air. Rozanoff's patrol was just climbing and the dawn patrol was just getting ready to come down. At this precise moment the generator, which was buried a little nearer the runway, elected to go off; there was no means of warning the escadrille. I crouched there in the round hole where the VHF (very high frequency, ground to air) telephone was installed and watched the struggle helplessly, making an occasional attempt to use the radio on the off chance that the generator might have gone on again. Ten Messerschmitts came in to the attack, ran rings around the French, peppered them and the field with machine-gun fire, and swept away again with their usual virtuosity. One of the P-40's, piloted by Sergeant Raymond Delannoy, was shot down east of the field and went deep into the earth with a terrible thud. Another, with Lieutenant Hébrard as pilot, made a crash landing right in front of us with a fuselage and wings that seemed to be all lacework. A third French P-40 was badly shot up and had to crash land; it, too, was a total or almost total loss. The pilot of this one, Sergeant Lestume, was taken out with a wound in his head and was rushed off to Tebessa at once.

Thus, by 8:15 in the morning, having started with eight of their ten planes operational, my French friends only had five left—which was not enough to ensure the protection of the field. Cochran's system called for so many in the air and so many on alert; today it was two each. It was necessary to assign planes from the 58th squadron for the next tours of duty, and from the 59th afterwards, to keep up the schedule. At 11:15 of this harassed morning a formation of seven or eight Messerschmitts attacked while there were two P-40's of the escadrille and two of the 58th in the air. By this time, having struggled in vain with the French pilots on the VHF and found it an almost impossible task—they all talked so loud and so fast—I had relinquished the control to their chaplain, "Padre" Bougeron, who was wild with excitement over the battle. A loss which saddened the whole field came in this brief clash: Lieutenant Watkins, "Horse" Watkins of the 58th, one of the best, was badly damaged by an Me-109 and had to jump. His plane crashed on the north side of the field. There was a heavy wind and when he landed his parachute dragged him. From all over the field we watched this in horror. We were told afterwards that he was dead before he landed, and we hoped so. The Messerschmitts in this action, being two to one, had everything their own way and it was impossible to watch their performance without wondering—as Cochran said—"whose air" this was. A sinking feeling was beginning to come over some of us: there were not enough aircraft here to protect the field for long against such odds.

In the middle of the day—wind of these events having reached all the higher headquarters—it so happened that about five generals visited the field, including General Doolittle, Commander of the Twelfth Air Force to which we all belonged. He came in a Spitfire; some others came in a transport plane which had, we all felt, little or no business in these regions; General Craig came in a jeep. So many stars had never been seen in one small dugout in Tunisia before. But as chance would have it they missed all the attacks, arriving after the second and leaving before the third. I believe their visit was, on the whole, encouraging, because they promised reinforcements.

The role of luck in these matters was never demonstrated more conclusively than in the case of those C-47's which came in that day. There were three or four of them, bringing mail, spare parts and a passenger or two. They came lumbering in over the mountains with their usual air of leisurely confidence, just as if this was healthy country for the unarmed. One of them was actually on the field, pulled up beside the runway, during the attack that took place at 11:15, and in spite of the sprinkling of machine-gun fire it was not scratched. This one took off immediately afterwards, with Joe Liebling and Hal Norgaard as passengers back to Algiers; but no sooner had it been removed when two or three more came in. They, too, took off in another hour or so, and not one of them was any the worse for their visit. If they had come in a little later or a little earlier their chances of survival would not have been great.

The gloom of the day was to be lifted dramatically before long, but during those mid-day hours it was thick over all spirits. To be subjected to repeated attack by superior force is not an experience Americans suffered much anywhere in this war after the initial surprises of the Japanese attack; above all it did not come to many airfields. Life at Télepte was made arduous enough by climate, by supply difficulties, by shortages of men and equipment, but all this could have been easily enough overcome if there had been any assurance that the air over the field could be defended. It was this—the sense of being too far forward with too little force; of having nothing to anticipate but an endless series of such attacks in superior numbers—that made some moments on this field unlike those on any other in Africa or Europe. It made us think of what we had heard of Guadalcanal, or, even earlier, of the desperate withdrawing action in the Philippines and the Dutch Indies.

That afternoon at 2:35 when I answered the French telephone in the operations dugout I learned that a formation of Ju-88's was approaching from the east to bomb the field. The warning was specific; I think it even said how many aircraft, bombers and fighters. There was plenty of time for the alert planes to get up and for those already on patrol to choose an altitude and wait for the attack. There was, in fact, so much time that after ten minutes had passed most of us on the ground were inclined to think that this was a false alarm—that the formation was bound elsewhere or that the French observation had been mistaken. But at 2:50 exactly, fifteen

216

minutes after the French warning had come through, the Germans appeared in the west—right in the sun—and came down out of it, crossing the field diagonally from south-of-west to north-of-east in an absolutely regular bomb run at medium altitude. There were ten of them, with an escort which remained high in the sun—scarcely to be seen—and the air battle was immediately engaged as they thundered down upon us; in their escape they were closely pursued by the P-40's; we saw one after the other go down in the valley beyond the field.

So much was going on in those few minutes that it was impossible for us on the ground to be sure of anything at first. The thing had to be pieced together, the wreckage examined, the survivors questioned; it was not until well on during the next afternoon that we got all the evidence together and could make out just what had happened. There were four planes on patrol when the alert was given: two Frenchmen and two Americans of the 59th squadron. Two alert planes from the 59th took off immediately and were ready on the west of the field when the attack came. The Frenchmen, Lieutenants Hébrard and Tremolay, climbed into the sun together to await the attack and then found the Ju-88's suddenly in front of them. Each picked a Junkers and pursued it, and neither was aware that there were enemy fighters behind them still higher in the sun. The escort seems to have emptied its lead into Lieutenant Tremolay's plane and then disappeared without attempting to protect the bombers any further. This escort—which we on the ground of course assumed to be Me-109's—stayed so far away, and so high, that the German survivors afterwards swore they had not been there at all. They were Italian fighter planes, Macchi, which the Ju-88's had picked up at Gabès on the way in to us. Tremolay kept after his Ju-88 and claimed to have damaged it so badly that it must have crashed afterwards; he then made a belly landing with a plane full of holes, but was himself untouched. The other

217

Frenchman, Hébrard, pursued his Ju-88 until he saw it crash in the valley beyond the field.

Captain Boone of the 59th—"Dan'l" Boone, they called him; stark new to combat—saw two Ju-88's shot down before he could get in close enough to shoot. He closed in after the bomb run and poured his fire into the tail of one Junkers which then crashed into another; the two went down in flames in front of him. Dan'l Boone continued his pursuit toward the northeast as long as he had any ammunition and in so doing shot down two more Ju-88's—both confirmed; the wrecks were found. The commander of the 59th, Major Hubbard, shot down two Ju-88's, one from the rear and one from the side. Two lieutenants from the same squadron (all new to combat), Smith and Beggs, shot down one Ju-88 each. The roar and thud of the falling Germans was something we could all vouch for, but we had no means of knowing just how many, or where, in the excitement of the afternoon.

It was hours before any of us could credit this extraordinary performance even though we had seen it. At first Momyer and Cochran, like everybody else, thought it certain that the boys must be claiming the same victories two or three times over, as so often happens—three pilots might have been shooting at the same aircraft; in the wild speed and fury of the combat no human being could be quite sure. But as the afternoon and evening wore on the telephone began to ring from outposts of the French, from the British anti-aircraft people, from American posts, all up the valley to Kasserine and beyond. As we counted up these reports it appeared that all ten of the Ju-88's had been destroyed. There was one unaccounted for late in the evening, when a call came through to say that it had been seen to fall inside enemy lines beyond Hadjeb el-Aioun. This could not be officially credited, of course, but it seemed to me the next day after I had talked to the French G-2 officers at Kasserine, who had the best information from the Arabs up and down the countryside, and who had immediately questioned the German survivors, that in all probability the boys' claims were literally correct and that they had, in fact, shot down every one of the German aircraft, even though only eight or nine might go on the official record.

It was a weird evening in the dugout, pilots coming and going, asserting with vehemence their version of events, comparing notes, disputing over trifles. The most experienced of our P-40 leaders, Momyer and Cochran, had watched the battle from the ground at a great pitch of anger against Fate because they were not participants, and this may perhaps have made an unconscious contribution toward their effort to be moderate in assessing the victory. In the end they had to give in and concede that in all probability all claims were correct, even the most astonishing one of all, which was that of Dan'l Boone.

I saw Dan'l along about dusk of that day, when he was brought into the Château Cochran by his squadron commander, Major Hubbard. Dan'l was a thin-faced lad with a slight stoop and a pointed chin and nose which, under his peaked flight cap, made him look for all the world like a trapper in the Western woods of a hundred years or more ago. His real name was Carman Boone, but his squadron had dubbed him Dan'l from the beginning; he was in fact a collateral descendant of Daniel Boone—in a straight line from the pioneer's brother—and came from Boone Mill, Virginia. He had never been in air battle before and he was fully aware that his claim to have destroyed four German bombers in a very few minutes was a startling one, but he was stubbornly unwilling to doubt the evidence of his own eyes: he had seen what he had seen. The story was compared in detail with those of other pilots and of ground observers and proved out very well; even so, perhaps it would not have been fully credited if it had not been for the messages that kept coming in by telephone, giving the exact situation of each Junkers wreck as it had fallen up the valley. There then appeared to be no way of refusing the boy credit for an astonishing achievement in his first action. Momyer removed his pipe for long enough to grin and speak. "Well, Captain Boone," he said, "it looks as if you'd really done it. One more and you're an ace." I could never forget Dan'l Boone's grin as he stooped to go out of the dugout. "One more and it's my ass," he said quietly, using the universal, conventionalized idiom for grim death.

In the morning Léon and I rose before dawn to go to the funeral of the French pilot, Raymond Delannoy, the first to be killed. The escadrille had rigged up an altar in a shed near the French engineers' barracks at the crossroads. The morning was bitter cold, with a knifelike wind sweeping down from the mountains, and the wait was long. Finally the Padre, Père Bougeron, hardly recognizable in his priestly vestments, declared himself ready and the coffin was brought in and placed before the altar. The terrible thing was the size of the coffin: it was a box small enough to have contained the remains of a small child. It was covered with the flags of the two Republics.

After that I walked across the field to the 59th squadron for breakfast. On the day before, as I had been scurrying down the runway to the area of the escadrille in order to give them some message, I had been hailed from a P-40 on the line. "Hi, Major," a voice said. I looked up and saw in one of the alert planes, all coiffed for combat, the face of young "Pinky" Johnson. Pinky was one of the pilots I had known in Casablanca, one of those who had been quartered above the Coup de Roulis, our favorite restaurant out on the shore not far from the airfield: one of those who had been most impatient at the "long wait" (a few weeks) before they could go to the front. On state occasions we had been known to sing "Carry me back to old Virginny" and other anthems in the Coup de Roulis. I asked Pinky how he liked Télepte and he said: "It's all right except this waiting on alert. It's all right in the air. This sitting here and waiting isn't. They could come in so fast that we wouldn't have a chance to get up." His squadron was dug in beyond the field to the southeast and he asked me why I didn't come over there for a meal. Without any clear idea of how far it was I said, "O.K., I'll be along for breakfast in the morning."

The walk was truly epic; after an hour or so I felt that I must be almost in the outskirts of Tunis. The dispersal and camouflage on this field—done with practically no equipment except the native ingenuity of our youth—were so successful that it was hardly possible to see the dugouts until you were on top of them. Sand and scrub had been used with artful simplicity to cover every hole, and the immense, undulant plain in the cold, bright morning looked like a desert. I followed a jeep track until it seemed to vanish and then turned by sheer hazard—because I had to turn somewhere—into a path over a low hill. Perhaps I was too abstracted to be very good at finding directions. The whole Télepte experience seemed to me to contain an echo of our past in this war and an earnest of our future, as if it occupied a precise point of balance in time in which all elements (past, present, future) were co-existing, a point never to be found again in the swift development, but never to be forgotten, either, so that its memory would pop up to illuminate events still undreamed of. The manner and moment of our victory were still very deep in the unknown, but after what I had seen of the youth which swept us onward I could have no doubt, no shadow of doubt, that it would be complete; that is, of course, remembering the industrial might which supported them from afar and must support them more fully as time passed. Who could defeat so many Dan'l Boones? I sat for a while on a hillock and looked up the valley to the northeast, where the Ju-88's had fallen, and did not much mind being lost in the desert, the semi-desert, the empty high-colored plain. Eventually I retraced my steps and made an-

221

other turning and, after perhaps two hours of this wandering, found myself in the midst of the 59th squadron.

Pinky had had his breakfast, having given me up for the day, but the mess was still operating and I could still have mine. Since there were but two meals a day, and duties (especially patrols and alerts) paid no respect to hours, the time for eating was made elastic. Pinky and some of the others—Walter Scholl, for instance, who shared his pup-tent—sat around and talked while I ate. The one subject of conversation to which everything returned was the astounding victory of the preceding afternoon; the same episodes were recounted over and over again. We wandered over to the squadron operations dugout after breakfast and sat on the ground outside it for a while, talking to Major Holliday, the intelligence officer (afterwards intelligence officer for the whole group). Dan'l Boone, who managed to be both radiant and bewildered in his realization of what had happened, came and joined us and told his story over again. He was hardly able to believe that he, Dan'l Boone of Boone Mill, Virginia, had done this amazing thing. Probably, like most young men—like Stephen Crane's soldier in *The Red Badge of Courage,* prototype of all such—he had doubted his own ability to face these grim alternatives and do what was expected of him until it had actually happened. A correspondent with a jeep (the United Press correspondent stationed with Colonel Raff at Fériana) rolled up and asked us if we would like to go to Kasserine and see the German prisoners who had been taken out of some of the Ju-88's. It was, in fact, part of my job to do so and I had intended to take the trip later in the day; Dan'l and I climbed onto the jeep.

Somewhere between the field and the village of Kasserine, up the long valley, one of the Ju-88 wrecks was visible in the sandy waste, surrounded by a crowd of Arabs. We got the jeep across the trackless plain—a job at which our jeeps were always an object of wonder—and found the German bomber. An

222

American sentry, harassed and uncertain of his powers, was trying to keep the Arabs away from the machine. There were so many of us on the jeep (five or six, perhaps) that we dispelled the crowd without difficulty and looked over the wreck, of which, in spite of burned-out engines, the fuselage seemed remarkably intact. Two survivors had been taken to the French hospital in Kasserine, the sentry said. We made our way back across the sand to the highway and headed for the village again.

Kasserine was a little Arab settlement with two or three modern French official buildings in it. It could have had a couple of hundred inhabitants, perhaps, but it was no metropolis. The picture of this little cluster of huts came irresistibly to mind when we listened to the B.B.C. a month or six weeks later: "The enemy are in the outskirts of Kasserine," or still later, "Our troops are in the outskirts of Kasserine." We made short work of the outskirts and went to the white hospital on the hill, a building the French had built two or three years before to house various offices as well as a ward or two. The French G-2 officer there (*Deuxième Bureau*, that is) showed me the results of his interrogations; he was an Alsatian with an ample knowledge both of the German language and of the Luftwaffe, and his work was good. He said one of the German survivors from yesterday was not fit to be questioned, but that there was one whose condition was not too serious.

This conversation, which occupied half an hour or more, took place in the shaded office of the G-2 officer. Meanwhile Dan'l Boone and the others had been wandering about on the dazzling little terraces of the building. Dan'l was a little nervous; as the moment approached, he did not think he would much like to talk to the prisoners. "If they're badly wounded, I'd rather not," he said. I told him there was no reason why he should if he didn't want to. I went into a small ward with the French G-2 officer. The only occupant of this room was the German airman whose condition was not serious; his head and arms were bandaged and he seemed to be asleep. "Let him sleep," I said. "I can speak to him later." I went on out and joined Dan'l on the terrace. "Well, then we can get back to the field," he said in obvious relief.

The French G-2 officer came out on the terrace after us. "The Austrian has wakened up," he said. "He wants to speak to the American pilot who shot him down." Dan'l was reluctant. "How do we know I shot him down?" he asked. "But if he wants to talk to me, all right."

We went into the room and the Austrian, whose face was clean and uninjured, smiled at us from the frame of his head bandages.

"Which is the American pilot who shot us down?" he asked. When I translated, Dan'l came forward rather unwillingly and stood beside the bed.

"Ask him where he was attacked," Dan'l said to me. "That is, from the rear or the side or where." The German airman answered in some detail: his plane had been attacked from the side and never from the rear. "That must be one Major Hubbard got, then," Dan'l said with obvious relief. "I didn't shoot any of them in the side, all from the rear."

Once this point had been established a brief, awkward conversation took place with me as interpreter. The enemy airman was the gunner-observer of his crew, an Austrian boy of 22 who had been fighting for sixteen months without leave, most of that time in Russia. He was from Kg 77, which (like Kg 76, the other Luftwaffe bombing unit with which we had mainly to deal) had come down to Sicily and Tunisia straight from Russia without any time at home. His wounds were numerous but not serious, and were accompanied by some burns; he would recover. I thought he seemed content to be a prisoner; he asked if he would be sent to America. He seemed to want Dan'l Boone to say something more to him, and I passed on the request.

224

"Tell him," Dan'l said with some difficulty, "tell him I hope he gets well quick."

I translated this—*gute Verbesserung*—and the Austrian stretched out his bandaged hand, the fingers alone of which protruded, in a gesture indicating a handshake. We left the room and returned to the airfield, Dan'l a little subdued at first until the brilliance of the day and the swift drive home began to revive his spirits.

The Télepte airfield, which according to captured documents had been the primary objective for all German air attacks in this part of Tunisia (Fériana and Gafsa next), was not attacked again for nineteen days. What story the Italian escort told we never found out; but it would have had to be a good one. Perhaps the command of the Luftwaffe decided on the evidence that the Télepte field had received formidable reinforcements. In any case, until the pressure on our ground forces compelled the retreat from the whole Kasserine valley, the squadrons at Télepte were able to use their strength, such as it was, for air cover to ground troops and for roving missions of attack against German communications and movements. In the defeat which brought us back on the Algerian side of the Kasserine Pass the one detail which meant most to me and to many of us was—perhaps it should be confessed with shame since a great deal was lost—the loss of that field on which so much that was vital had been proved at a price. Among those who paid with their lives were Dan'l Boone and Pinky Johnson, on the same day (February 16th) at Sened, and along with them others whom I knew less well or remembered less vividly, but whose combined aspect of brave and dogged youth gave me, lasting over from the strenuous days into the time of our air mastery, a concept which I can perhaps call the face of the Air Corps—something it was necessary to know in adversity if it was to be properly known at all. Civilians, war correspondents and even to some extent the combat infantry had a tendency later on to think and speak of our airmen as pampered and spoiled favorites of destiny, almost resenting, as it seemed, the very condition of air mastery for which the whole nation had worked and which as one inevitable result made our airfields in Europe relatively safe, reducing our casualties—which for a long time were the highest of any service—and increasing our results in destruction of the enemy. When I heard such talk in the next few years I was likely to think of the windswept field, the cold holes in the ground, the crackle of machine guns in the upper air: of Télepte and of the American cemetery at Gafsa.

The field at Biskra was a vast area in southern Algeria on the edge of the Sahara, where our two B-17 groups were based in January for their daily attacks upon the Germans at Tunis, Bizerte, Ferryville and Gabès. This field, too, had its hard beginnings and its own epic stories, but it was never so exposed to the Germans—was never so near them—as Télepte. Our big bomber fields around Telergma (near Constantine) were, for some reason of German economy, never attacked at all. But all these fields experienced the same bitter winter of privation and daily battle—a battle which continued for many weeks during which no other of our forces were engaged in this theater. At the time when our logistical problems were being solved (those problems which, according to the press politicians of New York and Algiers, did not exist—during those months when, according to the same strategists, we should have been waging civil war among the French) the war was sustained most of all by the advanced air units, preparing for the great infantry and artillery effort which in the end gave us the Tunisian victory.

It was an astounding experience to be immersed, even if only for an hour, in the atmosphere of Algiers just then. I had to go to Algiers on a mission for a day and was weathered in for five days by fog while no aircraft could take off; that was during the time when the Germans were pressing up to the mountain range behind Kasserine; it was there, in Algiers, that I heard we had lost Télepte. In Algiers there was talk of French politics from morning to night—this one and that one; Bob Murphy had had lunch with Tiddledewinks; de Gaulle had sent a message to Foutenlair; appointments of this and that, prospective trials of Whoozis and Whatsit, were in the air; it all seemed just about the last word in futile nonsense. All de Gaulle had to do was to contain himself until we were able to win the victory in Tunisia; after that he could do what he liked with Africa. This was foreordained, was clear from the moment we landed. But the press, the psychological warfare experts, the political warfare strategists and even a good many of the higher staff officers were having such fun with their E. Phillips Oppenheim dramas that they hardly even spoke about the events which at that very moment, from Gafsa to Kasserine, were involving us in defeat and heavy casualties. One day I went to lunch with Ernie Pyle, who had just come from Sbeitla, and we carried on one of those unresponsive double monologues which under certain circumstances of gloom and sorrow take the place of conversation among men. I told him about Télepte and he told me about Sbeitla; I spoke of the 33rd Fighter Group and he talked of the First Division; we mourned over what we had lost and cursed Algiers. Even though we were talking about different subjects we thought (or felt) that it was the same thing. It was at this point, perhaps even on this day, that Ernie decided he would not continue on the world journey he had begun, but would stick to this army, in which by now he had innumerable friends, until it had reached its victory. So far as I know Ernie never had the slightest interest in anything else from the time of the African landings; and I wish there had been more like him.

Against the secret-papers-and-dirty-teacups atmosphere of

the Hotel St. George, the whisky-and-Gaullisme of the Hotel Aletti, the black-market chickens and burgundy of the illicit restaurants, the mind set up violently contrasting pictures of those great purpling plains on which, at first light and at last light, the aircraft were rising: of those cold holes in the ground where the boys took shelter two by two, as in the ark of Noah; of retreat from an earth we had paid for in blood. If the Germans had possessed sufficient strength to push on through the Kasserine Pass and exploit their success immediately, they could have taken Tebessa and Constantine without much further trouble, but their weakness played its part as well as our strength. On return from Algiers (on Washington's Birthday, it was, and the day after) I stood on the field at Telergma and watched the squadrons go off to bomb the Germans in the Kasserine Pass—the first time we had ever used our strategical bombers for tactical purposes—and the realization that we had been brought to such dangerous expedients was not good. It was on Washington's Birthday at Telergma that I saw the blue-and-white patches of the Third Division on the highway, moving up to the front—an inspiriting sight. And on that day, also, the French commanding general at Constantine sent for me and demanded that he be given adequate notice for the evacuation of the city and district by all civilian and military personnel, since the revenge of the Germans (as shown at Gafsa) would be severe. These were the states of mind even in higher headquarters as you approached the zone of battle, and they differed sharply from the states of mind in Algiers. One staff officer in Algiers had actually assured me that our bloody retreat from the Gafsa-Kasserine valley was "in accordance with plan." People in Algiers could believe anything.

The might with which we finished the war was so overwhelming on land, at sea and in the air that it has been easy to forget how long it took to achieve it, or how delicate was the balance at times between success and failure. I think of Télepte not only in its physical aspect and in the faces of those, living and dead, who gave it value as a symbol, but as a point of equilibrium in time, summing up our past and anticipating our future in this struggle, holding the remembrance of bitter suffering and the assurance of triumph together for one breathless moment like the glint of the sun's rays on a naked sword.

CHAPTER IV

A SUMMER DAY

per ch'io, che la ragione aperta e piana
sopra le mie questioni avea ricolta,
stava com' uom che sonnolento vada.

PURGATORIO, XVIII.

WHY TOM DARCY chose August second for our expedition to Regalgióffoli would be hard to divine, except that all the operations for the day appeared to be well in hand and there was nothing much to do but wait for results. In any case it was a beautiful day: the sea and sky had the soft, gleaming radiance of the Sicilian summer and the brown hills enticed the imagination back over uncounted years to the day of the Greek who built his temples there. We were soon out of Palermo, a city of the dead when I had come into it ten days before, now already crowded with jeeps, trucks, tanks and half-tracks, the resurgent cart and even the civilian car. We went out by way of the coast road to the south, through all those villages of fishermen and peasant markets which string along the sea in a life of riotous dirt, color and obscure excitement; I bought some grapes out of one cart and we ate them as we drove along in the jeep. Scarlet petticoats and yellow shirts against a biscuit-colored wall, dark, dusty grapes in the hand, shrill melodies in Southern voices, all filled me with the awareness of an Italy I had loved too long to understand as enemy, as conspirator against the world. The harbor was filled with our own ships, but as we passed along the Southern shore of

the Conca d'Oro we began to see the occasional white sails
of the fisher people, painted, sometimes, with lavish instinct,
shapes cut softly against the brilliant sea, and the smell of the
fish-rich water and the rotting wood of minor piers came to
us through the sunlit air. Tom had a map by which he drew
our course, away from the sea now and into the hills, while I
waited, looked, pondered, quite content to pass like this along
the brown Sicilian road without any idea of where we might
be going. As soon as we got out of the area of Palermo we removed our steel helmets, which regulation still compelled us
to wear in the city, and except for the pistols at our belts we
might have been peaceful travelers on a foray to learn the
shape of the yellow-white asphodel or the gamut of the shepherd's pipe. The brown, cheerful faces with the shining white
teeth were all turned toward us as we went through the single
street of the occasional village, and until we got well into the
interior there were shouts of welcome now and then, especially
from agile, tattered children. Then we came to the high, rocky
hamlets, the poverty-stricken gray hamlets of the rocky high
hills, where the highroad invariably turned into a village
street of rough stones and queer gradients up or down, open
gutters on each side and colored clothing hanging like pennants from the open windows of the high gray houses. Sometimes there would be three floors to such a house on the street
side and only one floor, the top one, at the back where the
house met the hill. Few Americans had come this way and the
inhabitants had not yet acquired the habit of yelling "Cara-
mele!" at every passing vehicle. It was mysterious and, to
many of our soldiers, disgusting, to observe that no animosity
was ever shown to us; this was a country which had declared
war upon us—upon which we might never have declared war
otherwise in spite of its German and Japanese alliances—and
we had come as enemy invaders, with great engines of death
and destruction; at this moment Italian troops were fighting

231

our own and allied troops at Catania and just above Troina (which had been taken that morning), yet the people of the country had for us only a variety of friendly grins, ranging from frank welcome to ingratiation to mendicancy, and never was there a sign of pride, of resentment, of restraint or shame. The whole campaign had been like that for nearly a month, since the landings on July 10th, with the Italian and German armies firing at us and the population throwing flowers. No wonder many of our soldiers were bewildered, especially those who had a smattering of Italian or were able to find interpreters, since it appeared from every slight word of the inhabitants that they considered the war now to be over. It was reminiscent of medieval conflicts in which the professionally armored combatants, the knights and their squires, had all the fighting to do, and the countryside knew and cared nothing of their reasons. The news of Mussolini's fall on July 25th merely served to confirm the people in their belief that the war was over, and that all that remained to be done was for the Americans to repair all damage, feed the hungry and introduce a regime of unrationed plenty and limitless opportunity.

We encountered the same strange expectancy everywhere, of course. It had been so in Africa, all parts of Africa from Casablanca to Tunis; it was to be so later in Italy, France and Germany. These people had made war upon us and expected us to come in laden with gifts for them. One might have been less surprised, perhaps, if the attitude had been common only among the educated, those who were familiar with the legends of a munificent America, but it was, quite simply, universal. I had not been in Casablanca more than two or three days when I met a charming lady who said, "*Mais, enfin!* Tell me, what have you brought for us? Aside from cigarettes, that is— which is not bad to begin with." This charming lady was the wife of an aviator who had fought our planes on D-day, only

232

a few days before. I was a little startled at this, even among the French, who had not, after all, declared war upon us, however much damage they may have done in one way or another; but to find it again among the Italians, all Italians, from the peasants of remote villages to the recently ex-Fascist officials, was at first extremely annoying. Once when I was attempting to disperse a crowd from in front of our headquarters in Palermo—our sentries were much too good-natured to do so, and it usually fell to me, as the only Italian-speaking officer, to order the people away—I was accosted by an elderly bourgeois with a small, round paunch and a large, warty nose, no doubt a prosperous merchant or banker, who said: "Tell me, *Signor Ufficiale,* when are the Americans going to start repairing the damage done by the war?" This was while Mussolini was still in power and the Rome radio was threatening us with total extermination several times a day.

Now, going through the hill villages, climbing higher and higher on the road to Enna, we did not meet quite such glib and confident clients, but there was never an unfriendly face or gesture. Tom and I fell into talk about the campaign, and, as we came up to the bare summit of a range and surveyed a valley strewn with German wreckage, he told me of our purpose in this journey.

Tom was Colonel Darcy, A-3 (that is, assistant chief of staff for operations) of our Command. He had come through the desert with the Eighth Army as an American operations officer with the Desert Air Force under Cunningham; he had only lately been transferred to the Twelfth Air Force and this Command (Air Support, afterwards called Tactical Air Command or Tac). During the early stages of the Sicilian campaign, its preparation and the landings and just afterward, Darcy had still been permitted to fly on combat missions. Now he was, to all intents and purposes, grounded, since a staff officer in his position was not supposed to run any risk of capture by the

233

enemy. Among the combat missions he had flown some two to three weeks earlier had been one in an A-36 aircraft under a certain squadron leader whom we may call Major X. The mission assigned was to dive-bomb the German troop and vehicle concentrations at Lercara-Friddi, which was amply protected by anti-aircraft guns and had been repeatedly attacked during just those days. The leader of the mission, Major X., had taken his formation on a long and beautiful detour up Palermo way (this was a week before the capture of Palermo) and then down on a course which Darcy felt sure must be wrong. Darcy, of course, outranked the flight leader, but it would have been a heinous breach of airman's protocol for him to say a word while Major X. commanded. The position here was delicate in a way difficult for civilians to take in fully: not only was Major X. the squadron commander and in command of the mission, but Darcy was, in the fierce unspoken code of the air, a sort of intruder, in that he did not belong to the squadron, was a staff officer of higher rank and from a higher headquarters, and had in fact been obliged to borrow an airplane from some disgruntled pilot and get the group commander's permission to go at all. Consequently he was obliged to follow along obediently and obey orders although his gorge rose at what was happening. The leader took them down a course which Darcy followed on his map and then led off in a dive-bombing attack upon a sudden valley in the hills. The A-36's all made their dives, dropped their bombs and returned to their base on the South coast. Major X., who made the operational report, said that he had attacked a concentration of German troops and vehicles and done much damage.

Now, to do Major X. full credit, he may perhaps have thought so. The A-36 is a very speedy aircraft; it is, in fact, a dive-bombing version of our P-51 (the Mustang). We had two groups of these slightly revised Mustangs in Tunisia,

Sicily and Italy, but they were the only ones—for some reason I never knew, their manufacture ceased and we got no more. In an A-36 in its powerful screaming dive it might be possible to mistake anything for anything else. At any rate, the fact was that Darcy did not agree with the squadron commander either in his navigation, in his attack, or in the report he afterwards made upon it. And, as a thoroughly conscientious and methodical officer, he made up his mind at the time to keep his own counsel but verify the facts when opportunity offered. He had studied the map with care for some days and had come to his own conclusion about the point attacked, when chance threw in his way an Italian aviation officer who spoke English and knew Sicily. By questioning this prisoner he obtained indications which confirmed his own belief that the point attacked on July 15th was the mountain village of Regalgióffoli; this was a hamlet so small that it appeared only on the largest maps, but both by co-ordinates and by the contours Darcy was sure of it. He had bided his time until an opportunity came to make a quick jaunt down through the mountains to find the place, and had spoken to me some days earlier about my availability as interpreter on the expedition. Now, today, the day of the fall of Troina, enough stability had befallen the operations staff to make the trip possible.

It had been a surprisingly swift campaign, on the whole. The Sicilian landings took place on July 10th at points on the South and Southeast coast; Patton's army (called the Seventh) had pushed on up the coast road from Gela to Agrigento and had then turned north to Palermo, finishing the whole western part of the campaign weeks ahead of the scheduled time. Montgomery's Eighth Army had moved up to Catania and stuck there, pinned down by some good German units and the best of the Italians, but its immobility signified little while Patton was on the move. My old friends of the Third Division had played a notable part in Patton's advance and had—up to

Palermo—suffered remarkably few casualties. The second battalion of the Fifteenth Regiment had its bivouac in the lemon groves of the Duc de Guise's house in Palermo, the Palazzo d'Orléans, and there we had had some fine sessions with remarkable "liberated" food and wine, Bill Billings and I, the Pasha (Captain Emil Bitar) and the rest, while the story of the campaign came out bit by bit. We of the Air Support Command had not landed until several days after D-day; as a matter of fact, I had had three weeks at home in America after the Tunisian victory, on a mission (with Phil Cochran) and was on my way back to General Cannon when the Sicilian landings took place; he sent me off on temporary duty with the Air Support Command when it flew over from Tunisia on July 18th or 19th. Followed Licata, Agrigento, the southern hills and temples, the eternal search for quarters and headquarters; and then, one fine day, an order to go to Palermo and get the best available space for the air corps offices and installations. There was no other officer in our staff with any knowledge of Italian, and consequently my first occupation everywhere we went (Licata, Agrigento, Palermo) was to survey the field, ask questions, and determine to the best of my ability where and how we should be established. My colleague in the enterprise was always Eugene Cropper, the lieutenant-colonel who commanded our headquarters squadron, an inveterate seeker after antiquities and curiosities, a wry, sly bird with a small, humorous face and a quizzical manner, who availed himself of every opportunity to have a little innocent fun at my expense.

When we drove into Palermo on the 24th of July (it had fallen to the Seventh Regiment of the Third Division the day before) the ruined port and seafront, the deserted streets and much-damaged houses, the general air of death and disaster under the summer sun, appalled us into silence; we had not then acquired the habit of ruins, and the city—not really so much damaged, as it turned out—seemed to us tragically impaired, so that it might be long indeed before it returned to life. I had then no general experience of the resilience of the Italian populations which spring from the ruins or stream back to them with such indomitable vitality. To Cropper, I said: "I hope nothing has happened to the mosaics in the Cathedral of Monreale," and told him, idly, that I had made a strong memorandum to General Cannon about that cathedral early in May when the bombing of Palermo had been decided. Cropper bore this in mind and took the earliest chance of going up to Monreale, a day or so later, to see the mosaics, which were indeed intact under a layer of what looked like cheesecloth; so were the Romanesque cloisters, one of the great beauties of Sicily (so, we found out later, were the mosaics at Cefalù, by some miracle, although bombs had fallen near the church). As we stood verifying the immunity of the mosaics, a dark wraith, a priest of sorts, approached us and said that the Archbishop would enjoy the privilege of a word with the American generals. Cropper, with a glint in his eye, said that we were only lieutenant-colonels but we would appreciate the honor, and we were ushered through a corridor from the cathedral to the palace of the Archbishop, where Monsignor Filippi, once attached to the Apostolic Delegation in Washington, greeted us in rusty English. Then Cropper's design became manifest; he informed the Archbishop, solemnly and as if there were no question about the case, that I had by my personal intervention with the highest authorities preserved Monreale from any share in the attacks made, through the necessity of war, upon Palermo. Monsignor Filippi, who had hitherto attributed the immunity of his cathedral to the intercession of the Virgin Mary, was overcome by this and showered me with attentions; we were asked to lunch two days later to a meal which, although obviously cooked by the priestly secretary who put it on the table, was so ample and

237

various that it suggested a ransacking of the whole neighborhood for victuals, and although neither the Archbishop nor
his secretary had quite the courage to deal with every dish all
the way through, Cropper and I took shameless advantage of
the situation and cherished the meal in memory for weeks
afterwards. I never ate Byzantine-Saracenic mosaics which
tasted quite so good.

At some period after the Hitler-Mussolini alliance had
blighted the Italian tourist traffic, some enterprising company
or individual optimist had built a big hotel, a whacking big
semicastellated or castelliferous structure of stone with turrets
and balconies and terraces, on top of the hill to the west of the
Conca d'Oro, just beyond Palermo on the way to the mount
and shrine of Santa Rosalía. This masterpiece rejoiced in the
name of Castell' Utveggio and had been the headquarters of
the Luftwaffe up until shortly before our arrival, as well as of
the German anti-aircraft system for the Palermo area. It dominated the city, of which it had indeed become the most conspicuous landmark by this time. (I suppose it to have been
built in 1939 or 1940—certainly long after the last time I had
seen Palermo.) When Cropper and I arrived in Palermo,
scarcely twenty-four hours after the first American troops, and
perhaps three days after the departure of the Germans, the
Castell' Utveggio was still empty and had been visited only by
a few stray infantry soldiers in search of loot. We had hit
upon it almost at once, partly because it struck the eye immediately and partly because the Luftwaffe had been there;
consequently we stopped the looting—to the disgust of the
Third Division soldiers who had been enjoying themselves—
and stuck up a sign saying that it belonged to us. This was
always the system at the beginning of the occupation of any
town; later on, when things fell into better order and all the
administrative officers arrived with their staffs and files and
desks and papers, requisitions were regularized, authorized

238

or abandoned. It was my original idea that the Castell' Utveggio would serve both as quarters and as headquarters; such had apparently been the Luftwaffe's system, for we found both office equipment and living gear of the Germans in considerable quantities throughout the hotel. Some charming Italian prisoners trooped up and surrendered to us in the street the day after we arrived—about fifteen of them, all gleaming teeth and good nature—so we ferried them up the towering cliff, over the excellent Fascist road, in about three jeep trips and put them to work. The rubbish and havoc wrought by Germans and Americans between them were somehow cleared away (nobody ever worked more willingly and indefatigably than our Italian prisoners) and the place was ready for the arrival of our general and staff, except—alas!—for the water, which did not run in pipe or tap, kitchen or toilet, anywhere in the hotel. We used our prisoners under one guard, who was actually superfluous except as a jeep driver, and thus fetched water from down in the town, but it was an unsatisfactory system. At this point the manager of the Castell' Utveggio, a calamitous, bent and quivering wreck of an old man named Signor Collura, put in his appearance with many a wail and moan over the fate of his beautiful hotel. From him I learned the water system, discovered the pump at the base of the cliff, determined after many trials that the motor was irremediably damaged, and made a trip to the West coast to a hidden refugee village to requisition another motor—all of which took just five days of unremitting toil, arguments, journeys, hysterical scenes with Collura, engineers, repair men and the like, capped by hilarious uproar among our own Italian prisoners who enjoyed the whole problem more than anything they had met with in this mysterious and profoundly undesired war. In the midst of my travail (which of course was a source of great merriment to Cropper and to the staff officers who had now arrived) Franklin Roosevelt's destroyer, the *Mayrant,* limped into the harbor in a very bad way indeed, having been bombed and all but sunk on the high seas; when Franklin came to see me I had vain recourse to him to inspect and perhaps explain the unfathomable secrets of the pump, the motor, the "tubo" and the rest. Then, that same night (it was the last night of July), my efforts were crowned with triumph; the water, which had been coming and going capriciously for days, but seldom at an hour when it was needed for meals or washing, flowed upwards (incomprehensibly) from the base of the cliff to its summit and filled every pipe in the whole Castell' Utveggio, so that the entire staff could have had baths if they had so desired. The reservoir at the top of the hotel filled up gloriously, and my emotions were rather like those De Lesseps might have had if his dream had come true; but *es wär zu schön gewesen, es hat nicht sollen sein.* That night of triumph ended with a daring and persistent air raid by the Luftwaffe, the best job of its sort I ever saw them do against us (the Americans, that is—I had seen much better in England) with the single exception of their attack on the port of Bari the following December second; and thereafter the Castell' Utveggio was no longer habitable.

It was an extremely spectacular air raid, the first of a series which did us small material damage but sounded magnificent in the German and Italian communiqués. It started at about four in the morning of August 1st and finished at about half-past five, just after first light. The aircraft were Junkers-88, two of which were shot down on our hilltop, one of them going up in flames where we could plainly see it. (The Germans never told the truth in their communiqués—for example, in this raid they said they lost no aircraft.) The attack began with the release of flares by which the whole dark harbor was lighted up and the incoming Ju-88's could bomb with considerable ease, making their runs from the sea and returning to it in what sounded like a huge semi-circular movement at top speed. I slept on a balcony overlooking the Conca d'Oro, as did a number of staff officers, and was awakened by the first flares and the anti-aircraft guns which accompanied them. We had no idea that so many A.A. guns were placed around the port, and their lines of tracer bullets made a night of wonder. Then the bombs began to land, and one of the very first ones hit a munitions train which had been left unloaded on a pier (a circumstance for which undoubtedly somebody suffered thereafter). The munitions train went off in a stupendous pyrotechnical display and continued to go off for about two hours, illuminating the entire city and its surroundings as if by the most blazing sunlight. Colonel Darcy, who slept a few feet down the balcony from me, took an educated professional interest in all this and commented upon each circumstance in the spectacle before us with considerable detachment. Then bombs landed very near us, two of them, shaking the hotel and causing us to hurl ourselves to the floor; after each one we got up, dazed, and returned to gaze again from the open balcony; but it was dawning on me, at any rate, that the Castell' Utveggio, as the most conspicuous landmark in all Palermo and as air headquarters which had been Luftwaffe headquarters so short a time before, was in all probability a target of the German mission. Just as I had begun to realize the implications, we were mightily shaken by a roaring hit which sent the glass and plaster crashing throughout the structure. In the pitch darkness we made tracks for the stairs, through air thick with plaster dust, and skidded down as best we could toward the front door and the cave which served as shelter just beside it. The bomb had, in fact, hit our reservoir on the roof (my reservoir!) and seemed designed only to make my work on the water supply useless, since the rest of the building was relatively undamaged. There were no casualties, and we spent the rest of the raid in and in front of the cave shelter; but on the next day an order was issued to find new quarters. It appeared that the Castell' Utveggio was, indeed, a German target—I never knew exactly how this was confirmed; probably the German pilots talked of it in the air, as was a habit of theirs; they were always remarkably indiscreet in their talk to each other.

Thus it was that our Commanding General (Major-General Edward House) with his operations and intelligence staff, moved to a villa on the beach at Mondello, near Patton's, where two nights later we were neatly bracketed by two bombs in the very peak and middle of the night, one on one side of us and one on the other, just to teach us that nowhere in the area was safe. But the most memorable thing in the raid of August 1st, to me, was Franklin Roosevelt's exploit in carrying a badly wounded boy from his disabled destroyer across two other ships alongside to find a doctor just when the raid was at its most intense—a feat of such difficulty that I could never have accomplished it even in daylight, owing to the obstacles the navy so generously strews in the path of those who wish to set one foot in front of another. Franklin, who was in command of the *Mayrant* that night (his skipper being ashore), had behaved with exemplary coolness and decision, as I found out when I went down to the docks to see what had become of him. The sailors called him "Poncho" or "The Big Fellow" and their regard for him was no secret. When I asked him how he had ever managed to walk through that inferno with the wounded sailor in his arms, stepping over rails and stanchions and other obstacles innumerable with names maritime, he said: "I didn't think of the thing as a whole—just one step at a time. I thought, I'll take this step and then maybe I can get the next one." He also said he gave a shot of morphine to the young sailor, one of whose legs had been shot clean away and the other injured, before they started their journey across the ships alongside, and the boy said: "All right, sir. Will it hurt much?"

On the way to Regalgióffoli, Colonel Darcy and I talked of this raid, which we knew had accomplished nothing of consequence to either our shipping or the port. I had listened to the Rome radio the night before—an evening task which was also of the keenest interest, because one could detect from day to day the fluctuations of the Badoglio government's will or spirit. On one night they put on old Orlando to talk to Sicily—Vittorio Emanuele Orlando, he of the Versailles peace conference, whose demise long since I had assumed without evidence or, indeed, concern. And Orlando said, in so many words, that the beloved island would not much longer be separated from the mother mainland, adding, "I know I am speaking to my Sicilians, for whom a mere signal is enough—do not lose heart." This was afterwards, of course, but nods and becks and wreathed smiles of the same general nature had been put on the government radio in Rome from time to time almost from the moment of Mussolini's downfall, so that, even when they were followed by straight German propaganda from Russia or about our own campaign, it was not at all difficult to perceive that the Badoglio government was looking for a way out of the war. The thing had been so obvious since July 25th that for my own part I never understood why it took so long. Long afterwards some of the story came out: the conspiratorial conversations here, there and the next place, unbeknownst to the Germans (supposedly), during which German divisions up to the number of twenty were steadily moving down into the peninsula to meet us when we should come.

Tom Darcy was the kind of soldier who would never dream of discussing high politics: his not to reason why. At the same time he had an obstinate feeling that air bombing should be on defined targets and should be carried out with the maximum precision in attack and the most conscientious exactness in subsequent reporting to base. This was why his West Point

soul revolted at the execution of the mission he had flown on
July 15th. It was, I think, for the good of the service and the
honor of the Air Corps that he had determined to investigate
it. Tom was young—ten years or more my junior—but not
young enough for what he had most wanted to do in the war,
which was to fly in combat, and his relegation to a higher
shelf, but nevertheless a shelf, irked his pilot's glands; only
a few years less, three or four, would have made him a group
commander rather than an operations executive on the staff,
and he regretted those few years with, as he said, the feeling
of a professional soldier: "You must remember that war is
my trade," he would say with a certain grimness lightened by
a characteristic sidewise smile that left you wondering how
much he meant and how much was ironic parody. That he
would be a general officer sooner or later (as he was within
the year) could be forecast by anybody who saw the operations
of this command, but the prospect of such advancement held
no allure for Tom in comparison with the thing he most
wanted to do. With his cool eyes and sardonic voice, his professional guardian-of-the-arcana manner heightened by the
scar which traversed his cheek in the most approved Wehrmacht style, Darcy overcame his own considerable natural advantages of appearance and nature and succeeded in appearing
rebarbative, even to some degree frightening, toward those
who had to deal with him at headquarters, but I had very
early decided that it would be childish not to discern how
much of this was a vocational crustaceous acquisition created
by his idea of duty and serving in the office of a mask, perhaps,
to much simpler and more familiar sensibilities. Like Cochran,
Dick Carmichael and a considerable number of other Air
Corps officers who had already struck, or were to strike, my
imagination in series, each with the sharp and distinct note
of a rare personality, like the plucking of a harp string, Darcy
had, so to speak, his particular irredeemable separate tone in

244

the moral air, and like theirs it had an original wood-wildness, but with him it did not sound out unconfined. His disciplinary armor, monkish or soldatesque, could not be put off, so that it was startling to discover any weakness in him, even a liking for the art or science of poker playing, which, in any case, he played so superbly that what with others might have been a weakness was transformed into a strength. The romanticism common to those who, on leaving West Point, deliberately chose to fly in the air rather than adopt any of the military *métiers* which were so vastly easier in peacetime, lurked in Darcy's interior like a dark secret over which he attempted to draw innumerable stratifications of military science, history, doctrine, discipline and duty. He was forever on his guard against any form of display, influenced to some degree by his desert days in the R.A.F., a service which regarded "shooting a line" as even more repulsive than did the Americans; and nothing would have induced him to admit aloud the concepts by which, nevertheless, he clearly lived: duty, courage, honor, justice, patriotism. These large high virtues were less rare in the army, or at least less difficult to identify, than they seemed to be in civil life, but they were so implicit that only the most partial statement ever expressed them, and that only under the stricture, the emulgent stricture let us say, of a crisis involving the persuasion of others. I knew how Cochran could talk when he had to, and wondered what straits would be required to squeeze out of Darcy the same profane and dashing eloquence, the same unpremeditated art, which quite certainly existed there underneath the armor as it did in virtually all other Air Corps leaders, old or young, who ever came under my observation in the conduct of the actual war.

The day was of that kind which, in Sicily, is bound to thrust the name of Theocritus into the current of thought—Theocritus, for whom I had no Greek and knew only in lame paraphrase, but whose hills and flocks were certainly not greatly different from those we saw from the mountain road. These people, African, Greek, Saracen and Norman, had as little reason for participation in Mussolini's ill-calculated war as in any of ages past, during which their history, by and large, was one of frequent and principally unregarded conquest. The violence was not alien—there was plenty of violence in the Sicilian tradition—but the ideas or purposes of the conquerors were. We, the Americans, rolling over the lovely, ancient island in our jeeps, affected the shepherd and his flock not at all, or at any rate no more than had a dozen other conquerors (Anjou and Aragon, for example) in the long, unnoticed past. The dust of the road grew thick when we turned sharply off at a point Darcy had pin-pointed on his map: here a narrow side road led up the mountain side, unpromising but in his mind quite certain to lead to Regalgióffoli, somewhere beyond.

And when we passed the near summit of a gray hill we found ourselves looking down into a small valley more fertile than the slopes we had left. It had pasture and orchard and a cluster of houses with a small church tower down toward the middle, above a meandering and almost dry stream which descended through rocks from the higher mountain on the right. "This," said Darcy quite firmly, "must be the place." We drove on down until we were in the middle of the one street with half a dozen houses on either side, and here, by the church, we left the jeep, which was instantly surrounded by a circle of gaping children who, unlike the children of larger towns or more frequented places, kept their distance and marveled in silence. No Americans had ever been to Regalgióffoli, we soon learned, and it was quite ten or fifteen minutes before the wild denizens of the vale had overcome their diffidence to the point of

246

clambering over our vehicle and rifling its pockets; even then they stole nothing, content with wonder.

The largest of the houses was the one I chose to try. I knew that there was unlikely to be anybody in the hamlet, aside from priest or schoolmaster, who could speak or understand Italian, and so it turned out: the two men we encountered before the house made incomprehensible but polite sounds and motioned us in. One house at the foot of the village street, just by the stream, had been partially demolished and Tom pointed it out. "You see," he said, "that must have been done by a bomb." I knocked on the door and when a woman's voice called out we pushed it open and went in.

We were in a square room of some size, with earthen floor beaten smooth and swept clean, lighted by doors opened at the side. Three women were sitting on the floor winnowing grain in a large, round, flat sieve about the size of a big drum, running their slim brown hands through the golden grain to pick out and throw away what I supposed to be the chaff. They were all young women, one of them a slip of a girl—a "young thin pale soft shy slim slip of a thing then," says Joyce—and the dominating character, the one who rose to her feet and assumed with easy grace the role of *padrona di casa,* was round and soft and full, the bright-eyed mother of two children who quickly materialized in the open door at the side and stared at us with lustrous, awestruck intensity. The mother understood Italian, of which she could manage a few words at a pinch, and told me that her husband, who was by the look of things the principal man of the village, could speak Italian well; she sent the children off post-haste in quest of him and then returned to her winnowing. As she made the long, graceful motions with the big sieve she glanced up at us with flashing eyes and gleaming teeth and asked questions which showed that she, perhaps as a result of more assured social position in the village than the others, was not intimidated. Now that we had arrived, was the war over, she asked artlessly; and would grain rationing cease? I said that we were only soldiers and knew nothing about the rationing system, which was an affair for civil authority. She burst into a tirade against the system, whatever it was, by which I gathered that she was compelled to deliver her grain to a mill run by the local Fascist authorities, and was only permitted to withdraw a fixed proportion of it afterwards for the use of her household. This mill and these Fascist authorities were tyranny itself, in her view, and the first thing the Americans should do was to abolish the system. She said that in spite of a good property and much hard work she and her husband could not obtain the necessities for themselves, notably shoes, and pointed to her own feet shod in a kind of canvas *espadrille*. Had the Americans brought shoes, she inquired, and when would they begin to distribute them? I gave up trying to explain anything to her and sat there wondering how, in this far fastness, the legend of an all-munificent America had come to be so calmly taken as fact. Colonel Darcy, embarrassed and a little surprised at all this talk, sat on a deal table and watched the long movements of the women's arms, their brown swift fingers in the grain. The *patrona di casa* was still endeavoring to make me understand, in bursts of Sicilian broken by phrases of more or less comprehensible Italian, what the American authorities must do in the village of Regalgióffoli when her husband came in and spoke his welcome. He was a well-made, sturdy and handsome farmer of perhaps thirty, cleaner and with better clothes than were usual in the countryside, who spoke clear Italian with a dragging Southern accent. With him, since he understood at once that we had not come for the pleasures of conversation, it was possible to start our inquiry. If the *Signori* would come upstairs, he said, we could get to our business.

Upstairs in a truly wonderful bedroom he produced a bottle of local wine and three glasses; we sipped the heavy, sweet stuff politely and complimented him upon it. His name was Antonino Capuana and he was, as all the externals demonstrated, the principal citizen of the village. Had there been a bombing at Regalgióffoli on July 15th? Yes, indeed, yes, there had been a bombing; the most extraordinary event in the history of Regalgióffoli. Had it done damage? Very little, but the bombs were still to be seen; three of them had not yet exploded. How many planes? From which direction did they come? At what time of day? How many bombs fell? And so on.

Antonino Capuana was perfectly distinct and precise in his answers to all Tom's questions, which I relayed as fast as if we were conducting an examination in court. By the time we had fixed the hour of the bombing and the number of aircraft and bombs, Colonel Darcy was quite certain: this was the place, this was the bombing in which he had participated on July 15th.

We finished our glasses of wine, refused another and went downstairs. Antonino Capuana undertook to guide us through the village and down through the orchard to the stream where the unexploded bombs lay. The last house in the village, beside the stream where it turned down to the bottom of the valley, had been damaged, but, Antonino said, nobody was in it and nobody was hurt. One bomb had fallen just there, harmlessly (we could see the crater from the road); another over there, another on the upper slope. Antonino thought there were twelve bombs in all; Tom said this would be the correct number for his bombing, but he was professionally hurt to learn that three of them had never gone off. We went and looked at the duds and Tom told me to instruct Antonino to keep everybody away from them until an American ordnance officer should arrive to make them harmless. Antonino understood, indeed, and had been doing precisely that ever since the day of the bombing.

"You'd hardly say there were many results from that attack," I remarked to Tom. "Three duds, one shack partly damaged, the rest of the bombs scattered on the hillside."

"I know," he said with a kind of gloomy ferocity. "It's just as I expected. I knew it at the time. You ought to have seen the report the guy made . . . ! German concentrations . . . Well . . . Ask our friend here if anybody in the village was hurt."

Antonino said that one boy of fourteen had his head blown off by a bomb which landed in the pasture higher up, beyond the village, off the road we had used to come there. This boy was, Antonino said kindly, as if to console us for any remorse which might be thought to come upon us, a half-wit whose parents were quite glad to be rid of the responsibility for him, even though they had been obliged to go through the conventional acts of grief and commemoration. He was standing in the middle of the pasture when the bomb started to fall and had not had sense enough to run or to take shelter. The bomb took his head right off, said Antonino with what sounded like esteem for such efficiency, and no part of it was ever found again. The body and its clothing identified the boy.

By this time, having strolled down through the orchard of apple, plum and almond trees to the stream at the bottom of the little valley, we had returned to the roughly paved street of the village and were surrounded by the entire populace. They had learned by observation and eavesdropping what our errand was and they were all eager to help. The great difficulty came in trying to get them to talk one at a time. Each had a tale to tell of the great event, the unimaginable event which had shattered the life and mind of the village more than any mere earthquake or volcanic eruption—those familiar catastrophes—might have done. Actually there had been no casualties at all in the bombing attack, with the exception of the imbecile boy who was beheaded in the pasture, but the effect on the mind of the people in Regalgióffoli could not have been more apocalyptic if the dread horsemen themselves had descended from the sky in a physical charge upon the forty or fifty inhabitants of the place. All of the villagers had at some time seen aircraft passing overhead, all knew what they were, all understood that such engines were employed in blasting the resources or refuges or bodies or vehicles of the enemy, but none had ever witnessed bombardment from the air or expected ever to do so. The event of half-past three in the afternoon of July 15th therefore struck upon every mind with the disintegrating power of a wholly new horror, something which mere second- or third-hand narratives from the cities had never even vaguely conveyed.

"I was in the courtyard feeding the pigs . . ."

"I was sewing on Talinu's Sunday jacket . . ."

"We were sitting on the step in front of the house . . ."

The surprising thing to me was that no resentment of the event appeared in any of the words I could understand. All the talk was in the most turbid Sicilian, of which I seized only a fragment on the wing, but Antonino was there to translate for me and to make them repeat when necessary. Not only were these men, women, boys and girls unresentful, but each one appeared to have a pet explanation for the bombing and introduced it in the course of conversation to show that Regalgióffoli was not too stupid, or too provincial, or too bucolic, for the most modern of wars. It actually does not seem to have occurred to one creature in that village that we, the supreme and superb Americans, had made a mistake. One man thought we bombed the place because there had been some German gasoline dumped down at the road junction on the other side of the hill; a woman said there had been German military vehicles parked beside the main road at the Regalgióffoli junction for two days before the bombing; another was certain that Regalgióffoli looked from the air exactly like another village where there was a German installation of some

251

electrical mysteries and some anti-aircraft guns. That in reality no reason whatever existed for the bombing of Regalgióffoli was the only hypothesis that did not seem to have been considered in the weeks since that afternoon of terror. The eager voices, the crowding gestures, were all friendly, and I could not make out even a hint of blame toward us for what we had done, which, indeed, they had long since explained to themselves satisfactorily. If there was any resentment shown, it was towards the Germans who were held to be responsible (by their parking of vehicles or dumping of gasoline) for bringing on the attack. This promptness to find excuses for us, whatever we did, was a notable characteristic of the Italian masses throughout 1943 and 1944, and made it so much the easier for our wise and great to multiply their errors. In the case of Regalgióffoli, Tom (my superior officer) told me not to ruin any of the people's illusions about American logic or military efficiency, and in fact to make no choice among the many reasons they offered for our action, but to say, without further ado, that we regretted the bombardment and would not forget the village.

When we came back to Antonino Capuana's house the *padrona di casa* had stopped her work and was on the threshold waiting for us with the two other young women, who might have been her sisters. We stopped to talk with them for a few minutes, refused more sweet wine and wrote down their names. Signora Capuana, all curves and quizzical merriment, said in her mixture of Sicilian and Italian: "Have you found out all about the terrible day? Do you know that all the people ran away and it has only been in the last two or three days that they have all returned?" I asked where they had fled and she said, vaguely, "To the mountain. They were afraid to come back to the village at all. Only the boys, the very lively young boys, would come down to the houses to get supplies or anything to help. Most of them lived in the mountains for ten

252

days or so." The implication was that she, Signora Capuana, was of a social and economic order which did not share such superstitious timidity. I asked if she, too, had gone to the mountain, and Antonino answered with a sudden flash of laughing teeth: "She went, too. She wouldn't allow me to remain behind. We had to stay up there for three or four days, sleeping on leaves and among the rocks. Finally I forced her to come home." Her eyes and teeth and hips all spoke to him as he laughed at her.

"Tell them we'll not forget them," Tom said. "Let's go."

On the way out of the village, alongside the pasture where the imbecile boy had been decapitated, we ran into the parish priest. He was a thin, scrawny young man with spectacles and protuberant purplish lips which he was moving over an open book which he held in his hands as he walked slowly along: his breviary. He wore the rustiest, flimsiest sort of cassock of brownish black and had on a hat which could have done service in the *Barbiere di Siviglia.* I asked Tom to stop the car while I verified all that we had heard with this local oracle.

The young man, who had of course studied somewhere, spoke Italian well without any of the characteristic Sicilian absences of grammar and syllables. He said that indeed a half-witted boy had been killed in this pasture by a bomb; his parents were poor people and could ill afford to bear such a cross as an unproductive, helpless son, so perhaps it was for the best, it was the will of God. Indeed, yes, one house had been damaged and there were still unexploded bombs. Yes, it was also true that the whole village had fled to the hills after the bombing, taking mattresses and such cooking utensils as were considered necessary. It had required days of patient persuasion to get them back again.

"These are very simple people, *Signori,*" the young priest said with a tolerant smile and a half wink, as of one man of the world to another. "They understand nothing. Of course

253

I understood that the bombing was because of the German gasoline dump down the road there, and as soon as I saw that was moved I knew there would be no more bombings. I convinced them at last, and they are all back now."

I warned him about the unexploded bombs, which an American officer would come to remove soon, and he said he understood. His wide black eyes gazed upon us with a wonder as frank as that of his parishioners, and his purple lips and scraggly Adam's apple twitched in excitement. His whole external person was such that he put me irresistibly in mind of Chaliapin's stories of Spanish and Italian priests, all dingy black and dandruff and spectacles and umbrellas, whom he studied in streets and railroad trains while he was composing his Don Basilio. This was a young Don Basilio whose contribution to the character might have been that extraordinarily expressive Adam's apple, which twitched most frenetically just when he was trying to convey that to him, as an experienced and educated person, there was no surprise in bombardment from the air.

We went on. Tom sighed deeply.

"Will you do anything?" I asked.

"I'll send somebody out to study those duds and find out why they didn't explode," he said.

"Is that all?"

He drove along for a while without speaking.

"Oh, I'll send them something," he said. "Did you get that man's name? Capuana—what was it? I'll send them something. It's a kind of a pity. Just a mistake. An ordinary mistake. Scared hell out of all of them. Makes you think what it would be like if—well, if it happened the other way round."

We did not discuss the matter further. Days later, when I asked about it, I learned that an American ordnance officer had visited Regalgióffoli to study and make harmless the unexploded bombs, and that gifts (food and useful articles) had gone to Capuana and the parents of the half-witted boy who was killed in the bombing. On that afternoon, which was rapidly fading and dwindling and amortizing itself in a wash of color all over the sky and the land, the episode had made us both a little pensive. It was not unusual to find a forgotten hamlet where the Americans had never been and the inhabitants looked upon the stray soldier visitor as an emissary from on high. Some weeks later the headquarters doctor, Colonel Nelson, took me on a brief expedition to one of those mountain-top towns on the north road toward Messina—the village of Tusa—on a search for eggs, and we were greeted by a popular demonstration and asked to appoint a new mayor and chief of police. In the simplicity of the Sicilian peasant's world there had been one golden thread for generations past: the journey to America, the rich relatives in America, the cousins in America. Now that Mussolini's war (as they had always considered it) was over, had ended in Mussolini's defeat, it was only logic and common sense in their eyes that the victorious American army should take them under its all-provident wing. The expectation of beneficence was so obstinate that it took weeks for it to sink, and as it was always being revived again by the careless good nature of our G.I.'s, with their anarchistic attitude toward army property, it can never be said to have become wholly extinct in the lovely, melancholy Greek isle. One of the ironic aspects of the situation was that Sicily, which hated Mussolini with such whole-hearted sincerity and was so happy at his downfall, was in fact a region which had demonstrably benefited more than most by the tyranny of his strong central rule. He had exterminated the Mafia and made ordinary justice, as distinct from political justice, more independent than ever before, and he had done something tangible in the way of roads, communications and ports. In his attempt to Italianize the island and the whole peninsula he had shifted civil servants everywhere, so that

Florentines ruled in Calabria and Sicilians in Venetia and Lombards in Catania, and whereas this may have been an un-necessary vexation in the advanced and cultivated regions of Central and Northern Italy, it could have brought nothing but good results to Sicily. Yet these scraps of good in the deluge of unwanted Fascism were forgotten now, and the people turned to us like so many refugees hopeful of food and cloth-ing, shelter and kind words, ready always to find excuses for any inadequacy, any mistake. The war? The war was not our fault; the war was Mussolini's fault, simply, solely his.

War is a calamity so immense that only fools can hope to regulate its scope or define with assurance the consequences of its concrete enactment in the lives of men. Even the most inevitable and necessary conflicts, those without which the progress of human society would be arrested or turned back, strike off innumerable undesired and unforeseen effects which in turn help to determine the anfractuous channel of persistent life, pushing it this way and that until it runs where no man had thought to see it run, and the event of December bears small resemblance to the plan of May. When such reflections push their way up from the spectacle of our half-ruined and half-aborning world, my mind is inclined to turn to Regal-gióffoli, to the soft brown arms of the women over the big winnowing sieve, to their slim fingers in the golden grain, and to the calm pasture where the half-witted boy was beheaded on a summer's afternoon.

CHAPTER V

ITALY

chè in la mente m'è fitta, ed or mi accora,
la cara e buona imagine paterna
di voi, quando nel mondo ad ora ad ora

m'insegnavate come l'uom s'eterna;
e quant' io l' abbia in grado, mentre io vivo
convien che nella mia lingua si scerna.

INFERNO, XV.

THE INVASION of Italy took place under circumstances of peculiar uncertainty and tension. Between July 25th, when Marshal Badoglio assumed the government in Rome with the clear intention (clear, that is, to all Italians) of making peace as quickly as possible, and September 10th, when we landed on the beaches below Salerno, the German High Command had moved twenty divisions with all their equipment into the peninsula. It was an open secret during August that conversations of some kind were taking place between the Anglo-American allies and the Italian government. The journeys of large, escorted transport planes, particularly since they clearly bore enemy markings and were tenderly guarded by our own Spitfires, could hardly fail to occasion comment on our airfields, not to mention the whispering set up by the necessary instructions to our fighter patrols, radar stations and air controllers. All this involved not only definite knowledge for some hundreds of officers (who, I assume, kept the secret rigidly)

257

but the observation of thousands of men who could not help seeing what they did see and consulting each other privately over what it might mean. We all laughed a good deal over a directive which came down to us from the highest headquarters, asking us to "discourage rumors" on the airfields; it was impossible to discourage people from using their eyes and ears and native brains. All we could do was to deny all knowledge whenever our lads asked what was going on. For my own part, I hoped that the Italian armistice which was obviously in the making would be made quickly and would be at least fractionally the work of somebody who had heard of Italy before. A good deal of our difficulty everywhere was due to the startling novelty of the non-American world to the overwhelming majority of our officers, even those of highest importance, and the concomitant distrust not only of foreigners but of those who (like myself, on some occasions, or like a certain number of others) had been too familiar with foreign faces and places in the time of peace. So far as the Italian armistice was concerned the main consideration was speed, and as the weeks passed without a known result, this desideratum seemed to have been—inexplicably—shelved, and it appeared that we were to sit forever in our exquisite Graeco-Sicilian idleness and discuss plans which might never come into effect. We had a whole series of plans for the invasion of the Italian mainland, each one with a picturesque code name, and for some weeks we had no idea (on my level, at any rate) which was to be adopted. There were Baytown and Barracuda and Avalanche and I can no longer remember how many others, each of which had been worked out to the tiniest detail by the planning boys back in Algiers, with the details of how many aircraft would be needed to protect how many troops on how much beachhead for how long, and how many ships would be required to feed them for a week, and how much ammunition for anti-aircraft defense, and so on and so on, the most specific calculations imaginable, all of which came remarkably near to concrete realization in the operations of which I had first-hand knowledge. I do not mean that it was possible to calculate everything in advance and execute an operation (any operation) "according to plan"; this would be contradictory to reason and common sense. There were many unexpected deviations from plan in the field, thanks to the weather, alterations in the enemy's strength, disposition or tactics, sudden accidents of war or other ever-changing circumstances which affect or determine the decisions of a commanding general. But in the broad, general lines of an operation, especially in the big calculations of strength (air strength, ground strength, fire power, etc., etc.) and what we called "build-up" (the logistical problem) the event never was far off what had been estimated in a tranquil villa on the hill in Algiers. Again and again we were ahead of our plans; indeed, in some important respects, such as the building of air-strips by our aviation engineers, we were practically always better than we were supposed to be. But this is the most pleasing of faults, and we can hardly complain if our plans sometimes erred in underestimating our abilities; what was more important was that there very seldom occurred a case in which our advance planning had been wrong in the other direction—that is, in assigning us more than we could do. The exceptions which will occur to every informed person are Salerno and Anzio, but I think it is indisputable that the air plan in both of these instances was fully adequate and was carried out with remarkable precision; it was only on the ground that the manipulation of the troops gave the Germans opportunities which they, as experienced campaigners, could hardly pass up even though most of them were well aware that any advantage they gained could only be temporary.

On August 24th I was ordered to La Marsa to a new job, and General House sent me over in an A-20. From the nose of an A-20 the Sicily-Tunis trip was lovelier than I had ever imagined (I had done it often, but always in C-47's), the whole haunted land and cobalt sea rushing up at the eyes with no interfering medium at all, as if at every moment you were about to embrace it all physically with immensely outstretched arms. La Marsa was the beach town outside of Tunis where the North African Air Forces had their headquarters and the officers lived along the sea in little white villas with sandy gardens. The bathing was wonderful and the headquarters officers, who were no more overworked here than they usually are, took full advantage of it. Old friends from Washington or Casablanca or Constantine—Dewitt Sage, Palmer Dixon, Jack McGuire and a dozen others—made a visit to Tunis a little bit like a class reunion, and in this atmosphere I spent the time until it was necessary to go to Algiers to get on the *Ancon*.

The new job was that of executive officer, as they decided to call it, of technical intelligence, on the operation we called Avalanche—that is, the invasion of Italy by way of the Salerno beaches. Technical intelligence had two main parts to it, the first of which included the work of those who classified enemy matériel and either reported on the enemy's mechanical secrets or sent the captured objects back to the War Office in London or Wright Field in America for study. The second part of the section was the interrogation of enemy prisoners of war. A third part, for which I was only briefly responsible (D-day and two days afterward) was a combat camera unit which was supposed to get photographs of the landing and the immediately ensuing action and then get out to America with the results. My function was to hold these parts together, keep in control at least of their movements, relate their activities to each other when necessary, and report on what they were doing (as distinct from their own technical reports) to the higher headquarters in La Marsa. The whole personnel

involved in these detachments, even with part of a British
air regiment (aviation ground troops) assigned to us to guard
prisoners, came to something like two hundred. Of these only
about ten were technicians concerned with enemy aircraft and
matériel, with their jeep drivers and party, and another five
or six were prisoner of war interrogators with an equal number of jeep drivers. My people were mixed British and American, with one South African lieutenant who happened to speak
Italian and German; the guards were British, the jeep drivers,
cooks and personnel attached to the technicians were Americans; we drew American rations through the Air Support
Command, had vehicles from the North African Air Forces
and appeared on the strength reports of nobody, so far as I
ever found out, in the entire field. Such an anomalous situation had never come my way before, because I had always
served with purely American units (the Air Support Command, the Bomber Command, the Training Command and
again Air Support, all of our own Twelfth Air Force) and had
no experience of the peculiar "sandwiching," as they called
it, which went on in the more exalted headquarters. In this
"sandwiching" an American commander was supposed always
to have a British deputy, a British commander an American
deputy, and all the highest levels were thus to be more completely Anglo-American than would be possible or desirable
lower down. I suppose it worked well; it seems to have produced good results on the whole, and was the principal invention (I think) of General Eisenhower in that realm which he
made peculiarly his own, that of amalgamation with the British. On my own very low and obscure level I did not much
like it, because it was without legal basis as everybody knew;
consequently I was in no real position to give orders to the
British officers who were the chief components of the unit
for which I was responsible. I had no legal command functions
of any kind. The whole "technical intelligence" detachment

was an invention, a convenience, a way of expediting information back to London and to Wright Field and Washington on certain things we considered important, but there was no machinery known to military science by which an American officer could legally hold command over British officers (or vice versa). In other words, the "North African Air Forces" themselves did not legally exist, and any unit or detachment which was made up of British and Americans working together was a bastard child of this wholly fictional command. If a British officer chose to disregard my requests, wishes or orders, as the squadron leader in charge of prisoners of war did more than once, I was without authority to enforce them. (I could, of course, have made a pompous report against him, which in due course would have reached the War Office and caused some action perhaps of some kind, but hardly during the present war.) It even proved rather difficult to keep track of the movements of all the personnel for which I was responsible, since they had acquired in the Tunisian and Sicilian campaigns the habit of accounting to nobody for their actions so long as their technical information was regularly supplied. They had vehicles from Tunis, which did not have to be checked in at any motor pool in Italy, and consequently it was never possible to be sure where they all were at any one moment; nor, in the nature of their work, would this have been invariably necessary; and I would have cared nothing except that I had been instructed to keep them within reach. Thus I turned into a kind of anxious hen for some weeks of the Italian campaign, with sections of my detachment dotted here and there over the countryside and me never able to get them all quite under my wing.

Some days passed in the rather torpid atmosphere of La Marsa, where the war was so distant that nobody even bothered to keep up the blackout. One night Thornton Wilder (then a major) turned up at the officers' mess with a friend from

Cairo who had brought French brandy all that distance, and we drank it on the balcony of Thornton's quarters, a part of the mess building built right out over the sea. This was the harem of the Bey's beach palace there, and the middle of the house had a roof covering but no floor, so that the sea water at a respectable depth formed a sort of swimming pool for the ladies of the household, with their balconies and sleeping quarters all around it. Thornton and his friend and I drank the exquisite Bisquit Dubouché (exquisite to us in 1943— more so in 1945) above this plashy interior and tried to imagine what the scene had been like only a few years before. On another occasion all my friends of the old Bomber Command had a splendid dinner at the hotel in Tunis—the Bomber Command had now become the Strategic Air Force, and was before very long to blossom out as the Fifteenth Air Force, free and independent—where we sang songs and felt that the campaign of the winter before had happened in the days of Queen Elizabeth. Then, one day, I had been sufficiently instructed in my coming duties and took the plane to Algiers.

Algiers was no longer so much the center of the allied world at war, since a great deal of the "brass" had moved to Tunisia and Sicily. The Hotel St. George was still surrounded by sentries, red tape and secrecy, and the supreme military powers (Eisenhower, Tedder, Spaatz and the like) still dwelt in villas on the hills near by, but the streets of the town were no longer thronged with G.I.'s and it was occasionally possible to get the attention of a barber or bookseller. I encountered my old friend "Sully"—Commodore Sullivan, chief salvage officer of the navy—within the first fifteen or twenty minutes of my stay in Algiers, and moved into his quarters for the duration of the wait. He, too, was going on this expedition, and we left together for the *Ancon* late on the night of September 4th.

Sully has not hitherto figured in these memoranda, but his part in the work and life of our advancing forces had been important from the beginning. It was he who came into Casablanca as soon as the fighting was over and cleared the port, struggling hard to raise and save those French ships which we had been obliged to sink. He did the same in Algiers and Oran, Bizerte and Tunis and Palermo. He was soon to do the same in Naples—as he did in the Pacific, in Normandy, Belgium and everywhere else during these years. If we got a port opened and working in good time it was owing to the work of Sully and his boys, who were without hours, schedules or the conception of fatigue during the first period of any occupation. Aside from his very respectable contribution to the winning of the war, Sully was a superb morale officer—nothing seemed to shake his amiable spirit or cause him more than a passing worry, and his quarters anywhere in Africa or Italy were always a place to which I most willingly repaired in moments of gloom or difficulty, certain that the clouds would be blown away. He had the bluff and candid appearance which we associate with seafaring men of experience, but along with this sea-dog air and manner he carried a shrewd intelligence with respect to whole worlds of problems which most of our officers were content to leave completely unplumbed. Sully had been aware of the Fascist-Nazi conspiracy for years and did not in the least feel that the war was becoming "less ideological" with success. This alone differentiated him sharply from most of the men with whom, in his service as in mine, the conduct of the war produced association.

The *Ancon* put out to sea sometime on the early morning of September 5th and we described a course which took us in a big arc around Sicily and on to Salerno beach from the northwest. The convoys were huge, some of them from Oran, some from Algiers, Bizerte and other ports in our area, and some actually from Tripolitania or even Egypt, with appointed rendezvous here and there in the ocean. When we came round the northern corner of Sicily I saw, or imagined

I could see, the rocks of Mondello, where I had been living up until very recently, and no doubt the enormous convoy was seen from there and from other points, not to speak of the ports of departure. In any case one thing is sure, the landings at Salerno did not surprise the Germans. If we could calculate the extreme limit of fighter protection from our new fields near Milazzo in the tip of Sicily, so could the Germans; and any such calculation brought your pencil precisely down on the Salerno beaches.

We expected attack from the air, but it did not materialize until the night of September 8th, two nights before the landing. The Germans were not unaware of our convoys, but they probably wished to save their attack until it could be most effective, and we took the brunt of it on D-day itself and the next day, when the ships were conveniently (for them) close together and busy. I felt at the time and have felt ever since that this was the last big effort of the Luftwaffe, which actually did throw in force from all parts of Italy and Southern France to damage our shipping. It also afforded some of the last spectacular examples of sky battle between fighter aircraft in this theater, high in the dazzling sky over the crowded gulf and encarnadined (not to say bloody) beaches. Our arrangements to beat off attack from the air were all centered in the *Ancon*, which also was the control ship for the army and navy communication nets as well; as a result the ship bristled with rods, wires, cables and gadgetry of all sorts which could be seen from a considerable distance with the naked eye, and it was inevitably the primary target for German bombing. If I am not mistaken we got nineteen bombings in twenty-four hours, and although a considerable number of bombs fell in our immediate neighborhood, causing much noise and agitation, we were never hit. (The German radio spoke of "a control ship of a new type," obviously the *Ancon,* and said with the coolest mendacity that it had been hit, but this was not so. The *Savan-*

nah, alongside, damaged on D-plus-one with a radio-directed bomb, and some other of our neighbors may have been meant, but it is fairly safe to assume that German lies were merely lies and nothing more.)

Our first bombing at sea was a sight of great and terrible beauty. Our Beaufighters, controlled from the *Ancon,* pursued and shot down two or three of the German attackers, and our anti-aircraft from the ships made splendid the night. On the night before the landing we had the same attentions and the same spectacle, with the added tension caused by the extraordinary happenings of the hours just past and those just to come. For at six o'clock in the evening our supreme headquarters at Algiers had announced on the radio (heard, of course, on all our ships) that an armistice had been signed with Italy; Marshal Badoglio later in the evening had broadcast orders to the Italians to lay down their arms; but we were to make the combat landing the next morning just the same. I listened to the Rome radio as best I could, down in the bowels of the *Ancon* where all our radio controls for the aircraft were, but could not make out what was happening there. I knew that one airborne division (the 82nd) had been supposed to jump there over the airfields, which Badoglio was to have clearly marked and guarded for our use; I did not know for a day or so how the Germans had taken control of Rome and arrested many responsible Italians while Badoglio, King and Cabinet all escaped to the south. The German air attack that night, prolonged and determined, served at least to let us know that these events—this "armistice"—would mean nothing to our troops, who were going to have to fight for it just the same. The admirals and generals aboard the *Ancon* had decided to explain the plan, in its larger lines, to all on the ship that night, and chose Quentin Reynolds, who was aboard as correspondent for *Collier's* magazine, to speak in their name. Quent's rolling basso, rich with humor and sympathy, has seldom been heard to greater advantage in my experience; he did a great deal for the spirits of the sorely bewildered G.I.'s that evening. On the following evening (D-day) he performed the same function, explaining the results of the day's work to all the soldiers and sailors on board our ship. On the night before D-day a weird thought occurred to many of us: we hoped that the Germans had no device by which they could pick up Quent's speech from our local loudspeaker machinery, as it gave not only our plan (which by then was fairly obvious) but also our strength and dispositions. The technical people said such a thing was impossible, but the ignorant, like myself, had seen too many impossibilities given concrete existence during the course of this war to be incredulous any more.

The dawn brought our naval bombardment to its climax and started our infantry landings. It was an exquisite dawn and a blazing sunrise—for many of our boys their last. Through that day and most of those which followed during the next week the gulf of Salerno was brilliant in sunlight, although a white haze sometimes gathered in the upper air and there was, after the radio-directed bomb became the focus of our anxieties, a lavish use of smoke-screening by the navy. From the air point of view our chief interest in the day's work was that the field at Montecorvino, one of the best in Southern Italy, should be seized at once so that we could use it; but it did not fall into our hands for two days, and then was so effectively commanded by German artillery in the hills behind it that it was of no use for aircraft. Aside from this, the chief preoccupation for Tom Darcy—who as A-3 had direct responsibility—was to see that our fighter patrols covered the beaches and the ships in the order established, kept their due twenty minutes or whatever it was and got back to their Sicilian bases. (The length of time a fighter patrol stayed over the battle area depended, of course, upon the type of aircraft: the P-38's stayed a great deal longer than the Spitfires, for instance.)

There were sharp engagements in the air. The Luftwaffe was unquestionably making a real effort, and before D-day was half over we made acquaintance with the radio-directed bomb, which for a week or so caused a great flurry of concern throughout the allied world, particularly in the navies.

This device was one with which we had some acquaintance (through British Air Ministry Intelligence) although we had never met it before. It was a carefully guarded German secret, and although all German airmen had heard of it in a rather vague way—as they freely said under interrogation—only the members of one Kg. (bomber group—*Kampfgeschwade*) had been entrusted with it. The unit in question was Kg. 100, based in the South of France, and composed of Dornier aircraft (Do-117). These ships began to come over the gulf on the morning of D-day and continued for some days thereafter, doing considerable damage and stirring up such excitement in London and Washington that whole relays of experts were told off to investigate, and continued to arrive long after the device was no longer used and the Luftwaffe had, to all intents and purposes, given up the battle. In so far as I understand this or any other gadget of the kind, the bomb was released at some distance before the target and then controlled by radio in its descent. The aircraft had to slow up at the moment when the bomb left the ship, and the pilot then had to keep his position very exactly, as any deflection impaired the accuracy of the bomb's aim. The slowing-up naturally made the aircraft more vulnerable, and the device depended to such an extent upon the impassivity and superhuman control of the pilot that it was not, in actual fact, a very good weapon. It had two good hits: the British battleship *Warspite* and the American cruiser *Savannah*, two which were quite enough to justify the stir caused in London and Washington. The *Savannah*, alongside our ship, was hit at half-past ten on the morning of D-plus-one, and the bomb went straight down amidships, killing some two

hundred men. My friend Sully had to deal with the results
of all such attacks, and I remember one occasion when the Germans (at night, not with a radio-directed bomb) attacked a
hospital ship of ours and created some horrible carnage; Sully
came back looking very solemn and said to me gravely, "After
a sight like that I know that I can never like war. Any war."

Naturally the advent of the radio-controlled bomb was
something which made my technical intelligence detachment
more important than before. The messages from higher headquarters began to arrive on D-plus-one and continued steadily
for days. The technical experts (Wing Commander Turnbull
and Captain Getty) were implored for any detail on any scrap
of bomb, aircraft or radio; the interrogators were urged to
question every German prisoner in hope of getting some light.
Actually one of the Dornier planes which launched these
bombs fell in the water on D-2 and we had a chance at their
pilot and navigator, but German airmen in those days were
much harder to "crack" than they afterwards became, and we
got little. As it happened the bomb which fell on the *Warspite*
was reconstructed by the experts in London and, with such
indications as we were able to give, pieced together with bits
from here and there, a fairly satisfactory notion of the device
was obtained, which did us no great good as the Germans then
ceased to use it. Our immediate task was, during the whole
period of the Salerno battle, to try to find out how we could
jam the apparatus by radio. This involved a line of interrogation and investigation which need not be detailed here (even
if I understood it, which I do not). In the most immediate
sense, on D-day, my job was to find my technical detachment
and tell them what to look for; but the *Ancon* was so isolated
from the shore that I found no means of getting off until
D-plus-one (September 11th), when Sully acquired a boat and
took me to the beach.

The shallow beach all round the gulf was one on which

"ducks" (I know no other name for the big amphibian truck) and other special craft had better luck than ordinary small boats, and Sully and I got over the last bit of water by "duck" and an improvised pontoon pier. Rations, ammunition and every other kind of supplies littered the beach. The unloading was incessant, the movement of LST's and LCI's and "ducks" scarcely interrupted even by German attacks from the air. The beach where we landed was (I believe) Red Number One, which was directly behind the temples of Paestum, and the narrow half-sunken road from the beach to the ruins was choked with American vehicles. At the place where the beach road joins the main highway from Naples to the south there was already an American M.P. stationed, directing traffic, and a Signal Corps company was installed in the Temple of Neptune, stringing its wires from column to column.

I found my technical intelligence detachment all together —for probably the last time in the campaign—in a rose-colored villa to the north of the ruins of Paestum, just beyond the airstrip which the aviation engineers had started to make on D-day. The strip had been completed at noon this day and the first two of our aircraft which attempted to land on it, both disabled, had been shot down by our eager anti-aircraft. These were a P-38 and a Spitfire. I saw them both, and wondered sadly at the inevitability of such tragic accidents in war. The infantry headquarters (both of the VI Corps, the Americans, and of the 36th Division which was a part of it) had been established in a tobacco factory a little farther up the highway —a long, low barrack of a building in which the tobacco leaves were still hanging, setting up a perpetual dusty cough-laden air. The fighting had been sharp here the day before but had now moved to the hills just beyond; the 36th Division had deployed (how it had deployed!) to the east and south, the 45th to the east and north, but through some startling circumstance which I was never able to understand, the Germans had remained along the Sele River and in the towns of Eboli and Battipaglia north of it, so that the American VI Corps on the south was separated from the British X Corps on the north by a band of enemy. This circumstance—the German salient between the two halves of the Fifth Army—was what caused all our alarums and excursions of the succeeding days and nights.

My orders were to stick to the Air Support Command and have the parts of my detachment report to me there. After passing on what I had to say of the radio-directed bomb I asked Turnbull and the others to check in with me daily at the Air Support Command, but when they asked where that might be I could not answer. The fact was that the Command was so dependent upon radio equipment that it was now facing a crisis: its apparatus for operation had been, through some fantastic misunderstanding, taken off a ship and left at Milazzo, so that all the controls had to remain on board the *Ancon* until the error was rectified. When our general and staff would land, or where, were not to be guessed yet. And indeed on that day there was no possibility of establishing the air controls on shore, and it was not until D-plus-two that we piled up in an LCI and made for a beach above Montecorvino. I had, in the meantime, gone on shore each of the two days to keep in touch with my detachment, and had observed in some consternation that while our troops pushed east and south, the Germans seemed to have been getting stronger in the area they held in our middle, on the Sele River. When we did land with bag and baggage, on a littered beach in the British area, we were above the German salient and could not communicate with the American army corps by the highway, which the Germans held, but only on a sort of goat track down by the shore, which in turn was none too safe from artillery fire. It looked very much indeed as if our army had been cut in two.

Those first days were strange and fruitful in impressions of strangeness. It was odd indeed to come back from the beaches, on which nobody had anything to eat except K rations, and find our navy mess running in its usual luxurious plenty. We had everything—meat, ice cream, fruit and vegetables—on the *Ancon*. But the control ship had been fitted out at great expense and was the only one of her kind then in existence; threatened, as she was, by incessant bombings, the *Ancon* gave the naval High Command an altogether special headache, which terminated in a kind of ultimatum to us all (air and ground commands) to get on shore so that the ship could be removed to safety. Thus on D-plus-two (September 12th) toward the end of the afternoon, we moved at last to a bivouac in an apple orchard near the village of San Antonio, on the road below Salerno. It was singularly ill-chosen for our purposes, since the Germans lay between us and our army headquarters on the other side of the Sele River, and the next day we had to move south; but on that night the soldiers walked almost reverently through the green grass and touched the apple trees and said, "This is not a bit like Africa." They were so used to baked, unyielding earth and cactus and olive groves that grass and apple trees seemed a little unreal, a little too much like home. They had never been able to think of Sicily as anything but an island belonging to the coast of Africa, and the notion that Italy was in fact the beginning of another continent was slow to make its way in their heads.

On the next day I had to take two trips between the halves of our army, across the area held, in part at any rate, by the enemy. It was an unpleasant business because it was impossible to tell just how far down the Germans had come toward the sea; we knew they commanded the highway, but in the fields below the highway their whereabouts were still, for a little while, uncertain. The only road open to us was the wretched little goat track down by the sea, which, since it was commanded by the guns of our ships, was apparently a little too risky for the Germans. They were, however, able to lob shells into it from time to time. North of the Sele River the detour came back again to the highway and we crossed the river in a traffic block which was being handled with special zeal by the M.P.'s. All south of the river was ours, between the highway and the sea and for some few hundred yards up from the highway. The Fifth Army headquarters (General Clark's) was in a red villa directly beside the Sele River on the south. I had to find my detachment and return to the Air Support Command north of the gap; upon doing so I discovered that they had moved in the interim and I had to come back again. The bivouac, when found, was in the dustiest olive grove to be found south of the Sele, next to the headquarters troops and staff sections of General Clark's headquarters, which had also hastily moved. The amount of moving that had been done that afternoon set up a haze of dust over the bivouac area, and during the week or more that we remained there the dust never settled. We used to take baths in our steel helmets and achieve a blackness of resultant water such as would have been startling in the muddiest river; the dust settled in our noses, lungs, throats; it grew caked with perspiration in the most inaccessible corners of the body. Our name for this bivouac was "the Dust Bowl." Its main advantage, indeed only one, was that the olive groves were so extensive that our tents were presumed to be invisible from the air, and indeed the German aircraft seemed all to pass over us to attack down on the beach, as our naval bombardment passed over us to land further inland.

That night—September 13th—was "the battle of the bedding-rolls" for our headquarters squadron. To reduce congestion in the bivouac area these troops had been ordered out just after sunset and found still another resting place in low-lying ground just beside the Sele River. In the soft light evening we all went down and bathed placidly in the cool water without any idea of how near we were to the Germans; we were perhaps visible to them, as they had crept down the stream

273

during the afternoon and were about to attack parts of our 45th Division, on the other bank, as soon as it was dark. I had acquired an Italian student pilot during the late afternoon: a young man—let us call him Mario Mario—who had stolen his single-seater training aircraft on the field near Forlì in Northern Italy and flown it down to us on the shell-swept field of Montecorvino. The boy had heard Badoglio's orders to join the allies and obeyed them, no doubt without any real conception of the risk he was taking; he had flown right over the city of Naples and over part of our own fleet without drawing much anti-aircraft fire, and he burned with a simple zeal to fly and fight on our side. Mario was turned over to me because we had—strange as it may seem—no clear idea of what to do with such volunteers; on the following afternoon I got him on a transport plane to Sicily, where a number of others were collecting; what became of him afterwards I never knew. On that night he was my responsibility, and I had to find bedding and a mosquito net for him on the long grass in the valley by the Sele. It was an astounding evening. The searchlights from the fleet were incessant; there was fire of all sorts in the air, and at about ten o'clock one of our Beaufighters pursued and destroyed a German bomber directly in front of us—a wild fury of flame, a comet-like descent and a thunderous explosion on the ground. Mario said to me: "Of course you are used to this. To me it is very remarkable. I have been a student for two years and have never seen anything of the war. I envy you, being so used to it." The poor boy apparently thought that a three-ring circus of this sort, combat by land, sea and air, which happened seldom enough in anybody's experience, was the merest commonplace to us.

At midnight a runner from the Signal Corps unit further up the river reached us and gave Cropper, the headquarters commandant, some verbal orders: we were to get out immediately, taking only the clothes on our backs, small arms and

274

ammunition, and retire down the highway with all possible speed, as the Germans were near at hand on the Sele. The task of dealing with them was to be left to the 45th Division.

We only half believed what we were told, but the orders were explicit, and we got out with all the speed and silence of which we were capable. Our vehicles were crowded enough with men alone, and Cropper insisted on leaving every scrap of our belongings, strictly as ordered; there was many a moan and groan over the bedding we had to leave in that grassy vale, in the midst of which there was my rare and wonderful air mattress, the Télepte mattress. In that calm, moonlit night, as the firing had died down and the air was for the first time almost cool, it seemed difficult indeed to believe that the Germans were almost upon us, but we learned afterwards that there had been no error; they did indeed creep down the river practically to the sea. The bombing attack in which our Beau had shot down a Ju-88 a little earlier had as its primary target "American troops beside the river." That disturbed and sleepless night, with the agitated day that followed, constituted our big Salerno crisis, during which the German salient threatened the whole American army corps and there was a serious possibility that we might have to evacuate the beaches altogether. What turned the Germans back and forced them in a few days to pull out altogether was the relentless use of our whole Strategical Air Force for tactical purposes on September 15th and 16th.

These bombardments we saw with something like awe. Our B-17's, B-25's and B-26's came over in large, compact formations again and again, at medium altitudes, and poured destruction down upon the German troops at Eboli, Battipaglia and the highway on either side. It seemed impossible that anything could live under such a rain of explosive; as we stood there and watched the bombs fall in the dazzling sunlight we knew that the danger of defeat on this beach-head was over.

Owing to the delays of communication and censorship, our perils were past before they became known to the world at large, and just when Washington and London grew most worried about us was when we needed their solicitude least. We had gathered under the olive tree in which our radio was set up for two or three nights, listening to the B.B.C. say that "everything was proceeding according to plan at Salerno," and the irony of that bland optimism was compensated for during the next two nights when we heard—now that we felt safe—how serious our situation was. The tremendous naval bombardment from the British and American warships which augmented the efforts of our Strategical Air Force played its part, no doubt a vital one, in the destruction of the German salient, and the day came soon when we were able to go straight through on the wrecked highway, through the rubbish of what had once been Eboli and Battipaglia, to Salerno.

Before that day came the Third Division was with us. I remember the sharp delight with which I saw that blue-and-white patch again, coming in on the beach road by the temples of Paestum, a week or so ahead of the time scheduled for its arrival, and the instinctive response of so many of us: "Oh, we're all right now, the Third Division is here." It pushed out north of the Sele at once, and with the 45th and 36th played its full part in the advance on Naples.

Then, at the end of the month, when we had moved from the Dust Bowl to a leafy, wet and much-trenched area where the Germans had been a short time before (and what holes those Germans dug! I nearly broke my neck in them in the dark, more than once) Naples fell: it was one of my duties to get there as quickly as possible, to take charge of whatever the Germans and Italians had left on the big field at Capodichino. We drove in on the first of October in an endless line of American army vehicles which traversed the endless ruins along the Castellammare road. The spectacle had a curious

276

and almost repellent pathos. On both sides of us, for mile after weary mile, were the rubbish heaps which had once been dwellings, and we were fully conscious that the destruction was our work, our necessary and inevitable but heart-sickening work; yet from these heaps of dust and shattered stone the people, women, children, old men and even young ones, came out to cheer us and throw flowers, lining our way with the signals of relief and welcome. It did not seem possible that so many thousands of Italians could be glad to see us in the midst of all this devastation, and yet we could hardly doubt the sincerity of the feeling which found such emotional or even hysterical expression. In front of the great Fascist post office in the heart of the almost deserted city of Naples, from which the last Germans had only that morning made their way out on the road to Pomigliano, a man who seemed delirious with some stormy joy for which he had no words poured red wine from a Chianti flask down my surprised throat. The woman who was with him was weeping with excitement. The agitation died down within three or four days, but while it lasted it gave powerful evidence of the intensity with which these Southerners had disliked the war, the Germans and the tyranny which wartime made heavy upon them. I should be slow to attribute all this show of feeling to any true or reasoned revolt against Fascism, for I had seen the Neapolitan populace going mad with joy too often over Fascist shows in the past, but there was no doubt that at the present moment (October, 1943) the Fascist buffoonery had lost all its charm, the Fascist gamble was seen to be an unrelieved disaster for Italy, and the first impulse of the weary, resentful people was to rejoice over the advent of a conqueror whose tradition or legend— well supported by a serious propaganda effort—was one of magnanimity. It was to be my doubtful privilege to watch this hopeful excitement die and change, in successive months, into a cynical determination to make what could be made out of the individual generosity or gullibility of the Americans since nothing, it seemed, was to be expected of their collective activity. The very bread which we brought with us, which came off the ships within a week of our arrival, had to be distributed "through regular local authorities" (that is, chiefly through Fascists and neo-Fascists) and thus reached the black market within the hour. I myself bought American bread, that is to say white bread made with American flour, on the black market within a very few hours of its first appearance on the Italian mainland.

In the early days in Naples I was quartered with my technicians in a great white tenement not far from the Capodichino airfield; later I briefly inhabited a highly furnished and decorated apartment in the Palazzo Caraffa, holding it for a general; still later I rejoined the headquarters staff in a tent under the wet trees of the park at Capodimonte palace, above the city. During my time in the baroque splendors of the Caraffa palace I had engaged (for the general, who never used the place) two domestics of the feudal entourage of Prince Caraffa. They were, inevitably, named Gennaro and Maria, from whom I learned a great deal about the life of the people of Naples, bewildered and harassed as they had been throughout the war by exactions undreamed of in other days, and struggling now against malnutrition and despair in a city which had neither water nor electricity nor means of transport. It was Maria who bought on the black market for me, and although the prices she mentioned with consternation did not seem too exorbitant for us with "occupation" lire at one hundred to the dollar, they represented an unimaginable disaster for the Neapolitan poor.

With my friend Eugene Cropper I visited the antiquarians' shops which, within three or four days of our arrival, began to open their doors and mark up their prices. Tortoise shell and coral, neither of which I wanted, were swept off the mar-

278

ket within a few days of the allied occupation, and it was interesting to see the spurious concoctions which rapidly began to take their place. The bourgeoisie, now more beset than ever—since many of them drew their incomes from Rome and the North—began to sell objects of art and curiosity within the week: laces, wedding veils, linen, tablecloths, ivory, silver, jewels and all sorts of little minor treasures like painted boxes, fans, miniatures and the like. Once as I was standing in a shop in the Strada di Chiaia a fresh-faced girl dressed in dark, worn clothing of good quality came in and unwrapped a sword for the dealer: it was her father's sword, she said, and from what I glimpsed of it it must have been a presentation weapon of some kind. The dealer said he could not buy it; the Americans were not interested in swords, he explained. She went out without a word. Phallic symbols from Pompeii—in which a flourishing industry was soon established—were perhaps the chief object of interest for the American soldier purchaser, with saints, madonnas and other holy images or paintings a poor second. The officers bought tortoise and coral until there was no more, and then searched for laces and fans.

On the public food markets very little was reaching the city from the rich plains near by. It was extraordinary indeed to see Naples without oranges or tangerines, for example, when the whole Sorrento peninsula groaned with the fruit. The prices for what vegetables reached the market were startling to the Neapolitans, and their *tessera,* the ration book, would not buy its quota of flour or cheese since there was almost no flour or cheese. Naples without spaghetti was as startling as Naples without oranges. Prostitution, which had grown apace during the months of German occupation and food shortages, now passed all bounds, and the army prophylactic stations became the most frequent and noteworthy landmarks of the city. The Germans had so drenched the town with sulfonamide drugs that the venereal microbes were immune to them, and our doctors had a first-class problem on their hands. They bitterly disliked using penicillin for such cases, since their supply was so urgently needed for the treatment of wounds at the front, but they were driven to it in due course. When typhus made its appearance the medical authorities seized the opportunity to put Naples out of bounds to all troops stationed elsewhere, which was one way of dealing with the problem but made combat troops and air corps units bitter at the favoritism shown the base supply soldiers (the despised "rear echelon"), who had the city to themselves.

Long before this semi-quarantine took place I had been transferred from the wet park above Naples to the cold seaside cottages at Santo Spirito, above Bari, where the Tactical Air Force had its headquarters. General Cannon was the deputy commander of this air force, which included all our fighter, fighter-bomber and light bombing aircraft (the B-25's but not the B-26's, which belonged to Strat—the Strategical Air Force). The Tactical Air Force—Taf—included the American Twelfth Air Force, to which I had belonged since the original D-day, as well as the Desert Air Force (British) and the tactical bomber command. Even at the time it was difficult to explain these transitory arrangements by which the Americans and British air forces were fused in operations, and by now no doubt the words have lost all meaning; but it can at least be said that Taf was mainly British, the surviving headquarters of Air Marshal Cunningham after his journey across the desert and junction with the Americans. In the senior mess of Taf there were four American officers and some twenty-two British. Lower down, on the actual airfields and by the actual count of aircraft, the Americans preponderated, but in this high headquarters an American was a foreigner and—owing to the differences in our staff systems—felt strange indeed for a long time. I was often on our airfields, at Foggia, Manfredonia and elsewhere, and often in flight or on the road between Bari and Naples, so I did not languish too monotonously amid the alien corn; but I did so enough to get a shrewd idea of how and why the Americans and British failed to get along together as well as the inventors of this system had hoped.

My principal source of disquiet, both in Naples and in Bari, was in a region which theoretically did not concern me at all: that is, in what I could not help observing of the relation between the allies and Italy. It had been part of my functions to receive Italian volunteers coming to us from all parts of Italy, the Adriatic and Greece. There were some remarkable examples of reckless bravery among these young airmen. Most had stolen the aircraft in which they arrived, very few came to us unscathed, and all were subject to killing on sight by the Germans as "traitors" under the German view of Italy's surrender. One crew, if such a makeshift collection of adventurous youths could be called a crew, brought a Savoia-Marchetti bomber from the Peloponnesus to the field at Crotone by means of a map about the size of a playing card, on which the amateur navigator had drawn two converging lines. I was always being struck by the courage and spirit of these boys in coming to join us at such risk, and it occurred to me that some public announcement of what they were doing might encourage others to do the same, or might at least show that there was some gain to us in making the armistice with Italy. The ruling of a high authority in Taf (British, of course) was that "We don't want to make heroes out of these bloody Eyeties." Consequently nothing of all this was made public at any time, although it could only have strengthened our position and encouraged our friends to do so. What was even more disheartening was that the only thing I could do for any of these Italian volunteers was to send them to the Badoglio government at Brindisi—an almost purely Fascist organization which had as its chief aim the maintenance of "discipline" in the remains of the Italian armed forces. The interpretation of "discipline" was, of course, that any wild youth who came to us to fly combat or to jump from aircraft in espionage missions should be severely reprimanded and put to opening and shutting doors for Fascist generals. That is what actually happened to some in my knowledge.

These things I saw were a small part of a large allied failure—a failure to understand the nature of the Italian problem and our relation to it. I had thoroughly understood and approved of our policy toward the French in North Africa, and consider it the only possible policy toward a friendly nation with which we were never at war. But Italy was the origin of the evil we had set out to cure; Italy was the breeding place of Fascism, the instrument of Mussolini. We should in common sense have had a rigid system of differentiation between friend and foe in such a land. The known anti-Fascists were *ipso facto* our friends (at least to begin with) and the known Fascists were our enemies. Italy had declared war upon us; we were at war with Italy; we were not bound to treat Italian jurisdictions, susceptibilities or nationalistic suspicions with the same tactful reverence that was bound upon us by common decency in dealing with the French. It was quite possible to find out in Italy who was Fascist and who was not; all this was a matter of public record. And yet . . .

Well, the whole world knows what we did. We forbade the anti-Fascists even to assemble, for a long time; even their funeral processions or memorials were forbidden; we installed Fascist officials on the ground that they were the "only competent officials"; we requisitioned the houses, properties and printing presses of the anti-Fascists while the most notorious Fascists went untouched; we treated the whole population with the same wholesale visible contempt, Fascist and anti-Fascist alike, all "bloody Eyeties," and the only privileged exceptions were those disreputable elements which clung about the thrice-dishonored King and the wretched old Marshal. For a long time we did not realize that this incredible course *was a policy*: I, for one, thought our consistent wrongdoing was the result of ignorance, confusion, the lack of firm directives and, in short, the *lack* of a policy. It was not until much later, until Mr. Winston Churchill showed his hand in speeches in the House of Commons, that it was proved how clearly this had been a policy from the very beginning—a policy of neo-Fascism based upon the monarchy, the Marshal and the so-called "elements of order." That we drove even the most favorable of Italian democrats into an attitude of skepticism toward us, and prepared the way for a hospitable reception to revolutionary novelties of which we (presumably) did not approve, that we effectively destroyed the House of Savoy by insisting upon supporting its discredited representatives, that we greatly enlarged the Socialist and Communist parties by delaying their legality, that we made it difficult for Italian patriots in the North to work with or for us, that we strengthened the hands of the Germans throughout the area they occupied by our course in the area we occupied—all this could, I think, be abundantly demonstrated upon the public record from the time of the Italian "armistice" until the spring of 1945. American misgivings upon the whole business began to appear very early, and were strong among those who had most directly to deal with Italians; yet in all these matters Americans were subsidiary to British officers who apparently knew what they were doing and why. Only later did we begin to hear how this came about—how that Italy and, indeed, the whole Mediterranean had been assigned to Britain as a zone of political operations; how British policy under Mr. Churchill had been conceived as a whole in a neo-Fascist pattern in which the "elements of order" were always to be preferred to popular forces; how Italy was only part of a pattern which also included Greece, Spain and—until force changed this detail—Yugoslavia as well.

At the time only part of this was apparent, and even that part seemed hard to believe. It was difficult for me to see how even Mr. Churchill, whose Tory and imperialist temperament was perfectly well known to me, could have any faith in a course which alienated the Italian masses for the benefit of a worthless King and his worthless son, or salvaged whole sections of the Fascist hierarchy for the service of Badoglio. The whole thing was contrary to common sense, and I never understood how it came to be accepted by Roosevelt—Roosevelt who had once said to me with obvious conviction, "I have always been a man of the Left." Meanwhile food and transport showed no improvement, the cold of the winter was only just bearable, the military campaign itself was costly and useless, and the anti-Fascist Italians of my acquaintance were growing more and more inclined to think that Soviet Russia provided the only possible hope for the future. I shared this belief for a while, thinking in my innocence that Vishinsky, when he came to Naples as Stalin's Ambassador, would put a stop to the most arrant of the allied nonsense; but Raimondo Craveri[1] disabused me of this notion. "You are quite wrong if you think the Russians wish to correct your errors and save you from them," he said. "They are on the contrary pleased to see you blunder on such a scale. They will even help you blunder." And when I went to see Croce on New Year's Day he had just had a visit from Vishinsky. "I tell you," he said to me in amazement, "Vishinsky is a monarchist." Not long afterwards the Soviet Union recognized Victor Emmanuel III and Badoglio, provoking an outcry in the allied capitals which I can only paraphrase thus: "How dare you recognize our puppets?" By this time we had so embroiled ourselves that it was the merest

---

[1] Craveri was a leader of the Actionists, both in the underground before our invasion and among the Northern partisans afterwards; he is a son-in-law of Croce.

child's play for the Russians to make us ridiculous without themselves undertaking the slightest responsibility.

Two elements must be isolated in the British behavior in Italy and, in due course, studied by those who will eventually have access to all the documents. The first was political: it was directed from on high, and its original source was undoubtedly Mr. Winston Churchill. I have already recorded my opinion that this was a reactionary policy, both wicked and foolish, directly contradicting the purposes of our war; but I should also hasten to record that a great many Englishmen agreed with me, even among those who were charged with carrying it out. They tried, for the sake of self-respect, to blame a good many of the errors on simple confusion and muddling. "You can't explain these things to soldiers," they would say when something really startling, like the seizure of the Laterza presses in Bari, took place. (The Laterza presses, which had never been seized in twenty years of Fascism, although they were the main source of anti-Fascist literature in Italy, were now commandeered by the Eighth Army.) There were also a great many Americans who were fully in accord with this policy, among them some of our Military Government officers who said, "We are not here to distinguish Fascists from non-Fascists." Thus, although the policy was unquestionably British, it cut across the lines of nationality. It was a Tory policy and as such appealed to Tories of all countries. The second element was psychological, or, to put it broadly, merely human. It involved the feelings, instincts, natural responses, of British soldiers who had been fighting Italians in the desert for more than two years and had never found any ground for respect or esteem toward them. In the Eighth Army you heard many stories of the nasty, bullying cruelty of Italians toward British prisoners of war—the blow in the face to the defenseless prisoner; the insults and jeering. No doubt these are mostly true, for in the nature of things the inferiority sensations of the Italian army, kept so vividly alive by their German allies, were bound to come out unpleasantly upon the captured Englishman. The Eighth Army and the Desert Air Force did not forget any of these things and had acquired an almost instinctive contempt for Italians as a result. Up to a point, it was mutual, because the Italian professional army and air officers felt that they had fairly beaten the British more than once, and that without the entrance of Russia and America into the war they would have been masters of the Mediterranean. In expansive moments one or two of them said so pretty plainly to me, and short of throwing the Germans in their teeth it was difficult to know what to reply. Relations between the British army and the Italian "co-belligerents" were not, therefore, based upon naturally favorable circumstances, and in my time were never very good.

The Americans, thoughtless, careless, unaware of anything important about the "wops" or their country, had no policy to guide them and no prejudices to wreak. Their generosity with army rations and their natural good nature made them individually popular among the Italians, although collectively they were soon seen to have brought no good to the country. At a later stage (in 1945) bands of American deserters roamed the country with Italian kindred spirits and produced a greater wave of lawlessness than Italy had known since the Risorgimento; it was no longer safe to go out at night in the streets of Rome; crimes of violence had increased beyond anything known to Italians. But in that first crucial winter these inevitable resultant stages of a dreary and depressing campaign, a drearier and more depressing meaninglessness in the whole situation, had not yet been produced; all that one saw was their generous embryo, the innumerable nits of a moldy future.

I withdrew at times into an almost totally civilian abstraction in which it was possible to communicate with the Italy that had existed before these events and would long survive them. A powerful assistance in this consolatory process was afforded by the bookshop of Laterza e Figli, at the corner of the Via Vittorio Veneto and the Via Dante in Bari. The Via Veneto is a main cross-street with a tramline on it; Via Dante Alighieri is a lengthwise street, one of those conceived as being parallel to the seashore, which, at some little distance toward the rising sun, gently curves and twists and returns to its main direction from north to south.

The Via Vittorio Veneto was lined with shops which still, at the coming of the allied armies, contained wares not often seen in cities at war. There were cameras and watches, the two objects most insatiably desired by the Anglo-Saxon soldiery; there were silver plates and cockleshell china, Venetian glass and carved wood. All day long the soldiers came and went in the street, staring through the glass (the shining, unbroken glass) at what still remained to be sold, breaking off with their own sudden unreasoning laughter, with incomprehensible conjointed whim pursuing in pairs whatever momentary diversion the street had suggested, or, occasionally, going into the shops to buy, with signs and signals and a word or two of bad French, kickshaws to send home or to place, unused and unusable, on the crowded table in the cold barracks, littered already with the empty bottles and tattered magazines, the dried figs, the canteen cups and the service caps of a dozen inmates.

The Via Dante Alighieri had fewer shops along its greater length. There were, to be sure, the café and pastry shop at the top, near the Corso, and there were some baskets, corks and sponges in a little hole-in-the-wall lower down, and there was a typewriter shop along there (with no typewriters), but most of the street was given over to the heavy stone *palazzi* of Italian city dwellers, apartment buildings which unsuccessfully imitated the façades, at least, of signorial establishments that were no more. It was a gloomy street in cold or cloudy weather because it was narrow and gave an effect of blank and sightless expanse with no windows to suggest an interior life behind those heavy walls; the soldiers did not walk here; there was no dawdling; those with business to do in this street went about it hastily, that winter.

At the southwest corner of the crossing of the two streets was the bookshop of Giuseppe Laterza and Sons. Behind one of its plate-glass windows there was displayed a selection of the works of Benedetto Croce; in another window were to be seen some mystic literature, Buddhist and Christian, some desk furniture, and a beautifully printed Italian translation of H. A. L. Fisher's *History of Europe*. But you would rattle the knob and tap on the glass in vain at the locked door between these two windows; nobody would come to open; the shop was shut.

When you knew how, you could go around to the side, in the Via Dante, and by ringing a bell you would be admitted to the great hinterland of the shop, a region where thousands of volumes, old and new, filled the shelves and the tables, reminding you with lavish and sudden emphasis that the world was not all B-17's and P-38's, hunger and blood and ruins—that there had been peace and would be peace again. Here were the books which, along with the lovely hills and warm valleys, the painting and the music and the wine, formed the Italian spirit in its specifically enduring, specifically Italian quality.

"Why," you might ask one of the Laterza brothers, "do you keep your shop locked up?"

"We tried having it open for a while," they would tell you. "It didn't work. A lot of soldiers bought books they obviously couldn't read, just for the pictures, or for the look of them. It hurt us to see books going out when we knew they would not be read. And we haven't enough left to waste books. We can't print anything more—the Allied armies take all our presses—and our stock would soon be exhausted. We're taking an inventory now, and we'll sell what we think we can afford to sell.

But we prefer to sell only to those who really want or need the books."

Fortunes are seldom made on such principles, and the Laterza brothers are not rich. But one soldier, at any rate, approached their door with deep respect, and ever revisited the silent and remembering poets in that vast interior with gratitude; none were exiles here, none strange or forlorn; all the stilled voices of the centuries made welcome the humble heart. In the half-light and the silence they came and went, these many men and women—Madonna Laura in her distant beauty, the sensuous laughter of the party at Fiesole, the haunted face of the grim Florentine; there the Venetian abbé trailed a white hand in lagoon water, here the peasant lovers bade farewell to their lakes and mountains; what Italy had said, felt, loved and suffered drifted through the air of the quiet room, suffused, penetrated, interpenetrated, lived again in the mind as men's dust does in the growing plants of the earth. Here in the back room of the Laterza bookshop in Bari we could see that time's reality lies not in its extension, which manifestly must to all men be more apparent than real, since no man can see beyond the time limit of his own life, but rather in the concentration upon one aware moment of all that most powerfully speaks to the consciousness out of innumerable moments past, giving sense, direction and organic continuity to what must otherwise be as fugitive as the single tick of a clock.

The Laterza brothers, as a firm of publishers (Gius. Laterza e Figli, Tipografi-Editori-Librai) were the institution most worthy of respect in Italy after 1922. Their course was undeviating, their courage and fortitude equal to the task. The task itself, in its scope and limits so wisely defined, must, I think, have been set out for them by the genius of their house, the august and venerable Benedetto Croce. They were always themselves the first to claim Croce as their guide; they were known most of all as his publishers, and for years prefaced their catalogue with a paragraph ending as follows:

"Our house, which owes its rapid development to the authoritative advice and assiduous co-operation of Croce, is proud to have contributed toward diffusing the entire work of this great Italian thinker, whom foreign authorities have judged 'master of literary and philosophical criticism.' "

To have made this claim or acknowledged this allegiance required fortitude in the era which ended July 25, 1943. Croce himself was at no time safe from Fascist malevolence, which surrounded his house, family and friends with unfriendly attentions; his mail was always read, his correspondence abroad interrupted, his finances made difficult. When the young Fascist ruffians broke into his house in Naples the police made no effort to protect him, and it was the fearless, indignant protest of Signora Croce which shamed them into going away after only minor violence. Every word Croce wrote was scrutinized with the utmost care by the Fascist authorities, but the essence of the matter always escaped them; they allowed Laterza to publish, again and again, matter which, if they had understood it, outraged every rule and fetish of their regime.

Laterza as a publisher carried out a task which was analogous to that of Croce as a writer. That is, he set rigorous standards of purely literary excellence, remained aloof from contemporary politics, gave thought and love to the Italian past, and approached all subjects in a mood of liberal Socialist idealism which was the precise antithesis of the Fascist mood and temper. Whether this mood was indeed Laterza's or was Croce's own does not affect the result. In the result, clear and beautiful, a shield of honor on the long record of the printing of books, what happened was this: for twenty years the house of Laterza in Bari never ceased to publish work which was animated by the love of justice and liberty, which denied in every line the ignorant assumptions and anti-historic claims of Fascism, reminded Italians that they had not always worn bondage willingly, and called upon them in the voices of Dante and Leopardi to come into their heritage.

This was done, of course, by indefatigable attention to the letter of the law. Laterza father and sons were none of them politicians or conspirators; they never published clandestinely; the books they published did not (could not) openly attack Fascism. Croce's principle appears to have been to *appear* to ignore Fascism—not to mention its ugly name or those of its leaders, but to address himself to the Italian mind on terms which tacitly involved the recognition of Fascism as a monstrous aberration from the historic continuity of Italy's development.

No other principle would have worked. Thus in Croce's books for twenty years past there has sung out—whatever the subject—a sort of hymn to liberty which echoed in hearts that did not dare acknowledge it. And so with time's revenges the kings and the marshals came to wait on the doorstep of the old philosopher who was too wise to serve them, as he had been too noble to serve their discredited master.

It gave me pleasure to think of what Laterza was most carefully seeing through the presses in July, 1943—the month when the Fascist despotism collapsed under military defeat. It was the fifth revised edition of Croce's superb essay on Dante (*La Poesia di Dante*).

The Laterza house did not, in those twenty years, escape the notice of the Fascists. Even though the police were often unable to understand the danger, there were plenty of quite literate persons in the Fascist ranks who knew that such books as those published by Laterza were attacking the foundations of the regime. Why Laterza continued to exist, why Croce was permitted to go on publishing his books, why the review *La Critica,* edited and mostly written by Croce and published by Laterza, was never wholly suppressed, were questions which agitated Fascist writers again and again, and sometimes the magnitude of the exception to an otherwise tyrannical rule seemed inexplicable even to its beneficiaries. The reasons may be explored—when cold evidence is available—in the character of the Duce del Fascismo and some of his earlier advisers. Like all self-educated men, Mussolini had a great respect at one time for the masters of thought and expression. He took pains in his autobiography to say that no book had ever influenced him, but at other times and places he owed a debt to Sorel and to Pareto; thus he could not have been unaware of Croce. Croce's international fame never reached into the masses in Italy or any other country, because it was based on a system of thought deliberately maintained at the difficult level of speculative idealism, but in spite of this restriction it achieved validity everywhere. His work was translated into all languages of the East and West, and the universality of this prestige was what influenced Mussolini to lenience toward Croce and his publisher—that and a feeling, which those who had the honor of the Duce's acquaintance say he often expressed, that Croce's ideas made no difference among the people. The latter reason exempted *La Critica* from any but the most cursory censorship, and so long as the review did not openly attack Mussolini by name, it was allowed to print critical studies which destroyed the whole intellectual basis (such as it was) of Fascism. The distinction made here by the Fascist authorities was that *La Critica,* which had a small international circulation, was "read by nobody," whereas the same studies, in more popular form, would have been accessible to the masses and therefore dangerous.

The gross ignorance of history's processes revealed by this reasoning was obvious. The synoptic Gospels, written in Greek, could have been read by very few of the poor Jews and Latins who made up so large a part of the early Christian community, yet the influence of these writings upon the Christian revolution was direct. Sorel was inaccessible to the multitude, but Lenin read him; Clausewitz means little to the masses, but the German general staff studied him. And then, too, what of Hegel? His books belonged to a category which neither Hitler nor Mussolini would have considered politically important enough to be banned; and yet, in a sense, did not the dead hand of Hegel hurl immense armies against the Eastern front of Germany? A philosophical writer who, like Hegel or Sorel or Croce, is read by "only a few" is more to be feared by tyrants than any deliberate polemicist, because that "few" will one day include a Lenin.

What Laterza and Sons published during the era of delusion constitutes a claim to immortality in the history of their profession. Aside from the whole work of Croce in a uniform edition, they undertook important new translations from English, French and German, such as Professor G. M. Moore's *History of Religions*, Karl Vossler's monumental work on Dante, H. A. L. Fisher's profoundly liberal and liberalizing *History of Europe*, A. G. Baumgarten's *Aesthetik*; they collected or reissued neglected work by the best of the Italian liberals and Socialists (Labriola, De Sanctis); they issued two small philosophical libraries, one of the ancients and one of the moderns, which are models of editing and bookmaking; they made a series of "esoteric and religious studies" which ran from Buddha to Rudolf Steiner; they became the Italian publisher for the Carnegie Peace Foundation; they instituted a "library of modern culture" which included the widest variety of enlightened thought on literature, philosophy and history.

Hardly a line in all these books could have been of any use to the Fascist regime, and most of the work was profoundly at variance with the concept of dictatorship. But the greatest achievement of the Laterza house, aside from its steady diffusion of Croce's writing, was its library of Italian literature under the name of "Scrittori d'Italia." This collection, which will eventually include four hundred titles and now has about half as many, is one of the most admirable efforts any publisher has made in our time. It involved the preparation of pure texts by the greatest academic specialists in each case—texts which have become definitive for almost every writer, dislodging the variants; and it involved printing these texts clearly, beautifully, on good paper with impeccable proofreading.

There must be hundreds of men who obscurely and devotedly have given their lives to this work, putting into the hands of many Italians just those masterpieces (Dante, Leopardi, Foscolo, Vico) which the Fascist despotism was impotent to suppress even though they constituted the most relentless and ultimately invincible charge against it. It was Croce's idea that a man who really read Dante could not possibly be a Fascist; and the house of Laterza applied this concept, by the "Scrittori d'Italia," to all that was best in the Italian past.

Croce's own work was, year by year, the most important new material offered to the public by Laterza, and its influence grew through the dark decades. Those who never lived under a dictatorship cannot easily imagine the effect of these austere and lofty criticisms, these Bach-like contradictions to the operatic melodrama of Fascism. Croce was never read by the wide masses, it is true, but he was read by thoughtful Italians in all parts of the society, no matter how difficult they found the task, because his was the only voice in Italy which steadily maintained that justice and liberty were the permanent aim of mankind, despotism a temporary phenomenon, and the judgment of history inexorable.

These things were well understood in the Via Dante. The Laterza family, through all the difficulties of the two Fascist decades, never regretted their course. Fevers come and go, but the general life endures; Fascism, deriving in part from the sensual and megalomaniac posturing of D'Annunzio, was unable in its twenty years to produce so much as one good writer;

the essence of falsehood is its sterility. Croce had already influenced the mind of Europe (with his book on historical materialism, for instance) before D'Annunzio had even celebrated his first Black Mass, and Croce will do so today and tomorrow because he belonged to the main stream of life and thought on the European continent and not to any of its deviations.

The Laterza brothers were proud to have served, for twenty years, by good workmanship and loving care, the whole Italian spirit and its principal living representative. But what good fortune was his! Every writer, of whatever kind, knows that the rarest and most valuable collaboration is that of a publisher who fully understands and loyally carries out the purpose of the work. This rare good fortune came to Croce abundantly, for the Laterza brothers not only gave his own writing to the public in exact and harmonious form, but suffused their whole publishing enterprise, the choice and treatment of other books, with the luminous honorability of a kindred purpose.

As I came out into the Via Dante from the bookshop, evening after evening, the early winter night of the Adriatic, sharp and cold, would be lying along the deserted street like a shroud. It was just as well I had stored up the promise of spring from the eternal voices inside, for here, in the cold and dark, there was none. Yet I did know, with a certainty which no external event could or can alter, that those who have loved Italy and hated Fascism connect, and they alone do connect, surviving the wintry season as best they may, the haunted immemorial past and the unknowable future. They stretch out their hands through the darkness to the time that is coming, when in Italy, too, there shall be hearts at peace under the starry sky.

Our men fought for the future through the most dismal, bloody and indecisive campaign of the whole war; of their misery I saw enough to make me miserable, even though I seldom had to share it physically. On our airfields around

Foggia, where we went to sleep at night in cold tents with the guns roaring to the north, or in the mud of the fields north of Naples, or in the high mountain villages where the snow lay all winter long and the cold wind cut through any number of layers of clothes, the thought of what we were doing here, and why, oppressed and perplexed and made doubtful not only my own mind, but many others. Field Marshal Alexander had told the whole press at Santo Spirito, his headquarters, in a public interview given October 13, 1943, that he had no real hope of conducting his campaign in Italy unless he was allowed enough ships to make a series of landings along the two coasts, the Tyrrhenian and the Adriatic, behind the German lines so as to force withdrawals; this fighting from mountain crag to mountain crag with machine guns might, he as good as said, take for ever, and he was firmly against it as a scheme of campaign, but the higher powers had left him no choice in the matter. In fact, the landing craft and other ships necessary to a "scalloping" operation up the Italian coasts had been sent off as soon as we captured Naples. Most of them went to India to be used by Lord Louis Mountbatten in the projected invasion of Burma. By the time they got there the Teheran conference had taken place, Stalin had made his pointed inquiry, "What do you think you are doing in Italy, anyhow?" and the ships were turned around again and brought back to Italy for the Anzio operation. The whole business, on the public record and not from any information available to me as an army officer, was a deplorable breakdown in the firmness and coherency of our strategical high command (that is to say, effectively of Mr. Roosevelt and Mr. Churchill). Either the Italian campaign was worth doing, in which case it was worth giving the means necessary to an early victory; or it was not worth doing, in which case the men and ships could have been used elsewhere. But to do it halfway, then move the ships away for a Far Eastern project which had to be postponed, then to bring the ships back again for a landing project which alone, in its force as applied, was not sufficient to achieve its objective—all this betrayed indecision in the highest places and had to be paid for by our poor lads in blood. Before the awful wall, the sheer rock wall, at Monte Cassino, and in those wild hills where no real "line" existed but death stalked incessantly, and out through the regions which our fighter-bombers attacked day after weary day on "pin-points" marked on a map, the campaign was dragging on without respite, bringing the war no nearer a conclusion and attracting no German troops away from the desperate struggle in Russia, but costing us, every day, costing us wearily and dismally what we should have paid (if at all) only for some real advantage, some positive accretion of power or value in time or space for the winning of the war or for the greater good or happiness of humanity. Yet no such advantage appeared. And in the increasing misery of the Italians, the obfuscation of all the purposes for which we had gone to war, the hollowness of our proclamations in the face of facts, the deterioration of our own morale and the cynicism that was beginning to surge up upon us, we passed a dreary winter. In the Via Roma in the heart of Naples (January, 1944) I saw streamers in front of the new office set up by the Psychological Warfare Branch: they enumerated the "Four Freedoms" in Italian. The sheer irony of the display can seldom have been equaled in recent times, for none of the four—except the freedom of religion, which is the least difficult and the least valued in this era—existed in our part of Italy. At one point, feeling singularly useless in my own position and agitated beyond measure over the moral bankruptcy I felt creeping over us all, I asked General Cannon to release me for special duty in the O.S.S.—the Office of Strategical Services. The Commanding General of that service, Major-General Donovan, had come to Italy to oversee certain operations in connection with the Anzio landing, and he was willing to use me in a field which strongly

297

attracted me. (I had my eye on Yugoslavia, of course—the contrast between our course in Italy and what we appeared willing to do in Yugoslavia was great: who would have thought the Adriatic to have had so much water in it?) General Cannon felt, perhaps, that the particular task I had in mind was too small, too hazardous, too detailed for an officer of my age and rank, and he seized upon a request which arrived at that time from Washington as an excuse for sending me back to the Air Staff. I think he was probably right. There was no doubt a vein of sheer romanticism—not to speak of a desire to escape—in my longing for the ditches and derring-do of the O.S.S. If the O.S.S. story, even in some small part, should ever be told when the war has receded enough into the past to make it safe, the lure of that highly variegated, esoteric enterprise, in which nobody was ever *gleichgeschaltet* and nothing was thought to be impossible so long as its objective was the winning of the war, would become instantly apparent to all who have not finally taken leave of their youth. Even upon the slight acquaintance which I had, perforce and for other reasons, with the O.S.S. in Italy—reinforced later in France and the East—I had acquired the feeling that this was one undertaking where race, color and previous condition of servitude cut no ice whatever so long as one actually wanted to get into the fray and help to win it.

So (*addio mia bella Napoli!*) one day I crawled into a B-25 at our air-strip not far from Caserta and set out on the long flight home: Algiers, Casablanca, Dakar, Fortaleza, Borinquen and Washington. The new wonders of our Air Transport Command on so many far-flung fields set me to wondering, as usual, what was to become of all this effort when the war was over, and whether Americans in general were fully aware of the extent to which we had sprawled over the face of the earth. There were memorable glimpses of man and nature, the laugh-

ing naked blacks hauling in the fish on the golden beaches below Dakar, the high dreaming Atlas below Marrakech, the
cloud cathedrals at dawn on the South Atlantic; but mostly I
brought home a depressed and sour perplexity over our war.
It seemed somehow to have changed into a different war from
that which we had set out to fight only two years and a half
before. To some extent this may have been a psychological constant—the inevitable progression of feeling in all men and all
wars—and chance has lately put under my hand a paragraph
by William James (in *Memories and Studies*) which states that
point with brutal clarity: "Man lives *by* habits indeed, but
what he lives *for* is thrills and excitements. The only relief
from habit's tediousness is periodical excitement. From time
immemorial wars have been, especially for non-combatants,
the supremely thrilling excitement. Heavy and dragging at its
end, at its outset every war means an explosion of imaginative
energy. The dams of routine burst, and boundless prospects
open." It does not seem possible to me that what James wrote
of the Russo-Japanese War in 1905, from his academic distance, could be true of myself or of anybody else who participated, even in a so-called "non-combatant" capacity, in the
campaigns of *this* war, but I put it down as a thesis: perhaps
it may be imagined that this alternance of mood, as of a fever
abating, could account for what happened to me and to others.
I do not think so. I think that the Italian experience was for
us crucial; it called into question the purposes and meaning of
the conflict, and we met it with what can only be called a spiritual inadequacy of the most frightening nature. Not only did
our soldiers display at all times the most callous indifference
to the land and its people—with an invincible ignorance of the
past—but those who were most qualified to see past, present and
future as a whole got their historicity so muddled, by deliberate intent, that they encouraged the suspicion that only the
past had any value to them. I can leave to others, who had more

299

continuous direct experience of it,[1] the task of describing what our foot-soldiery and our army in general went through on the Italian front; I saw enough to realize that these errors in high places fetched a high price. To me King Victor Emmanuel III and his superfluous son taken together and squared were not worth the life of one American fighter pilot; yet this one obstinate peculiarity of Mr. Churchill's retarded our advance in Italy more than any other political factor and gave the Germans time to stiffen and hold fast. From that time onward I lost faith in Mr. Churchill's leadership, for which nobody in existence had had more fervent admiration than I in 1940 in England; and I counted the days until he and his party should cease to direct Britain's course—and lead America's—on the continent of Europe. For a year and a half longer these errors were to continue, and their legacy may trail across the future indefinitely, but their sharp, clear, unmistakable inception came with the negotiation of the Italian "armistice" in the summer of 1943.

Once more, for the sake of lucidity, I must differentiate between our policy with the French, of which I wholly approved at the time and since, and our policy toward Italy. The French were a friendly nation in grave difficulties—conquered by a powerful, relentless enemy, attempting in spite of that to hang on to a huge empire, governing in extra-legal fashion and committing innumerable faults, but not, in spite of that, absorbed by Hitlerism. When all this dust and smoke have cleared away it will probably be seen that the essential failure of Hitlerism, of the "New Order" in Europe, was its failure to obtain the whole-hearted collaboration of any important section of the French people. The Lavals, Déats, Doriots and the rest of the traitors were a tiny, criminal minority in a nation which as a

1 Ernie Pyle's *Brave Men* has not yet been surpassed for detail; the drawings and text of Bill Mauldin in *Up Front* supplement it well. No objective military critique of the Italian campaigns may be expected until long after the war.

whole steadfastly rejected membership in the Hitler empire; rejected that, but clung to the only government it possessed. The French regular army and administration, the whole body of French officialdom, the mass of the French people, the teaching profession, the arts and sciences, in a word, the French, were loyal to their pitiable government at Vichy and their own wretched old Marshal. We came to them in 1942 professing friendship to all Frenchmen, and we could not impose upon them the unknown, the dictatorship of the Gaulliste exiles who had as yet made little or no impression on the mind of France. We allowed them to come to that dictatorship by themselves over a period of two years in which the Vichy expedient became more and more discredited by our victories, as was inevitable from the beginning.

But Italy was the enemy—not only the enemy, but the *original* enemy, the source of Fascism, the prime mischiefmaker in Europe and the world. To Mr. Churchill the war grew "less ideological" with success; he reverted to his old admiration for Mussolini, perhaps, who had "done so much for Italy," and forgot that the destruction of treaties, law and the comity of nations was begun not by Hitler but by Mussolini as early as 1923; for Mussolini he substituted Badoglio and considered the revolution achieved. This was so downright childish that it reminded me of H. G. Wells' celebrated story of the last war, which he tells somewhere in his *Autobiography*. He was summoned to Crewe House to undertake a job for Lord Northcliffe, who was then Minister of Propaganda. Northcliffe looked at him as they sat in the huge drawing room and said, "Well, H. G., here are you and here am I, and isn't that enough social revolution for you?" A mere change of masters at the top, with scarcely any alteration elsewhere in the structure, was considered enough for Italy, and even the military campaign itself was allowed to languish in the most half-hearted manner for lack of the necessary force and equipment to push it on-

ward. The war had certainly not grown "less ideological" for
the peoples of the world, but the suspicion arose that it had
become so for those who governed on our side, and that they
would thus throw away every good result of all this suffering.
The notion that American boys could be asked to give their
lives to install a reactionary neo-Fascism in Italy or anywhere
else was to me infinitely revolting, and the consent of our own
government to any such proceeding left me dazed, uncertain,
more wretched in what, for lack of a better word, I might call
the political sensibilities, than any event since the Munich
Agreement. There was also in all of this a strictly material concept which seemed to govern all minds from those of our highest potentates to those of our young soldiers: it was that Italy
"did not matter," that the campaign itself did not matter and
our policy even less, because Italy was not a great military
power and our main concern lay elsewhere. What this contributed to the demoralization of some of our troops is a story that
may be told in due course. For me the hideousness of the concept wore many faces. If this were true, why waste so much as
one life on the Italian campaign? But it was not true; it was
grotesquely untrue. There was no part of the mind of modern
Western man that did not owe some of its substance and texture to Italy. The continuity of the Italian contribution was as
remarkable as its quality; the sciences and arts of life owed
as much to the Italians in the nineteenth century (now tardily
ending) as to any other people; it was by no means an affair of
what our boys called "the dark ages." The fertility, the life-
giving abundance, of the Italian spirit was not to be estimated
by Mussolini's criminal speculation upon the forces of history,
as Italy's secular wealth did not lie in barren hillsides and
crowded cities. To approach this country at all without a concept of its true nature in the evolution of mankind, its permanent value and significance, was to release a bull in a china
shop. As one who had helped to play the hind end of the bull

I resented the whole enterprise and regarded it as a contradiction of what I had conceived to be the meaning of the war.

This is not to say that the Italian people as a whole were to be (in any solution I might have accepted) absolved of responsibility for the part they had played in supporting, or at least in enduring, Mussolini's schemes for the war gamble. To them as to the Germans I would have applied the words of Goebbels: "Every people remains responsible for the government which it tolerates and must pay for all the crimes committed by its despots." The doctrine crudely proclaimed, Nazi fashion, with regard to Soviet Russia was one which could apply to Italy and to Germany; but precisely here was where our own course lacked coherency. We could have punished Italy for war guilt without supporting an administration which shared in that guilt; we could have held all Italians responsible without showing ourselves prejudiced *against* anti-Fascists; our failure was the worst of those possible at the time, because it consisted in making a political and ideological *parti pris* the only excuse for our presence in Italy—a *parti pris* which to simple men looked remarkably akin to the official doctrine we said we had driven out. I would have been severe with the Italian Fascists; but I would have offered the popular and democratic forces, such as they were—and Fascism had left them feeble indeed—something better than a harsh word and a blow.

From the whole experience what came through best (pure, unalloyed) was the element of character in our own troops. An awareness of Italy was not among their virtues; for weeks or months the word "Africa" continued to designate the theater of operations—"ever since I came to Africa," they would say, seated upon a hillside in Apulia—and their contempt for the population was undisguised, unthinking, unashamed, mitigated only by their good-natured recklessness in scattering largesse. But among them was to be found the unswerving loyalty, the consideration for each other, the brave front against the enemy, all the familiar qualities of a time before the war had grown "less ideological," and in them no change except a hardening, a tempering, had taken place. The war could not become "less ideological" for them because it had never, except in the vaguest sense, been ideological at all. When I thought of our 57th and 79th Fighter Groups, which had flown and fought all the way to Foggia from the Egyptian desert, or of the 33rd Fighter Group—my own, it almost seemed for no good reason—I thought of the keen, wild, sure young eagles. This was a superb weapon, and it was not merely air-corps prejudice that made me think there was no better in the world. What saddened an older and perhaps more prescient observer was the use to which this weapon was put; for if we are to choose our weapons, even more must we choose our cause; and what we did in Italy was not worth the hazard of this pure steel. Thus I came home equally despondent over our achievement and its cost, Italy and America, our future and Europe's, for it was now the eve of the climacteric D-day, and it did not seem to me likely that history would afford us many more such opportunities to throw away.

CHAPTER VI

TING HAO!

To the Winds they set
Thir corners, when with bluster to confound
Sea, Aire, and Shoar, the Thunder when to rowle
With terror through the dark Aereal Hall.
PARADISE LOST, Bk. X., 664-7.

JUST AS THE JAPANESE war had hung upon Germany's course
from the beginning, and had broken out at the precise moment
when German victory seemed virtually secure, so its prosecution attended upon events elsewhere and could not attain full
impetus until the German military power had been destroyed.
This is blatantly obvious now, but was not apparent to all
Americans in the earlier stages, especially in those sections of
opinion which confounded every topic or item of human experience with an all-comprehending hatred of the Roosevelt
administration. Roosevelt's strategy, displayed in action everywhere, was to hold the Japanese in check where possible—particularly at the approaches to Australia, Australasia, Alaska
and Hawaii—while a mighty land, sea and air power was
amassed for the annihilation of Germany. To those for whom
everything Roosevelt did was automatically a work of the
devil, this was opposed in immoderate language and General
Douglas MacArthur was cast in the role of hero-martyr who,
practically with his own bare hands, was holding off the Japanese while all our resources went to the unnecessary or undesirable or at any rate less important defeat of Germany. I have

already said that in my opinion, which, although relatively humble, is not without plenty of material to support it, this was the only possible strategy in a war which—although most Americans will never really believe it—we could quite easily otherwise have lost. The Roosevelt strategy, we say; but it was the Churchill strategy too, and the Marshall-King-Arnold strategy as well as that of the Imperial General Staff in London. It might be said (and was!) that the British had no choice in the matter because their case was more desperate; but it has never been sufficiently or plainly enough said that our case was desperate too. By the skillful surprise attack at Pearl Harbor the Japanese removed our Pacific fleet from action for a period long enough to accomplish the conquest of the "Co-Prosperity Sphere of Greater East Asia including the South Seas," as Japanese official terminology named it. This took six months, at the end of which the Anglo-American allies had lost the Philippines, Malaya, Burma and the fortified bases at Singapore and Hong Kong; Siam (Thailand) had been overrun; the French in Indo-China accepted Japanese overlordship, and the incalculable wealth of the Netherlands East Indies had been easily gobbled up; Australasia was invaded (New Guinea, the Solomons); Australia itself was threatened and India was far from safe. It was not until August 7th, 1942, that the Americans could begin even the most modest offensive in the Pacific —the small but tremendously important action at Guadalcanal. From that time onward, with heartbreaking slowness and at times heavy losses, our army, navy and air forces, devoting what they could to the task, pushed steadily against the Japanese in the steaming jungles, the coral strands of the South, the misty crags of the North, the middle islands of the Pacific, everywhere at once and nowhere with enough to assert and maintain clear material superiority. The vast distances over which men and supplies had to be transported made this war unlike any other and reduced the minimal requirements of the American soldier to a point far below anything known in Africa or Europe; the area of conflict was vast and unfamiliar, the climate and topography almost always horrendous to the newcoming troops; worst of all, the attention of the United States seemed to be concentrated upon the Atlantic. This probably hurt our Pacific warriors in 1942 and 1943 worse than anything else in the whole chain of circumstances: that their hard, cruel struggle was not sufficiently known or understood at home. I remember an evening at the Waldorf in New York, when I was on leave after my return from Italy (spring, 1944), when a Marine correspondent got up and spoke with passion about this state of affairs. "I have listened to six speakers," he said (or seven or eight, whatever it was), "and every one has talked about Europe. Nobody here seems to realize that there is a war going on on the other side, too." He spoke of the "low priority" of the island fighters on all materials. "Our priority is so low," he said, "that we didn't even get Mrs. Roosevelt until this year." He had that tone of resentment, anger, impatience, which was common to all who returned from the Pacific during the first two years. It was more than comprehensible; they saw their comrades die and knew that with more force much of this loss might have been avoided. It was no use telling them that those who died on Guadalcanal died also for the ruling purposes of the war everywhere; in a jungle filled with snakes and mad dogs young men do not usually think loftily of the whole world. Their frame of mind was perfectly understood by our armies in Europe, which, indeed, displayed a kind of awe toward all they knew or heard of the war in the Pacific, and treated the occasional transfugitive from there with deep respect. As all know, the gradual development of our power in the Pacific followed this necessarily painful course until our resources were finally equal to the great efforts of 1944 and—at last—

1945; but it was not until the end of 1944 that MacArthur was able to return to the Philippines.

High military authority had always been, so far as I know, alert for every opportunity to strengthen our forces in the Pacific without impairing our chances of destroying the more dangerous enemy. An opportunity of this precise kind arose in the Army Air Forces with the development of the ideas and designs to which we referred as VLR—very long range bombardment. The first in the field was the B-29, developed in the Boeing establishment and approved by the army as soon as its prototype had been created. General Arnold produced this novelty at the Cairo conference at the end of 1943 as a way of taking the offensive against Japan even though we were as yet far from the island empire, and the acceptance of his suggestions by—particularly—Chiang Kai-shek led to the signal of full-speed-ahead on the production of the required aircraft. Chiang Kai-shek returned from Cairo and put an immense number of conscripted men, women and children—250,000 according to one figure I heard; others were higher—to work in the great plain of Szechuan building airfields for the new monsters. In that remote part of China's interior, where in the "old days" (that is, before 1931) foreigners had seldom visited, runways and camps were created as China was wont to create all things, by labor alone, and the fields were ready, we heard, in the spring of 1944. The B-29 had been produced in operational quantities only just in time to use them. The whole business—Chiang's astonishing speed in the building of the mammoth airfields far from all modern engineering science; our equally astonishing production of the aircraft many months ahead of schedule—may have had a sort of Sino-American competitive rivalry and pride as part of its incentive, but the dynamo at the heart of it all was, as at every period known to me since Pearl Harbor, General Arnold himself. This pink-faced energumen was more responsible than any single man for the creation of our tremendous air force in a period of time which, up to 1942, any sane authority would have considered impossible. He had a habit of demanding the impossible, insisting upon it and getting it. When I first went into the War Department my admiration for our supreme air commander was a tepid quantity; like most civilians, I supposed it to be vaguely scandalous, in some way, that we did not possess a strong air force already, and I was inclined to take the usual course of blaming the most conspicuous person. I had also read a book, then widely circulated, by Alexander de Seversky—*Victory through Air Power,* it was called—which, along with some lively perceptions of the possibilities of design and production, contained, explicitly and implicitly, an indictment of the plodding, unimaginative, old-fashioned, etc., etc., minds at the head of our military aviation. As I sank more and more into the documents of the war, of aircraft production and the organization of the air forces, the gross injustice of such judgments became apparent to me. From 1942 to 1944, as I became more familiar with the truth, General Arnold's central importance in the unprecedented development of our air power was increasingly revealed, and in nothing so much as in the documents concerning VLR in general and the B-29 in particular. Indeed on every one of the once controversial points—every one of real consequence to victory—General Arnold was proved right by 1945. The concept of precision bombing, for which he was mainly responsible—with Generals Harold George, Lawrence Kuter, Ira Eaker, Giles and some others—was rejected by our allies and doubted by our ground army; yet its results are now in the main irrefutable. Specific aircraft which General Arnold insisted upon for practical reasons were in the practical result invaluable: P-40, for example, the most controversial of all in the early stages, played its part nobly in our war because it was available in quantity at the right time and because its armor (which of course reduced its

309

speed) saved hundreds of pilots' lives. The long-range fighter concept (P-38, P-51, P-47) was abundantly vindicated in practice, and although it might be argued that we should have taken Spitfire and produced it when we could get it, the air war did actually develop in accordance with General Arnold's ideas and not in accordance with the British and German ideas of 1939-1940, which in turn made the spectacular short-range fighter less valuable than our own. Another sore point at one time was B-26; and yet, after it had undergone some modifications, what aircraft was more vital in the attack on such small targets as bridges, or more useful in the "isolation of the battlefield," as it is called, the circumvallation of bombardment which sealed off the German army in Normandy and in the Ardennes? Point after point (there are many more) justified Arnold's general thesis of air war, which, if it had to be put into a word, consisted of *attack*—the greatest possible concentration of attack. The defensive concepts of the British and Germans (crystallized in Spitfire and Me-109) were never accepted as valid for us; and why should they have been? For men who knew, or dared to guess, what the United States could and would produce, why was any weapon of pure defense regarded as necessary? The running defense of the attacking plane—at first defective—was brought up to the level of its punitive powers as experience dictated, and all these ideas were, of course, restudied and ceaselessly modified with the lessons of combat, but the main lines were constant. The argument can be made (I seem to hear it now) that with the resources of the United States a purely numerical and quantitative victory is always possible. "You can win the war with Piper Cubs," a friend of mine used to say, "if you've got enough of them." But anybody who has had any direct experience, however slight, with the operation of our air forces will not accept the suggestion that our victory is quantitative; when I hear such words I think of Télepte.

310

In the spring of 1944 the B-29 operation against Japan was, miraculously, ready to begin. The first B-29 mission was actually flown against Bangkok (secretly, from the Indian bases) on the day before the invasion of Normandy. All through March, April and May the B-29's had been assembled and flown to the East by crews which, in some cases, had never seen the aircraft before. There had never been enough B-29's in existence up to that time to give training on them; the original groups were trained on B-17's and B-26's. The British and Indian governments had agreed to lengthen some of their airstrips in India to accommodate the big ships, and somehow or other the necessities for base supply were moved to Calcutta; against difficulties innumerable—I have only indicated a few —VLR was about to become a reality.

At the time I was depressed enough over the war and my part in it to wish, half-heartedly, for release (on "inactive status," that is) from the army. I wanted a part in the invasion of France, but every job in that operation had been assigned for weeks or months past, every part of the machine oiled and ready. My friends in the Air Staff suggested a mission to India and China for the summer, reporting on the first phase of the B-29 operation for the Chief of Staff of the new (and still secret) Twentieth Air Force. This was to be, it seemed to me, the last distinctive or novel contribution of air power to the winning of the war—I did not expect jet-propulsion or rockets to play any real part in the present conflict—and the service to which I had hoped to be useful when I joined the army had benefited singularly little, by and large, from my activity; this might give me a chance to contribute some trifling bit to its store, even though I was well aware that "reports" were not what the higher staffs needed most. I refrained from putting in my bid for "inactive status" (to which I was entitled under the regulations then obtaining) and received orders to report at the headquarters of the XX Bomber Command—the field unit, and at this time the only field unit, of the Twentieth Air Force.[1] The Twentieth Air Force had been conceived as a mobile strategical striking force, like a "grand fleet" in the navy, which could be moved from theater to theater as necessity required, and which was commanded from Washington by the Chief of the Air Forces himself, with General Hansell ("Possum" Hansell) as his Chief of Staff. There were to be, eventually, two or three Bomber Commands, each with two wings or more under it; but we started out with only one of each higher staff—one Air Force in Washington, one Bomber Command in the field and one Wing under it. The Bomber Command had its staff, in fact—as I found out when I got there —in the same building as the Wing, a short flight of steps dividing them, and the duplication of effort was, as usual when there are more staffs than airplanes, something phenomenal. These were the penalties of an expanding air arm: we had to have "room to grow in," staffs to work when the aircraft were produced and ready.

This time I flew a new route: Newfoundland-Azores-Casablanca-Cairo-Karachi. Some time after midnight on the night of June 4th, as we were winging through chaotic cloud formations in mid-Atlantic, the co-pilot came back into the C-54 and told us that General Clark had occupied Rome. The successful termination—at last—of this campaign left me pensive through most of the cool indifferent night while the other passengers (mostly very young pilots on their way over as replacements) gave way to a few minutes' chatter and then sub-

1 The alternation of Roman and Arabic numerals in army units may be worth a word, since civilians so seldom understand it. We are supposed to say the 33rd Group of the XII Fighter Command of the Twelfth Air Force—or 5th Division of the XII Corps of the Third Army. The alternation between Roman and Arabic numerals was rigid in the Luftwaffe, as I believe also in the Wehrmacht, and went straight from the lowest to the highest, so that actually the numbers gave their meaning by form alone—e.g., 103/II Kg. meant the 103rd Gruppe of the II Kampfgeschwade. It could be carried on much further—103/II/3/IX, 103rd Gruppe of the II Kg. of the 3rd Luftgau of the IX Luftflotte. We were neither so logical nor so formal, and often broke the rules.

sided into sleep. We had expected to take Rome in November, then by Christmas, then as a result of the Anzio operation. Here we were in June; the whole Italian campaign lay like a question mark across the logic and meaning of the war. At Casablanca there was a day's delay while the plane for Cairo was subjected to treatment, and on the morning of the sixth of June I heard on the radio at the Hotel Anfa that the invasion of Normandy had begun.

Casablanca seemed, by some fatality, to be the point in space where I was to learn a good many of the culminating events of this war, and chafe at being there. Coming or going I was at this crossroads when the impassive radio announced the invasion of Normandy, the fall of Paris, the death of Roosevelt. The white city which had provided my first impressions of the war was in the later stages like a conning tower, in which every visit chanced to provide some sharp glimpse of the great sea upon which we were launched, its steadily prospering sunshine after the storm strewn with wreckage as the waves subsided. On that day I scarcely left the radio, imagining with the aid of the B.B.C. that vast scene off the Norman beaches where so many men I knew and so many thousands I did not were casting the die in the impartial sunlight. All the way to Cairo and to Karachi these cogitations accompanied me, and every scrap of talk overheard was on the same subject: D-day (*the* D-day) at last. For some reason I had resumed the keeping of a notebook just then, and I wrote in it that night in Casablanca: "Well, it has begun, and I suppose I can only look at it from an immense distance all summer long, reflecting that if I had remained a civilian I should have been there. The irony of it is that the army is keeping me away from the war."

In Karachi, along with the notes on time which are Air Corps habit ("Lv. Cairo 6:07 A.M. arr. Abadan 11:15 A.M.") I wrote—and why it is in French beats the bejeezus out of me

313

—Mon corps semble avoir devancé mon esprit: ces voyages vont trop loin dans l'espace pour le peu de temps qu'ils prennent. Perhaps it was in French because the other notes there that day concerned Caen, Bayeux and Lisieux.

India was the only country—except, briefly, Iceland some months later—of all those to which the war sent me, that I had never visited before. Some instinct of caution or inadequacy had always deterred me from going to India. I kept putting it off as you might put off a visit to the dentist, or as a child defers the hardest problem in the arithmetic lesson to the last. For twenty-five years I had been reading the learned, perspicacious or humorous observations of travelers—chiefly British —on that country; I knew my Kipling; I had absorbed a very considerable amount of Indian Nationalist argument, along with the flux and transflux of recorded events in the newspapers of the two decades; Nehru's *Autobiography* was a book I esteemed beyond most in the present century; certain works of the imagination, particularly E. M. Forster's *A Passage to India,* had seemed to impart a sense of the mystery rather better than most expository efforts; I had read Rabindranath Tagore in my childhood and reread him ever afterwards, as I do now. This, except some slight exposure to ancient texts (the Bhagavād Gita) and to history, constituted my whole equipment for approaching the most subtle and involved of the contemporary collective difficulties; and it was not enough. I knew so well that it was not enough that before I left Washington I made up my mind to stick to my onions. I was an officer in the Army Air Forces and could be or would be nothing else during a summer's visit to India. The B-29 and nothing else was my business.

The trouble with such a resolution was that it could not be carried out. I might physically restrict myself to the airfields and army bases, but those fields and bases were in India, and their labor was all Indian; I might avoid talking to any Indians at all and still I could not avoid seeing them in their pullulating clotted numberlessness; I might ignore everything of their social economy but I could not help being overwhelmed at every turn by the evidence of their unequaled poverty, the most unrelieved, squalid poverty I had seen anywhere in the world; under no circumstances could I or anybody else escape the impressions of geography, climate, topography, vegetation and animal life; in a word, India was too much for me. Impressions, perceptions, nervous resentments and awarenesses, all those complicated and ineluctable little devices for admitting even the most unwanted parts of external life to the areas where they do not properly belong, combined perhaps with a professional and habitual noticing proclivity or capacity which continued to function even when it was not called upon, made India for weeks on end more real to me than the task with which I was actually concerned, and gave it a kind of enveloping reality, dense, opaque, unfathomable in any direction, which made the precise job very small and transitory, like an ice-cube in a jungle. I penetrated nothing of this encompassing immensity, but I felt it all around me with oppressive, constant force, a kind of indifferent force—indifferent to me or mine—which was either altogether undirected (sheer inspissated chaos) or was directed by a whole complicated world of laws and motives and minutely intricate determinisms which were so different from those with which I had any traffic that I might as well have been at the bottom of the sea. True, I saw very little of India "on the ground," as we say—I had the most limited and superficial acquaintance with a part of Bengal and a tiny sliver of Bihar; this acquaintance was one of the senses only, for I made no attempt to talk, question, investigate, explore; the few books I did try to read succeeded chiefly in bewildering me, particularly when I tried to understand such things as the caste system or the variations in even a single religion; it was a process divorced from conscious observation or reason, beginning with the most active resentment and ending with the feeling that what I had here been plunged into was so far as I was able to determine a new element.

Let me see if I can be precise about a subject which in many respects defies words more than others do; it is perhaps worth the effort because, allowing for all the obvious differences, I think that many thousands of American soldiers passed through the same *kind* of experience, only to throw it off, some more uneasily than others, and to conclude that "India stinks." Or (another very usual remark) "They can give it back to the Indians any time." Or, "The only thing I can't understand about the British is why they want the damned place."

It begins with the most disconcerting experience of all, which is that of the servility of the population—any part of the population to which the newcomer is exposed. Things happen which never happen anywhere else on earth. A man creeps up and puts sugar in your tea; and as if that were not bad enough, he stirs it for you. If you laugh or speak harshly he looks at you with a dumb, suffering look that seems to come from somewhere a thousand years ago and a million miles away. The "bearer" in an officers' barracks near Calcutta actually holds your underwear out for you to climb into; you are not permitted to carry anything, to lift anything, to do anything; intent brown eyes follow you everywhere; on my first day at Hastings Mill, outside of Calcutta, when I finally got into a bathroom I locked myself in and felt relatively alone for the first time since I landed at Karachi. These are the slightest, smallest, most immediate impressions: and yet if you stayed in India forever they could not be eradicated. I have seen Englishmen who were never out of India (a pretty sight!) and Indians of high degree: no person anywhere else expects or receives such docile servility as they do, because they have known this all their lives. In the bazaar of any vil-

316

lage or town—along with the brazen insistence of the vendors and beggars—there is the same cringing, doglike attention, the ever-present fear, the old sorrow and pain in the silent eyes. How *dare* any people be so subservient, so inhumanly docile? How dare they make you feel so sorry for them? Have they no spirit, no human dignity, no pride? So you rail at them in your mind; but beware of a harsh word, for their revenge—the eyes of the wounded deer—will haunt your night.

These exasperating qualities in the population go fairly high in the social and economic sphere, at least as high as any American soldier is likely to go. They afflict, in different ways, the voluble Babu who keeps books and answers questions at the railroad station, the smooth rascal who sells rubbish as souvenirs to foreigners, the correct student who works in the big Calcutta department store and the girl with downcast eyes who stands by the flame-tree outside the village where the soldiers pass on their way to the Red Cross canteen. "Educated Indians"—by which the British and Americans usually mean only those who have been to some degree Westernized—are not exempt from the heritage, although they are skillful in concealing it in the ordinary affairs of life until some chance word or careless phrase lays it bare. Such humility is an offense in the nostrils of all Americans: but so are all the other impressions which come flooding in afterwards, the unconscionable filth, the innumerable diseases, the crowding, the religious abstraction in the midst of material horror. ("What can you do with a people who eat shit?" the American soldier says; and the habits of the Hindus with cow dung are perhaps the most specific shock of all these I am enumerating.) To this revulsion against India the heat, the dreadful, clinging, gasping, clawing heat, only intermittently and relatively mitigated by torrential rains, contributes as much as anything else, as does the lush jungly luxuriance of plants and animals. I never saw an American soldier who professed to like India and I en-

317

countered very few who were able to overcome their impatience, exasperation, irritation at its oppressive life, its creeping, crawling aliveness, the very sight and sound and smell of it. But within the week—within a day or two—the newcomer is confronted by the evidence of special power, skill, disciplines or resistance on the part of these people who seemed too humble even to live. It may be only the most vulgar snake-charmer playing with death, but it is something he has never seen elsewhere, and it makes him wonder. In our village there was a little naked black mystic who always rolled—never stood up or walked—and never talked; he would lie motionless in the foul dust of the blazing afternoon, hour after hour, perhaps in catalepsy, perhaps in dreams, with his wretched scrawny legs drawn up in what looked like a position of excruciating discomfort, while the occasional passing soldier would gape and curse with obscure and covered anger at this confrontation by the completely unknown. In the same way the humility of the Indian laborer or servant or countryman was in itself a kind of power which, after some weeks, defeated the most brutal attacks upon it. "You can't do anything with these people," the British would say (How often and with what pleasure they would say it!) and indeed nothing seemed to make much difference to them. Watching coolies, men, women and children, moving stones to make a roadway in front of our headquarters, hour after hour, day after day, singing doleful melodies from time to time, never smiling, seldom talking, patient and inexpugnable like a part of the landscape, it was impossible to avoid the uneasy impression of some strength —some quite possibly collective, or more than collective, rather co-conscious and earth-born vegetational strength—among these indistinguishable millions of the most materially disinherited people on earth. The forces inimical to their life are tremendous; every year vast numbers of them are wiped out by famine or epidemic or flood; in the year before I went there a million had starved to death in Bengal alone; and yet the forces favorable to their life must be even more tremendous, because the waves close over the hecatombs without a trace, and the population not only survives but increases at a rate unequaled in the world.

A year after I had left India I found in a little work of Tagore's [1] some clue to the kind of impression of another life, another element, which had almost overpowered me that summer. The sage is trying to say in simple, pure words what he believes to be the difference between the philosophical systems of the West and the East. Western civilization arose in the cities of Greece, he tells us, and from the earliest times has been conceived of as the result of man's struggle with nature, its fruits the fruits of the conquest of nature. Indian civilization arose in the forest and was from the beginning thought to be a part of its natural environment, man and plant and animal all forms of the same living truth: no struggle, no conquest, all love.

The development of the thesis leads through some familiar concepts (soul and over-soul, *maya* or illusion, truth above facts) with which, doubly distilled as they are in Tagore's high laboratory of poetic purity, the most confirmed materialist can scarcely quarrel until the enchantment of the reading is over. But, leaving that in abeyance, what served my turn as a clue to these impressions of India is the original statement. *If* it is true, which I have no means of knowing—if, that is, the Indian mind or consciousness *is* pantheistic, instinctively aware of a life shared with all nature, the insects and the fish and birds as well as all other like-minded men, with a god or gods dwelling in these innumerable forms and all somehow in communion with a larger life above appearance (as might have become psychologically true after so many thousands of

1 *Sādhanā*. This is a collection of the lectures he delivered at Harvard University in 1915 on aspects of Indian religious experience.

years), then there actually is some reason for the sense of a new element given off by the crowded existence of these countless millions, and my feeling of an immense, indifferent force inhabiting the very air and soil about me was no heat hallucination, but a perception at least as respectable as those of the ordinary physical senses, and not, perhaps, very much different in nature. I regard myself as a socialist materialist, but if I have learned anything at all from a somewhat checkered existence it is that we are only at the outset of our discoveries in matter and energy; in the relatively simple chapter of electromagnetics alone what we have found out and exploited during the present war would have made Huxley himself give a superstitious shudder; and I do not find it necessary to seek a religious explanation for every unexplained fact. All these facts will be explained in due course before the sun of this system cools, postulating, that is, the continued existence and curiosity of mankind. And I take it to be a fact, if perceptions are facts—a fact which has not yet found an appropriate concept to clothe it in my mind—that there is a power in India which arises from the consciousness of the people and their relation to the land, that this power is totally different from anything known to us elsewhere, that it is singularly oppressive and disturbing to the stranger, and that so far all the knowledge and techniques of the West are helpless before it. Unquestionably the Indian explanation is religious. Religion dominates life in India as it never did the West except just possibly in the thirteenth century and, what is more, the religions tend to run into each other in a way baffling indeed to the Western mind, with Mohammedanism itself osmotically Indianized and mysticized from sources too obscure and remote to be tracked down, the innumerable Hindu sects wearing a strong family resemblance over their minute and rigid differentiations, and movements of "higher unity," from the earliest centuries through Asoka and Akbar to the Brahmo

Samaj of Tagore, arising like steam from the whole boiling whenever a creative spirit is appalled by so much subdivision. Something in it is so specifically Indian that the religion transplanted from India changes its character, as that transplanted into India does, and Japanese Buddhism is as far from the Himalayas as Indian Mohammedanism is from Mecca. To me these religious phenomena by their very sensitivity to race, geography and climate betray a contingential, non-absolute character which contradicts their essential claim, and makes them totally inadequate to explain the philosophical or social systems based upon them. It should be possible by the study of anthropological origins, climate, diet, traditions and collective experience to make some scientific beginning upon Indian psychology and sociology and relate them, more than they are now related, to those of the rest of the world. I believe that if this were done the residuum, the specifically Indian power to which I have referred as a perceptively known fact, would be identified as clearly as we now identify magnetic curves, types of electromagnetic radiation, testosterone or anything else in nature of which the effects have been known and the causes adumbrated through the ages; it would be physical, i.e., not supernatural, but subject to a set of laws not hitherto known; and the Indian religious talent would slip out of this as it slips out of everything else, by saying that nobody ever pretended otherwise, nature as a whole being the expression of the universal spirit. There would, however, be an alternative presented to the Indian mind (the ordinary Indian mind, not those of the handful of Westernized types) to set up against the excessive religiosity which has governed Indian life for myriads of years, and it would be possible to see the undoubted peculiarity or peculiarities of Indian consciousness without thereby falling into mysticism. It seems to me that the Indian religio-social culture is so extremely old, so much older than any other in existence, that it might quite possibly have produced some kind of psychosomatic variation by this time—not a crude biological variation, of course, like the zebra, but something a little more difficult to explain to the children. After all, the most *terre à terre* inhabitant of New York knows that he can go into a department store and buy a whistle which makes a sound audible to dogs alone. This physically and financially verifiable phenomenon should make him a little more humble than he usually is about the limits of the physical universe and what may or may not be contained therein.

The existence of a co-conscious mass-and-nature Indian reality, somber in its awareness of endless time, fatalistic and productive of an almost inconceivable passivity before social circumstance but at the same time slithering with a life-principle hardly sexual at all in our individualistic Western meaning, but intimately connected with the communal rites from the dim original forest, a sexuality at the same time social and religious, animistic and purposive and central in the whole collective existence as well as in that of the single being—all this intellectualized by sages, of course, but existing on the simplest physical and instinctive plane for uncounted millions—became irrefutable for those who had, as I did, to pass frequently between India and China. I had hardly been in India three days before I made my first trip "over the Hump"; I made six thereafter; the summer passed in an alternance between the light and the dark. The oppressive awareness of an alien life-force in India, resentment against it wearing off into perplexity over its nature and wonder at its function, was constantly being followed by the quick, delighted recognition of China's brave gaiety and charm. In this respect I am quite certain that I am characteristic of all American soldiers because I have heard them say it, in other words, many times over. "God, what a relief!" they used to say as they got out of the airplanes in Szechuan. This was not a matter of temperature or

322

climate; it was just as hot and wet in Szechuan in August as it was in Bengal. The relief consisted in escape from the consciousness of India, its tragic eyes and helpless, brooding eternity. Here in China everybody smiled, worked, moved about with energy and a sense of purpose; the smallest children, once they were able to walk or control their movements, would make the thumbs-up sign of victory at us and yell *"Ting hao!"* [1] There was nothing gayer than the Chinese boys who took care of us at the mess or quarters on the fields; they cooked and handed round the food without a trace of servility, friendly and ready for a joke at any time, approving highly of our whole enterprise and considering us to be a part of their own struggle. It was a clear fact that hardly anybody in India (except Nehru and a dozen or so other men whose culture was completely European) understood even the first principle about our war, which seemed to them an affair of no interest to India; they looked dully upon British and Japanese imperialism and said they could see no difference; indeed, in 1942 the Nationalist Party under Mr. Gandhi (not Nehru) conducted a disgraceful campaign of sabotage and violence which the Mahatma disowned after having started it off; the inevitable deaths in that affair are a very queer result of the doctrine of *ahimsa,* under which even a fly or a mosquito ought to be safe. You never got a smile or a good word, if you were an allied soldier, out of any Indian man, woman or child along the road, in the country or in the villages, in the city or the hills. The Indians were temporarily obsessed by the British occupation of their country—a tiny episode in their whole history and a rather irrelevant one; the British have done nothing in India to speak of, and if they leave tomorrow their historic function will have

---

[1] *Ting hao* literally means "very good," or "extremely good," but is used by the Chinese as a sort of cheer. Naturally it caught the ear of all our youth, who romanized it phonetically as *Ding how* and named jeeps, trucks and aircraft after it. We had a B-29 called the *Ding how.*

been merely the opening of the country to some slight traffic with the West—and in that mania they were unable to see anything else, including their own advantage. They had nothing whatsoever to gain by sympathy for the Japanese or Germans; a victory of the Axis would have meant the permanent enslavement of India (and with Japanese or German overlords they would have learned what imperialism means); if they believed in principles at all, those for which the Western allies professed to be fighting were clearly more universal than the tribal maxims of the Fascists. Their inability to understand that India, for all its distinct peculiarity among the races and nations, was situated upon this planet and had as yet, in spite of the wisdom of its sages, discovered no reliable way of getting off it, was a key to the general intellectual inadequacy of the Indian Nationalist movement as a whole. Only Nehru among the great leaders of the movement had a sense of the world; when the others talked about the world they meant India. Normally this was a fairly good way for Nationalist politicians and agitators to talk, because it suited most of their listeners and avoided many difficulties; but in the supreme crisis of the present war, when what was at stake was nothing less than —as Hitler said—the whole order of the world for the next thousand years, Indian Nationalism betrayed the pettiness of its aim by saying, in effect: "Good! The British are in difficulties—let us try to make things worse for them." This was about all any sensible man might have expected of a movement which—aside from Nehru—has shown scarcely an inkling of the fundamental problems of human society, including Indian society; and a political party of which the chief practical objective is to dislodge the British from their jobs so as to fill them with Indians. Of course the British ought to get out of India, to whose long history their intrusion was a silly impertinence, however profitable it may have been to England; but from this rather obvious generality to the statements

324

made by Indian Nationalist propaganda is as far as from George Washington to Huey Long. I have sat quiet and listened while Indian Nationalist leaders on visits to America said in so many words that the British regime in India was indistinguishable from that of Hitler in Europe—this because a few hundred political leaders were in a mild imprisonment (unavoidable from the British point of view) which they had as a rule themselves invited. Any comparison between the treatment of Indian political prisoners and those of the millions who died at Maidanek, Buchenwald and the like—any comparison of ordinary liberty of assembly, communication and press in India at its very worst and Hitler's at its very best— would show how absurd such statements are. And yet this loose talk from the Westernized Indians, and the oppressive consciousness of another (and of course quite different) life-force in India itself, were about all the Westerner had of a semi-intelligible nature to go on, the only data offered him by his surface experience. It was not surprising if, in his uneasy resentment of so much impermeable autochthonic self-responsive misery, he came into the light of rational China and felt reborn.

Some of the difference—a very thin shimmer on top of its final polish—was due to the fact that we were fighting as China's allies in the war against Japan. This was why every one of us got the victory sign from every Chinese in the countryside. Larger than this (much larger) is the fact that the Chinese are a people who feel themselves to be free and independent and are in fact so, as much as most people are; they have had no experience of slavery as a people, even from such military conquerors as the Manchus, who supplied them merely with an imperial family and a few commanders and little else; they exploit each other ruthlessly, but success in such exploitation is rather admired than condemned. The sense of being a proud race, invited by life to much activity and profit, with no need to feel less important than any foreigner, is something either born into the Chinese or taught them so early that they never remember where they first heard of it. If we were to use the slipshod language of department-store psychoanalysis, it might be possible to say that the Indians have an "inferiority complex" and the Chinese none; but the humility and pantheism of India are something which do not fit these mass-produced price-tags. Rather, let us say that in the talk of a very hasty American, loaded down as he is with such slang, the expression "inferiority complex" might sometimes, unfortunately, slip out with respect to an Indian, but practically never with respect to a Chinese. The Chinese meet the world on equal terms, at least until it beats them down into illness, old age and despondency. Poverty never bothers them much; the poorest Chinese are often the gayest; their city and country masses are just as poor as the Indians, but it does not seem to affect their spirits, their activity, their energy. There may be some simple physical reason or reasons (chemical content of waters; prevailing diet; average yearly temperature or rainfall) but whatever they are, along with them there is a powerful *apport* from the immemorial past, which in China has been almost as consistently, homogeneously rational and ethical as India's has been mystic and metaphysical. The distinct antithesis is an encouraging phenomenon to those who feel, as I do, that all the talk about a natural antagonism or incompatibility between the oriental and occidental nations is foolish. No Western people could be more unlike the Indians than the Chinese are. These claptrap ideas of the Hearst press ("yellow peril" and the like) get along without any debt to fact, but they are bolstered up from time to time by fortuitous circumstances, such as the natural tendency of Eastern delegations at an international conference to vote together on any question involving the so-called "white" race's claim to supremacy over the others. Solidarity between Chinese and

Indians on such questions means nothing; the gestures of sympathy to India made by such Western types as Mme. Chiang
Kai-shek mean nothing; all these notions of oriental as opposed to occidental are recent innovations and are alien to
the spirit of both Chinese and Indian ideas, which, although
profoundly different, are alike in considering mankind to be
a whole. What does mean something is that the cheerful,
acquisitive, energetic Chinese are incapable of understanding Indian humility, Indian passivity, Indian resignation—
just as incapable as we are. There does exist a Chinese mysticism, but it would appear to be a ritualistic affair of disciplines and precedents rather than a pantheistic dream; and
at all events it has little effect upon the stream of ordinary
life in China.

When we get out of the airplane at Kunming or somewhere
on the vast plains of Szechuan we feel immediately the release
from Indian gloom; the bustling, laughing Chinese inhabit
another world. Labor, danger and privation have attended
the lives of all ordinary Chinese with more fidelity than usual
during the past seven or eight years, and not only the national
"resistance war" against Japan has brought suffering and
sorrow, but an outrageous racketeering has gone on practically without concealment or shame in the highest places
through this whole epic, the great Chinese "patriots" robbing
their people with as much zeal as any Japanese could have
shown. And yet the Chinese, out of their unique strength,
have still the art of making the best of it; they can somehow
contrive to get more active enjoyment out of less material than
anybody else, and despair or even cynicism in the deadlier
sense do not seem to exist for them. What they have been
taught by all these misfortunes is, instead, a kind of healthy
skepticism, a frank expectation of scoundrelism on all sides
but a preference for one's own scoundrelism as being better
business and more fun. It would be pretty difficult—I dare

327

say downright impossible—to shock any Chinese who had lived through the present war under the Chungking government; he has seen everything. But the Chinese zest for life accommodates itself to all its forms and surmounts them, overshadows them, survives them, goes through terrible suffering and sacrifice and comes out on the other side still able to crack a joke and relish a meal. All the Americans felt this life-warming, friendly practicality from the moment of arrival in China; after the indifference of India it made those first days sheer pleasure. But a few weeks on our great fields in the empty country and almost all of our people were ready to go back to India, not that they liked India at all—nothing ever made them like India—but because poor China, blockaded and starving, had very little comfort or luxury to offer, not even much food; in unrationed India everything was to be had for money. Thus a trip back to the Turkish bath of Calcutta and the doe-eyed humility of its inhabitants could be endured for the sake of its ice and gin; but after a bit in India everybody in our outfit (which was, of course, unusually footloose) was glad to get across the Himalayas again and breathe the air of a country of free men.

Against this alternation between heroically happy China and the dark indifference of India the first phase of our B-29 operation took place. Our home bases were in India, at a string of former R.A.F. fields in Bengal (Khargpur, Chakulia, Charra and Piardoba). For each mission against Japan or Manchuria it was necessary to build up a supply of gasoline on the advanced field in China from which the mission took off, and the only way to get such gasoline into China was to fly it in. Long before, the Air Transport Command had served notice that it did not have enough planes and pilots to haul gasoline for us on top of all its other duties, and if we wanted gasoline we would have to fly it "over the Hump" ourselves. Thus weeks went by—on an average, one month—between missions, because it took so much time to get the necessary amount of gasoline up to Szechuan. At first the crews, unfamiliar with the aircraft, were able to get little gasoline over the Hump; some trips actually operated at a loss (i.e., consumed more gasoline coming and going than they were able to haul). It was by the utmost ingenuity, stripping the ship here, there and the next place to get in extra tanks, and by the develop, ment of special skills in slow climb, etc., etc., to save on gaso, line, that the B-29 finally became the most superb flying tanker in existence, hauling a maximum of 3,600 gallons of fuel from Khargpur to Szechuan in a single journey, and taking the Hump on the way at 24,000 feet. The use of this beautiful aircraft, perhaps the most beautiful aircraft to behold that was ever built, as a draft horse through the upper air seemed to me at first one of the most grotesque extravagances I had yet heard of, but the simple pragmatic attitude of our people soon convinced me. They did not like being made into tankers, either, but they could not fly combat missions against Japan unless they had gasoline and they could not get gasoline unless they flew it up there; so they set to and invented ways and means of doing it, developing an elaborate competition be-tween ships of a single squadron, between squadrons inside the group, and between the four groups themselves as to which could transport the most fuel in the course of a month. Of course it was a wildly uneconomic scheme altogether, but it was the only way by which we could reach Japan at the time, and the moral advantages in China and the United States (not to speak of the actual damage done to the Japanese) would be worth it—war being, at best, an enterprise in which it is not reasonable to count material costs.

I reached the XX Bomber Command headquarters at Kharg-pur on June 11th and left on June 14th for Jorhat, Chabua and Kunming on the way to Szechuan for the first mission against Japan. The B-29's had already flown one mission as a "shakedown," to get used to the airplane, its central fire-power control and numerous other gadgets, and to learn how to keep formation on such tremendous long distances through cloud fronts and unpredictable weather; this was the mission against Bangkok on June 5th, a "practice run" as the boys said, notable chiefly for the extraordinary dispatches the local Japanese authorities sent the Tokyo government. When I realized —new as I was to this war in the East—what barefaced lies the Japanese field officers told their own superiors, I understood that the Tokyo government could have no very clear idea of any specific military situation. The same thing (claims of many B-29's destroyed, and details of aerial combat which never took place, with Japanese fighter aircraft performing miracles of strictly imaginary valor) occurred after the other missions of the summer, and unless the reports I knew about were augmented by some others of which I knew nothing, the Tokyo authorities must have been hopelessly misinformed on each one of these events. Perhaps they had some scheme for detecting what was true underneath the lies, some of which— like a good deal in Japanese behavior—may have been purely conventional and therefore meaningless.

The Hump was one of those experiences which withheld its true meaning for further acquaintance. My first journey across, as well as the return two days later, might have been any flight anywhere except for the altitude. We were in a C-47 piloted by the skillful and experienced Colonel Ellsworth, who had flown the Hump about eighty times then; he put us "into the soup" soon after we left Chabua and kept us there all the way across. Only once or twice, for the briefest few moments, the drifting mists would thin enough for us to see the far-off empty valleys below us in the desolate mountains. Ellsworth knew his way so well that he was able to corkscrew through the perilous beclouded peaks at only 18,000-19,000 feet and bring us down through a very low ceiling to the mud and safety of Kunming. We sucked oxygen at intervals most of the way—a commodity which seems to me better than beer; I always enjoyed that part of a high flight.

Kunming was the headquarters of Chennault's Fourteenth Air Force, which, we had heard, was a little annoyed at the expenditure of gasoline and other valuables on the B-29 project; in spite of this some of their officers (not their celebrated general) came up to the Szechuan fields to see the take-off. We got to Hsinching, the field where Bomber Command made its headquarters—with the 40th Bomb Group occupying the field—on the afternoon of June 14th, and the take-off was at four on the next afternoon.

It is hardly possible to exaggerate the tension with which that first take-off was accompanied. Nothing quite like it ever came my way in the war. Every B-29 take-off was a bit tense ("never a dull moment," Blondie Saunders said) because we were loading them so heavily, but the first take-off for Japan was an occasion upon which every string had been made so taut and vibrant that the whole field seemed to echo with their twanging. I had hoped up to the moment of my arrival in Hsinching to be able to go on the mission, but when I reported to the commanding general—K. B. Wolfe, who played a vital part in the development and execution of the project; he went back to head the Matériel Command in August—he cut me short with a word. I did not realize until afterwards that he had hoped to go on the mission himself, and had received the fatal telegram from Washington about half an hour before, forbidding him to do so. Naturally my application was ill received. "K. B.," as they called him, said a little later: "Well, you're only going on one, I suppose, and it'd better be a good one. Wait and go on one where you can see something." For this first mission to Japan every ounce of gasoline, every scrap of weight, had been carefully calculated, and in the stage of familiarity which the boys then had with their

331

machine—to be blunt, a very early stage—there was risk in overloading as in underloading. It was important to get to Japan and back, but it was also important not to crash in the take-off or in the crucial period before altitude was gained. These were the considerations (among many) which furrowed the young brows on the field. There were half a dozen representatives of the world press who were going on the mission, scattered through the four groups, and this little extra weight was also an occasion for misgiving among the pilots. The press thought the mission was to Tokyo, which was just a little beyond the range of the B-29 loaded as we were loading them then, from these particular fields; the target was actually Yawata, on the island of Kyushu, an iron-and-steel mill town of such consequence that some of our information ("poop") about it called it "the Pittsburgh of Japan."

For the take-off I stood on the wing of a B-24 on the left side of the runway, along with some operations officers and crew members. During that period when, one after another, the great silver ships were gathering speed on the runway, struggling to get off into the air, I doubt if anybody standing on that wing drew breath; every inch of the rise in the air seemed to be happening inside one's chest, somehow. I discovered afterwards that no such anxiety obsessed you when you were actually inside a B-29; it is only from the outside that this slow take-off is so agonizing. The climb was so gradual that it seemed to us the shining ships barely cleared the little bunch of low scrub down at the end of the field. On another of the fields a few miles away in the great tawny plain, at about half past four or thereabouts, a tremendous explosion and clouds of smoke warned us that elsewhere tragedy had attended such a take-off. In half an hour or so the whole sky seemed to be full of B-29's wheeling around and setting their course; they came from all of the bomber fields, near by and far, one of them actually thirty miles away—the 40th Group, the 444th, the 462nd and the 468th, commanded respectively by Colonel Franklin Z. Harman, Colonel Alva L. Harvey, Colonel Richard H. Carmichael and Colonel Howard E. Engler—and turned to the east, to the half-mapped and half-known regions of Central China, where neither the mountains nor the military "front" could be depended upon to fulfill paper specifications. In the orange-and-gold dust of the June evening their departure had something fateful about it; nobody would have been much surprised if they had never come back.

The Chinese stood in awestruck but happy crowds well away from the runway and watched the departure of the planes. Nothing had been explained to them, we understood; but as hundreds of thousands had been working on the fields, and flights of B-29's had been coming in with gasoline for weeks past, they must have been able to guess with some accuracy what was intended. The Japanese themselves, at any rate, were very fully informed. They used the names and ranks of many of our officers in their radio broadcasts, spoke of our bases both in India and in China by name, and made clumsy, stupid efforts to ridicule or minimize the B-29 (as by saying it was "made of shoddy, inferior materials," for example —this of an aircraft which, you might say, was built of platinum and diamonds). Every B-29 on the field had been guarded by two Chinese soldiers; the Bomber Command headquarters, the hostels for officers and enlisted men, the camps and the whole area around these fields, were similarly controlled by the Chinese military. The poor barefoot boys, who looked fourteen or fifteen years old, stood with fixed bayonets—usually much taller than they were—beside the powerful wing of the massive and beautiful airplane day in and day out; they were not aware, I suppose, of the contrast they made, in their threadbare gray scraps of uniform and their unshod feet, with the triumph of modern design. Out here in the great flat space of Szechuan, where a model-T Ford would have been anachronistically modern, the B-29 occasioned no particular astonishment in itself; for, by a "law of combined development" peculiar to this war (not Trotsky's law!) the airplane has become a familiar sight in many areas which have not yet seen a good wheelbarrow. But it was—as all understood by telepathy—going to Japan to bomb the enemy on his native heath, and the Chinese even in this remote region, who had probably never seen a Japanese, knew enough about the increased hardships forced upon them by this savage enemy to be glad.

At eight the next morning the planes came back—most of them—to the wet morning field, the tired crews garrulous in relief. We had waited through a good part of the night until the message came, the single word "Betty" (from the name of Jim Garcia's wife) which indicated that bombs were away over the target. Jim Garcia was the A-2 of the Command and had played a considerable part in the preparation of the mission; he was on it himself, flying with his own brother-in-law in the 444th Group. The first bombing of Japan had taken place with success so far as the B-29 was concerned—that is, the planes got to their target and back again (most of them) without undue mechanical trouble; the thesis of VLR was proved. The accuracy of the bombing, owing to a series of reasons which then belonged, and perhaps for a little longer still do belong, to the realm of military secrets, was not all that might have been desired, and appealed to Dick Carmichael, for example—ever a perfectionist—as being "piss-poor." But the main point had been proved and the rest was a matter of development, practice, familiarity with the resources of the aircraft and all its applied and attached gadgetry.

China, India, India, China: thus passed the summer. I think the beginning of the B-29 operation meant a great deal in the Far East, where in spite of everything that had recently

334

happened the Japanese still retained an aura of good luck and success; the fact that they could actually be bombed on their home islands from thousands of miles away disturbed this impression (or superstition) and led the Chinese and even the apathetic Indians to look forward to a time when they would be more severely punished from bases closer in to their heartland. The operation was fantastically difficult and expensive, but it was worth it in effect upon enemy and ally alike, not to speak of our own soldiery and public at home. And in the meantime the Marianas were being taken by the doughty Marines and regular infantry, to serve as bases for a more efficient B-29 operation in which we should not be dependent upon our allies (British, Chinese or other) for any of our essential supplies or logistical work. One of the chief headaches of an unconscionable number of our staff officers (A-4 and Service Command people) was the inability, real or imagined, of any non-American person to understand what we meant by schedules of delivery, "build-up" and the rest. When—as at the Port of Calcutta—the Indian Civil Service was added to the difficulties normally experienced even with our British allies, there was a good deal of bright blue language shot into the air. "The British," these supply officers would say—I had a great friend who was one and said it often, "have been here well over a hundred years and haven't built a decent port or highway in the place, and not enough railroads to fit out a small state at home. What the hell have they been doing, anyhow? I'd like to tell a few of them to take their fingers out and go to work." To which they would answer themselves, American fashion: "But I guess they don't want to do anything in a place like this. It's the ass-hole of creation anyhow."

During the weeks when gasoline was being monotonously hauled over the Hump for the next mission from China, I made the rounds of the four B-29 groups. All were on fields enlarged from former R.A.F. stations and thus had the usual *basha* arrangement—long huts with thatched roofs for quarters and offices. There were some troops in tents on each base as well, because even these shacklike buildings could not be put up in enough quantity or with enough speed to accommodate all our men. The runways were, of course, very long, and in some places (as at Piardoba) there were concrete chevrons; dispersal was on the whole good, although nobody really expected that the Japanese would be able to come in and bomb us. (Their last bombing at Calcutta had been two or three months before, and with the fighter strength we were now acquiring it would have been expensive for them to come near us.) Life in the jungle was a little outside the normal expectancy for most of our boys, but they applied their best talents to the job of making it tolerable, and the most captious visitor would have been compelled to admit that they had succeeded. They wore few clothes—practically none when they were working on the ships—and seized every chance to get cool or keep cool; the clubs or canteens on every base were able to get ice, at least for certain hours a day, and cold beer was a great help; somebody could always do something to decorate or make agreeable the rooms they had in common in the *bashas*. The Officers' Club at Piardoba, decorated by a lieutenant who had been a commercial artist in peace time, and run by a captain who had come to the air corps straight from the hotel business, was something startling to find in the Bengal backwoods in the midst of the monsoon: it had a proper bar, made of bamboo, and two or three spacious rooms with bamboo furniture and pleasant lights; Casablanca, Tunis, Cairo, Rome and Karachi looked down from the walls in the sprightly designs of the lieutenant-decorator; there was an apparently inexhaustible supply of what was needed to keep a club going, including buffalo steaks.

Piardoba was perhaps the base where I felt most at home. This was the field of the 462nd Bomb Group, one of the organizations—along with the Lafayette Escadrille, the Third Division and the Fifth Division—of which I was for a moment or two an honorary (but proud) member during this war. The 462nd Bomb Group was commanded by Colonel Richard Carmichael (Dick Carmichael was as well known in the air corps as almost any of our most famous pilots; he had commanded the 19th Bomb Group in the South Seas just before it came home); his next in command was Colonel A. F. Kalberer—Kal—who had had more than 1,500 hours of flying time on transport aircraft before the war; they were a great pair. In their *basha* were Col. T. B. Storey and Major Lewis—Tom and Doc—executive and medical officers of the group, and Don Roush, the S-3 (operations officer). These five men ran a bombardment group which had about as constantly high a collective spirit as any I have seen in war. Dick, the commanding officer, probably had more to do with this than any one man, for all these B-29 groups were spanking new and their group character had to develop or be created in accordance with a whole new set of circumstances; Dick had the legend, the good looks and the brilliance in actual performance to impose his personality without an effort, but he also had the administrative capacity and judgment which so often our best air corps combat men (the "dashing young pilot" types) could seldom acquire. On his return from the South Pacific with the 19th Bomb Group he had spoken very frankly in the Air Room in Washington before all our generals, and instead of being reprimanded for disrespect he had been taken into General Arnold's office, where he remained six or eight months. One day while he was driving me around the standings at Piardoba, looking at the airplanes, Dick said about General Arnold: "That's the most man you'll ever see in one chunk." Apparently his incarceration at the highest headquarters had been less painful for him than it usually is for his kind of airman; he did not regret it, and professed to have learned a lot. His place, however, was in the field, preparing and leading missions, criticizing them mercilessly afterwards, "riding herd" without respite in matters of maintenance and everything else concerning the airplane, but, with air corps insouciance, permitting the kids to do almost anything they wanted between times. His rigors with respect to the aircraft and the mission were extreme. I never heard anybody who could speak more sharply and coldly, or whose words were listened to with more shamefaced contrition, more eager respect. He had a vein of sarcasm which was justly feared by air and ground crews alike. But in other matters—in anything concerning the club, for example, or games, or leeway on those parts of army discipline which only remotely concerned our conditions of life—he was gay, light-hearted, easy-going, much more inclined to laugh than to frown at any unexpected event. As may be imagined, his popularity among those he commanded was instinctive, unanimous and profound. Twice I heard Carmichael brief his pilots for long missions—once in China, for the mission on which I accompanied him, and once in Ceylon for a very long mission to Sumatra—and his care and patience, his attention to detail, were only equaled by the religious hush with which his pilots listened. I should find it difficult indeed to remember anything to equal the perfect and total attention they gave him when he spoke. Indeed Carmichael had to a very high degree the quality of direct leadership, natural command over men his own age and younger, which I had seen before in Phil Cochran and Art Salisbury, among airmen-commanders, and was to see more than once among the company and platoon leaders of the Third Army during the last phase of the war. (This junior leadership, so essential to any campaign, is something the war developed brilliantly among the Americans; we were not strong in that department to begin with; everybody with any first-hand knowledge of the war has seen dozens of good ex-

338

amples.) Carmichael's age might have been 30 or 32, which made him a little older than most of his pilots but a good deal younger than many of the men under his command— younger than his friend Kal, his *alter ego,* who made the other half of the partnership. They could argue for hours on end, particularly on air subjects, but I never heard of a real dis-agreement between them. Kal had the smooth, cool and self-possessed manner, appearance, style of behavior, of a transport pilot who never under any circumstance is supposed to show excitement in front of his passengers; Dick had the tigerish temperament of all great combat pilots, with supersensitive fingers on the controls and a strictly instinctive response to the crucial situation as it took place; this contrast between them was no doubt more apparent than real, and Kal's maturer mind no doubt appreciated every peril and every possibility just as much as Dick's did, but without betraying it in the slightest movement. Tom, Doc and Don, the other three in-habitants of the *basha* where Dick and Kal lived, were happily conscious of being in the best of the B-29 groups, under the best of commanders, with all sorts of special dispensations— such as the Coca Cola machine Kal had brought out, which cooled the beer—to constitute a regime of special blessedness.

The monsoon had started on the 23rd or 24th of June and was in full tilt during the rest of my time in India. It seems to have startled me. "Now that the monsoon has really come," I find in my notebook, "there are multitudes of flying insects at night, some as big as small birds; the termites eat the beds, the chairs, the houses; the roads are half washed away; the whole plain is drenched." A lifetime of reading or hearing about this abrupt seasonal change is not enough to prepare you for the actuality of a shift in a few moments from desper-ate, unabidable heat to the dark steaming cool (relatively cool) sogginess of the monsoon. At Chakulia, where the jungle seemed to enclose the airfield, the drenched undergrowth and

339

dripping trees appeared to exude totally new life, life which had not been there before, innumerable forms of flying and crawling bestiality, all apparently created by the cataracts of water which so discouraged human activity. I saw a naked Indian boy (of the adult age which usually wore clothing— therefore worthy of remark) dancing and singing in a clear space there one day during a brief sunny moment between downpours; I never knew why; I assumed it to be part of the life I recognized without understanding. On another occasion I was driving back to the Charra airfield with a pilot friend after a visit to the near-by town and we came to a long avenue of trees with water on both sides. On one side was a stagnant pool with both scum and lilies upon it; women were washing at one edge; men were performing their natural functions at another; children were bathing in it here and there. On the other side of the tree-lined avenue, which was like a causeway between the two bodies of water, there was a much larger lake which looked cool and clean in the evening light. Out in the middle of it was a green small island dotted with white flowers which looked to me like what the British called *frangipani*—a white, odorous flower, very common in Bengal, not a bit like what is called *frangipani* in the West Indies. We stopped the jeep to look. The silver lake, the green island and the white flowers seemed startlingly lovely in that light, arrested and held there for a moment in a kind of eternal abstract truth bearing no relation to the day, the place or the circumstances. As we gazed in silence, something very surprising happened—for pure, unalloyed surprise without past, present or future, for isolated distinct surprise, it was unique in my experience, and I doubt if the words will convey its sharpness. The splashy white flowers, perhaps disturbed by some sudden veering of the wind or shout of a passing boatman, took wing all together and flew away into the red and gold of the evening sky. They were birds; perhaps they had always

340

been birds; I was willing to admit it, reasonably, but the fact is that so far as my sense perceptions went they were flowers and they had nevertheless taken wing and flown up into the sky. Unless it is instantly apparent, the astonishment of this event and its curious, lasting impression upon the mind will not be understood with any number of words.

The mission on which, as General "K. B." said, I could really see something, took place July 29th and its target was the Japanese coking ovens and steel mill at Anshan, near Mukden in Manchuria. It was our first B-29 mission in daylight. There had been attacks upon Sasebo, Yawata and Omura in the meantime (night of July 7th-8th). The first daytime mission had been anticipated with very mixed emotions by everybody concerned, since it seemed beyond doubt that the Japanese would put forth their best fighter effort to meet an unescorted bombing attack. Aside from anti-aircraft fire, which could be quite accurate at the altitude from which we were to bomb, the Japanese fighter aircraft were a real question mark; in spite of all the antiquated types known throughout the East, there were surely some good ones in the Yellow Sea region, and the B-29 was so far an unknown quantity in battle. Moreover, at this time and from these distances—flying without the advantages of accurate weather prediction or even really good maps; altitudes in China had never been properly determined—it was virtually impossible to keep a formation. The night bombing at that time was done singly, with no attempt at any particular order; our day bombing was to be done in box formations of four if possible—at least all aircraft were to meet and form immediately after take-off, and what happened thereafter depended upon cloud fronts and the forces of the universe in general, including our unfamiliar enemy.

I joined Dick Carmichael and Kal Kalberer at Piardoba two days before the mission. The planes were already leaving to cross the Hump and continued to do so all day. I went with Dick, and we were among the last to leave (July 28th), arriving at the 462nd Group's Chinese field, Chunglai, fairly late that afternoon. At Chunglai a variety of things took place before dawn the next morning, when we took off on the mission. In the first place a message was decoded along toward sunset which informed us that a Japanese parachute attack upon the field was to be expected during the night, and that American armed guards should be put on the aircraft instead of the weary Chinese boys who usually stood there. This order was almost impossible to carry out; I still do not know exactly what Dick did, but I remember that he spent a great deal of time trying to make the available men twice as available, so to speak, as they could be. The trouble on all these Szechuan bases was that we had barely enough men to maintain the aircraft; if the aircraft were to be maintained, ground crews had to sleep; air crews which had been flying the Hump all day had to sleep before the mission at dawn; where were American sentries to be found? In the little flurry which accompanied the parachute alarm I noticed for the first time the Chinese defenses on the perimeter of the field; every gun, I need hardly say, was pointed in toward the center, which could have been of some use against parachutists if they dropped precisely on the runway but not otherwise.

Another event of the night was a torrential rainstorm, a sort of cloudburst and tempest all at once, which knocked down some tents and swept others with wind and rain. I was drenched to the skin and almost choked by my wet mosquito net. Life at Chunglai was entirely in tents, the only huts on the field having been taken over for offices, briefing and interrogation. We never really knew about the report on Japanese parachutists; it may have been Chinese G-2 (probably was), but if it was a well-founded report, as so many of these Chinese G-2 titbits were and so many were not, at all events the tempest

342

must have made the execution of the project impossible. In the cold gray morning—"first light" as we say, that is, before dawn—we were hauled down to the field in trucks and found our aircraft intact, standing in proud rows alongside the runway while the ground crews made the last checking and rechecking with anxious care. They used to do the same thing over and over again; they reminded me of a favorite line of Pope:

> Venus oft with anxious care
> Adjusted twice a single hair.

Dick was cold, sharp, incisive, giving orders and poking his nose into every part of the aircraft. I had been an awed listener at his briefing the evening before and knew the plans about as well as anybody in the squadrons did; all I had to do now was to make my large carcass as unobtrusive as possible and watch, look, listen. As usual, my first and most persistent observation was that those who had work to do in combat were as intent upon it as actors on a stage; the whole ground personality seemed to be left behind when the deadly work that these boys were trained to do began its calls upon them.

We took off at 5:15 A.M. in our local time, which was at about dawn, with rose-pink streaks lying along one side of the runway, over toward the purple hills we were to penetrate on our way to the sea. The rain did not seem to have made the runway difficult for our take-off, although there were big pools in the softer ground alongside; we rose easily and went into the long, slow climb; we were to assemble over the field at 1000 feet, form in a box and head east with Dick in the lead. Kal, who led the next element, was to assemble his four planes at 2000 feet and do likewise.

Everything proceeded according to plan for about fifteen minutes, when our right-wing man developed trouble in his

343

Number 3 engine and had to go home. The tail plane in our box (Number 4) then closed up to the right wing position and flew that way for hour after hour, all the way to the Yellow Sea, in fact; but when we got there we lost him. There was considerable cloud cover as we approached the Yellow Sea, and Dick coasted down into it; when we came out our right wing man had disappeared. We learned afterwards that he had stayed upstairs and then joined another element to go in over the target.

The flight across China to the Yellow Sea was otherwise completely without incident. We were at medium altitude most of the way, in perfectly clear view from the ground, and why we were never attacked mystified all of us. It was a beautiful day without much cloud—better than our weather forecasts, made with insufficient data, had indicated—and we passed in the immediate neighborhood of several Japanese fighter airfields. Once we flew directly over a Japanese airfield which was so new that it did not even occur on our maps; it was near the provincial capital of Kaifeng, had concrete runways and some camouflage, and there were ten fighter planes lined up right beneath us. They did not budge. The big Japanese fighter field at Tsinan in the province of Shantung had been confidently expected to give us trouble, and this one we skirted carefully; but there, too, nothing moved. Hunched up in flak suit and the rest of my accoutrement behind Dick Carmichael, I could see his incredibly sensitive fingers (like the fingers of a safe-cracker) fiddling with the controls, a fraction here, a fraction there, as we kept on what seemed an iron course. Everybody maintained a keen lookout all the way, and there was little relaxation on the part even of the observer-passenger. It did not seem possible that so many aircraft—about a hundred in all—of such exceptional size and appearance could be roaming across occupied China without giving the alarm. At this moment, as at other moments in the

Japanese war from now on until its sudden end, the B-29 was a leading character on the principal pages of every newspaper on earth, and an incursion of B-29's in broad daylight (the first) might have been expected to stir the Japanese dovecotes more than a little. Today not.

At the Yellow Sea Dick sloped down into some cloud cover, skillfully accompanied by our left-wing man (Captain Alley, in a plane called "King Size" which I could see at every moment throughout the day). When we came out of this, expecting to face Japanese opposition of an intense sort both from the ground and in the air, we were leaving the Yellow Sea, precisely on course, at the mouth of the river (Liao-ho) into which, a little higher up, the Hun-ho entered. By following the water bed around to the right we came in what seemed no time at all to our target, the Showa Steel Works at Anshan, below Mukden.

We were supposed to go in over the target in boxes of four: under no circumstances, Dick had said more than once in his preliminary instructions, was an aircraft to bomb unless it was in a formation of at least three. In daylight it would be by no means safe to do so. And here we were, very much up in the air, because after many hours' flight to get there we had lost two of our aircraft: we were only two. Above and below us, right and left, could be seen B-29's coming in to resume their formations, many of which had been broken by penetration of the cloud front over the Yellow Sea; stragglers "stooged around," as pilots say, looking for some group they might join. In the brilliant sunlight at upwards of 20,000 feet we could see nobody who looked likely to join us.

"I don't like the way this damned thing is heating up," said Dick, frowning, and brought us down lower. At that altitude —19,000 feet, six thousand less than in the field order—we started in on the target, the two of us, No. 474 (Dick's) and our left-wing man who had never left us.

We were among the very first over; our bombs were away at 11:03 A.M., local time. As we swam over the target, neat and clear as a model beneath us in the summer sun, no apparent damage had yet been done to it. The concentration of pilot, co-pilot, bombardier and navigator in their respective tasks left me a somewhat limited opportunity to see the ground. We went over the target fast—around 300 indicated air speed —and everybody in the plane was tense with that peculiar, active tension which occurs only in that precise situation. No fighter aircraft were to be seen anywhere. Coming back from pulling the bomb pins, the bombardier thrust one at me. "For your kids," he said, and crawled into his place. Just as we were about to bomb, a terrifying thing happened—the most terrifying and unexpected possible. Two sticks of bombs fell alongside us, one on each side. Every man in the plane made some kind of startled cry and looked up (in so far as it was possible). A perfect formation of B-29's was above us, five or six thousand feet above, and we might easily (so easily!) have been blown to smithereens in the air. I only saw one of the sticks of bombs, because I could only see out on one side, but Dick saw both.

As soon as our own bombs were away we veered sharply off the target and made for home at a good tilt, giving ourselves a broadside view of the target. It was partly invisible under a dense cloud of black smoke which rose at least 1000 feet, perhaps more. The part hidden was the coking ovens, our principal objective. In the sparkling sunny air the puffs of anti-aircraft fire were coming up, but I only saw one puff anywhere near us; Dick saw three. In another minute or two we were roaring down beside our I.P., the river mouth, and were back over the Yellow Sea.

From there on a certain relaxation set in—not that we were at all safe; we were not; the Japanese had plenty of fighter air-fields all along the way, and we still had about five hours or more of enemy air to traverse. But the let-down after bombs away, except when combat is taking place, is inevitable and not to be overcome by discipline. Sleepiness, jokes, candy bars —these are the signs of the psychological change that has taken place. The boys have a tendency to tell stories and break forth into irrelevant autobiography, like characters in a play by Chekhov. "In the town where I came from nobody had ever seen an airplane. I wonder if they've seen any now? There were seven in our family, two brothers and five sisters. We had a dog named Rover." Almost in that vein—a curious release. I have seen it on various types of combat mission, big, medium and little, and the process is exactly the same always, the lifting of a weight and the expansion of a gas. The air corps psychiatrists who ordered the distribution of candy and chewing gum to the kids immediately after leaving flak areas in Germany (we did not have this in the East) knew what they were doing.

We were on the ground again at Chunglai at 5:07 in the evening (local, that is Chinese war and summer, time). Dick, who had been all electricity in the air, soon became all exhaustion on the ground; after he had found out all he could about the planes of his own group and the fate of the mission as a whole, had given orders for the return to India and had made sure of a few more duties, he took to his tent and stayed there. He had flown the Hump the day before and was to fly it again in the morning, with the combat mission between.

The flying of the Hump was a perilous business to begin with, remained only a little less so in the summer of 1944, and no doubt still is far from easy. There was no possibility of accurate weather prediction over the towering mountains; there were not enough weather stations even on the Indian side, not to speak of the Himalayas or China. The shifting whims of cloud and wind, the uncharted mountains, the strange effects of atmosphere and temperature on machines, metals and fuel—all this played its part in making pilots and crews a little apprehensive, and perhaps their apprehension in its turn contributed to the sensation of adventure with which each journey was accompanied. It is a cold, grisly thought, that of the numbers of our youth who died in the snowy tempests of that far height, died and were never heard of again. We did get whole crews back from the valleys of the Himalayas, and everybody who went on such a flight was prepared to trudge for weeks, if necessary, to get back to friends; but many an aircraft simply vanished in the wastes without another sign. In the eight flights I made across the Hump something went wrong on every one except the first one (the one in the lowly C-47, with the expert Ellsworth). In all subsequent flights we either got lost, or got water in our gasoline, or had engine trouble, or wandered into Japanese territory and expected attack, or something else of sufficient consequence to warrant the order to put on parachutes and prepare to jump. I had flown uncounted hours in the Twelfth Air Force without ever having a parachute on (except in actual combat); usually I had used it as a cushion; but out here in the C.B.I—China-Burma-India theater—the parachute was ready at all times and was the most essential part of all gear for crew and passengers. Even with Carmichael, on our return to Piardoba—after some irritating engine trouble at great altitude had passed without a crisis—water appeared in the gasoline and an engine went out. The same order ("get ready to jump") woke us up during the last ten minutes of our flight, as we were floating down through monsoon clouds to our base. But of all the episodes of this kind, the most startling was that which enlivened the journey of a certain B-24 which went to China for the small (or smallish) mission of July 7th-8th. I was one of half a dozen staff officers who made the journey with "Butch" Blanchard, then operations officer of the Command—he was soon to be C.O. of the 40th

Bomb Group—and, like a good many of our young pilot colonels out there, a West Point footballer. "Butch" flew the mission at night (it was to Sasebo) and then got a little sleep the next day and elected to take off for the Hump flight at two in the afternoon. It was not a propitious hour under the best of circumstances, and we knew nothing of the Hump weather; the navigator refused to fly with him. The rest of us went along anyhow, with an inexperienced navigator who proceeded to lose us very thoroughly before we had been long out; uncertain where we were, "Butch" decided to evade the Hump and fly down through Burma. We made a roundabout trip through Japanese territory, everybody on the lookout for enemy fighters, then tried to get in somewhere in Assam (Jorhat, Chabua), had a series of difficulties with the radio and then found ourselves lost, without a radio compass and with our gasoline running short. This time all hands donned parachutes and prepared to jump again (as twice before on this journey) with noses glued to the windows, looking for airfields. The whole Brahmaputra Valley was flooded; it was the height of the monsoon; the sunset light pushing through mottled clouds fell on only the most occasional and immaterial-looking little tussocks of green above the flat wide water. The thought of jumping from such a low height (we could not have been above 400 feet) into mud or Brahmaputra water was not cheerful. We found a field (Lalminarhat, an A.T.C. field which the Americans pronounced Lamnerhat); we had enough fuel left for perhaps another ten minutes. Some such contretemps seemed to occur on every journey across the Hump.

And yet those journeys had a stupendous, unearthly beauty which made them unlike any other—indeed, unique in experience. Sometimes at sea or in the air the universe presents its forces on a scale so grandiose, and with so little restraint, so little regard for the puny human intruder, that whatever philosophic or religious concepts a man may have are likely to rise to the surface. On this particular journey (the one with "Butch") while we were in the midst of the cloud pinnacles at a great height, with snowy mountain peaks suddenly rising against the intense blue sky not far away, I observed that my friend and fellow-officer X. was studiously counting his rosary. I said nothing then, but the circumstance led me to wonder —gazing out on this world of cloud and cold, high splendor —what, actually, I did believe myself, and what might be my last thought if the word came now to jump out of the airplane. I thought of Goethe's *Ganymed*—the bosom of his father—and reflected that some kind of relation must be felt to exist between all these phenomena and the human being who was set in their midst, sentient and aware, and that the sense of this relation was what betrayed most people into religious acceptances of one sort or another. My friend X. with his rosary was consulting a higher authority on the probability that his life on earth might now be over; but he was doing so because the grandeur of the lofty stillness all about us had awed him into it. It was not fear, precisely; it was a sense of mortality. But although I knew exactly what he meant by counting his beads, nothing would have induced me to do likewise, because I felt quite certain that the forces of the universe would receive me back into their complex enclosing non-human but living time-space continuum in the most perfect indifference, and I did not want to spend my last moment on idle gestures. Better to look out and recognize that this life existed, that human existence was probably a minor aberration from it, and that in a very few minutes these specific entities (X. and I) might have returned in material, that is, in carbon and other elements, to the materials of the earth, and in breath perhaps to the wind of the mountains, passing from one part of this nature to another without a disturbance in big or little, and if the life of the whole race was recapitulated in one human life, or the solar system mirrored in nuclear systems, then the only sensible thing was to look upon the wild glory of these deserted altitudes as being your own distant kindred under the laws of a common nature, and forget these supernatural inventions. Somewhere in his *Reisebilder* Heine tells about meeting some Germans in Northern Italy who kept talking about the Russians (then, in the 1840's, much in favor with Germans) as being cousins, inhabitants of the same space in Europe; they were like herrings, says Heine sourly, claiming relationship with the whale because they inhabit the same ocean. So I, too, like a herring, could look steadily at the cloud and the mountain and say: O Whale, you and I inhabit the same ocean, we are akin.

At any rate I counted no beads. When X. asked me rather curiously if I had no impulse toward prayer in these very unearthly moments, I said no; I thought of things that might fall under the same general classification in human activity, but I did not pray, because I did not believe in any force outside the forces of nature, and to these it would be useless to pray. X. then made the religious answer which infuriatingly slips out of all discussion: "I prayed for two," he said.

In August there was a mission from Ceylon to Sumatra, our longest during my period with the B-29's, and I flew to Ceylon with the advance party for it. All our groups, their staffs and the staffs of the Wing and the Command were accommodated at an R.A.F. station on China Bay, near the British naval base at Trincomalee. At first we were guests at the R.A.F. mess, with the usual results. In my notebook on August 7th I wrote: "Our officers do not hesitate to comment aloud on the food at every meal. True, it is impossible to tell the coffee from the tea, and the standard of cooking is very low, but we must make it difficult for the R.A.F. officers to be silent. Our enlisted men are complaining bitterly of the British soldier food they get. They are not used to the extreme difference the British make between officers and men. (Flogging was only abolished

351

in the British army in 1881, and to this day there is no relaxation in the assumption of power by officers in ordinary affairs whether they have it or not. We think they treat their men "like dirt"—and this we often say.) All these forms of disagreement are pointed up by our manners, our way of stating our opinions out loud. I saw all this in the Tactical Air Force in Italy; it is the same everywhere. Our combined interallied effort gets along better when the relations between British and Americans are confined to the highest ranks, with everything below the top staffs kept separate." And on August 8th: "We left the R.A.F. mess at breakfast this morning (an excellent thing for the Grand Alliance!) and henceforth are to have our own mess. We eat out of mess kits, stand in line without regard to rank, sit at very crude wooden tables, and wash our own kits afterwards—all things which the R.A.F. would no doubt consider *infra dig.* (as my Frenchmen of the escadrille did a year and a half ago). But the food is what we like and we have our own cooks and food now. Our satisfaction must be felt with equal keenness by the R.A.F. officers on the station. We have heard that they were made to leave their extremely comfortable quarters here on the hill (where we are all crowded in now—a huge, airy building like a summer hotel) in the middle of last May, and have been waiting for us to come in ever since. I don't imagine this increases their enthusiasm for us as they watch us take over their beautiful station."

The B-29 groups arrived on the 9th and the mission took off at 4:15 in the afternoon of the 11th. Like all "firsts," it had been the cause of much apprehension. This was the first very long over-water mission, and some of the airmen were exchanging farewells like this: "So long, Red, see you in San Francisco." As it turned out, fifty-four aircraft took off and fifty-four crews came back, although one of them had to be rescued in the middle of the Indian Ocean by the British Navy, which had set up an admirable air-sea rescue service for the occasion.

One of the last planes back on the field the next day had been in the air for almost twenty hours and still had a thousand gallons of gasoline left, having bombed the primary target (Palembang refineries, in Sumatra). As proof of the beautiful performance of the B-29 in long over-water hops, a matter of the utmost importance in its subsequent use against Japan, this mission was decisive, and its accomplishment without the loss of a single life was inspiriting to the whole command.

The take-off and return were spectacular. There did not appear to be any monsoon in Ceylon, or if there was it did not impair the brilliance of sea and sky. The runway went to the water's edge, and each B-29 seemed to be skimming the blue sea as it left the land. Behind the field was China Bay, filled with warships of every class, including the *Richelieu*. On the day before the mission some of us had visited the *Richelieu* and had seen the nostalgic maps of France which were posted on every bulletin board there, with pins indicating the positions of allied and German forces. French, British, Dutch and Americans—there was some representation from each in this military area—seemed to share a common excitement over the B-29's and to hope with us that this machine might conquer geography in the war against Japan. From our hill beside the field we had the best possible observation post for the departure and return of the ships, Carmichael first, Kalberer next, the others one by one in single flight off to the sea and the night, and back again the next day in the golden sunlight, having proved their point—having abundantly proved their point. Saipan had been captured a month before, and the time was not far off when the B-29 operation would all be based in the Pacific isles and would consist entirely of such long water jumps to the enemy's heartland.

Thus the few missions we were able to carry out during the summer of 1944 from bases in India and China, a great and costly effort to overcome natural disadvantages, had a pioneering value far beyond their statistical achievement. Dick Carmichael, who had been through the early days with the B-17's in the South Pacific—the very grueling early days—sometimes said, particularly when bombing results did not please him, "We seem to be starting all over again." He was right, because the weapon was new and the methods had to be entirely new; there was much of trial and error; a technical complexity and wealth unknown in earlier aircraft had to be mastered and sometimes modified in accordance with the lessons of experience. But the machine survived every test, and although maximal performance was never achieved during these months, the way to achieve it was shown. As remarkable as the machine itself had been these young men chosen from all parts of the air corps to put it into operation. A good many came from the B-17's of the early days—as did "Blondie" Saunders himself, the General commanding the Wing—and others from the B-24's in Africa. Kalberer was from the Ninth Air Force in Egypt (before it became tactical) and had been on the first Ploesti raid. Howard Engler, who commanded the 468th Group, had been our operations officer in the Bomber Command during the early days in Africa, the days of Biskra and Télepte. The increased demands made by the B-29 were met by its human material with the qualities of stamina, skill and determination which had mastered all our earlier aircraft, and it is a curious thing to record, but true so far as visual observation goes, that the fatigue resulting from twenty hours on a dangerous mission did not seem proportionately greater than the fatigue resulting from five hours. The stuff—human and mechanical —was good.

The scenes against which this stuff was tested in India and China were weirdly alien to it; nothing could so telescope the centuries and continents as a B-29 field beside an Indian village in the lush Bengal plain. Many of the Szechuan peasant women who worked on the B-29 fields near Chengtu had bound feet; the planes were guarded by Chinese soldiers in rags; the Himalaya valleys over which we flew had never even seen a good modern wagon. But if your conviction of the meaning of the war was broad enough and solid enough you had to believe that by winning it we should bring the fruits of life a little nearer to every inhabitant of the planet, including those who suffered famine and injustice in indifferent or despairing masses. It was often difficult to be sure that our victory would mean anything to India beyond merely saving it from the tyranny of the Japanese; but if you disregarded official statements on all sides you could be sure that the reality lay beneath them and pulled in a certain direction. Thus a whole act of the drama of Indian nationalism and British imperialism was played out this summer: a letter from the Viceroy to Gandhi, a reply, a proposal for Hindu-Moslem unity, a meeting between Gandhi and Jinnah, a series of advances and retreats, skirmishes and disappointments, known to us merely as a continuing story in the newspapers, but indicating, at a minimum, that things would not be left forever in the uncomfortable state of suspended animation which succeeded the events of 1942. Some of my British liberal or Left friends (Frank Owen, for example, in Calcutta, then an officer editing Mountbatten's army paper) seemed to think that there was no "Indian problem," that Britain would "get out of India as soon as the war was over," and that the next phase was a "relentless exploitation by American capitalism." I did not believe this because I saw no evidence either of British willingness to abdicate or of American willingness to build such a risky economic empire; but if it should be true, it might perhaps—along with many evils—bring that industrial revolution in which, so far as I could see, India's hope of development lay. But all that was outside the realm legitimate for the activity, or even the speculation, of an air corps officer; and similarly the political dramas of Chungking, which were also active that summer, took place on another plane far away. What remained was the somber impression of India's distinct quality, unlike any other collective reality elsewhere, and of the cheerful voices of the Chinese peasants shouting, from their poor lives and high hearts, *"Ting hao!"*

CHAPTER VII

DEATH IN SPRING

> . . . not always died
> Sooner than their mates; and yet
> Their fall was fuller of regret:
>   It seem'd so hard and dismal thing,
> Death, to mark them in the spring.
> G. M. HOPKINS (*a posthumous poem*)

THE LAST WINTER of the war in Europe was the coldest there had been in many years, according to those calm peasants whose lives are regulated by weather. In the great middle valley from Holland to Switzerland there was war of varying intensity on successive river lines. In Alsace, in Lorraine, the Saar, Luxemburg and Belgium the snow gripped the land firmly until the early thaw of February turned it to cold mud. The war should have ended in September, 1944, but the racing American armies were stopped by the necessity to wait for supplies, and the respite afforded Germany a chance to make one more attempt at victory. The attempt came on December 18th, 1944, when highly prepared forces under the command of Field Marshal von Rundstedt broke through the American positions in the Ardennes and made phenomenal progress for a few days, only to be beaten back in a slow and bloody battle, lasting about a month, to their steel and concrete in the Siegfried Line. The head-on assault upon the Siegfried Line which followed was, according to excellent authorities (including General Eisenhower), one of the most remarkable and de-

357

cisive actions of the war. By mid-March the German army was surrendering by the hundreds of thousands; by early May it was all over. The whole campaign of the winter and spring was unnecessary, the cruelest waste of human life and energy imposed in the whole struggle, since the Germans were already defeated and without any possible hope except the illusory notion—cultivated to the last ditch by the Nazi organization—of a falling-out between the Eastern and Western allies. Sometimes when I attempt to estimate Hitler's responsibilities, so numerous and complicated, I think the greatest of them must be this hideous prolongation of the useless slaughter by six whole months after the issue had been decided. It classifies with that other monstrous horror, the reintroduction of human slavery in twentieth-century Europe, and is not even surpassed by the systematic extermination carried out upon helpless prisoners. A decision like any of these (to exterminate whole classes of prisoners; to prolong a bloody and destructive war after its end is certain; to reintroduce human slavery as an institution on a vast scale with the idea of maintaining it "for a thousand years") is almost impossible to understand, and yet, as the evidence accumulates, it seems more and more certain that these decisions were actually taken by Hitler himself. Thus one man could deliberately choose, elect, order and impose courses which are very nearly unimaginable, and obtain obedience, full obedience, from an entire nation. I used to spend hours talking to German prisoners and I never found one who had an idea of the monstrosity involved in this. Some of them quite freely admitted that they had no idea of how the war was to be won for Germany, but they always said that there must be some way, or otherwise the Fuehrer would not continue the war. They were never in possession of enough facts to know the how or the why of anything; but they obeyed. Even men who did have the facts (such as Rundstedt and Kesselring) obeyed. It is most probable that by this relentlessly cold winter of 1944-1945 the astonishing elements of genius which Hitler had once displayed had merged into his fundamental madness, and the German nation was now, finally, in the extreme stage of what had been partially the case all along: helpless, blind and drugged obedience to a lunatic. No stranger conjecture can be ventured upon than to wonder, as I sometimes did, upon what could be taking place in Hitler's mind between January and May, 1945.

My own acquaintance with this last phase of the war was in a new-old capacity, as a war correspondent. On my return from India I took advantage of the regulations governing the release of officers over thirty-eight (I was well over it!) and was put on inactive status by the first of November. I then engaged upon the process of getting overseas as a correspondent accredited to *Red Book* magazine, which took a little time (there were already too many correspondents in the field); and it was the end of December before I got started. I was actually at the Air Transport Command's camp on Long Island, waiting for an airplane, when Rundstedt's counteroffensive in the Ardennes began, and those days—Long Island, Iceland, England—were punctuated by anxious efforts to get news on the radio. Bad luck dogged the journey; there were delays everywhere, a host of new and unfamiliar regulations to learn, and I did not reach Paris until early January.

One day at last I got to Chantilly, then the base headquarters of the Ninth Air Force, and on by the mail truck to Luxemburg, where there was an advanced (or "forward") press camp. How advanced or forward was shown by the shells which the Germans tossed in from time to time, and by the fact that on two sides the front was very near. Luxemburg was the headquarters of General Patton's Third United States Army, to which I was assigned by SHAEF in London, but for some reason or other—perhaps by the habit of three years—I gravitated into the Air Force press camp and stayed in it until the

Third Army press moved up. All this machinery, press camps, communications, censorship and the like, was new to me; I had seen none of it in Africa or Italy, where my own duties were so different, and in India and China I had seen only those relatively modest arrangements which accompanied the first B-29 mission to Japan. The feeling of being a freshman all over again, learning again how to do a job, did not leave me for the first few weeks, since I found myself mostly with men who had been attached to the Third Army or the Ninth Air Force since the Normandy campaign. Such a belated novitiate had its comic moments, particularly as all the techniques of communication had been greatly improved in the recent months, and when I first had to broadcast to America it was only the special good nature of a broadcaster for a rival network (Bill Shadell of Columbia) that got me through the unfamiliar routines. But there were new and special interests in being, for the first time in my life, an American correspondent attached to an American army: one was the quite different feeling engendered toward events, persons, units, equipment and movements ("ours," everything very much "ours") and another was the genuine welcome which the front-line units always gave the stray reporter. I had learned by previous experience that the non-combatant was a nuisance at or near the front; I now learned that the American soldier, conscious of the press as no other could be, attached real value to the chance of getting his name in his home-town paper. "That's the only way my folks can ever know what I'm doing," they would say. The American way of writing about the war was, in fact, as it had now developed—partly under the influence of Ernie Pyle—to get as many names of infantry and artillery soldiers into print as possible, and thus to establish a channel of communication between the soldier and his family at home. The trick was much overdone. I soon saw war reporters who did nothing whatever at the front or near the front *except*

360

to write down the names and home towns of soldiers, conveying private information at the expense of what was, or should have been, a public interest; but so long as it gave any solace to the men in the lines there was justification for it. The best of the new crop of correspondents—such as Meyer Levin of the Overseas News Agency and Morley Cassidy of the Philadelphia *Bulletin*—seemed to combine the two with great skill, weaving into their accounts of an action in progress a considerable number of names without sacrificing the general contour or meaning of their stories. This was, journalistically, a technical development or adaptation so purely American that it mystified people of other nationalities and made much American war reporting incomprehensible to, for example, the English.

Another curiosity to me was the extent to which censorship had grown liberal under the pressure of American demand for more and more information. During my early months in the army we, that is I and other officers as I knew, were extremely conscious of military security, and it had not greatly relaxed when I left the army. Now I discovered that almost everything we intelligence and staff officers had thought of as being ultra-secret was very fully explained to the press at regular intervals, with maps, diagrams and generous response to questions. Certain parts of this information were designated as secret, and such parts would be rigidly censored if any correspondent attempted to write about them; but the censorship was indulgent in the extreme on such matters as the identification of units—far more indulgent than it had been in any campaign I had known. Such things as military plans were much more freely communicated to the press than I had believed possible; even dates of movement were sometimes given, under caution against printing them. When I remembered how fearful we had been in earlier days—how we could not speak even to a fellow-officer of a plan unless he was also involved in it—this struck me with wonder. The truth of the matter was that by this time we could have given all our plans and all our information to the Germans on a silver platter without greatly helping them; their alternatives in any case were strictly limited; but it was also true that the American High Command (starting, I believe, with General Eisenhower) had a new idea of press and public information and had learned, with only a few unhappy exceptions, that the press could be trusted.

The city of Luxemburg lay under the snow in a picturesque and miniature Germanic prettiness, like those small court capitals which flourished in the nineteenth century German novels. The fortifications which had made these ravines famous in the old days (the last were by Vauban) served no purpose now except for the curious visits of our G.I.'s on leave, and the valley of the Pétrusse—more like a gorge than a valley—which runs down the middle of the city was photographed in its wintry magnificence by a thousand eager soldiers. Our press camp (the Ninth Air Force's) was a modern hotel which had hot water at all hours, and was consequently known as "the fur-lined fox-hole." From its jeep park on the north bank of the Pétrusse the correspondents sallied forth every day, or nearly every day, for visits to the divisions which were in action near at hand. To write anything about these visits it was necessary to come back to Luxemburg or even— in January—as far back as Esch, where the Third Army press camp then was with all its panoply of communications; but if you were not held to daily messages home you could stay out for a day or so with the troops, sleeping in the farmhouses and barns which were usually battalion headquarters. The Fifth Division's front, in January, was very near—only down at Diekirch, less than an hour's drive away; the Twenty-sixth (Yankee) Division was moving up in the direction of Wiltz across a bitterly cold plateau; the Fourth was up at the top of the army's territory, in the region where it joined the United States Ninth Army; the Fourth Armored, Sixth and Tenth Armored, the new (new to combat) Seventy-sixth and the well-seasoned Ninetieth were among the other divisions we got to as often as we could.

Who could forget the rigors of that winter? It seemed so cold in the snowy forests of spruce and pine that two suits of G.I. underwear, with thick coats and army blankets, did not make an hour in a jeep much more bearable. Our infantry soldiers at first did not have either the boots or the snow-suits they needed, and it was infuriating to see that the Germans, even in their extremity, even at this moment when they had clearly lost the war, were better off in these respects. Their padded snow-suits were warm and well made, field gray inside and white outside; they had warm boots and very thick socks. By the end of January the new boots were arriving for our army, too, but February's thaw had set in before everybody had them. The campaign, after tense days around Christmas, was going well and the German retreat was accentuated every day. The initial advantage of Rundstedt's assault came from weather: our air power, the eyes of the army as well as a formidable weapon of attack, had been canceled out by a week of impossible weather. Whole divisions (the 106th, for example) of our army were almost plowed under by the weight of the German attack; the Fourth suffered cruelly; non-combatant services saw their first fighting; the 101st Airborne Division had held out at Bastogne. Patton, whom I came to regard as our most remarkable field general (army commander, that is), had performed his astounding transfer of the whole Third Army from the Saar to the Ardennes, relieving Bastogne and forcing the German back by head-on assault. In the Twenty-sixth Division I was told that the march against Rundstedt's counter-offensive had been a "meeting engagement," an operation very rare in any war after the opening; that is, nobody knew where the enemy was or how strong he was, and the division simply had to march until it met him and then attack. The confusion of those days—which I, of course, did not see; I was on my way across the ocean—must have been extreme. The forest was full of strays trying to find their outfits, and it was a long time before all the survivors of the 106th Division got together. The casualties were heavy and the fatigue of our sorely tried troops was pitiful even when I arrived; two weeks earlier the ordeal must have been heartbreaking. By now the weather permitted the use of the Ninth Air Force (tactical—fighters, fighter-bombers and light bombers only) practically every day, with devastating effect upon the retreating Germans, and it was only a question of days until they would take refuge again in the steel and concrete of the Siegfried Line.

It is not my business to give an account of that campaign, which should before long receive the attention of the qualified military historians; it was a hard and bloody battle and I had only brief, partial glimpses of it. What I should like to convey, if I could, would be some notion of its bitterness, of the cold and lonely unhappiness of death in the snow. At my age I could not see our lads as they sometimes see themselves (as young Bill Mauldin's cartoons show them, for instance), in the role of great, tough, bristling warriors; I saw, instead, extreme youth, bewilderment, eyes and voices of an all-unconscious pathos. Always the same questions: "How much longer do you think this is going on?" And always, "Where are the Russians now?" In Russia itself the progress of the Red Army could not have been followed more anxiously than it was in the Ardennes. Our soldiers, with all their lurid language and their admiration for toughness, never had any real inclination for warfare—as the Germans or Japanese have—and I never met one who did not long for home and peace. They were, in spite of that, very good soldiers. Nobody who saw them at the river crossings, at Echternach or anywhere in the Siegfried Line, could take that away from them. They stuck to a plan, carried it out, did what they were supposed to do, often in disgust and (I suppose) always in fear, their sole purpose, really, to "get this God-damned war over with," and their hearts always in America. You could not see much of this business without feeling humble toward our G.I.'s, who—in spite of all our advantages in technique—still constituted the essential sacrifice, the conscious and deliberate sacrifice. I have seen them in a fairly wide variety of behavior, sometimes weeping with pain and fright, sometimes stiff-lipped and silent with a kind of scornful, angry courage, sometimes merely drugged with boredom and depression, but I never saw them fail to try conclusions with their fate. That was the thing, really, that made them superb soldiers—they had the presumption or assumption of general victory and took the chance on sharing in it (however unwillingly at heart) by doing their appointed task.

One night in late January Meyer Levin and I found ourselves in a snowy forest where all these observations found precise, if limited, enactment. We had been moving forward in the Ninetieth Division all day, from division headquarters to regiment to battalion and now, finally, to the two companies of the front line at a village called Lascheid, in Belgium. Levin was a good man to go out with on these expeditions because he always wanted to keep going and thus you would find yourself propelled forward, whatever the conditions. On this occasion two companies had taken the village of Lascheid during the afternoon and had spread out over the snowy hills on both sides of it. Then, just a few minutes before we arrived, some German tanks came back and counter-attacked in the village, producing about ten minutes of wild fighting in which men who had never used a bazooka before did some of the best

365

work. Levin and I, with Lieutenant Glenn Rugh from Norristown, Pennsylvania, who had brought us forward in his jeep, came into the woods above Lascheid at dusk and found some tank destroyers waiting under the fir trees. The radio telephone was working overtime, trying to find out and pass on information. It was, of course, bitter cold, and there was no way of telling what parts of this track through the woods had been mined. At one point in our cautious progress through the woods we found three G.I.'s from L Company who had been lost since morning; Lieutenant Rugh sent them back to battalion headquarters. The guns—mostly our own—were roaring fairly steadily, and the Germans had just been using a peculiar rocket shell with a screaming trajectory unlike anything I had ever heard before. As we waited in the edge of the woods above the village we had, on that very small scale, all the uncertainties and rumor-mongering of war: one group of five or six G.I.'s, breathless and agitated, arrived from the village and reported that the Germans had counter-attacked in strength and "I Company was wiped out." One of these boys had been shot through the arm and was crying with pain. Lieutenant Rugh turned him over to a medical detachment in the woods and then took the remaining five stragglers and marched them down the slope into the village from which they had just fled. The matter-of-fact way in which he did this, and the immediate obedience of the soldiers who had been in sheer panic ten minutes before, were demonstrations of the qualities I have been attempting to indicate—the willingness to try conclusions with fate; the thing which made our unwarlike and homesick youths excellent soldiers, more or less in spite of themselves and against all their instincts. Levin and I waited for what seemed endless hours in that freezing coppice while the moon came up and the whole Christmas-tree landscape was bathed in light; then he decided to go into the village and I followed him. The road down was deep in snow and impassable for vehicles; we plowed through on foot, falling now and then, and passed the holes from which the Germans had resisted the advance of our two companies that afternoon. The village, at last, proved to be a double row of houses in the shape (roughly) of the letter Y turned upside down, and the lieutenants and sergeants of I Company—far from being "wiped out"—were having their K rations and coffee in the kitchen of one such house by the flickering light of a candle.

It was strange to sit there in the smoky kitchen and watch the story of the evening's episode narrow down and become exact. There had been about fifteen German riflemen in the counter-attack, instead of fifty; there had been only one tank instead of three; and Item Company had never really lost control of the situation. Lieutenant Fred M. Phillips (from Weston, Ohio) who commanded Item Company was a quiet lad with a slow and thoughtful way of speaking; he had manned a bazooka for the first time in his life and frightened the German tank by peppering it with noise. I Company at this moment consisted chiefly of replacements who had never been under fire before, but their platoon leaders were boys who had been all through the Ninetieth Division's very considerable battle history. Another of these lieutenants (Bernard Meinschein from Cockeysville, Maryland) had manned another bazooka, and between them it seemed clear that he and Phillips had frightened off the German tank, which could not actually have suffered any damage.

Another lurid detail of the story as it was relayed up to the top of the hill had concerned the loud grief of a village woman that evening, who had been screaming frantically in the street. The panicky G.I.'s who got up the hill told us that one of the foraying Germans had taken this woman's baby and dashed its brains out. By talking to the woman I discovered that her hysteria had been caused, instead, by the loss of her three cows,

367

which had been shot during the sudden outburst of firing when the Germans came.

Some of the wounded Germans were kept in a house near by, moaning frantically; one of them died in the night. The American wounded were able to walk and could get up the hill to the vehicles. Only one had been killed. The episode took shape and sense in Lieutenant Phillips' narrative, but when I reflected what a distorted version had come up the hill I wondered (not for the first time) at the myth-making genius of war. It sometimes seemed that a distance of a few hundred yards in wartime produced more complexities of legend than so many thousands of miles might do in peace.

Levin and I slept on benches in what seemed to be a beer house and got back to our base the next day. Even then, only twenty-four hours after our trip forward, the roads were already crowded with transport; where engineers had been carefully searching for mines the day before, now Signal Corps people were at their eternal task of repairing telephone wires; and by another day probably both Item Company and Love Company had forgotten all about Lascheid—even to its name. The campaign was made up of hundreds upon hundreds of such small actions in which the platoon was the unit and the single G.I., his sergeant and his lieutenant, were the critical materials.

Through January and February I acquired an even healthier respect for our junior officers than I had ever had before. It was the company and platoon leaders who made these detailed advances possible and held the whole thing together: second lieutenants, sergeants, youths who had been in high schools three years before. The soldier depended on his platoon commander more than upon any other person in the world, and if that second lieutenant was not good (as had to happen sometimes) the results were deplorable. But on the whole we had, by this time, so shaken and burned out and tested all the men of the fighting divisions that their platoon leaders were very good indeed, created by conditions in which only the best would do. They stick in my memory more than many a general or other dignitary before whom I had, in my army life, to stand at attention, and I think if I had soberly and truthfully to define the greatest instrument of our victory I should reply that it was our second lieutenants. Later on, in the Fifth Division on the eve of a river crossing, I saw three platoon leaders with an average age of about twenty-two sitting around the stove in a German farmhouse while they discussed the plan for their attack at dawn. They had all been doused in a shell hole full of water some time before, dodging some *Nebelwerfer* fire, and were hugging the stove to dry out their long G.I. under-wear. One of them was picking his toes reflectively throughout the discussion, but his contributions to the morrow's plan were as sharp and exact, on the scale involved, as the field orders of Napoleon. When I saw this action carried out the next day (it was the crossing of the Prum at Schankweiler) the merit of these detailed decisions in advance was shown as if by diagram. The name of the toe-picking junior strategist comes back: it was First Lieutenant John D. Kennedy of Baltimore, known in the company as "Peanuts." Such as these it was who won the war.

At the end of January the Germans had been wholly driven back into the Siegfried Line, and the next phase, the attack upon the Siegfried Line itself, took place in early February. I saw a number of these headlong assaults taking place, from Brandscheid, up at the top of the Third Army area, where the Ninetieth Division had to walk into the dragon's teeth, to Echternach on the Sauer River, where the crossing had to be made in small boats straight into the Siegfried positions. The most startling of these attacks were made by the Fifth Division across the Sauer (or Sure) River between Bollendorf and Echternach, which Patton himself, in one of his off-the-record talks to the press, characterized as a "magnificent feat of arms." It was unlike anything I had ever seen, certainly. Our infantry platoons had to get across a river in its spring flood-tide and assault the strongest steel-and-concrete positions in the world as soon as they got on the other side. The crossing itself was made extremely difficult by nature, even if the Germans had held their fire altogether, for the premature thaw of early February had converted the little Sauer River into a torrent, and many of the small boats were washed downstream; hundreds of our boys had to swim ashore on the German side. When they got there they faced the murderous fire of machine guns from the intricate and numerous pillboxes, forts and strong points of the Siegfried Line. At one place called Weiterbach, where the Second Regiment of the Fifth Division crossed, it would have been difficult to the point of impossibility for anybody not in first-rate physical condition even in peacetime. The men had to crawl down the sheer face of a clifflike river bank, launch their boats into the torrent and get out on the other side between the German positions. As I lay on the top of the river bank and watched them crawling about on the other side I felt that this crossing was the most daring I had ever seen. It was, however, no more remarkable than that accomplished at the town of Echternach by the 476th Regiment of the Seventy-sixth Division, which I saw the following day.

Echternach was a little Luxemburg town which had enjoyed a reputation as a summer resort in peace; it was now a ruin. Amidst the ruins, which were amply commanded by German shellfire from the hills across the stream, the new regiment (new to combat and still on the secret list) had observation points and first-aid stations. The crossing was made at dawn on February 7th and a withering fire then descended upon the river; for three days, while the engineers struggled to construct a bridge under fire, the platoons which had crossed were cut off and had to depend upon supplies dropped to them from Piper Cubs. At the observation post by the river, a religious school which was now gaping with shell holes which grew more numerous every hour, Levin and I had a direct view of our platoons crawling up the hillside to their assault on the pillboxes. I sometimes think that this is perhaps the clearest picture I ever had of war—the platoon on the hillside, strung out at intervals, crawling up to win or die; that, and perhaps, too, the smiles on their mothers' faces.

When the Siegfried Line was pierced and taken, these divisions swept on in a series of flanking movements to capture Bitburg, Trier, Coblentz, all the towns and villages of the Rhine-Moselle triangle, and then, in another daring movement, to cut off and capture the whole German army in the Saar. By now it was March; spring had come; the Germans were surrendering by the tens of thousands. I spent a good many hours talking to them when they were still new prisoners —that is, at the front and just behind the front, where they were as a rule more communicative and the rules had not yet begun to operate. They seemed to me a totally different breed from the German prisoners I had seen earlier in the war, and by March there was no doubt whatever that theirs was a demoralized and broken army. Our neighbors to the north (the First and Ninth United States Armies and Field Marshal Montgomery's army group) had moved decisively, and although the Third Army was at this point supposed to be on the "active defense," its defense was indistinguishable from an offensive; as a matter of fact, the Fourth Armored Division and its flanking cavalry groups cut straight through to the Rhine at a rate of about a mile an hour, sixty miles in sixty hours. When I followed their advance I had the feeling of being deep into Germany with no American holding forces in the neighborhood; for miles your jeep would roll along without passing a single American; but the Germans you saw would snap their hands up in the air and pass you in cadenced step, walking back to the prisoner collecting posts. When we reached and crossed the Rhine the decisive phase of the war was over—as, indeed, it had been for some time. I now was headed for home, for San Francisco, to see what, if anything, was going to be done about the peace.

The campaign of the winter and spring left some vivid impressions of this grim business, all dominated, I think, or given cruel distinctness, by the feeling that the whole thing was so unnecessary. The decision was already past; Germany had no longer any hope whatever of avoiding unconditional surrender. This was what made each day's sacrifice (reduced, as it was, by the mounting tide of victory) so painful. It was very difficult for me to understand how any human being, even a Nazi, could wish to continue this senseless butchery, from which every element of struggle for defined goals had departed. I had already seen so many friends disappear into the darkness that as April came on I had only one wish left about the war: that it would end at once, totally, everywhere, with its objective realities conforming at last to what had been essentially true for months. Thus I was more than ready for Paris, Rome, Casablanca and San Francisco.

That was an extraordinarily gloomy journey and it is difficult to give a rational explanation for the apprehension with which it was surrounded. There is nobody who hates, dreads or fears war more than I do, and yet it almost seemed that with the end of this struggle I was afraid of the peace. I have since discovered that something of the kind, something not altogether dissimilar, has afflicted many of those who had concentrated upon these matters for years past. Questions crowd in, and the faces of the dead look inquiringly from the shadows, asking if we can make use of what they gave. The time when a single simple purpose governed everything was now gone. In Rome in April I learned the final plans for the

Italian offensive which was to clear Northern Italy of the Germans, and so far had I traveled from any warlike spirit that I could not convince myself that it was even necessary. The war is over, something kept saying in my mind, and why not just sit it out here, wait until Germany surrenders? The attack upon Bologna took place before I left Italy, and the Fifth and Eighth Armies fought their last battle in a moment when the issue had already been fully decided. In Rome there was little cheer to be found for anybody who was interested in the *purposes* of our war; Italian anti-Fascist friends had found no reason for encouragement in recent months. The only thing more disconcerting than our record in Italy was, it seemed to me, the question I began to hear in March and April from Germany on south, a really hair-raising question, phrased usually something like this: "How soon are we going to have to fight Russia?" The conviction of all Germans (planted there by the Nazis, of course) was that America and Russia would come to blows, and by some mysterious osmotic process the idea had made its way into a good many American heads, particularly among our more thoughtless officers. Under such circumstances the meeting at San Francisco, to which I was going, took on an aspect of fatefulness which did not truly belong to it, and events in the Balkans and elsewhere seemed to contribute to the most dangerous and pointless of antagonisms.

Over the Mediterranean the mood of gloom engendered by these and other reflections took the form of maddening reiterations, lines of poetry which kept running through my head and would not be driven out. One was the words of Massenet's song, *Elegie,* a most lugubrious affair (*tout est flétri pour toujours*), and try as I might I could not get rid of it. Into the midst of this affliction there came sharp interruptions from the Whitman refrain: *O heart, heart, heart, O the bleeding drops of red, On the deck my captain lies, fallen cold and dead*. These words kept coming back all the way across Africa, although I do not suppose I had thought of them for a very long time. At the time, struggling to clear my head of such incomprehensible obsessions, I was inclined to attribute the trouble to the tendency which, perhaps, we all had, in taking our leave of this frightful struggle, to remember the dead and how they died; to weigh their lost youth against what we can or will do with the time they give us; to assess and evaluate a little. One's mind is a rag-bag at best, and it is never sure what scrap will come up when the hand of Fate stirs in it. When I went on a night-intruder mission over Germany this last spring in a Black Widow my thoughts were not on what we were doing; the swift flight of the powerful aircraft, its diving swoop on the few lights of German transport or barracks, its extraordinary maneuvers to escape searchlights and anti-aircraft fire, were only partly present to my consciousness; what I clung to was the only fixed points I could see in the world just then, the moon and the evening star, which sometimes appeared on one side of the plane and sometimes on the other, sometimes above us and sometimes almost below us, but at least always there; and the actual words which ran in my head ceaselessly were: "My sister the Evening Star, my sister the Evening Star." Why sister? Who is to know what queer shapes or sounds this kind of consciousness (half aware) is to take? Certain it is that I was beset by the odd mixture of Massenet and Whitman all the way to Casablanca, and that when, at midnight on April 14th, a lieutenant in the Air Transport Command telephoned to tell me that the President had died, I made the natural, erroneous but inevitable human connection between my own apprehensive gloom and the dire event on the other side of the world.

This is not to say that I had ever been among Mr. Roosevelt's familiars or even among his more fervent admirers. I had known him and had experienced from him great kindness.

But the weight of the event was due not to any such merely personal accidents; it was due to a much wider and deeper phenomenon, the national unanimity of which must have been apparent that day at home. I am quite sure that even Mr. Roosevelt's most violent enemies felt a little lost, a little strange, at his departure. He filled so much space; he had been there so long; he was the "Great White Father." It was difficult to think of how we were to go on without him. To the young—to our pilots, for example—there never had been any other President of the United States, and although I was no longer young, it was still true, even of me, that no other President had ever really existed for me. The effort to accept the fact, to take it in, to realize it, occupied the next days, and I could tell on the airfields that even our most careless youths were going through the same process. I heard them on the field at Casablanca and in the Azores saying, "I can't believe it. It's hard to believe it." The voice now silenced was, to all Americans, the most familiar voice in the world, and there was probably not a squadron in our whole air force which did not contain at least one duly accredited official imitator of it. The place Mr. Roosevelt filled in all our lives—even in the lives of his enemies—was greater than we had ever fully realized; so much greater that even months later it was still a constant source of astonishment that we could keep going without him. I observed, and still observe, that his successor benefited by the immensity and pervasiveness of this Roosevelt influence upon our lives and minds; that is, whatever the new President did was bound to be better than had been expected, for the truth of the matter was that we had, almost unconsciously or perhaps even against our wills, fallen into thinking that only Roosevelt could deal with what we now faced. Certainly there has never been any time in my experience, not even in the adversity which befell us everywhere in the spring of 1942, when I felt such sharp anxiety for my own country.

The situation Mr. Roosevelt left to his successor (any successor) would have been difficult at any time; at this precise moment its complication and danger seemed too much for any less expert hand and mind than his. Perhaps these were unnecessarily dark forebodings, but they filled the hours just then, and not for me alone.

Over the sea then, at last, I carried the consciousness that this tremendous drama of the war was now over. There was to come a week, a single week, in which the chief protagonists on the other side would disappear and the surrender of the whole Fascist conspiracy, with the exception of the jackal Franco, would be complete; this was near at hand. It was perhaps only to be expected that a sense of what this victory had cost would somewhat lessen the joy with which we hailed it—that, and the certainty that the Japanese would fight on for at least a while—but even so, few happenings of such consequence have gone so coldly by. In San Francisco, where I was on V-E Day (and where there were riots of joy three months later at the Japanese surrender), there was hardly a sign to mark the event. The dreamlike completeness of the drama may have dulled the edge of its reality; it was too much to follow all at once. In my own case hardly any move had been possible for years without some reference to the progress of the Fascist conspiracy, even before the war; it had been for so long the enemy that for years my comings and goings, my work and thus to a considerable extent my life, had been ruled by it. I had actually been hired in my first job as a correspondent because of the March on Rome, and my whole adult and professional existence had exactly coincided with the development of the events now culminating, from which, even when I most wished to escape them, my mind had taken its color and pulse; small wonder that I was a little dazed, a little unsure of the pavement beneath the foot. Only a few years ago, when I read in the newspapers that Hitler and Mussolini had met at the Brenner Pass I telephoned for reservations on a steamship to Europe; still earlier, when a certain momentous editorial appeared in the London *Times* I went to Prague; thus—like all my colleagues—my own private decisions were governed by the doings and sayings of these monsters who had set out to enslave the world. For a great part of the whole period I had been so strongly engaged that I had no room for doubt or question: *écrasez l'infâme* was enough. Now, in the sudden and total victory, the piling up of ruins, I still was— and am—quite certain that this thing had to be; the alternative (Fascist victory) would have been incomparably worse; but there was, even so, a desolate question extruded by the wreck of half a world. It was, simply, what are you going to do with all this? What now, little man?

What, indeed?

PART THREE

SHADOWS OF THE PEACE

An Anticipation

O, if you raise this house against this house,
It will the wofullest division prove,
That ever fell upon this cursed earth.
Prevent it, resist it, let it not be so,
Lest child, child's children cry against you woe.
King Richard II, **IV, i.**

§ 1

THE LOBBY of the Palace Hotel in San Francisco, thick and murmurous with the gathered clans, greeted the newcomer like a summing-up of twenty years. The very first persons I distinguished in the crowd there on the night of my arrival, even before I had been given a room, were two Hungarian caricaturists whose work and presence had been a familiar element in every international conference at Geneva and elsewhere in the 1920's. When the League of Nations was new they used to sketch its council meetings, its curiosities and its characters, and I had known them first at the peace conference of Lausanne—that which made the Turkish settlement—in the spring of 1923. The mere sight of them, however welcome, threw my mind back across the years to a time when every aspect of international politics had been new to me, including the journalistic function therein; when I had accepted almost every public speech by a reputable politician as meaning what it said; when, in a word, I was young. And in the days that followed I was to be reminded successively of intervening episodes by some face glimpsed in the crowd, by the experts, the delegates, the hangers-on, so that sometimes there came powerfully the sensation we have all experienced: I have been here before. It was almost as sharp as the American byword, "This is where I came in." But not quite: not quite because in spite of familiar faces and a familiar air, change had struck through this world to its very roots. In the old days at Geneva all the powers dreaded disputes and fled from them timorously; now the greatest of them had learned to be ruthless. One such was concocting, and would before long use, a weapon of almost unimaginable horror; another had completely revised the concept and practice of national independence for its neighbors. These were the United States of America and the Union of Socialist Soviet Republics, two which now overshadowed the world and had not usually, in the old days, even been represented. Indeed much of the unreality of the old conferences had arisen precisely from the fact that the Americans appeared in the role of "observers" and the Russians, for many years, not at all. Many old and famous states—Mr. Churchill's phrase —were too feeble now to play their dominant part in the discussions of mankind, and had to rely upon intelligence or skill rather than power to compel a hearing. With the single exception of Great Britain, which by its central position in capitalism (in such matters as banking, shipping and insurance), by its dominion over important sources of raw materials overseas, and by its crucial part in the common victory, had retained enough weight to command respect, none of those European nations which had governed the world for a thousand years could impose anything here. The world history we used to learn in school consisted largely of the doings of France, Spain, Germany, Italy and England; in its last phases Russia, Japan and the United States had been added; from time to time Holland, Portugal and Sweden had played parts in it. Now, of all this, what essentially remained, what governed or really "counted," was the Big Three, and where an opposition of points of view occurred most sharply it seemed, or was made to seem, that these three were in fact two.

Here was the greatest change in the political relations of the world since the fall of the Roman Empire, and although it had not happened suddenly (this century is largely the history of how it happened) it was made clear to all, under a very brilliant illumination, at the San Francisco conference. We are not all dolts, and the truth had been widely suspected for some time; but here the thing was flung out on a stage visible to all, with such emphasis and simplification as only the conditions of American life can provide. Its outlines might have been softened a little in some other surroundings, but in San Francisco there was no evading the sharpness with which two gigantic silhouettes, the United States and the Soviet Union, America and Russia, Gog and Magog, stood out upon the somber gray curtain of the future. Every discussion fell into terms of that opposition, and although much of this suffered every form of technical exaggeration known to the engines of American publicity, it was all, even so, true enough to remain true however fantastically it was contorted in the blaze of these lights. Your head might swim; you might close your eyes; when you opened them again the silhouettes were still there.

Years ago, when I first read Georges Sorel with the excitement of unaided discovery, one concept in his *Réflexions sur la Violence* burned itself into my mind. It was the theory that in this world of most unsatisfactorily operative thought and action, an idea derives its validity by reflection from the act to which it leads. That act is not necessarily much like the idea, or may be only a distorted and partial version of it, but the act, the deed, is what refracted validity upon the idea from the mirror of the future. Sorel uses as an example the idea of Revolution, which derives its validity, says he, from the act to which it leads, which is the General Strike. His example is much less powerful, because more transitory, than his general concept, as often happens; but the concept recurs in life

383

and particularly in our time with force and frequency as it is recalled by numerous outwardly unrelated aspects of contemporary thought. Here at San Francisco it obsessed me for some days in the specific example before us. That is, had our anti-Fascist struggle, in which I had been immersed for many years, had the anti-Fascist idea itself, derived its validity by reflection from the act which had now taken place? That is, from the ascension of the United States and the Soviet Union to supremacy in the public affairs of mankind?

Merely to ask the question was to open up an endless interrogation into the meaning of history. For myself I believed, or thought I believed, that history progressed dialectically, by the opposition of forces and their synthesis followed by new antitheses; therefore this development was massively and overwhelmingly confirmation rather than refutation; yet I was well aware that most of the anti-Fascists I had known throughout the world for ten years and more had not fought for this. This was not the result they had in mind. More: it was the result they most vehemently repudiated when it was put forward—in other terms, of course—by the enemy. I well remembered one day in the late summer or autumn of 1940 in London when a gentleman who had every right to know told me about one of Hitler's most recent approaches to the British government. In this tentative effort (repeated the following spring by Rudolph Hess under more dramatic circumstances) the question the emissary raised was this: Why should the two leading Nordic powers continue to fight each other for the ultimate benefit only of the "mongrel Americans" and the "Bolshevik barbarians"? The German-Italian-Japanese conspiracy used this language whenever it wished to speak to English, French or any other nationalism which it wished, at whatever time or for whatever reason, to conciliate. Was it possible, then, that the enemy had foreseen the result of his own defeat more clearly than we had foreseen the result of our victory? The speech of

Hitler on January 31, 1944, a year and a half before his *débâcle,* had come nearest to a plain statement of the German idea: *if* we are defeated, he said, our enemies will have to take up our work, and the work itself will never be defeated. This notion (I have only paraphrased it briefly) permeates the epigonic neo-Fascism of Germany and Italy today, and in San Francisco I had it stated to me in the baldest language by an American newspaper columnist who was and remains a fanatical isolationist. All these people, in all parts of the world, considered that Hitler's "New Order" in Europe and the Japanese order in Asia would have been better for human civilization than the uneasy equilibrium of two tremendous powers, one capitalist and one Socialist, and they so considered because in their view this equilibrium could not be perpetuated and must break up in war.

All such arguments (I have stated them as fairly as possible, giving them the benefit of the doubt on their sincerity) reposed not only upon fear of any great social and economic change, but also upon a strange confidence in certain races or nations and repulsions against others. The American newspaper columnist who felt that our victory was wrong—that Hitler and Japan should have won—had all the characteristic delusions about Jewish machinations, British greed and American simplicity; he seemed to feel that our enemies had more capacity for dealing with difficulties than we; he had a sort of trust in the Germans. Such aberrations from reason have been characteristic of the whole National Socialist movement, and of Fascism in general, since the very beginning, just as much in the United States as anywhere else, and have often kept us from taking dangerous men seriously. The fact remains that they did say some time ago—stating it as the greatest of evils —that our victory would divide the world between American and Russian views and systems; the implication is that this must inevitably lead to a renewal of war. Many months after the San Francisco conference was over citizens of occupied Germany were saying to our soldiers: "Why don't you attack Russia at once? We will join you; all Germany will join you." I had the same sort of thing from German prisoners in the last phase of the war, over and over again.

Was this opposition at San Francisco a proof that our enemies had made one final calculation correctly?

I have said that the result was not that for which the anti-Fascists of the world had consciously struggled through all these years; but if my view of time relations in the consciousness is even partly correct, there must be some resemblance between the achieved effect and the desired effect. However remote this achieved effect might be, it should fulfill at least two conditions: it should be more desirable than the alternative against which the struggle took place, and it should contain an element of historical progress (i.e., of an advance made possible in the state of man).

The first condition I held to be fulfilled by the destruction of the Nazi power with its tribal manias and cruelties. Whatever smaller shocks might be in store, at least the scheme of *Deutsch-arisch* dominion over the world for the next thousand years had been defeated, and whatever we might now have was preferable to that alternative against which we had fought.

The second condition, historical progress, was more difficult to discern at once in San Francisco because, precisely, of the enormity of the change in the political relations of the world —that change to which I apply the Sorel formula, which our enemies had predicted, which many among us had not foreseen clearly, and which in notable respects affronted our libertarian principles. Was it progress, historically speaking, for America and Russia to dominate the fate of the nations, so that a distinguished representative of a country which fell early to Fascism (Jan Masaryk) could tell the press on his arrival at San Francisco that "small nations should be seen and not heard"?

It would be progress only if these new custodians of destiny showed the most serious consciousness of their responsibility and employed the simplification of powers toward ends socially desirable in the widest possible sense—that is, for peace, production and the raising of new layers of the world's population to the surface of life. If such purposes animated them, then the reduction of the dominant powers to three, and the reduction of essential points of view to two, was clearly better than the criss-cross of conflicting powers and points of view which paralyzed the old League of Nations and made any permanent solution of difficulties impossible during the period between the two wars.

At San Francisco I came to the conclusion that this was in fact the case, and that we stood a better chance of achieving and maintaining a world organization under the dominion of these fewer and vaster powers, for the reason that these few were desperately in earnest. Anthony Eden in his speech at the opening of the conference referred to it as "humanity's last chance." This mood of grim necessity had never to my knowledge penetrated the sleepy purlieus of Geneva in the old days; it was due first of all to the knowledge of our own capacity for destruction and self-destruction, which had grown apace during this war and was to reach an extreme point at its end. I knew only a little about jet propulsion, rocket and directed weapons, chemical warfare and the like, and nothing whatever about the atomic bomb beyond the suggestion of its possibility, but even I knew enough to perceive that the war-making faculty had now approached a technological development which threatened the survival of the race. How much more must this have been in the minds of those, American, British and Russian, who spoke for the great war powers? They were determined to make a charter for a world organization; that was what came out of the confusion and disputes of the first days at San Francisco. A friend of mine in the American delegation said to me: "I can tell you one thing. We are going to make a charter with anybody who will stay here and make it with us." This was during those early days when the disposition of the Russians to argue from the ground up had given rise to the wholly fallacious notion, much aired in the press, that they were going to go home if they did not get their own way. As a matter of fact, as the thing unfolded, the Russian desire to state their case on every question large or small became one of the most encouraging of all developments. It proved that they were taking this project with the most deadly seriousness—as they had never taken the old League—and were determined to make it work and to play their part in it. Since this was almost the primary condition, when it was accompanied by a similar determination on the part of the Americans and British, the first step—the acquisition of a charter for the organization of the world—was assured, and that first step was so momentous that it justified a belief that the simplification and intensification of powers was, in fact, historical progress. What fell by the wayside might, from any slightly detached or semi-philosophical point of view, be regretted, but in the turmoil of time it is necessary to put first things first, and our first need was a machine for peace.

I need hardly say that these impressions at San Francisco—first, of the bigness of the Big Three; second, of the unexpected seriousness of disputes; third, of the fact that this involved historical progress—were differently felt by different people. The ethical revulsion of some of my friends and colleagues was strong. One of them said to me at the Fairmont Hotel (the headquarters of the American delegation) one day: "But what's the good of all this? What do we the people get out of it?" I said: "We can at least meet." He said: "What's the good of meeting? Do you *like* meetings?" It wasn't, really, a question of what I or anybody else liked; it was a question of how to provide, as quickly as possible, an arrangement of a permanent character under which the victors of this war could regularly consult and agree upon major courses, and thus prevent a degeneration into opposing world groups with a gulf steadily widening between them. The moment of earliest maximum danger in this respect was (as our enemies had foreseen) the actual moment of victory, but it found the conference at San Francisco well started, its most difficult obstacles overcome; and although the danger would no doubt recur, it would find us at least in possession of peacemaking machinery and some directing or at least normative principles in recognized being, to which we could refer in the presence of what used to be called the conscience of mankind. And as the discussions went on I grew more and more to feel that my friends who disliked the blunt realism of their tone were sentimentalizing unduly over those small nations which, if we come to the horrid truth, have caused most wars and never fought them out; if it is the vast agglomerations of power which must fight wars, then surely they have the chief interest and responsibility in maintaining the peace; and the recognition of this objectively existing situation by the conference at San Francisco and in the new world order may not appeal to our inherited liberalism, with its tender heart for small nations and its knack of getting much larger ones into trouble, but even so it has a granite foundation of sense, and in the long run must—if it does keep the house of peace intact—be of the greatest possible service to the small nations as well.

§ 2

The scene was well chosen. Somebody (I forget who) told me it had been Mr. Roosevelt's idea. The incomparable beauty of San Francisco, its combination of natural splendor, importance in war industry and suggestive position as our gate to the Pacific all combined to make it a setting which in itself led the minds of the delegates into larger frames, looking upon larger vistas, than might have been possible elsewhere. Not all the United Nations were at war with Japan, but in this place no delegate could fail to have that war present to his mind, so that its implications were woven into the texture of the work done. All the delegates made excursions to Mr. Kaiser's shipyards, for example, and most of them had ample opportunity to contemplate the peace and plenty of the countryside; those whose countries now lay in ruins may have done so with mixed feelings, but at least with anticipation of possibilities which a more rationally organized world might generalize. The San Francisco Opera House itself, where the plenary sessions of the conference were held, was so gleaming new and speckless clean that it seemed to assert—all in remaining very much an opera house, architecturally akin to the ruined ones of Europe—how man could build anew whenever he had the will. Upon the tribune built under its flag-hung proscenium arch there beat such a concentration of lights that no speaker could be for a moment unaware of the forces of American publicity; the photographers crawled everywhere around that proscenium, so that to see one on the ceiling would not have occasioned surprise; where I sat (in the American Broadcasting Company's box) the glare was so great that I always wore sun-glasses, and no doubt the speakers would have liked to do the same; this, the newness and the glare, probably constituted the ruling impression for delegates from overseas.

All, by this time, were familiar with the primary importance of the press in American public affairs. If they had not been familiar with it, they would have learned in a day or two at San Francisco. The press, including radio and photography, became a recognized part of the tactical apparatus of the conference; delegations used it as an adjunct to the actual discussions in committee, at times an adjunct more important than the thing itself. The uses of the press for trial balloons, for mobilizing opinion, for starting suppositions and for suggesting undiplomatic truths have long been known to all governments, but at San Francisco there was such an opportunity as has probably never existed before, since the press was out in force. "Press" included practically every kind of writer and speaker, including straightforward propagandists for this or that cause who obtained press credentials and used the press conferences as a public forum. The primary purpose of a press conference, which is to give information to the public, sometimes appeared to be lost in the shuffle, but in the main it can be said that there were extremely few secrets in San Francisco, and what you did not get on the swings you got on the roundabouts.

The purpose of the conference was to draw up a charter for the world organization which had been proposed at the Dumbarton Oaks meeting the summer before. Its secretariat was provided by the American State Department; a steering committee, consisting of the heads of delegations, was to deal with the main lines of its work and push them off, when principles had been decided, into all the committees and subcommittees which had to draw up actual texts. The committees met in the Veterans' Building, alongside the Opera House; the plenary sessions took place in the Opera House; but all those innumerable smaller meetings in which so much was decided (including Big Three and Big Five) met as a rule in the Fairmont Hotel with the Americans, the Hopkins Hotel with the British, or the St. Francis with the Russians.

The atmosphere after a while was one of nervous exhaustion among those who had any real work to do. This is why the tremendous and incessant clamor of the American publicity machine, although it serves its function in our society well, does not recommend itself to those who have to carry on delicate and difficult negotiations; the press with its headlines and the radio with its bulletins are all too likely to make a crisis every hour or so, and thus increase the difficulties which they describe. The curiosity of the public in America also passes far beyond any matter of mere information, and attaches itself to the most inconsiderable details. Thus for many days it was almost impossible to get in or out of the St. Francis Hotel because of the crowds which collected to see—merely to see—a Russian go by. The phenomenon was less marked at the hotels where the Americans and British were, but it was there. The men involved in this work had to attend meetings from morning to night and often far into the next morning, with (during the first week) a sort of artificially stimulated hysteria in the air, a fallacious expectation of catastrophe which, even when you know it to be groundless, exhausts the moral oxygen, and the battering on their nerves was severe. I had one friend in the American delegation who used to totter to bed at the dinner hour rather than eat—and eating, by the way, except perhaps for the supreme dignitaries, was never easy in San Francisco. All of these conditions would exist in a much less exaggerated form in, for example, Geneva, where the press would be reduced in scale and the public stolidly indifferent. In San Francisco the flash and bang, the clatter and glare, never stopped; among other things, photographs were taken incessantly in all public places, including shops, restaurants and streets, and even at private parties. With sun-glasses, aspirin and Vitamin B-complex it might be possible to get through an occasional such meeting, but for the permanent work of a world organization these conditions were not favorable.

And yet the work was done. The concentration of the principal delegates and their principal aides was probably so intense that they were able to disregard a good deal of their environment, saving out of it the best: the unique loveliness of the bay and its islands, the hillsides blue with lupins in the country to the north, the wonder of the sea.

§ 3

From the opening speeches of the conference little would survive unaided by notes, I think, in any memory. Little survives even now in mine: the tone of Mr. Stettinius, which was the tone of a prayer; the desperate earnestness of Mr. Eden ("humanity's last chance"); the two points drily, even harshly, put forward by Mr. Molotov, that this organization should be built about a nucleus of the great powers which fought the war, and that the Soviet Union, after its great sacrifices, was resolved to find a way of keeping the peace. There was also, a day or so later, a speech by the representative of Uruguay which wore out the entire assembly and recalled all the worst aspects of the League of Nations, its juridical niceties and punctilios, its boredom and futility. Uruguay was a country which had taken no part in the war except, perhaps, to get richer by it, and yet its representative made the longest speech of all, in a language foreign to most delegates from countries which had taken part in the war, and in the full-blown style of the 1920's. The Uruguayan representative had once been president of the League of Nations, and even if we had not known it we could have guessed it.

The first controversy which produced the "crisis" headlines in the press (especially the Hearst press) had nothing directly to do with the charter of the United Nations. It concerned the seating of a Polish delegation at the conference; it had already been agreed that the *émigré* government in London would not be admitted, and Molotov, probably for tactical reasons and without any expectation of obtaining it, had asked that the Lublin government be admitted. There was no reason for elevating this discussion to the rank of critical consequence which might threaten the existence of a world organization; it was, rather, a problem to be discussed by that organization after it was formed, or by the interested powers apart from the organization. (It certainly had little do to with Uruguay.) As might have been expected, the whole subject was put on the shelf until the business of this meeting was over.

The second, and more pertinent discussion, arose over the organization of the conference itself. This was the so-called dispute over "chairmanship," which unnecessarily involved the personality of Mr. Stettinius. Actually it was a question of principle: the Russians wanted rotating chairmanships of the plenary sessions and main committees, keeping these chairmanships in the hands of the five greater powers (France and China as well as the Big Three). This would have amounted to a permanent presidium of this and future meetings, and shocked the democratic sentiment of our delegates; they felt that the democratic principle demanded elections for all such positions. In reality there is not much difference: the great powers dominate such elections when they are held; it is not conceivable that the Costa Rican delegate would either be elected if the American State Department did not wish, or would exercise his functions in any way against the wishes of the American State Department. What Molotov was attempting to impose was akin to the Soviet system of the presidium, with which he and other Russians were most familiar, but what we held out for and eventually obtained was the same thing in a democratic dress. Our conception of democracy, at San Francisco anyhow, often seemed a threadbare thing, concerned merely with the number of votes we could whip together on any question; and as we showed on several occasions—particularly in the astonishing spectacle on "Argentina day"—we could, of course, throw a whole gaggle of votes into Russia's face whenever we wished. The permanent chairmanship remained with Mr. Stettinius, as chief of the delegation of the country which was host to the conference; plenary sessions rotated once through the five delegates of the greater powers of this war; the principle of democracy was saved on paper and for the future. But the "presidium" did exist in reality, just the same, and it is difficult to imagine circumstances under which it would not exist and effectively control any such meeting.

The heat generated by these opening arguments increased during discussion of the unanimity rule for permanent members of the Security Council (the so-called "veto" of the great powers), on which the Latin-American states were particularly agitated, and on a number of other regulations to be written into the charter, including, at the beginning, the formulas for trusteeship of territories amputated from the losers in this war. The general line of discussion on details which no longer have much interest seemed to place the Russians in the position they had stated to begin with, i.e., that the world should be organized around the nucleus of the great powers which had fought this war and would have to fight any future war. It placed the British and Americans in the position of wanting, actually, much the same thing, but of attempting to soften the language and becloud the outlines of the cardinal statements so as to humor their flock of smaller nations. The positions were natural and inevitable because Britain and America between them controlled almost all the votes in the organization, and had nothing to lose and everything to gain by building their future on such votes, whereas Russia stood very nearly alone, and even with three votes (White Russia and the Ukraine having been admitted to the conference) could still be outvoted by Honduras, Costa Rica, Nicaragua and Guatemala. This curious situation should have compelled a good deal of thought over the meaning of democracy and the democratic principle when applied to an organization of national units. I for one was not convinced that democracy meant merely the number of votes you could hornswoggle, particularly under these circumstances. If you granted England her own seven votes (Britain, Canada, Australia, New Zealand, Newfoundland, India, South Africa) and those of Belgium and Holland; if you granted the United States the twenty-one votes of the Western Hemisphere (which, through some arrangement made by Mr. Rockefeller, did vote as a single bloc), there were precious few left for the Russians to pick up by hook or by crook, whatever they did. On any question, therefore, in any committee, the British and Americans between them could swamp the Russians with votes, and that is just what happened. It is the most arrant nonsense to suggest that the votes of either the American or British bloc of states are "free" or are ever likely to be "free" in the computable future. A certain foreign minister in the British Commonwealth—an amiable man and a good Socialist in theory—was extremely critical of the British and American course in these respects when you talked to him privately, and his castigation of the performance on Argentina was severe indeed; but he voted right along with all the rest when the voting came. Under these circumstances could any sane person have expected the Russians to behave otherwise than they did?

That is, they fought tooth and nail, and sometimes very rudely, to keep from getting themselves put at the mercy of a ready-made anti-Soviet majority. That is why they insisted upon the "veto" power—that is, the rule requiring unanimity among the permanent members (great powers) in the Security Council (plus two of the elected members) before action should be taken for the settlement of disputes. Molotov, who had never been to one of these vast conferences before, betrayed his impatience more than once, it seems, and was particularly short-tempered when he was harangued by delegates from countries which had taken no part in the war. San Francisco, of course, echoed with stories of what went on in the closed meetings, of which one often repeated concerned a passage between Molotov and the Mexican delegate, Padilla. Señor Padilla, a particular favorite of Mr. Rockefeller's and hence regarded as a possibility for the Mexican presidency, delivered a reproof to Molotov on the Foreign Commissar's manners in the presence of the other committee members. Molotov is said to have replied: "The delegation of the Soviet Union did not come here to receive lessons in propriety from the delegate of Mexico." Such frankness, although it amused the spectators, had the alarm of novelty in diplomatic behavior, and there can be little doubt that the agitation of the Latin-American states, their expressed fears for "regional arrangements" and for the rights of the small, were partly due to it. But it was also noticeable that Molotov himself acquired a milder manner as the days passed and the possibility of compromise was proved; Bolsheviks are human beings too, and what passed for harshness in Molotov's manner in the earlier days may only have been the natural effect of unfamiliarity with the environment of an international conference so huge —unfamiliarity and perhaps also the expectation, happily disappointed, of an anti-Soviet front on the part of the West.

The anti-Soviet front did appear in most dramatic form, of course, during the performance to which I have already referred as "Argentina day." How it came about does not really matter much; roughly speaking, it was the result of pledges made by Mr. Nelson Rockefeller at the Chapultepec meeting with Latin-American states some weeks before; but the way in which it was done gave Molotov his best opportunity and made our own State Department look very foolish. What the State Department asked was that Argentina, which had been blatantly pro-Axis throughout the war, should be immediately admitted to the floor of this conference. The question did not greatly concern the Soviet Union, which had already learned that one more or one less Latin-American state was unlikely to change the alignment of forces, but it did give Molotov a beautiful soap-box. The question had already been argued out in committee and was now suddenly (April 30) thrown into the plenary session for an open vote. Mr. Stettinius took the tribune—with Mr. Eden presiding—and moved for the immediate admission of Argentina. Mr. Molotov then took the tribune and asked for a brief delay so that the question could be further examined. He pointed out that the Soviet Union had not objected to the admission of India, clearly not an independent country, although he looked forward to the day when an independent India might be represented. He also said that Poland, the first country to suffer German conquest, had been denied a seat here. He quoted Mr. Roosevelt and Mr. Hull in statements of Argentina's pro-enemy activity, and then said that these "little sins" of Argentina might require further examination. He asked for a brief delay: "This is all the Soviet Union has to ask."

There then followed a vote which demonstrated more conclusively than any argument how well-founded had been the Soviet fear of hostile combinations in this organization. Of the European states, only Czechoslovakia, Norway and Yugoslavia voted with Russia for a delay of two days. That was the first motion; then, on the second motion (for immediate admission), Norway switched her vote, leaving only Czechoslovakia and Yugoslavia voting with Molotov. France abstained. On both motions, of course, the American and British blocs of states voted solidly with Stettinius. When one knew beyond any question, from statements privately made, that a great many of these delegates did not want Argentina admitted and considered the whole performance a disgrace to the organization, it was startling to see their sheeplike obedience to the State Department's wishes. The merits of the question can have played no part whatever; it was a matter of discipline. Molotov cannot have cared much one way or the other about the admission of Argentina; what he wanted to do was to demonstrate before the whole world how this thing was run; and it was nothing short of astounding that he was able to put on such a demonstration. Probably, I thought, the State Department did not realize until it was all over that the joke was really on them; they may have thought they were proving "democracy" by this absurd counting of heads; in reality they had merely played into Molotov's hands and enabled him to speak for the conscience of mankind at no cost to the Soviet Union. It would have been far more intelligent for our American ringmasters to throw a few of their numerous votes into Molotov's lap; we might easily have spared him Honduras or El Salvador, just for the sake of appearances; but no—they had to sling the whole packet in his teeth at once. And it was apparently not until they read the newspapers the next day that they realized how stupidly they had played into his hands. One very influential paper—the Washington *Post*—came out in black on white with the statement that "our amateur Machiavellis" were endangering our future by such performances as this, and there was a great deal of heat and personal recrimination in the air.

And by and large—let us be quite frank, taking the fullest advantage of our unimportance—there was plenty of reason for it. On most questions the minds of the chief delegates had been made up before they came to San Francisco. Compromises were possible. They were sought and usually found. But when it came right down to horse-trading there was never any doubt that this was an Anglo-American market. Certain questions could be discussed on their merits, and when this did occur the votes flew about in a surprising manner, with reckless disregard for the opinions of Mr. Rockefeller. A case in point was the dispute over official languages for the conference and for the world organization. The French naturally wished their language restored to its historical position as one of the two

399

principal idioms of diplomacy, and Russia supported them on this; when the votes were counted it was discovered that they had won, no doubt with many votes from the Rockefeller bloc in spite of the State Department's preference for English as the sole official language. Thus it was shown that some questions escaped the iron discipline of political arrangements. But whenever a matter of serious political or military consequence to any great power arose, the votes fell into regimented order and we could all anticipate them with precision. This was the pattern of behavior also at the meeting of foreign ministers in London the following September and may be fully expected to continue in the world organization for a good many years. Independent votes (i.e., votes not controlled by the great powers) were extremely few. The Scandinavian states, when they enter the organization, may keep their freedom of choice; France may alternate between support for the Russian and support for the Anglo-American points of view, or may abstain when things get too difficult; but the balance of forces was made absolutely plain at San Francisco and is unlikely to sustain much alteration in the period we are now entering.

This being so, the Soviet Union was compelled to seek solutions which, in their general character, safeguard the Soviet system from the hostile combinations that might so easily rise against it in the organization of the future. Such a safeguard was found in the Russian amendment to Section C of Chapter VIII of the Dumbarton Oaks proposals—an amendment which now stands in the Charter as Article 53—declaring "regional arrangements directed against renewal of aggressive policy" by enemy states to be free from the jurisdiction of the Security Council. By the phrasing of this article all of Russia's separately made treaties in the East of Europe, the arrangements with Poland, Finland, Rumania and Bulgaria for example, retain an autonomous existence and could be enforced, if necessary, without the authorization of the Security Council, although Anthony Eden obtained the addition of another phrase which looks forward to a time when the world organization itself would take over these responsibilities. In one rather extreme way of stating it, Russia exempted her own borders, and action to be taken there, from the world authority altogether. That this was done at all, or thought necessary at all, indicates the profound and serious distrust with which the Soviet Union regards a world organization dominated by the capitalist states. Perhaps this may be dissipated by experience, if determined efforts are made to convince Russia that there is in fact no hostile intention toward her, but for a long time to come the pattern of San Francisco is likely to prevail. In that pattern, as it worked and as it is written into the Charter of the United Nations, the Russians stand substantially alone in a wilderness of votes belonging to the Western powers. It will be impossible to understand Russian behavior on the international stage unless the psychological effects of this cause are correctly estimated.

§ 4

The Charter was signed at San Francisco on June 26th, 1945, and was promptly ratified by the American Senate, so that by the end of the summer it already existed as the constitution of the United Nations even though its machinery had not yet been set in motion. It is, as Mr. Stettinius said in his covering report to the President,[1] a document of dual nature, containing a declaration of purposes and a constitution creating four instruments for the achievement of these purposes. Mr. Stettinius defined the declaration as "a binding agreement by the signatory nations to work together for peaceful ends and to adhere to certain standards of international morality." The

---

1 Department of State, Publication 2355, Conference Series 72.

constitutional nature of the document gives realistic and practical effect to the binding agreement. The four instruments created under this constitution are the Security Council, the General Assembly, the Economic and Social Council, and the International Court of Justice, the functions of which "are the functions appropriate to their names."

The Charter, together with the Statute of the International Court of Justice, fills a volume [2] of fifty-three narrow pages, in which procedure is laid down for the pacific settlement of disputes, action to be taken against breaches of the peace, regional arrangements, international co-operation in social and economic matters, an international system of trusteeship for territories not ready for self-government, and a permanent secretariat. The resemblance to the old League and its covenant could hardly be avoided, but in two or three important respects a new power such as the poor old League never knew is injected into this organization. For one thing, the United States and the Soviet Union are founding members of the body; for another, it is to have a military staff committee and national contingents of armed forces to compel obedience to its rulings. These alone would be reasons for regarding it quite differently from the Geneva debating society. Additional reasons might be found all through the organization it establishes. For example, something very new in international practice is introduced by the Commission on Human Rights, which is to operate under the Economic and Social Council. Human rights are not defined in the text, but it was very much better to get them recognized, even without definition, than to leave that whole subject out of account. As the phrasing stands now (Article 68) the Economic and Social Council is to set up a commission "for the promotion of human rights," along with the other special commissions, and whatever such a commis-

---

2 Department of State, Publication 2353, Conference Series 74.

sion may do or not do, it can hardly fail to serve as a device for directing attention upon some questions which otherwise would be blotted out under the cloak of "national sovereignty." Supposing that any state—Italy, for instance—should introduce legislation of an anti-Semitic character, it would be possible for another state to get that legislation discussed in the Commission on Human Rights. It might even be possible to obtain discussion of the rights and treatment of American Negroes in such a commission, or, if not, by its very refusal to discuss the subject, to show that a sore place exists. "National sovereignty" has never permitted such subjects to be internationally considered, and although the effectiveness of the proposed commission may be limited, it does in principle open up a field which under the old order would have been forever closed. Similarly the trusteeship provisions (Articles 73 to 91 inclusive), although they create a system reminiscent of the League's mandates, do include explicit declarations of purpose which have little to do, in words at any rate, with old-fashioned imperialism. The "interests of the inhabitants of these territories are paramount," Article 73 declares, and the specific aims defined in the rest of that and succeeding articles can hardly be abandoned in practice without something being said or done in the world organization. Here, as in all parts of the document, one derives the impression that it is really intended to give this thing power enough to make it work, actually work.

That is perhaps the main difference between the League and the organization built at San Francisco. Of those who built the League of Nations it can be said that only one, Woodrow Wilson, regarded it as a serious instrument for the maintenance of peace. Clemenceau's attitude toward it was notoriously cynical and came out without much effort at concealment. Lloyd George believed in it, within limits, but spent his chief energy in attempts to get the treaty itself, the

Treaty of Versailles, to function independently of it. Once Wilson had been overthrown in America there was nobody left who put the League first and other arrangements or instruments second. In this case the world organization—the United Nations—has been put first, and all treaties are to be made a part of its system (with some notable but perhaps temporary exceptions). The very tenacity with which the Russians fought for their own amendments and the Americans for theirs demonstrates the earnestness which both of them brought to the council tables. So long as the structure is treated with such respect by those who have to use it, it stands a very good chance of serving its primary purpose—which is to provide a way in which disputes between nations can be peacefully accommodated and the causes of war (some of them) attacked with authority in early and less dangerous stages. It also has an extremely good chance, much better than the League did, of creating normative principles of behavior, standards from which a departure would entail certain penalties and would at least constitute defined aberration. In the old League this was scarcely ever the case, at least after the Corfu incident in 1923; in the League almost any power could do almost anything with the assurance that it would be somehow smoothed over and made outwardly respectable. Some residue of that timorous diplomatic tradition may remain in the United Nations Organization, but both the Russians and the Americans showed at San Francisco that a more vigorous and realistic style of argument met their needs and could produce acceptable results.

These are small claims, from the point of view of persons who expected a new heaven and a new earth to come out of this war. They are substantial claims when they are compared with what could be reasonably said of any previously existing international machinery for the preservation of the peace and the prevention of war. The machine we now have, for the first time in human history: what comes of it depends in part upon the spirit and intentions of those who use the machine, and in part upon that immense area in the life of man which can never be wholly governed by political arrangements—his social, economic and psychological development, his ethical imperatives, the extent to which he is willing to generalize the best he has been able to achieve in life and minimize the worst, his readiness, at last, to accept citizenship of the dwindling planet and adjust the rival assertions of clan and class and creed to the over-riding necessities of continued life. No less is required; and this much involves progressive, uninterrupted evolution of the human consciousness in society—its relationships in an ever-widening circle—at an accelerated rhythm of which there is little evidence yet. The single man could be happy in the aboriginal forest, as he was in Periclean Athens or the Renaissance, and as he may be today; but social man, man in society, courts disaster at a rate so vertiginous that his annihilation now becomes a matter of where next he plants his reckless step or how much he can learn to think in a few years of grace.

§5

The use of a bomb employing the actual process of atomic fission for its destructive effect was the culminating event of the war (August 6th, at Hiroshima, and August 8th, at Nagasaki) even though its military effects were negligible. The war was, in fact, already over, and the Japanese Emperor had made advances to Moscow some weeks earlier in an attempt to sue for peace. The entrance of Russia into the Japanese war (August 8th) would have hastened the surrender in any case, since it had already been determined upon, and the use of this weapon of desperation by a power which was overwhelmingly victorious must be regarded as an unnecessary touch of horror in the last moments of the war. The atomic bomb served only one purpose politically: it enabled the Japanese imperial government, who were defeated and had no recourse but to surrender, to tell their own people that this terrible invention had forced their decision (which is untrue but politically invaluable to them). It enabled them to create in a few days a legend which no censorship of the press or military "re-education" lasting a few months can touch—the legend of an undefeated Japanese army obliged to give up without fighting by love of the home country, its women, children and hearths, its shrines and haunts of sacred beauty. What this legend of the heroic surrender of the unbeaten will do to the special consciousness of the Japanese people—especially as it was followed by no serious attempt to touch that consciousness—will be unfolded inexorably in the years to come.

But although its military results had already been achieved and its political results were undesirable, the atomic bomb was still the culminating event of the greatest of all wars because of what it did to the future of mankind. There was no secret about the principles of atomic fission, which had been the common property of science everywhere since 1939: the only secret was how to make the bomb, which could scarcely remain a secret for long. Therefore a whole series of possibilities of destruction opened up before even the most literal of men. The qualitative and quantitative progress made in aviation during this war had already shrunk the planet to a fraction of its previous effective size. At the very end of the war, pilotless aircraft and jet-propelled fighters, as well as radio-directed missiles of various sorts, were ready for employment on a big scale, and in the mere matter of transport at "normal" speeds it was possible to go round the world in the time it once took to travel from New York to Charleston. To this sudden contraction of space (sudden because it was accomplished in about three years) was now added a device in which an actual process in nuclear physics, that is, in the structure of matter itself, was employed as a weapon in human war. Its difference from all other weapons was that, although so employed, it was not really a weapon at all. It was a *process*, the results of which were unknown and may never be wholly known, traced out and tabulated. It was, moreover, merely the first and primitive form of an atomic disintegration the limits of which no physicist seems willing to define—releasing energies which, under determined social control, might enrich the life of all men and bring the submerged hundreds of millions into existence at its fullest, or else, under the irresponsible rivalries of "rugged individualism," might dissolve the earth. These prospects were so evident to the scientists who produced the atomic bomb that they hoped, while they were working on it, that they would not succeed; after they had succeeded they protested—seventeen of the best of them, at a meeting in Chicago in August—that they had never intended it to be used as it was used; they had hoped it would be demonstrated on a desert island as a warning to Japan. Its use was the result of a political decision which, like all political decisions, depended upon the philosophical grasp of the minds that made it, as well as upon which advantages they valued most keenly, which costs they were most willing to bear; considered historically, once the decision had been made and the deed done, it entered into the record of the race as a fact to which all its future course must have some reference and bear some relation of effect, near or far.

Those who lived through any part of the V-2 period in London will have a rudimentary notion of what a war between well-prepared powers would be in the future. V-2 was a radio-directed explosive which traveled invisibly at a great speed and height: you had no idea whatever of when or how it would explode. You would be sitting talking with friends when, with no advance notice of any sort, the thing would explode somewhere and the walls would shake, the windows fall. Nothing but a statistical probability stood between you and destruction. In the case of V-2, which was cumbersome and expensive for the Germans, this statistical probability was of some comfort because it was low; the technological advance has now made it certain that the whole statistical balance—even without atomic energy—would radically change. With the use of atomic energy there is no part of the world that could not be obliterated. The devices with which this can be done are already in hand. Further experimentation along these lines may, even accidentally, produce various degrees of the disintegration or dissolution of matter up to an unimaginable total.

Well, now, of course, life has always been a precarious affair, at the mercy of the forces of nature, uncertain in the jungle and the city alike, bound between darkness and darkness. All kinds of relatively minor incidents in the sidereal universe could annihilate this small planet without disturbing the larger system of which it is a part, and even that larger system itself will, our science tells us, grow cold at last; but while we live we prefer life to death. That is the instinct that animates us, grubworms or lunar moths or men, except when it is overcome by irresistible death-determining attractions, and whether we live a day, a year or a century does not much change the case. Human society historically consists of men banded together in larger and ever larger associations for protection against the forces inimical to their life, amongst which the savage elements in their own nature have always been counted, but not always systematically identified. If what is predatory and anti-social is not brought under control in time, it produces social cataclysms which are just as destructive to humanity as any of the greater catastrophes of physical nature: wars, revolutions. To exacerbate these conflicts between men there are now supplied new instruments which can destroy

408

ten years" (in his speech of March 3, 1945) and said that between the prospect he offered and the "soothing shadow of decline" he knew which France would choose. Against the anachronisms (however appealing) of such a state of mind, the French people themselves set up more realistic vistas through the parties of the Left, and gave those parties a heavy vote in the municipal elections which took place while the San Francisco Charter was being made. To minds nurtured by the life-giving ideas of France no greater tragedy took place during all these years than the prostration of that country under Pétain and its delusive revival under de Gaulle, and a more accurate adjustment of means to ends, such as the Left parties proposed, seemed the best hope for the coming years. The elections of October 21, 1945, giving a clear majority to the parties of the Left, ensured that de Gaulle's patriotic romanticism would be held within limits by a parliamentary control, and created some hope that although he was himself to remain, his white horse would have to be tethered outside.

In the East the Soviet Union, having achieved social and economic stability at frightful cost—at a cost no Western mind would be happy to consider for its own kind—seemed determined upon the assertion of its rank and power, particularly in regions near its own borders and in the general councils of the nations. Strong sympathies for the Soviet Union among the organized workers and peasantry of Europe gave special advantages to the Russian policy on that continent and encouraged the belief that in some directions (Germany and the Balkans) its expansion could go on for a long time. The reconstruction of European Russia, particularly the Ukrainian and White Russian republics, would require years of work, vast quantities of material, and a period of uninterrupted peace; besides which there existed no reason to doubt the determination of the Soviet government to keep the peace. But in due course there would and must come confrontations, in Europe

411

as in Asia, of the Soviet system and the capitalist system most strongly represented by the United States and Great Britain; in such confrontations, unless they be governed by an irresistible will to peace on both sides, there does undoubtedly exist the possibility of war. To encourage or emphasize it would be to carry on Hitler's work, but to deny it would be sheer foolishness.

The physical contacts of the two systems are, up to now, limited, their conflicts few, their disagreements chiefly theoretical or, if practical, susceptible of practical compromise. No effort at compromise was made at the London Conference of Foreign Ministers in September-October, 1945, because the American high command (Mr. Truman and Mr. Byrnes), seem to have felt, with their Republican adviser, Mr. Foster Dulles, that a "showdown" with Russia was desirable as soon as possible after the war. This policy, which endured until the Moscow meeting at the end of the year, reposed upon the notion that although agreement with Russia was a necessity during the war, once victory had been obtained it would be salutary to make it extremely clear where our dissent and disapproval of Russia's courses would begin. This was pursued, after the London failure, by a series of notes from Mr. Byrnes, attacking Russian policies in the Balkans and elsewhere, not always on ground well chosen from the point of view of logic or consistency. (Thus it seems extraordinarily hypocritical for a statesman from South Carolina to take such a high stand about "secret ballot" and "single list of candidates" in Balkan elections, when no secret ballot has ever existed in South Carolina and only one ballot is normally presented to any elector there.) The "showdown" policy not only gave no results on the international scale, but encountered a groundswell of opposition in the one place which American politicians consider important, the region of mind and opinion among our own voters; it was therefore abandoned in favor of conciliation, and at another

412

meeting of the foreign ministers in December at Moscow, procedural accommodations were made between the opposing theses. This was in its turn subject to attack as being a surrender to the Russian claims, and could not be looked upon with any confidence as a permanent policy, since those who were so willing to change from October to December might easily change again before May. In reality these expedients, this vibration from one side to another, gave no sense of permanent line or defined objectives in the conduct of our foreign affairs, and made more than ever apparent our poverty of intellect in high places. Whatever may be the sequence of events after the Moscow-London-Washington statement of December 27, 1945, it can scarcely reassure a troubled world unless some firm resolution is taken on what, indeed, it is that we want. That is what we need most. But unless a true effort at comprehension and accommodation is also made, nothing can prevent a world-wide antithesis being established and cultivated by every malevolent influence at work in our society, year after year, until half the world is set against the other half in conflict. It is true that our own economic organization is no longer "pure" capitalism; according to the apostles of "pure" capitalism, such as Mises and Hayek, every influence which mitigates the "natural harmony" of the unregulated economic life keeps it from operating, and such mitigating or distorting influences include Christianity, social reform of any sort, humanitarian ideas and factory regulation as well as Socialism. But, whatever it may be called, our system remains the nearest thing to capitalism now in existence, and to it our people still have a strong instinctive attachment which only disastrous crises could impair. Those crises would, by any enlightened capitalism, be mitigated or in part averted by recourse to social controls, so that a process of steadily diminishing capitalism might be set up within the system itself and work a series of transformations along the pattern already established in Great Britain and the United States. Externally such transformations could minimize, but could never wholly eradicate, the opposition between economic operations undertaken for private profit and those undertaken for a rigidly controlled state Socialism. How, then, to deal with this opposition—accompanied, as it is and will be, by the political and military adjuncts to systems of power—is the dominant question among all those now set for the brain of man to solve. We may reach Socialism by our own route, as the British Labor Party wishes to do, or by a series of catastrophes, as a good many economists have foreseen; we may not reach it at all, and succeed in perpetuating a "spontaneous" economic order through some miraculous means never observed before; but there are very few among us who would want to reach it through the Russian way of wholesale bloodshed and unimaginable suffering. If the Russians can understand this—if they can understand that we are free born—and if we can understand the supreme value they put upon their own system, it should be possible for two views of society to share the same world, however shrunken it may be, so long as peace and production are the resolute purposes of both. Not to attempt these adaptations in an almost daily exercise of the reason, as distinct from the prejudices and appetites, would be to risk extinction. Societies began when men had to organize or perish. On the scale now established this is truer than ever, although our minds are not quite ready to take it in, our reach exceeds our grasp and our world is still dizzy with victory. The point of development at which we now stand is one in which the most extreme disaster has come within the range of possibility: the end of life on this star.

THE WILSON PRINCIPLES

THE FOUR PRINCIPLES
(February 11, 1918):

1. That each part of the final settlement must be based upon the essential justice of that particular case and upon such adjustments as are most likely to bring a peace that will be permanent;

2. That peoples and provinces are not to be bartered about from sovereignty to sovereignty as if they were chattels or pawns in a game, even the great game, now forever discredited, of the balance of power; but that

3. Every territorial settlement involved in this war must be made in the interest and for the benefit of the populations concerned, and not as a part of any mere adjustment or compromise of claims amongst rival States; and

4. That all well-defined national aspirations shall be accorded the utmost satisfaction that can be accorded them without introducing new or perpetuating old elements of discord and antagonism that would be likely in time to break the peace of Europe, and, consequently, of the world.

THE FOUR ENDS
(July 4, 1918):

1. The destruction of every arbitrary power anywhere that can separately, secretly and of its single choice disturb the peace of the world, or, if it cannot be presently destroyed, at the least its reduction to virtual impotence.

2. The settlement of every question, whether of territory or sovereignty, of economic arrangement, or of political relationship, upon the basis of the free acceptance of that settlement by the people immediately concerned, and not upon the basis of the material interest or advantage of any other nation or people which may desire a different settlement for the sake of its own exterior influence or mastery.

3. The consent of all nations to be governed in their conduct towards each other by the same principles of honor and of respect for the common law of civilized society that govern the individual citizens of all modern States, and in their relations with one another, to the end that all promises and covenants may be sacredly observed, no private plots or conspiracies hatched, no selfish injuries wrought with impunity, and a mutual trust established upon the handsome foundation of a mutual respect for right.

4. The establishment of an organization of peace which shall make it certain that the combined power of free nations will check every invasion of right and serve to make peace and justice the more secure by affording a definite tribunal of opinion to which all must submit and by which every international readjustment that cannot be amicably agreed upon by the peoples directly concerned shall be sanctioned. These great objects can be put into a single sentence. *What we seek is the reign of law, based upon the consent of the governed and sustained by the organized opinion of mankind.*

THE FIVE PARTICULARS
(September 27, 1918):

1. The impartial justice meted out must involve no discrimination between those to whom we wish to be just and those to whom we do not wish to be just. It must be a justice

that plays no favorites and knows no standards but the equal rights of the several peoples concerned.

2. No special or separate interest of any single nation or any group of nations can be made the basis of any part of the settlement which is not consistent with the common interest of all.

3. There can be no leagues or alliances or special covenants and understandings within the general and common family of the League of Nations.

4. And, more specifically, there can be no special selfish economic combinations within the League and no employment of any form of economic boycott or exclusion, except as the power of economic penalty, by exclusion from the markets of the world, may be vested in the League of Nations itself as a means of discipline and control.

5. All international agreements and treaties of every kind must be made known in their entirety to the rest of the world. Special alliances and economic rivalries and hostilities have been the prolific source in the modern world of the plans and passions that produce war. It would be an insincere as well as an insecure peace that did not exclude them in definite and binding terms.

THE ROOSEVELT PRINCIPLES

JOINT DECLARATION KNOWN AS
THE ATLANTIC CHARTER
(August 21, 1941):

The President of the United States of America and the Prime Minister, Mr. Churchill, representing His Majesty's Government in the United Kingdom, being met together, deem it right to make known certain common principles in the national policies of their respective countries on which they base their hopes for a better future for the world.

First, their countries seek no aggrandizement, territorial or other;

Second, they desire to see no territorial changes that do not accord with the freely expressed wishes of the peoples concerned;

Third, they respect the right of all peoples to choose the form of government under which they will live; and they wish to see sovereign rights and self-government restored to those who have been forcibly deprived of them;

Fourth, they will endeavor, with due respect for their existing obligations, to further the enjoyment by all states, great or small, victor or vanquished, of access, on equal terms, to the trade and to the raw materials of the world which are needed for their economic prosperity;

Fifth, they desire to bring about the fullest collaboration between all nations in the economic field with the object of securing, for all, improved labor standards, economic advancement and social security;

Sixth, after the final destruction of the Nazi tyranny, they hope to see established a peace which will afford to all nations the means of dwelling in safety within their own boundaries, and which will afford assurance that all the men in all the lands may live out their lives in freedom from fear and want;

Seventh, such a peace should enable all men to traverse the high seas and oceans without hindrance;

Eighth, they believe that all of the nations of the world, for realistic as well as spiritual reasons, must come to the abandonment of the use of force. Since no future peace can be maintained if land, sea or air armaments continue to be employed by nations which threaten, or may threaten, aggression outside of their frontiers, they believe, pending the establishment of a wider and permanent system of general security, that the disarmament of such nations is essential. They will likewise aid and encourage all other practicable measures which will lighten for peace-loving peoples the crushing burden of armament.